LIVING LIKE INDIANS

Other books by Allan A. Macfarlan

BOOK OF AMERICAN INDIAN GAMES

CAMPFIRE AND COUNCIL RING PROGRAMS

INDIAN ADVENTURE TRAILS

TALKING STICK TALES

CAMPFIRE ADVENTURE STORIES

NEW GAMES FOR 'TWEEN-AGERS

MORE NEW GAMES FOR 'TWEEN-AGERS

LIVING LIKE INDIANS

1,001 Projects, Games, Activities, and Crafts

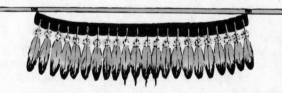

BY ALLAN A. MACFARLAN

Illustrations and Diagrams by Paulette Jumeau

Skyhorse Publishing

Skyhorse Publishing books may be purchased in bulk at special discounts for sales promotion, corporate gifts, fund-raising, or educational purposes. Special editions can also be created to specifications. For details, contact the Special Sales Department, Skyhorse Publishing, 307 West 36th Street, 11th Floor, New York, NY 10018 or info@skyhorsepublishing.com.

www.skyhorsepublishing.com

10 9 8 7 6 5 4 3 2 1

Library of Congress Cataloging-in-Publication Data

Macfarlan, Allan A.
  Living like Indians : a treasury of American Indian crafts, games, and activities : book of American Indian outdoor and trail activities / by Allan A. Macfarlan ; illustrations and diagrams by Paulette Jumeau.
      p. cm.
  Includes bibliographical references and index.
  ISBN 978-1-60239-983-9 (pbk. : alk. paper)
  1. Outdoor life--Handbooks, manuals, etc. 2. Outdoor recreation--Handbooks, manuals, etc. 3. Camping--Handbooks, manuals, etc. 4. Handicraft--Handbooks, manuals, etc. 5. Indians of North America--Recreation. 6. Indians of North America--Social life and customs. I. Title.
  GV191.6.M312 2010
  796.5--dc22

                                        2010010112

Printed in China

Contents

Activity Finder

To provide the reader with a quick, easy reference to some of the hundreds of activities which are described in this book, the following list has been compiled. The numerals refer to chapter numbers.

Introduction

Living Like Indians has been written especially for all leaders of recreation; directors of youth movement activity groups of all denominations; Boy Scout and Girl Scout executives and leaders; YMCA, YWCA, and YMHA leaders; Campfire Girls and campfire groups; Boys' Clubs; Girls' Clubs; camp directors and counselors; physical education directors; church groups; parents; Y-Indian Guides and all other Indian group leaders; libraries; colleges and schools, teachers' training courses, and all who plan and direct the recreation and instruction of today's youth. It is the sincere hope of the author that this book may blaze new trails which will lead to increased variety and more challenging activities in the field of recreation.

The greater part of the material is entirely new and an endeavor has been made to give that which is not, a new, more helpful and more vivid interpretation, in order to provide more original and exciting new activities and projects.

One important idea underlying *Living Like Indians* is to give authentic details of the way of life of the Indians of North America which can prove of service in modern life. It is written for the use of all individuals or groups which spend anywhere from an afternoon to several weeks at a time in the open. It is also a book for *all* camps as well as those which conduct an Indian Encampment Section during the summer months.

This book has a double purpose since it can be used as a handbook by leaders and chiefs, can be read with understanding by any young would-be brave, and also serves as a guide for all outdoorsmen and women, campers, boating enthusiasts, fishermen, amateur naturalists, nature lovers, and bird watchers.

Despite the fact that the author has sought to keep the Indian love of adventure, daring, and exploration to the fore throughout the book, due stress has been placed on safety and adequate safety precautions. The use of DARE WITH CARE! as a watchword has not been overlooked throughout the text, and practical pointers on outdoor safety and emergency measures which will serve to prevent accidents and save lives will be found in its pages. The challenge of the unknown, which was ever present in nearly all fields of Indian life is kept intact and vibrant as an incentive to seek wider horizons and as an antidote for today's more prosaic way of life.

Living Like Indians has been written as an authentic, informative, and comprehensive volume built on personal experience among the Indians and information given the author by old Indian chiefs, medicine men, and shamans. Because of this, it offers a clear insight into how the Indians of North America lived, worked, and played. It does not consist of tabulated, abridged programs but is a creative book of actual, fully detailed activities, with *How to* leading to *Let's do!* It combines theory and practice: the learning of skills followed by their actual application, based on Indian techniques.

The recorded activities of the Indians are those which tend to develop quick thought and action, self-assurance, control, concentration, co-ordination, desirable daring, dexterity, *esprit de corps*, and the spirit of fair play and unselfishness. The majority of activities, projects, and games in these pages can be practiced by individuals or groups of varying size, in large or small areas, as circumstances dictate. It is a book which can be used for educational as well as recreational purposes, because of its contents and their authenticity.

No suggestion is made anywhere in this book either to introduce or establish any new Indian or other group. Everything set down is for the use of existing Indian organizations and groups of all kinds as well as for those desirous of organizing temporary Indian programs for the summer months. The terms "modern chiefs, modern Indians, modern braves," are used only to distinguish the would-be Indians of today from the Indians of yesterday.

Indian woodcraft, woodlore and trailcraft are ageless, exciting, romantic, instructive, and helpful to all enthusiasts of all phases of outdoor life, irrespective of age. These pages endeavor to describe the American Indian of the past and picture the magnificence of their former unspoiled territories. Despite this, only a few paragraphs deplore today's rubble-strewn countryside, while many pages tell of challenging yet simple ways in which some of its former loveliness can be restored. CONSERVE—DESERVE! and SPARE—SHARE! are slogans put to practical use.

The author hopes that these pages breathe something of the fragrance of the forest, the rhyme of rivers, the lullabies of lakes, the wizardry of woodlands, inspired by the inward serenity of mind of the Spartans of the plains and forest who made this book possible.

May *Living Like Indians* help to promote the brotherhood which is born and flourishes in the crimson glow of the fire.

1

The Indian Way of Life

Practically all of the activities and projects detailed in this book can be carried out easily by a family, group, or individual camping in any one of the state parks or national parks—or even closer to home.

Much of the preparatory work for the more rugged forms of camping can be usefully accomplished before setting out on the trip. Anyone who has learned to set up a tent, lean-to, or any other improvised shelter quickly and efficiently in a back yard and has experimented with bedding, kitchen gear and building fires of various sorts, even if unlit, is a far better camper than one who sets out into the woods for the first camping experience without having practiced in advance some of the skills required for camping.

BRINGING THE OUTDOORS INDOORS

Many a practical tent on the market today began indoors as strips of tough paper or cloth, with a ruler, scissors, and paste handy.

Woodcraft, Indiancraft and naturecraft should begin indoors, graduating to outdoors later on.

Numerous knot-tying and lashing championships have been won by much practice at home.

The study of map reading and map making indoors will assure the ability to read maps accurately and quickly on trail or route.

Studying and making star charts indoors is fine preliminary training for further development of astronomy under the stars.

Compass work and route and course charting should begin at home and the practical results will pay off later on the trail and on the water.

First Aid and certain Lifesaving techniques should be started and practiced indoors—later on may prove too late!

Time spent outdoors is far too precious to waste on preliminaries and necessary skills which can be learned and developed at home and in the club room. With a little thought one can bring the outdoors indoors.

THE OUTDOORS AS EVERYONE'S HERITAGE

It is as much a joy as a privilege for a parent or youth leader to escape the thralldom of traffic lights, concrete, and city canyons by seeking out what still remains of the once "Great Outdoors" and telling the younger members of their safari about clean atmosphere, pure, natural water, soil particles, green leaves, and the wonder of quiet and open spaces. A father, mother, big brother, or family friend can be the "chief" who leads his "modern Indians" into such "Indian Country" and explains the vital, patriotic task and necessity of conservation.

Preserving our natural resources is one of the few issues of vast importance which are not controversial in this atomic age. It is everybody's privilege and duty to take a hand in helping to achieve this. In this age of rocketry, nuclear fission, and electronics, the basic things of life called natural resources are too often overlooked. When a modern youngster boasts that scientists have split the atom he can be reminded that no scientist has yet split a plant leaf to reproduce its green cell, which is the key to all earth life. When a youngster talks of the wonderful reproductions of the greatest modern chemists he can be told that not one of them has yet solved the mystery of chlorophyll, despite the millions of dollars spent on research in the attempt to reproduce it.

INDIAN TERRITORY

Modern boys or girls have the best chance of really living like Indians during the long summer holidays. This is especially true when the holidays are spent in the country. Though fun, adventure, and interest can be experienced in leading the life of a lone Indian, the Indian way of life can be made even more interesting by sharing it with a companion or, still better, by forming a band of modern Indians among those spending their holidays or living in a suitable location. Such groups can be organized as bands comprising six to ten Indians in each. Practically all of the activities detailed in this book then become possible and the band members will get the true feel and spirit of living like Indians. Six or eight braves to a band, under the leadership of a responsible senior or a mature chief, aided by a junior chief when necessary, will prove a suitable number. All of the Indian programs set down on these pages can be carried out successfully by almost any size group under the guidance of a leader.

There are fine opportunities for summer camps to include a certain amount of Indiancraft and trailcraft in their regular programs, thus adding additional variety,

incentive, and adventure to the lot of the campers. This is especially true of camps throughout the United States and Canada which are situated in almost virgin country which, fortunately, has not changed too greatly since the days when it was roamed by the Red Men. Unspoiled forests, woodland, lakes, rivers, and streams are there to be explored and enjoyed. Nowhere, except in very similar country throughout Europe, can one live the life of an Indian better than in such places, still unspoiled by the encroachment of modern civilization. Such sites are modern Indian country.

INDIAN CLOTHING

The types of improvised clothing for would-be braves detailed in this chapter illustrate how easy it is to equip modern braves of all ages.

Clothing for the happy, rugged, Indian way of life should be old, tough, and very comfortable. Breechclouts, which can be fringed and decorated in Indian style, can be made standard wear for at least a few sun-filled hours each day, when good weather prevails. Such garb should be worn in morning and afternoon hours until the braves become used to the sun rays and tan nicely. Seasoned braves who are conditioned to acquire a fine coat of Indian tan can wear breechclouts in the afternoon, too. Colored shirts, with fringes sewn onto the long sleeves, can be worn as protection against the sun during the first week of really hot weather. Of course, breechclouts are not suitable for roaming rugged country, especially where blackberry, wild rose, and thorn bushes lie in wait for thin-skinned modern Indians. Jeans or any sturdy, smooth-fabric long trousers *without cuffs* are standard attire for exploratory trips. Tough, smooth-surface shirts with long sleeves will afford necessary protection when the going is rough. Strong hiking shoes, or hard-soled moccasins, make the trail seem easier. Breechclouts are fine for games in the encampment and for hiking on brier and bush-free terrain. They are illustrated in Chapter 20. The Plains tribes rejoiced in the freedom of their breechclouts but the Woodland Indians usually wore tough trousers, in addition to breechclouts, for protection in wooded terrain.

HOW INDIANS LIVED

The purpose of this chapter is to tell as briefly, yet as concisely as possible, how the young people of the Indian tribes lived in their encampments and villages and how they occupied their time. It must first be said that a modern Indian village or encampment cannot prosper long, nor can a modern Indian tribe or band usefully exist, unless it follows the well-blazed trail which the Indians have left as a guide to their splendid way of life. Modern chiefs should study the ways and lore of the Indians. They must be able to set up and implement an authentic Indian program which is exciting, inspiring, and helpful to the braves-to-be. By their own knowledge and interest in Indian ways, they must be able to lead and inspire the braves in their bands to really live as the Red Men did, or as close to it as possible, and learn all they can about Indian lore, woodcraft, and Indian ways.

INDIAN YOUTH TRAINING

The early lives of the young Indian braves-to-be were devoted largely to building strong minds and bodies and having a good time while preparing for the responsibilities, risks, hardships, and adventures which lay only a few snows ahead of them. From their youth on through the devious trail of life they enjoyed being alive, with each day holding promise of a new adventure, a new challenge to be met and overcome and to accept both as treasured parts of their heritage. They acquired the priceless gift of culture and the joy of learning to be able to live without fear. As they lived and dared with high-hearted gallantry they developed spirit, mind, and body. They lived a simple, healthy, strenuous life and a happier one than that of most modern Indians because it was stripped of all non-essentials. When Indian boys learned something new that was helpful to their way of life, they employed and developed such skill to their utmost. An Indian boy strove to win but he also learned how to "lose like a chief"—gracefully.

Their schools were open-air ones. They learned by technical and strenuous play-ways to develop self-confidence and self-reliance and how to do well the things that would be most useful to them later on. Their training developed resourcefulness and ability to make split-second decisions, and inculcated habits of sportsmanship, loyalty, and generosity. The Indian youths were eager to accept the challenge of the unknown. They were taught how to get along with others, to speak the truth, to hold honor high, and to be ashamed only of lies and lying.

When a boy used a bow or tomahawk carelessly it was taken away from him and he had to convince a chief or chiefs that he was prepared to respect and take proper care of weapons and would use them with discretion. Only then were they entrusted to him again.

INDIAN ATHLETIC SKILLS

Indian youth learned to run fast and far without fatigue; to swim speedily and for a considerable distance, while ignoring cold and rough water; to wrestle and develop the arm muscles so that they would have strong bow arms, and to use and develop legs and feet so that they would acquire strength and balance.

Indians were extremely healthy before the coming of the white man. Most contagious diseases were unknown before they were brought as part of the many curses and scourges by the palefaces. Smallpox, scarlet fever, diphtheria, measles, and whooping cough, for instance, were alien and because of this the countless Indians infected were decimated, as they had neither cure for nor even partial immunity to such diseases.

Young Indians were taught how to really see; how to hear keenly, and correctly interpret what they heard; how to use their noses, so that the perfumes and smells of forest, woodland, and mountain held few secrets. These senses and skills were carefully developed and taught, and just as eagerly learned, for the sake of protection and achievement. Skilled instructors taught the young Indians how to move silently, skillfully, and craftily over all types of terrain. Ability to learn, develop, and use these crafts usually meant the difference between life and death to those who learned. Young Indians were taught to bear privations stoically. The pangs of thirst and hunger were accepted with good grace as a necessary part of life, at times.

MORAL CODE

Apart from physical training and development, the young Indians learned to live by a strict moral and religious code. They learned that it was cowardly and unsportsmanlike to lie. The Indians of many tribes had such a high regard for the truth and such contempt for lies that they lied only to deceive an enemy. When they could not speak the truth without causing trouble for a comrade, they kept silent and could not be made to speak. Of course, all Indians did not learn to "speak with a straight tongue"—which is why they had the "Telling The Truth" ritual before starting out on a war or raiding mission. This was a sort of confession in which braves, who might be going to their death, revealed hidden lies, sins, and unworthy thoughts to their closest comrades or a chief. Their statements were regarded as an oath and were never betrayed, even when those making them were only wounded or returned to their tribe unhurt. Even the most awkward of the secrets revealed in the moment of truth were considered sacred and never again mentioned. Indians never stole from others of the same band or tribe and if circumstances or privation forced them to pilfer, they made amends as soon as possible.

An Indian learned to be honorable, to live up to the trust imposed on him, to be loyal to his band, tribe and nation and to regard his word and promise as sacred. He learned that to be truly great one had to be unselfish and that to "give like a chief" meant self-sacrifice in the highest degree and the acceptance of charity and liberality as an integral part of his life. Indians regarded their personal honor and that of their band and tribe so highly that they were ready to die for it if need be.

INDIAN CLEANLINESS

The Indian learned to keep his body clean inside and out, and to be especially clean when he sought the counsel of or prayed to his gods. Many tribes believed that regular baths meant healthy bodies and took a daily bath in river, lake, or rain. Indian boys delighted in taking a bath during a heavy downpour of rain and modern Indians can have fun too by taking breechclout baths in heavy, warm rain. Indians often enjoyed mud baths, after which they lay in the sun until the mud was baked and then washed it from their bodies in stream, sea, or lake. Many tribes, when their habitat location permitted, also took advantage of bathing in mineral springs, long before spas were enjoyed by American palefaces.

INDIAN LIFE IN VILLAGE AND ENCAMPMENT

The life of a boy in an Indian village or encampment was happy and busy. He had periods of strict and intensive training in the course of most days but he also had ample time to think and roam and learn by personal experience. He had to be ready to lend a helping hand to his parents and chiefs when they required it, not when he felt like doing so. When an emergency situation affected the village in any way the youngest teen-age Indian ceased to be a boy and became a man. When the Indian boy had time to use in his own way he spent a lot of it in developing useful skills, such as woodcraft and tracking, and practiced various handcrafts, such as making bows and arrows, chipping arrow heads, and making many articles from skins and feathers. He loved to roam the plains, woods or forests in search of adventure and in the quest of strange or useful plants and flowers, and he often practiced with bow and arrow so that he acquired speed and skill in their use.

ADVENTURING

Though the young Indian was always ready and eager for adventure, he was not needlessly reckless. He learned from chiefs and wise instructors to DARE WITH CARE!, a motto which stands out here and there throughout this book as a reminder to modern chiefs, when their braves are all "dare" and no "care." Most Indian boys had one or two friends of about their own age who were almost constant companions in their adventuring. They were together when they roamed far afield or climbed, broke new trails in unknown and sometimes dangerous territory or swam in lake, sea, stream, or river. They made pacts of mutual help and quite often were able to save each other from serious accident. They stood together and were entirely honest with each other, sharing secrets of totems and trails of which others knew nothing. Together they wrestled, raced, and contested in games of war and peace, so that they were better fitted to meet other challengers from rival bands and thus uphold the honor of their band when grave chiefs judged the contests of strength and skill which brought eager spectators from the village.

FURRED AND FEATHERED WILDTHINGS

Indian boys learned to spot and name the "wings-of-the-air" and the furred wildthings of plains, woods, and forests. Chiefs skilled in woodcraft and wildlife told them whether they named the birds and beasts correctly. The names which

the various tribes gave to animals and birds were more descriptive and as correct as the names palefaces later developed, such as those devised by Audubon. Today, many of the names of animals and fowls of America are those given them by the American Indians. These names remain either in the original or translated forms. For instance, when an early pioneer asked an Algonquin what the ring-tailed, masked creature that looked like a dog was called, the Indian replied *arakun*. Since then, that animal has been known to us as a raccoon. *Musquash* is a more exact name than muskrat, as that amphibious rodent is not a rat.

Indian boys often made pets of animals and birds, such as raccoons, woodchucks, bear cubs, crows, ravens and blackbirds. Sometimes some of these pets were chased from a village back to their natural haunts so that they could tell the other birds and animals how well they had been taken care of and how kind the Indians had been to them while they had been their guests.

SUMMER SLEDS

The youngsters of many tribes found summer fun in coasting down steep grassy hills and sand dunes on sleds made from a piece of stiff buffalo, elk or deer hide. When there were no hills near the village or encampment, two boys pulled the sled by 6- or 8-foot thongs, one fastened to each side of the front of the sled. The modern Indian will have to replace the hide of these sleds by using slats of thin, tough wood, curved up at one end like a toboggan, when using them for coasting down steep hills of grass or sand.

Often such sleds were put to good use by loading heavier pieces of gear, which could not be carried in the arms of a man or the skirt of a woman, onto them. The sleds slipped smoothly along behind the puller, especially over grassy or sandy terrain. Modern Indians can make such sleds from oblong pieces of strong, heavy canvas, about 2½ feet wide and 4 feet long, with a 6-foot length of stout rope strongly sewn onto each side of the sled, directly at the front end.

An exciting game in which these sleds are used will be found in Chapter 17.

TRAVOIS TRANSPORTATION

This mode of transporting belongings and, at times, old people and children when a mass change of encampment was made, was common among Indians of many tribes. Plains Indian travois were usually pulled by horses but sometimes dogs were employed to drag heavy loads on small travois. When neither horses nor dogs were available, the Indians pulled the travois themselves.

The Squaw Hitch

The travois shown in the drawing offers a good opportunity to illustrate the Squaw Hitch which is useful for lashing both packs and gear onto either horse or travois. The travois shown is a dog-drawn one and the two ends of the poles fit through or onto a tough leather pad fastened on top of the dog's back, close to his shoulders. The pad was held in place by one or two leather straps which went through the pad and around the dog's belly.

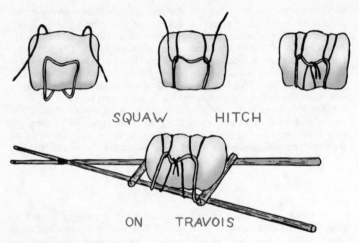

SQUAW   HITCH

ON   TRAVOIS

Tying the Squaw Hitch

The Squaw Hitch, which is effective and much easier to tie than the Diamond Hitch, is used also in fastening packs onto a horse's back or travois. This is how the hitch is tied.

The middle of the doubled rope used for lashing is brought around and under the horse or travois, as shown in Figure 1. Then the two rope ends are brought over, under, and through the doubled rope, as shown in Figure 2. The two rope ends are now pulled as tight as possible and then carried over and around the top of the pack, under the horse's belly or travois, then up to and under the middle of the rope, where they are securely tied.

SEEING LIKE INDIANS

Most American Indians had splendid eyesight not only because their eyes were naturally keen from childhood but also because they were trained to use their eyes to best advantage. Another factor that helped the Indians to guard their good vision was the fact that they had no fine print to tire their eyes and none of our intense modern lighting to wear them out.

Eye Focus

Instructors taught the Indian boys how to make the best use of their eyes and how to spot things which were most difficult to see under normal conditions. They were instructed in looking for and at things from certain angles which made hard-to-see objects stand out more clearly. The different ways of narrowing the focus of their eyes to see far distant objects and using wider vision when scanning country closer at hand formed a part of the training. They were given training in quick sight so that the smallest animal which quickly crossed the trail or darted from point to point in the underbrush was noted and described to the instructor.

Color Identification

Indian eyes could easily distinguish various shading of colors which only a white person trained as an artist would notice. The eyes of the Red Men were trained to see more colors and to observe accurately and with patience. When a modern Indian is shown an ordinary marigold for a moment or two and then asked to describe its coloring, few will have observed that the brilliant orange near the tip of the petals gradually becomes softer as it blends into a darker center, which enhances the brilliance of the petal tips. On careful consideration, one is forced to the conclusion that the average person sees without really observing and has made little, if any, effort to make his eyes work for him under difficult or unusual conditions. This is unfortunate, as life is only half lived when normal eyes work only half time in daylight hours and hardly at all in the darkness.

Observation

After a modern city dweller has spoken with an acquaintance for some time, were he asked the color of that person's tie or the sort of hat and shoes he wore, after his acquaintance had gone, in most cases he would give vague and quite probably erroneous answers. The Indian of the forest or plains really used his eyes to advantage on similar occasions, and even at long range his observation was accurate as to details. The headband or headdress worn by the Indian whom he saw could proclaim him friend or foe and moccasins often told the same story. So important were such things to the Indians that they developed not only the ability to see keenly but to photograph mentally the things they saw for future use.

Best Eye Forward

Although both eyes act as windows for the brain, there is generally one eye stronger than the other, which acts as the master eye. It is important for a modern Indian to know which is his master eye, as that is the eye to use when using a telescope or spotting tube and when looking around a tree trunk, rock or some other object with one eye. Here are ways to decide which is the stronger eye.

Two Eye Test

With *both* eyes open, the brave points his right forefinger held at arm's length, in line with the nose, ahead of him aligning it on a tree trunk at least 30 feet distant. Holding the finger steadily in this position, he then sights along the forefinger *first* with the *right* eye, then with the *left*. The eye which keeps the finger still centered on the trunk of the tree is the master eye. The eye which causes the finger to appear to move to right or left of the tree is the weaker eye.

One Eye Test

This test, though slightly different, will give the same result as the former one. The brave, with the left eye closed, points his right forefinger at arm's length and in line with his nose, at an object at least 30 feet distant, while sighting with his right eye. When the object is centered, he opens his left eye. If the finger is still centered on the object, the right eye is the master eye; if not, make the test with the left eye open to make certain whether the left eye is the stronger.

Making the Best of the Weaker Eye

By squinting with the weaker eye, keeping it about half closed, when looking at distant or nearby objects, a brave will offset to some extent its lesser vision, but a modern Indian should still use his master eye for scouting and observing animals and birds.

Further pointers in how to use the eyes to the best advantage, especially in a dim light, and at night, are detailed in Chapter 13.

Spotting Tubes

In order to make the best possible use of their vision, some of the woodland scouts and hunters used spotting tubes when they wished to fix an eye on some specific part of the landscape, thus limiting their width of vision and confining it to a certain spot. In such circumstances, it is easier to pick out and distinguish game or an enemy, which the use of both eyes may have discerned only vaguely. Naturally, it was the master eye which looked through the tube.

Though the Indians used rolled-up tubes of birchbark, modern Indians can make an equally good tube from either a piece of metal tubing, about 18 inches long and approximately ¾ inch in diameter. An improvised spotting tube can easily be made by carefully rolling a piece of stiff cardboard into a tube of the same size. The tube should be perfectly smooth inside and is used by the stronger eye.

Telescopes and binocular are not dealt with in this book but it should be kept in mind that even Indians of long ago sometimes got telescopes by trade and used them to great advantage. Even a fairly good telescope provided longer range vision than a keen pair of eyes, though it must be remembered that many Indians had phenomenal vision which required no artificial aid for their purposes.

Scanning the Terrain

Indian scouts used this method of searching the country in front of them for hidden enemies, animals, or objects. The spotting tube was used to center the vision on a certain spot, but the scanning method was used to sweep wider spaces. The observer first scanned the ground closest to him by making his eyes travel slowly from left to right over an area which covered a half circle in front and on each side of him. On the return sweep, from right to left, the vision was trained on the terrain a little further afield. Repeating this practice a few times allowed the eyes to cover the whole field of vision ahead and to each side, revealing any suspicious or sought-for objects.

HEARING LIKE INDIANS

Indians knew that ears could be trained to hear better and the boys were taught to use their ears to the best advantage. Indian instructors knew that one could hear better at night and that sounds carried further in the darkness. They knew that the wind could carry sounds for a long distance and that a scout could hear some sounds better when lying with an ear to the ground, especially when the sounds were made by horses' hooves or some large animal in flight. Young braves were taught that they could hear better with their mouths slightly open and that often cupping the hands behind the ears made sounds more distinct, when they came from in front of the braves.

There was need for a brave to know which was the master ear. Indian instructors soon discovered which ear heard better by covering one ear of the boy taking the test, while making slight sounds, which became fainter and fainter as the difficulty of the test was increased. Once both ears had obeyed the command of "listen well," the keener one was discovered. This was the ear on which the young brave would depend most in future.

The-brave-to-be was then taught to turn his keener ear toward the direction from which he believed the sounds came. Cupping it, by placing a hand directly behind it, so that the thumb and forefinger touched the back of the ear, was taught as an aid to the detection and identification of sounds. The Indian teachers knew how the deer and cow moose swiveled their ears toward a sound and they used that principle in their teaching. *But*, these listening tactics were mainly taught for use at night or when the listening brave was very well concealed or while hunting in territory which he knew to be free from hostiles. The eyes, the instructor pointed out, were more important in many circumstances than the ears. The teaching stressed that the combination of sharp eyes and keen ears was necessary on the hunting and war trails.

Though the weaker ear is never covered while listening, it is well for the modern Indian to know which one it is.

Indian pupils were taught to develop keen hearing by listening blindfolded for many varied, soft sounds made by the instructors. Sounds such as the slight movement of branches, the rustle of leaves or a leaf had to be heard at varying distances. The sound of a stealthy tread, or the dropping of a nut or dead twig had to be detected and, what was almost equally important, identified.

Other pointers on how to improve one's ability to hear well are given in Chapter 13.

PHYSICAL FITNESS

Indian instructors trained the boys to bear physical strain tirelessly. They would wake them up at dawn for a swim in a cold lake or river. Long, steady, follow-my-leader runs were taken and speed increased by training and contests. Wrestling was stressed and dodging, an important art, was taught. Soon a young brave learned to dodge not one but three attacking braves, inside a circle scarcely thirty feet in diameter. The Penobscot, Maine, Algonquin Indians trained young hunters to run down deer and kill them with a hunting knife.

INDIAN LANGUAGES

The Indian languages are too varied and too difficult to master easily, and too much research, work, and study are involved in trying to learn the language of even one Indian tribe for use in temporary encampments. Because of this, the author suggests that chiefs and medicine men learn to speak the picturesque English of the Indians, though it is well to remember that the Indian languages when translated into English lose much of their cadence and beauty. Despite this, the author, who has recently been in close contact with chiefs of Plains and Woodland, as well as Haida and other tribes of the Northwest Coast, finds their English not only picturesque but attractive and descriptive. An old Cree chief, who was disappointed with the broken promises of white men, said: "Words are not always as true nor as big as the *thoughts* you think when you say the words."

An Indian chief, speaking in English, once said to representatives of the United

States Government: "Listen well to my talk. Before you came, the wind blew free, and nothing broke the light of the sun. Why do you ask us now to leave the sun, the wind, the lakes, and the rivers and live in wooden lodges?" Here is an example of beauty, dignity, and clarity of speech which we shall do well to observe at our council fires.

Modern chiefs will find that the use of a sort of blank verse, poetical imagination, and the occasional displacement of a few verbs will greatly add to the effectiveness and interest of council fire talks and stories. It adds atmosphere when a chief in council says: "It is good medicine to gather here in our council ring— a circle is power." He can speak of big numbers as being as "many as the leaves on the trees," or being so great that "from a high hill one could not see all with one look." Such phrasing will not be found difficult when a chief writes what he wishes to say in everyday English and then recopies phrases which best lend themselves into the picturesque speech of an Indian orator. The few words and greetings of various tribes which follow may be of service to tribal and band chiefs for use in council, at council fires and on other ceremonial occasions. There is no reason why some of the older braves should not adopt some of them for their own use. Of course, tribes and bands should use the language of their adopted habitat group, as a Woodland Indian would be unable to make himself understood when trying to converse with an Indian of the Great Plains in Iroquian phrases and a Sioux would have to revert to Indian sign language if he wished to talk with a Pawnee.

The Chinook jargon was the simple, useful, and amusing trade language of the Northwest Coast Indians. This language not only was used throughout the vast Northwest Territories but spread to a number of tribes of the Great Plains. Today, *Kla-how-ya!* and *Hi ya!* are not heard only throughout the American and Canadian Northwest, because these salutations are frequently used by Blackfoot and other tribes of the Plains as well. The 350 words of the Chinook jargon take the place of 4,000 English ones. English, French, and the sounds made by birds, animals and things went into the jargon, making it colorful and colloquial. Take words such as that used for a clock or watch—*tick-tick*, for the heart— *tum-tum*, for a crow—*kah-kah*, for a duck—*kweh-kweh*, for a friend—*tilli-kum* and for family and kindred—*tillikums*.

Great Plains Tribes	*Greetings and General Expressions*
Blackfoot:	*Hai-yu!* means Hello! *Hai-yah-ho!* is an exclamation. *Wo-ka-hit!* means listen!
Sioux:	*How!* and *How, kola!* are general greetings, while *Ho mita koda!* means Welcome, friend! *Washtay!* means Good! *Palamo yelo!* is Thanks! *Hokahey! Hokahey!*—to horse; Away! and Charge!

Eastern Forest

Oneida:	*See-goh-li!* means Good morning!
Iroquian:	*Skansh!* means Power to you! *Kou-ee-e!*—Hello! and *Ha-oh!*— I come.
Seneca:	*Oh-neh-nih-hoh!*—that is all.
Northwest Coast:	*Kla-how-ya!*—How are you? *Kla-how-ya tillikum*—How are you friend?

AMERICAN INDIAN TERRITORY
AND HABITAT GROUPS

At one time, the regions of Indian life covered the entire face of the United States, and even today the habitats of the various tribal groups are far flung throughout the United States and Canada. The five main Indian groups are known to most modern chiefs as those of the Great Plains, Woodland, Southwest, Northwest Coast, and tribal groups of California. In addition, there is the Southeast habitat, in which the Seminole live. The Indian tribes of the California habitat made but slight impact on history and youthful minds and imagination. A modern brave may show indifference when he learns that he is going to be initiated as a Witun or Yokut but if he is told that he will soon become a Sioux, Blackfoot, Apache, Seneca, Mohawk, Algonquin or Haida, he will eagerly ask—"How soon?"

NAMING THE BAND

Once a chief has decided which nation or tribe is the best for his band-to-be to adopt—and this decision should be based partly on the site of the band's encampment, or recreational terrain, or hiking territory, and partly on the general interests of the braves-to-be, including crafts—the next step is to form and name the band and to name and initiate its members. They should be solemnly warned that Indians of all ages, from the oldest chiefs to the youngest children, strictly observed and obeyed tribal and band laws. Quite often their lives and success depended on their obedience. Even the dogs were expected to obey laws and all dogs which barked when security dictated silence were killed.

NAMING THE BRAVES

Many of the supposedly correct translations of the personal names of American Indians are incorrect and convey false impressions of the men involved and, frequently, of their actual ranks. The name Crazy Horse, for instance, is the somewhat misleading interpretation of the actual Indian name—"A Man Like a Wild Horse." The real name of Sitting Bull, of the Sioux, was "Buffalo Bull Who Waits." There were two famous Indians called Sitting Bull, one of whom was not a chief but a shaman and many stories told to this medicine man's credit were really stories of the great Oglala-Sioux chief of the same name.

Osceola, while a noted Seminole leader, was never a chief.

Unusual names for would-be warriors, in addition to the many names given in other books of the author, are: Two Strikes—Spotted Tail—Calf Robe—Crow Dog—Eagle Track—Yellow Elk—Red Beaver—Lean Wolf—Bear Claw Marks, and Walking Everywhere. The last name reminds the author of his friend, Chief Walking Buffalo, a Sioux, who was once a renowned scout for the Royal Canadian Mounted Police. This gallant chief, whose life trail has gone straight forward fore more than eighty-three winters, wears his buffalo horns headdress proudly and still takes his part in tribal dances. The Mounties honored him again, recently, for his past services and continuing loyalty.

INDIAN BAND NAMES

There is a wide choice of names which can be given modern Indian bands. A band may be called after a bird, animal, natural phenomenon, place, or star. Band names such as Eagle, Hawk, Flicker, Red Dog, Red Fox, Black Deer, Black Bear, Buffalo, Elk, Lightning, Thunder, Wolf Cove, Lone Island, and North Star are among the many names from which to choose.

WAR GROUP NAMES

The Indians organized War Societies, some for seasoned warriors and others for unfledged braves-to-be. Names were chosen or invented for such groups and among the Plains tribes such names as Fox, Buffalo, Drum, Big Pony, and Shield were used. The Woodland and Northwest Coast tribes used names more inspired by the animals and mystical beings associated with these habitats. The Six Nations, for example, had important societies named False Face, Bear, Eagle, Medicine Turtle, and many others. Northwest Coast tribes used such names as Killer Whale, Sea Otter, Raven, Thunderbird, Sea Lion, Lightning Snake, Dog Fish, Shark, and Wasgo (the sea-monster). All of these groups had certain initiation rites, strict rules, often totems, and usually taboos which were strictly observed.

MODERN TABOOS

Taboos for modern Indians can be imposed by a chief, or by the braves themselves, in encampments. The taboos should be neither too difficult nor too easy, nor yet stereotyped, but they should be very definite and closely observed. Modern braves will not suffer too much from such taboo impositions, as they will gain courage from the fact that they will be following closely on the trail of the Indians of yesterday and have a secret which they need share with nobody. Taboos may be rather complicated or they may be simple ones, such as deciding not to eat a certain food or fruit, which will help to strengthen the brave's will power when the thing which is taboo is something he really likes.

SECRET SOCIETIES AND SECRET MEDICINE SOCIETIES

Nearly all tribes in all habitat groups had secret societies and secret medicine societies. Such groups were organized by and for warriors and medicine men of certain attainments, and sometimes for those with the high possibility of achieving similar attainments. Medicine groups were not always formed of shamans who were already well versed in the secrets and mysteries of good and bad medicine. Sometimes warriors who were deeply interested, and who perhaps had high hopes of becoming medicine men, organized such societies. Membership and rank in these societies was decided strictly on the ability of the members. As in other groups of this sort, the choosing and acceptance of proposed members were followed by the initiation, and all belonging to the groups strictly adhered to laws of different kinds, depending on the type of society, without question.

Laws of the Societies

Though the laws which governed the various societies were serious and severe, some of them could be fun too. The members of most Indian Eagle Societies would not allow anyone to pass behind them while they were eating—because real eagles disliked that greatly. Members of different Turtle Societies moved very slowly at certain times, perhaps lasting for an hour or more and other members of the tribe who were in the dark concerning the rites and rules of these societies wondered what had suddenly come over tribal members who unexpectedly, and apparently for no reason, reduced their usual speed of walking and doing things to a strictly slow-motion basis. The members of a Buffalo Society would occasionally stop and paw the earth for a few moments. A Bear Society member would embrace the trunk of a tree, reach up as high as he could, claw the bark and, perhaps, scratch his back or shoulders against the trunk of a convenient tree. Most of the actions performed were symbolic.

Organizing Societies

Modern chiefs can form such groups within a tribe, or a band of six or eight members can become a group or society, with initiation ceremony, totems, secret signs, and all the other regulations which go toward providing the appeal of such groups.

When secret societies are formed within a tribe, modern chiefs have to exercise care that such groups do not develop into a *clique* which promotes snobbishness instead of the over-all, one-for-all spirit which distinguishes true Indian groups formed under wise leadership. Since such groups were formed for bands of practically all ages, there is no reason why a modern chief should not organize them, or suggest that they be organized, among groups of braves ranging in age from twelve years and upward. Care should be taken, as it was in forming Indian societies, that the leaders of such groups be boys with marked qualities of leadership and whose influence will be a good one on the society being organized.

CEREMONIES

Modern chiefs can work out little ceremonies of considerable importance in connection with tribal and band life. Among many tribes, for example, when a brave from another tribe was adopted he was given new moccasions of the tribe of which he had become a member. All braves selected for adoption by the Iroquois were given new Iroquian moccasins that they might, as the chief pointed out when the new tribal members were initiated, follow the right Iroquois path. In modern Indian bands this symbolic change of moccasins can be carried out most easily by simply painting new, suitable devices on the old moccasins or sewing on a gay-colored strip of cloth which the other members of the band may wear on their moccasins.

Indian Encampment Band Ceremonies

There were a great number of ceremonies observed by members of Indian bands, led by a chief in their performance. Since new ceremonies were frequently devised, to meet new situations which arose in the life of the tribe or band and the ceremonies varied vastly, according to the habitat and customs of the Indian groups carrying out the ceremonies, modern chiefs may not fear that they are being "un-Indian" if they devise and improvise to meet the needs of their bands. A few suggested ceremonies which are suitable for bands of modern Indians are set down here, and alert chiefs will add others to the number as the need arises.

Welcome Ceremonies

Special ceremonies are in order for greeting visiting chiefs, members of other bands, or entire bands or tribes, and other visitors. The importance and scope of such ceremonies will be decided by the size and importance of the visiting groups and the prestige and rank of the visiting chief or chiefs. Such greetings often include loud whoops of welcome on the part of the braves receiving the visit and a more formal welcome by the band chief, followed by a dance of some sort or an exhibition of prowess of one sort or another by the welcoming band. A small gift of a band-made artifact may be presented to the leading chief of a tribe, or to a band, or lone chief making the visit.

Departure Ceremonies

These rituals are used to "speed the parting guest." A talk is given by the band leader, who is host, thanking the visitors for coming and expressing the hope that they will come again. The artifact gift is perhaps best made at this time rather than at the time of welcoming, but either is correct. A guard of honor consisting of two to six warriors provides safe conduct for the visitors until they have traveled beyond the limits of the encampment. A sub-chief can be in charge of the guard when escorting an important visitor or group of visitors.

Medicine Shield Society Ceremony

If there is a Medicine Shield Society in the encampment, they can perform the traditional ceremony, on the morning of chosen days, of presenting the faces of their shields to the morning sun for five minutes or so, while some members of the group perform a Medicine Dance and appeal to the sun for guidance and help.

Sun Thanks Ceremony

A number of powerful tribes, including the Comanche, greeted the *first rays* of the sun on certain occasions in a manner which they considered suitable. The Comanche, for instance, had three of their best warriors greet the rays with three loud and prolonged wolf howls. The warriors, of course, were painted and dressed in full regalia, in order to extend full honor to the sun. Any tribe or band may use this sun greeting, at well-spaced intervals, the author suggests, as the howls will awaken all in the encampment, even if they are not lined up to give personal and moral support to the ceremonial greeting.

Such Sun Ceremony is especially appropriate after a few days of continual rain and generally bad weather. All of the tribe or band can participate in such an event. The chief can greet the rising sun with an appropriate Indian prayer of thanks and an offering of beads, feathers, or "sweet grass," burned before the band, or some other suitable gift substituted for any of those just mentioned, to welcome the return of the sun. Such a ceremony assures a very early start to a day's Indian activity program and plans should have been made in advance—or on the spot if there is no skilled weatherman in the encampment to make  a forecast—for fishing parties to set out immediately after the ceremony, while other bands commence suitable activities at the same time.

Passing of Time Ceremonies

There were a number of ceremonies which the Indians observed to mark or celebrate the passage of time. The Indians had many ways of "telling the time." Those whose territory lay closest to that of the Eskimo (who are also ethnically classed as Indians) set up stones to shadow-clock the length of days. Other Indian tribes told the time by shadows cast by hills, trees, or stones, or by when the sun rested exactly on a mountain peak or hill top when rising or setting. Modern chiefs can build occasional brief but picturesque and meaningful ceremonies around such times of shadow or sun positions.

Some American Indian tribes of the Southwest kept track of the passing of days leading to an important event by undoing a knot on a rope each day, the number of knots on the rope when first hung in position in a prominent part of the encampment indicating the number of days to the special event. This passing-of-suns indicator was operated by a chief or medicine man or in some cases by the camp herald, who was held responsible for undoing one knot each morning or at sunset each day. In the case of smaller bands, knotted ropes were distributed by a chief to each member of the band, with the number of days indicated on the rope by the number of knots. No excuse was accepted from those who failed to keep daily track of time, by undoing one knot with the passing of each sun.

When the author has set up such a time-recording device to call attention to some very special event, he has frequently seen serious-faced modern Indians gravely counting the remaining knots on the rope hung in front of the chief's tepee to find out when the coming pow-wow or council fire would take place! Apparently they had so thoroughly entered into the spirit of the Indian encampment ways that it did not occur to them that the event would be "a week from next Saturday."

Tribal or Band Initiation Ceremonies

These important events should be carried out with considerable ceremony, and though perhaps they may be carried out more effectively at a council fire, there is no reason why minor or even major ceremonies of this kind may not be staged at almost any other hour of the day. Full regalia should be worn by those attending the event and all ceremonial procedure performed so that the ceremony is significant and impressive at any time. Such schedules are best decided by the band chief, in council with the chiefs at the main camp, and the timing may often be dictated by events in the main camp's mass Indian activities. Naturally, no such consideration exists in the case of isolated bands or where the main camp is not concerned with Indian activities.

Initiation of Secret Society Band Members

Such initiations are far more effective when carried out in secret at some out-of-the-way place in woodland or forest site, selected by the chief in advance. Such a ceremony can be made still more dramatic when each brave to be initiated finds his way to the spot alone. It is strongly recommended that in such cases whistles be carried by each member of the band as a precaution, should one or more of the band stray from the unmarked or secret trail. When two or three chiefs or sub-chiefs are available at the time set for the ceremony they can be posted at key points to see that those attending the initiation do not go astray en route.

Modern chiefs will realize that much of the interest, thrill, and glamour of such events lies in the secrecy surrounding them. They should be shrouded in mystery and those to be initiated are sternly warned that the place, ritual, and everything else connected with the event is strictly secret and that any fixed taboos must be carefully observed.

Preliminary Coup-Claiming Ceremonies

These ceremonies can prove useful, interesting, and amusing at the same time. They provide practice for the braves who have decided that they have reason and right to claim coup. At the same time they allow the chief of the band to decide whether the claimants' reasons are sufficient and likely to cause the tribal chief to decide that the braves' claims are valid and the braves worthy of the honor of counting and claiming coup in council, or at a ceremonial council fire.

Special Offering Dances

Individual Indians frequently performed special dances as a thanks offering to the gods for aid in the fulfillment of vows or for special favors granted in response to prayers. Sometimes these dances re-enacted to a certain extent what had happened and at other times they were simply a stately, rhythmic, or whirlwind sort of dance conceived by the brave making the offering, in the firm belief that if his gods understood the meaning of the dance nothing else mattered. Two or three such dances can be given a place on a band assembly program, when the braves participating *really wish* to dance their thanks for favors received. Dances of special interest and merit can be noted by the band chief and these dances can be performed again at a tribal council fire at a later date.

Medicine Pipe Ceremonies

It is good practice and training for a modern Indian band to make a medicine pipe and, in consultation with the chief, to appoint a Keeper of the Pipe to take care of it for twenty-four consecutive hours. The Keeper should be changed daily since there are many taboos and ceremonies to observe as a Keeper of the sacred Pipe and it is well to distribute the responsibility for its safekeeping among all members of the band.

The pipe should be made with great care, each member of the band contributing something to its construction, such as cutting, carving, painting, and providing suitable feathers, fur, beads, short lengths of colored cords, and small strips of gaily colored cloth or leather for its decoration. The illustration shows one kind of medicine pipe, and how to make pipes is told in Chapter 19.

The pipe is kept in several wrappings of bright colored cloth or hide and is a separate bundle from other sacred bundles. The Medicine Pipe bundle must never be allowed to touch the ground. When the bundle has to be laid on the ground for some ceremonial purpose, a gaily colored blanket or strip of cloth or leather is first spread on the ground and then the pipe bundle placed on it.

The chief should devise special rituals, dances, songs and ceremonials to be performed when the pipe has to be unwrapped for any very special reason and when appointing each new Keeper of the Pipe. He may also decide, in council, on the specific taboos to be observed by the Keepers of the Pipe in his band. The following are a few of the difficulties which can assail the Keepers of the Pipe as they disciplined and plagued the ancient keepers among the Blackfoot, Arapaho, Sioux and other Plains tribes. The Keeper of the Pipe was often allowed to point only with his thumb and no other digit. He was forbidden to pick up any object which he found, no matter how useful or attractive it might be. He was not allowed to sit on his bedding, though he could lie down on it to sleep. He sometimes had to light a small smudge fire when the sun was directly overhead, while the pipe bundle lay close to the fire. The Keeper of the Pipe in some tribes had to move the pipe bundle several times daily, in sunwise sequence, among other strict observances.

CHARM, MEDICINE, OFFERING, PERSONAL, BAND, AND TRIBAL SONGS

A charm or medicine song, which is composed by a medicine man or brave in order to help to accomplish something special or work medicine or magic, often begins—"Ho Earth! Ho Sun! Ho Moon and Stars, hear me!" Help is then asked in a few short, concise phrases. The tunes composed for such songs are often not so important as the words, and quite frequently the airs are repetitious and rather monotonous, with unexpected high notes creeping into the melody at unanticipated places.

Many Indians composed personal, band, or tribal songs with simple words or merely syllables, such as *Hey-a-hey-hey-a-hey!* predominating. Many tribes commenced their songs with such expressions as, *Oh! Oh!* or *Sh-h-h-h!* or *Aah hey! Aah hey!*

Here, as an example, is the last verse of a medicine Sleep Song, sung very softly by Sky Bird, an Indian woman, on the counsel of a medicine man. She composed the song, as she sang, in order to put enemies to sleep. They had stolen her baby and she had come, alone, to rescue it.

> 'Sleep's silver stream sings a soft, sleepy song,
> Deep slumber keep eyelids closed all night long.
> Hey-a-hey! Hey-a-hey!—My sleep song obey!'

As the last note died on the lips of Sky Bird, the chief suddenly fell forward before the fire. She watched him closely but he did not move.[1]

[1] See *Indian Adventure Trails*, by Allan A. Macfarlan (New York: Dodd, Mead & Company, 1953).

Chiefs, medicine men, and braves who have little idea about composing songs or melodies can appeal to a musical member of the band or tribe to compose a song for them. The ghost-writer composer, once he has accepted the task, is sworn to secrecy, and when the song is finished and accepted he is paid for it by being given some small, suitable gift such as an Indian would give. A few good feathers, a necklace or an armband, one or two arrows, a piece of colored cloth or leather, are acceptable gifts. For such services, chiefs, who always tried to "give like a chief" (which is the reason so many of them were poor from a present day viewpoint) often gave a horse, a canoe, a tepee, or some similar gift of considerable value.

COUNCIL RING AND COUNCIL FIRES

This topic can easily fill several books, and has already done so. Because of this, only some council ring features are touched on here. The selection of a council ring site, the making of the council ring and its fires, ceremonies and programs have been covered in an earlier book by the author.[2]

The charmed circle on which the council fire burns should be regarded with respect and, whenever possible, should only be used for council fire purposes. Council fire activities can be greatly varied and range from grand and solemn ceremonies to lighthearted challenges and Indian games.

The council ring can be ornamented in Indian fashion, with a decorative entrance and a gaily colored blanket hung on a frame behind the chief's chair.

Painted shields can be hung from trees or poles prior to the council fire and taken down when it is over and the council ring is deserted.

The log cabin type of fire is often used for council fires. It has many things in its favor, such as good luminosity, the ease with which fuel can be added and its long-burning quality, especially when the fire tender is skilled in that craft.

Torches can be used to provide additional illumination in the council ring. They can be mounted on poles set firmly into the ground just inside the circle.

The council fire should always be lighted with ceremony, elaborate or simple, based on the council fire theme for that particular night. The fire should also be brought to an end with ceremony, which may take the form of some suitable closing words by a chief or medicine man or the recital of a suitable Indian prayer, such as the Omaha Tribal Prayer.

Simple but strict etiquette should govern the procedure at a council fire, from beginning to end.

Suitable programs for a council fire are varied and many. The activities can include dances, Indian and other suitable songs, ceremonies of various sorts, coup feather claiming and awards, dual and tribal challenges, acts of mystery and magic, short Indian stories, plays and pageants.

[2] See *Campfire and Council Ring Programs*, by Allan A. Macfarlan (New York: Association Press, 1951).

2

Indian Dwellings

The Indians built a number of splendid, substantial dwellings, the most durable and magnificent of which were the huge, cedar plank houses of the Indians of the Northwest Coast.

NORTHWEST COAST HOUSES

These structures were built to stand and serve for many years and defied the elements. Storm, cold, rain, winds, and snow had but little effect on these superb structures. They served their owners, and huge assemblies at potlatches, well in that rugged part of Indian territory which was their habitat. Such houses, as illustrated, took time, skill, and patience to construct. Though they stood on the

edges of great forests of giant red and yellow cedars, they were not dwarfed by their surroundings. It was hard for dwellings which often measured one hundred feet in length and sixty feet in width to appear small. They were built of thick, red cedar planks and were splendid without and within. They had huge, decorative house poles in front and wonderfully carved and painted house posts and screens inside. There are records of houses which measured as much as 500 feet in length and 75 feet in width. Such houses as those of the chiefs, princes, and some nobles easily held a thousand people. The massive roof of each Haida house formed a single gable, rising 20 feet or more from the ground in front. One main fire burned in the middle of the floor, often below the second terrace of beaten earth which was found in many of these houses. Such dwellings looked out over a pebbly, crescent-shaped beach with rugged islands and a stormy strait, which the Indians dared in their magnificent canoes. The building of one of these houses is not suggested as a summer project for even the most ardent band of modern Indians.

WOODLAND LONG HOUSES

The long houses of the Six Nations were also substantial, and made comfortable homes for many of the Woodland tribes. These dwellings are much easier to build than the huge, heavy houses of the Northwest Coast. They can be made by erecting a framework of stout poles or saplings, and covering these with squares of strong, waterproof canvas (instead of the thick slabs of elm or cedar bark covering actually used by the Woodland people). The drawing of

one of these houses shows just what they looked like, and the pointers given in this chapter on covering such frameworks will help in building one. The size of the long house is something to be decided by the band or tribe building it. These Algonquian dwellings varied greatly in size; the larger ones, sheltering ten to twenty families, measured about 100 feet long and 35 feet wide, and larger. The families lived in rows of small cubicles which ran along the sides of each long house. As a rule, there was a doorway at each end of the house. An open fire burned in the center of the house, filling the dwelling with heat and smoke, a good deal of which was carried off by the smoke hole, or holes, cut in the high, gabled roof. The size of a house for a band of eight could be about 18 feet long and 9 feet wide, the dimensions being based largely on the material and time available for building such a house.

WIGWAMS

Dome-shaped shelters of various kinds were built in different ways by a number of Indian tribes. These wigwams were comfortable, waterproof, and convenient, though they lacked the artistic beauty of the tepee and some other Indian dwellings. In some cases, the lower third of the wigwam was built by making a circular hole in the ground and building a dome over it either by using bent saplings, covered with bark or sod, or making a roof of thatched branches. Sometimes more substantial wigwams were built with planking of some sort, often covered with earth or clay, with holes cut for windows and a smoke hole in the center of the dome. The lower part of a wigwam built below ground can cause it to become damp and useless at times, so that one built entirely above ground is best, in addition to being the most easily built.

Mark a circle on the ground with a diameter of about 7 or 8 feet. With a pointed, hardwood stick about 1½ inches in diameter, punch a series of holes in the ground about 8 inches deep, around the circle, roughly 18 inches apart. Cut from four to six thin saplings (by thinning a stand in which the young trees are too thick) long enough to be pushed down firmly into the holes in the ground. Set a pole up on each side of the circle and bend them inward so that the tops can be tied together to form a dome 5 to 7 feet above ground level. Force somewhat shorter saplings into the other holes and lash them onto the longer saplings of the main framework at suitable points so that a framework that looks like a

beehive is formed. The illustration shows how it should look. Now, after stripping them of their leaves, lash withy branches horizontally around and onto the upright rods, with about 12 or 16 inches between the hoops. The wigwam framework is now complete. It should be strong and barely flexible. It is covered with wigwam "mats" which can be made from fairly heavy, or at least waterproof, canvas cut into squares measuring about 3 feet square. Such mats are always handy for erecting temporary shelters and they can be made still more practical by punching a small grommet into each corner, through which the cord is passed that ties the squares to the framework. These mats are used as shingles. The wigwam is covered by starting at the bottom and working upward, the upper mats always covering the lower mats, adding layer after layer until the entire framework is evenly covered.

THATCHING LEAN-TO'S AND WATERPROOFING SHELTER COVERS

There are only two or three sure ways in which a novice can be certain of roofing any kind of shelter so that it will be really waterproof, apart from covering the roof with a tarpaulin or some other waterproof cloth or material. One way is to use large sheets of bark, taken from a *dead* birch or elm tree. Other ways are the use of the canvas "mats" suggested for covering the wigwam, shingles of some material, or a tar paper covering, which always appears ugly when used on a wildwood shelter. All shingle types of roofing have, of course, to be started at the bottom of the shelter, or roof framework, with each upper layer overlapping, on top, the layer directly under it. Another important point in endeavoring to make any roof rainproof is to make certain that there are enough supports, upright and cross pieces, to assure an even, sloping surface, as any part of the framework which sags is certain to let water in.

This information may surprise the novice who has read how easy it is to go into the woods, set up a rough lean-to or similar shelter and then "thatch" it speedily with pine, spruce, or other branches so that it will be completely waterproof. Though the brave arranges the branches so that the leaves point downward, and begins his thatching at the foot of the roof and works upward, using a correct overlap, and even though he may add an extra layer of protecting branches, the sad truth remains—the roof will leak a great deal when it rains, or even showers. There is no doubt that an experienced woodsman with time on his hands can build a bough roof that is reasonably waterproof, but the real woodsman has enough foresight to take a sheet of tarpaulin or canvas along so that he sleeps dry.

These thatching details are not given to convince amateur woodsmen that good shelters cannot be built with wildwood material. They can, but it is not an easy task. The information is given in the hope that the difficulties pointed out will deter the novice from spending a miserable night in wet blankets in a leaky wildwood shelter.

Plastic materials are generally unsatisfactory as shelter coverings, chiefly because they shut out all air, so that the shelters become unbearably hot in summer. Eight- or ten-ounce duck, or lightweight canvas does a satisfactory shelter-covering job, as does unbleached muslin, which is also good for making tepees. Sailcloth is quite expensive, as is Egyptian cotton, for making or roofing outdoor shelters. Modern braves should know that the tepee of today is no longer covered with cow buffalo or any other animal hide. The practical Indian abreast of the times uses heavy cotton or unbleached muslin in the construction of both tepees and shelters.

To waterproof shelter and tepee covers, early in the morning—when the dew has been dried by the sun—rub a cake of beeswax over the material to be waterproofed and let the hot sun rays do the rest. Though there are a number of ways to do a more thorough waterproofing job, when linseed and other oils are available, the simple method described will be found effective.

INDIAN SUMMER CAMPS AND SHELTERS

A considerable number of Indian tribes built rather crude shelters of various kinds for use only in the summer months or as temporary dwellings at a hunting camp.

The Comanche used a shelter, among others, built in almost exactly the same way as the wigwam described in this chapter. It was called a *wickiup* and was a frame of hooped saplings covered with bark, brush, or skins, according to the season and the area in which it was set up.

This tribe, though it also used tepees, built open summer shelters with a brush roof supported on poles. The poles used were about 10 feet long and 3 inches in diameter. There were *always* an even number of poles, generally four or six, and they were driven into the ground to form an oblong or square with the tops of the poles about 7 or 8 feet above ground level. Four saplings were placed on top of these uprights, thinner ones laid on top of them, and the shelter was then roofed with leafy, green boughs. Such shelters were used as protection from the summer sun and often no attempt was made to make the roofs waterproof. The drawing shows what they looked like.

TEPEES OF THE PLAINS

The tepee was perhaps the most romantic, picturesque, and comfortable dwelling used by any Indians, and it had the additional advantages of being durable

and portable. In the days of the buffalo, from twelve to twenty cow buffalo hides sewn together with tough sinews were used in making one tepee, its size deciding the number of hides used. Today, heavyweight duck, cotton drill, unbleached muslin, or light canvas is used. The inside diameter of the tepee ranged from 10 to 30 feet. Indians of different tribes were known as either "three-pole people" or "four-pole people," according to the number of poles which formed the basic pole tripod and on which the other twelve to twenty poles rested. Among the well-known tribes using the three-pole foundation were the Sioux, Cheyenne, Pawnee, Plains Cree, Mandan, Arapaho, and Assiniboine. The four-pole foundation was favored by equally famous tribes, for instance, the Blackfoot, Crow, Comanche, and Omaha. The three-pole foundation gave a tepee a light, rather spiral, graceful appearance, whereas the four-pole foundation, which grouped the poles more to the sides of the tepee, gave it a somewhat stockier look.

The painted tepees were the dwellings of chiefs or medicine men, as a rule, and these lodges were artistically decorated with painted pictures of birds or animals, stripes, circles, various geometric patterns, and symbols in many colors. Generally, the tepee of a chief could be recognized by a streamer of colored buck-skin, cloth, or fur hung from the top of a tepee pole above the door. Often, there were fifty or more tepees in a Plains Indian camp and there were generally about four persons to each. There was an allotted place for each occupant. A rigid etiquette was observed which dictated, for instance, that visitors in a tepee must never pass between the tepee master and the fire, and that the chief's place was at the rear of the lodge, close to his bed. The rank and position of each tepee owner regulated its place in village and camp.

Though it is true that the tepee door of most tribes faced east, its position was not entirely governed by the rising sun. Many Plains tribes lived in areas where the prevailing wind blew from the west, and for comfort the doors faced east. Two wands crossed in front of a tepee door, whether the tepee flap was open or closed, meant either that the owners were not at home or that they should not be disturbed. This symbol also served as a lock and was strictly regarded as such by other Indians.

Tepee poles were made from lodge-pole pine, spruce, or cedar and other slim, straight trees which were not flexible. They were peeled and dressed down, generally to the heart wood, the men sometimes aiding the women with this work. When ready for use, the tapering poles averaged from 2 inches at the top to 6 inches at the butt and were from 12 to 30 feet in length. Much lighter poles are used today because the cloth covers are so much lighter than the hide covers were. Often the butts of the poles were sharpened so that they could be forced into the ground 2 or 3 feet for additional stability.

In erecting the tepee, the three- or four-pole foundation was tied together with a stout rawhide thong, the point at which they were tied being decided by the height of the tepee cover. The poles were then raised into an upright position, the butt ends of the poles being equally spaced in a circle. The remaining poles were then placed in the crotch of the tripod or four-pole foundation and spread into position, about 30 inches apart. In high winds, short stakes were driven at an angle a few inches above the ground, across the pole butts, inside the tepee. The average tepee measured from 12 to 18 feet in diameter at the base and was usually set up so that it slanted slightly toward the rear.

The tepee cover was hoisted on a single pole from inside the tepee framework and a woman, standing on another woman's shoulders, tied all the tops of the loose poles tightly together at the point where the tripod poles were tied and adjusted and fastened the cover at the top. Strong wooden skewers about the size of pencils pinned the cover together in front. The smoke hole in the roof of the tepee was made by folding the two flaps above the entrance back, each flap being attached to a long pole outside the tepee. By the movement of one or both poles, wind could be shut out, and the smoke hole functioned like a chimney. The draft was usually good enough to draw the smoke from the fire near the center of the tepee out through the smoke hole. The tepee fireplace, set just back of the center of the tepee, ranged from about 15 to 24 inches in diameter and was often a square of stones set into the earth. A very small fire kept the tepee warm. The smoke hole was protected by a bull cover, also known as a storm cap, placed over the top ends of the tepee poles during heavy rains.

The tepee covering was staked so that it touched the ground all around in cold weather but in warm weather could be turned up as high as required to cool the lodge. Many tepees had a buffalo skin lining, known as a dew cloth, encircling the entire tepee and fastened to the lodge poles about 5 or 6 feet above ground level. These dew cloths were often painted or beaded with colorful designs of various sorts. This lining hanging down inside the tepee carried the draft upward, so that it did not blow on the occupants, and insulated the tepee against heat and cold.

The tepee entrance, which often faced the rising sun, was usually about 3 feet high. It was covered by an oval of stiff pelt, generally weighted at the foot, so that this cover, fastened by a hide thong at the top, would close automatically. When the door covers were not fastened at the top of the entrance, they were fastened to the windward side of it.

When participating in *The Stampede* at Calgary and *Indian Days* at Banff, recently, the author was interested to see how the traditions of some of the tribes taking part were perpetuated. Men and women of the tribes piled practically all of their baggage and personal belongings on the ground, exactly where the center of the tepee would be, then set the three or four foundation poles up over it. This not only saved time and effort later on but indicated just where each tepee was to be erected. At one point modernism triumphed over tradition and instead of one woman's standing on another's shoulders to adjust and tie the top of the tepee cover, a short ladder was used.

MAKING AN INDIAN TEPEE FOR MODERN BRAVES

A colorful tepee can be made as an indoors or outdoors project by a band of modern braves. Many habitable and decorative tepees originated on a living room floor. A Plains tepee can be made as a family project at home, with mother contributing a big share of the work by operating the sewing machine. The entire tepee can be ready to set up when sunny weather invites the band or family out of doors.

The following directions are for making a 14-foot tepee. Tepees can be made larger or smaller, but a smaller one is not recommended, as the slight economy in cost of the material is not worth the tepee interior space sacrificed.

Materials Required

Even the Indians of today make their tepees from unbleached muslin, cotton drill, heavyweight duck, and occasionally light canvas. It is suggested that modern braves use unbleached muslin, 8-oz. duck, or some other tight-weave cotton in making their lodges. Acquiring tepee poles these days is a real problem when wildwood material is desired. Unless suitable poles can be cut from overgrown stands of really straight, suitable young trees, they are best bought at a lumber yard and tapered and worked by hand. White pine 2 x 4's can be bought in 20-foot lengths at some lumber yards, and such lengths can be cut diagonally to

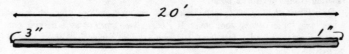

make two poles, as shown in the illustration. Fir and spruce also can be had in the sizes mentioned; these woods are considerably cheaper than white pine but not so good. A chief who can improvise metal ferrules, made from 8- or 10-inch lengths of lightweight but strong metal pipe, can not only use the more easily obtainable 10-foot lengths of suitable lumber but will have far more convenient lengths of tepee poles to transport.

Tepee poles can also be made from lengths of strong bamboo poles about 1½ inch in diameter, without splits or cracks. Lengths of 8 or 10 feet can be fitted below a joint with a strong metal ferrule about 10 inches long. Five inches of this brass or other metal ferrule is fitted and fastened to one end of a length of pole, and the second length is pushed into it so that it fits snugly into the open metal ferrule. The over-all strain from the tepee cover is not so great that these thin bamboo poles cannot be used; but slightly heavier lengths of bamboo, up to 2½ inches in diameter, can be used if desired. Because of their un-Indian appearance, the author is not keen on bamboo poles for tepees, but he has recently seen light metal poles used by real Indians. In the circumstances, such substitutes are made necessary by the usual inaccessibility of lodgepole pines and are suggested because of their convenience, straightness, and the ease with which they can be carried in a car or on a car top.

Whipping about 6 inches of the top and foot of each bamboo pole with strong cord or wide strips of adhesive tape will considerably strengthen these poles and prevent them from splitting if roughly handled.

The bamboo poles can be made to appear less Oriental by painting them in dull gray or dark brown.

The following materials are required to make a tepee.

Unbleached muslin, or other tight-weave cotton—46 yards, 36 inches wide.
Heavy thread—3 or 4 spools.

Poles—11 to 16 poles, 18 to 20 feet (approximately) long, tapering from 1 or 1½ inches at the top to about 3 to 4 inches at the butt. These poles should be strong and rigid. Two of these poles should be one foot longer but lighter. These are used for the smoke hole ears.

Cord—55 feet of strong cord, about ³⁄₁₆ inch in diameter.

Rope—12 feet of strong ¼-inch rope, for loops at base of tepee cover.

Rope—16 feet of ½-inch rope for lashing foundation and other poles together.

Rope—An additional 18 feet of stout, ½-inch rope is needed to serve as an anchor rope if using a 4-pole foundation tepee.

Lacing pins—14 smooth, straight hardwood pins 10 to 12 inches long, about the thickness of a pencil, rounded, and tapered to a blunt point at each end. Hardwood dowels, ¼ inch in diameter, can be made into lacing pins.

Tepee pegs—21 hardwood pegs, 12 to 14 inches long, straight, rounded and tapering from 1 inch to a point.

Door frame sticks—One ½ inch thick and 3 feet long, and one 1 inch thick and 3 feet long, for an *oblong* door cover. If a *horseshoe-shaped cover* is desired, one stick 1 inch thick and 3 feet long, and one 7½-foot supple willow wand will be needed.

Storm cap—A 5-foot square of lightweight canvas. This is to make a tepee top cover, often called a "bull boat" by Plains tribes, because it is shaped exactly like a bull boat. A 22-foot length of ⅜-inch rope is also needed.

Additional reinforcement—To give the tepee greater durability, a rope ⅜ inch in diameter can be sewn into the hem at the base of the tepee. This will require 44 feet of rope. The edge of the tepee door opening may be reinforced in the same way, by sewing 6½ feet of ¼-inch rope into the hem.

Making the Tepee Cover

The 46 yards of 36-inch material should be cut into seven strips, one each of the following lengths, as shown in the diagram: 29 feet; 28 feet 4 inches; 27 feet 4 inches; 23 feet 6 inches; 16 feet 4 inches; 9 feet 4 inches; and 3 feet. There will be a one-foot strip left over, which is used for facing and reinforcing.

First, mark each selvage except the 3-foot strip with a pencil at the center of each strip of cloth. Then pin each strip onto the next in size by overlapping them ½ inch at each selvage, with the pencil marks directly overlapping, the longer strip of cloth always overlapping the shorter piece. The only exception is the 9-foot-4-inch strip, which should overlap the 29-foot strip. It is imperative that the pencil marks be centered and directly in line. When all of the strips are securely pinned, spread the material out smoothly on the floor. Tie one end of a 14½-foot length of strong cord to a nail driven into the floor at the center of the top of the 29-foot length of cloth, marked A in the diagram. Tie the other end of the cord to a piece of colored chalk and use the cord as a compass, drawing a semicircle from point B to point C. Sketch in the smoke hole ears, as shown, 16 inches wide at each end of the 9-foot-4-inch strip and running diagonally across the cloth to its full width at the center. At points D and E, where the shorter strip joins the 29-foot length, cut a semicircle 2 inches in diameter. This assures a neat, snug fit when the tepee is set up. Cut evenly along the chalk lines and save the scraps for facing and reinforcing. Much time will be

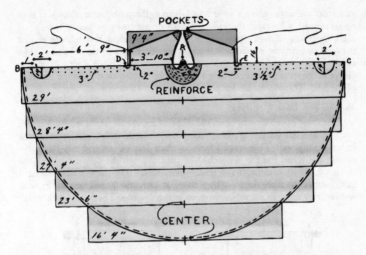

saved, and the sewing will be stronger and look neater, if the tepee cover is stitched on a sewing machine.

To make the work easier to handle and less bulky while sewing, unpin the 29-foot strip from the 28-foot-4-inch strip and work on this first section separately. Stitch the 9-foot-4-inch strip to the 29-foot strip on each edge of the ½-inch overlap, at the selvage. This double stitching makes the seam stronger. Complete all of the work on this piece. With the scraps, face the two front strips where the eyelets are to be made and turn them under, so they will be inside the tepee. Reinforce the edges of the door all around and if it is to be additionally reinforced with ¼-inch rope, for added strength, the rope should be stitched inside the hem. Make a small pocket, about 5 inches deep, at the top end of each smoke hole ear. Also reinforce the area around the tongue, marked A in the drawing, with scraps. Reinforce the edges of the smoke hole ears with the ³⁄₁₆-inch cord by turning the edge of the material over the cord, like a hem, and sewing the cord inside from point D to point E. Make each set of eyelets 3 inches apart on what will be the underside of the tepee cover and 3½ inches on what will be the side which overlaps it, as shown in the drawing, spacing them about 7 inches apart and ¾ inch from the edge. They should be buttonholed or served with strong thread to prevent raveling or tearing, and should be just large enough for the lacing pins to fit into easily. Finally, buttonhole or serve a ¼-inch eyelet in the lower outer corner of each smoke hole ear and pass a 15-foot length of ³⁄₁₆-inch cord through it and tie in place. Sew a strong one-inch metal ring securely onto the center of the little tongue, A.

Now stitch all of the remaining strips together, always overlapping the selvage of the longer strip over the shorter one and stitching each selvage edge to make the seam stronger. This overlapping prevents rain from seeping in between the seams when the tepee is erected and helps rain to run off easily. When this is completed, the 29-foot strip is also overlapped onto the 28-foot-4-

inch strip and sewn. Make a 1- or 2-inch hem in the tepee cover; then if it is to be reinforced with rope, the ⅜-inch length of rope can be passed through it easily by passing a large safety pin, to which it is attached, through one end of the rope and feeding it gradually through the entire hem to the other end. The ends should be securely sewn so the rope will remain in place. Every 24 inches, except at the entrance, securely sew a 6-inch loop of ¼-inch rope to the top edge of the hem. These loops are for pegging down the tepee cover.

Making the Door Covering

If the door covering is to be in the shape of an oblong, make a hem 3 inches deep along each selvage of the 3-foot strip of cloth which reinforces it and makes it hang well. Then make a hem one inch deep at one end and 1¾ inches deep at the other. Put the one-inch-thick stick through the deeper hem and the ½-inch-thick stick through the smaller one. Fasten the thinner stick about 3 inches above the tepee doorway by a thong at each end looped around the stick and securely sewn to the tepee cover, as in the diagram. The heavy stick at the

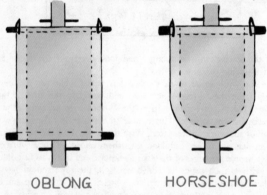

OBLONG   HORSESHOE

lower end is left free and will automatically close the door cover. If a horseshoe-shaped cover is preferred, it is easy to make by bending a supple stick, such as willow, about 7½ feet long and about one inch in diameter, into a horseshoe shape. Lash one end 3 inches from each end of the one-inch-thick stick so no ends of the willow extend beyond it, then sew the cloth over this frame. When this door cover is hung by two loops above the door opening, the straight stick should be against the tepee cover and the ends of the curved stick away from the tepee cover.

Before the tepee is erected, the cover should be spread out on the floor or other hard surface and waterproofed. Beeswax rubbed thoroughly over the entire surface will melt in the sun once the tepee is set up and does a good job. The door cover should also be waterproofed in the same way.

SETTING UP THE TEPEE

For a graceful effect, the tepee poles should show at least 4 feet above the tepee cover.

Raising the Foundation Poles

Setting up the poles is done in much the same manner for both the three- and four-pole foundation tepees. The cover is spread out flat on the ground with the foundation poles placed on it in order to find the correct place where these poles should be tied together. This point is usually about 12 inches higher than the point reached by the tepee cover and should be marked on all foundation poles to eliminate the need for future measuring. The three or four poles are then tied firmly together, at the marks, where they will cross, and the anchor rope is left hanging down to serve as the tepee anchor. This anchor is not necessary when a three-pole tripod is used.

The Three-Pole Tripod

The tied foundation poles are placed on end, almost evenly spaced, in the form of a tripod. One of the three poles should be placed so that it will form the right door post, as seen from inside the tepee. The other two poles are placed opposite the door pole and somewhat nearer each other than they are to the door pole. The first of the other poles to be set into this frame is placed so it will be the left doorpost. The remaining poles are fitted into the foundation poles crotch and spread out evenly around the circle, so the distances between the butts of the poles are approximately the same. The pole to be placed at the center of the back of the tepee should be kept aside. The tepee cover will be raised on this pole.

The Four-Pole Foundation

The four-pole foundation gives the tepee more of an oval shape than the three-pole tripod. The four poles form the corners of a rectangle, the narrow sides of the rectangle facing east and west, as a rule. The remaining poles should be set up first in the crotches on the wide sides of the rectangle, then in the crotches on the narrow sides. Two poles are placed for doorposts on one of the narrow sides of the rectangle. In this type, also, the poles should be about evenly spaced. Keep aside one pole to be placed at the center of the back of the tepee, as in the three-pole set-up, to which the tepee cover will be attached.

Fitting the Tepee Cover

Pass an 18-inch length of 3/16-inch rope through the ring in the little tongue in the center of the tepee cover, and tie the tepee cover to the pole which has been kept aside, so the tepee hem is level with the foot of the pole. A guy rope fastened near the top of this pole will help to raise the pole and tepee cover.

This pole is placed in the vacant space at the center of the back of the tepee, and the cover is raised with it. Pull each side of the tepee cover toward the doorposts, in front, and when they meet, pull the left side, as you face the tepee from outside, over the right side. Push the lacing pins into the eyelets from right to left and adjust them so the same amount of lacing pin shows on each side. When all the lacing pins are in place, step inside the tepee and push the poles out against the tepee cover all round until it is completely taut. This not only enhances the symmetrical appearance but also keeps rain from seeping through at any point which sags. When this is completed, the tepee cover is staked to the ground with the tepee pegs.

Smoke Hole Ears

Place the small end of one of the lighter poles in each smoke hole ear pocket and place the butt of each pole according to the desired position of the ears. Tie the cord at the lower edge of each ear to a peg in the ground.

Door Cover

Fasten the door flap to loops sewn onto the outside of the tepee cover about 3 inches above the door opening and 5 inches to each side of it. The oblong door cover is fastened by passing each end of the thinner, ½-inch stick through a loop. The weight of the heavier stick closes the door flap. If one is using the horseshoe-shaped cover, it should be fastened by passing each end of the one-inch, straight stick through a loop, with the ends of the curved width on the outside, away from the tepee cover, to avoid friction.

Storm Cap for Tepee

The Indians used this effective storm cover in the rainy season. Most tribes called it a "bull cover" because it resembled a bull boat. This is how such a cover can be made.

Fold the 5-foot square of canvas in half, as shown in Figure 2 in the diagram.

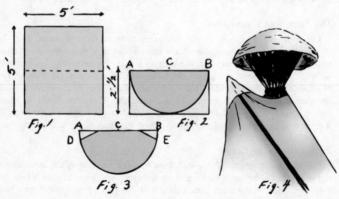

Tie one end of a 33-inch length of cord to a nail just above the exact center of the canvas, point C in the diagram. Tie a piece of colored chalk to the other end of the cord and use the cord as a compass, drawing a semicircle from point A to B.

Keep the canvas folded and make a pencil mark at point D which is about 8 inches below point A, in Figure 3, and another pencil mark at point E, about 8 inches below point B. Now, draw a line from D to a point halfway between A and C and another line from E to a point halfway between B and C. Stitch along these lines, keeping the canvas folded, as in Figure 3, then turn the canvas cover inside out and it will be somewhat in the shape of a coolie hat.

Sew a strong, lithe willow rod about 15 feet long and one inch in diameter into the hem at the foot of the cap to keep it evenly extended on all sides. A second withe can be sewn about halfway between the hem and the peak for extra support. Two withes, each about 8 feet long, lashed together can be used when a longer rod is not available. Sew one end of the 22-foot length of rope very securely inside the peak of the storm cap. This is to anchor the storm cap to a peg in the ground in high winds.

The cover is usually lifted into place with a long pole and sits on top of the tepee poles, as shown in Figure 4. The tepee poles must be fairly even in length at the top in order to use this cover to advantage. This storm cap should also be waterproofed with beeswax before using.

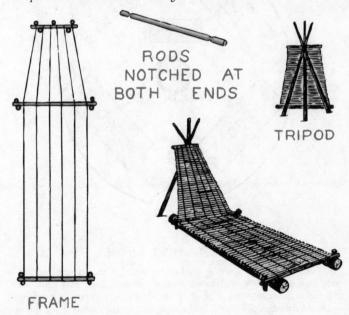

RODS NOTCHED AT BOTH ENDS

TRIPOD

FRAME

TEPEE FURNISHINGS

Usually the beauty of a tepee lies chiefly in its outside appearance. The graceful lines and colorful decorations lead one to expect equal beauty within the lodge. Despite these expectations, the interior of the average tepee even when set up as part of a permanent village or encampment, had few decorative features. There were sometimes decorated *parfleche* storage cases, colorful blankets, bear or other animal skins, an occasional painted dewcloth, weapon cases, and perhaps the willow bed of a chief. A bed was the only Plains Indian possession which could be classified as furniture; but no description of building a Plains Indian willow bed, like the one shown in the drawing, is given because at least seventy straight shoots of willow, arrowwood or other straight, springy shoots are required to make the bed, and each shoot is 30 inches long and about the circumference of a lead pencil. Such a quantity of wildwood material is required that, should half a dozen braves decide to make beds, a considerable dent in the available supply of this diminishing material will be made, so dowels, ¼ to ⅜ inch in diameter will do.

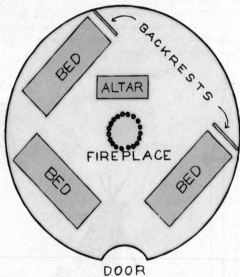

ENCAMPMENT LOOM

A loom is useful for weaving comfortable mats for encampment beds. It is easily made and will weave wildwood material such as ordinary long grass, straw, or sedge—a coarse, grasslike plant which usually grows in clumps on wet ground or around the edges of marshes. Sedge lends itself to close weaving and makes a compact, restful mattress.

There are several ways of setting up a loom and the number of rods and cords used decides the size of the mat woven. If six stakes are used instead of five and they are driven into the ground closer together than 7 inches, the mattress will have a closer weave. In such cases, a sixth strand of cord will be required. The 3-foot cross-bar can be securely attached to a tree or to the top of two stakes driven into the ground 3 feet apart. The five stakes, each 3 feet 8 inches long, are driven 8 inches into the ground and about 7 inches apart, at a distance of about 6 feet from the fixed cross-bar. The drawing shows how this should be done.

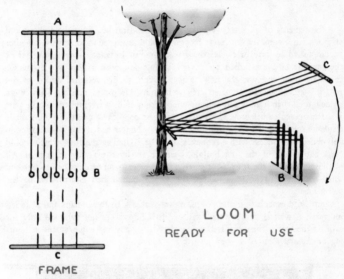

FRAME

LOOM
READY FOR USE

A strong cord or binder twine is attached tightly and securely from the top of each stake to the fixed cross-bar, as illustrated. Four longer cords, each about 10 feet long, are now attached to the fixed bar, each cord being tied exactly halfway between the places where the fixed cords (running from the fixed cross-bar to the stakes) are tied. The free ends of these cords are tied firmly to the binding-bar, spaced as on the fixed bar and the loom is ready.

One brave can work the binding-bar, raising it as high as his head and lowering it practically to the ground, while a brave on either side of the loom lays long bundles of the material being used to make the mattress, first above the fixed cords and then below them, as the binding cords rise and fall, weaving the bundles firmly in place. The thickness of these bundles, which should be uniform in bulk, decides the thickness of the mattress and also the length of the cords required to bind the bundles together. The loom bar is worked slowly enough for the braves feeding it to arrange the long tufts smoothly enough to assure a comfortable mattress.

3

Indian Warriors and Scouts

Achievements of all sorts were considered good medicine by the Indians and all worthwhile achievements were recognized and rewarded in some way, whether accomplished by boy or by seasoned warrior. For instance, when a squirrel or the smallest bird was killed by a very young boy with a bow and arrow or throwing stick and was the first "game" which his prowess had added to the pot, it was considered quite an achievement by his proud family. They were so delighted that friends and at least one ranking chief were invited to take part in a feast given to celebrate the youngster's first coup. The guest of honor made a solemn speech in which he said that the young hunter had reason to count coup and ended his remarks with a request that he be invited to the feast which would mark the killing of the first buffalo, bear, or elk by the young marksman. All of those invited to the feast were given a small piece—and often it had to be very small—of the bird or beast which the young hunter had contributed to the lavish menu.

Coups, and especially grand coups, meant real risk to the Indians and it added incentive as well as zest to their way of life. Coups were not awarded only for skill on the war path; many tribes considered that any big achievement in hunting or artistry merited a coup award.

RAIDING AND WAR COUPS

The risk involved in cutting a horse's rope in a hostile camp and making off with the horse was more important to a brave than killing an enemy warrior in the raided camp or village. Cutting a horse loose and stealing it on the open plain, where little risk was run, was not considered a coup.

Striking an armed enemy in battle with hand, bow, quirt, or butt of lance was counted a greater coup than killing him, even at close quarters, with lance, tomahawk, or club.

A brave shouted for a coup or kill and his name was mentioned in council. Braves-to-be who did not shout were, by their acts, noted by the chiefs. A Blackfoot warrior often put a black stripe on his deerskin shirt for each battle in which he took part.

CLAIMING COUPS AND DECLARATIONS
OF TRUTH

Coups were claimed in different ways by different tribes and varied ceremonies were held at the time of claiming and at the final granting of these claims. Coups were awarded by chiefs and councils of chiefs for many reasons. Though Indians rarely lied about their achievements when claiming coups, there was always the off chance, especially among fishermen, that some exaggeration might creep into their claims. For this reason, many claims had to be substantiated, when the council of chiefs considered it necessary, by on-the-spot witnesses. When, as was sometimes the case, there were neither witnesses nor direct proof to support a claim, the claimant took an oath that his claim was true and justified. When an Indian swore to the truth of a statement, even by the simple statement "on the pipe," even the most skeptical chief in council would not hesitate to accept the claim as factual. What were some of these oaths? Many tribes used different forms, but the essence of most of them was the same and compelled the claimant, through fear of the consequence, should he lie, to be accurate in his claims.

A Dakota would declare—"My words are true! Earth hear me! Earth, withdraw all help if my words are false!"

Warriors of other Siouan groups would swear—"This did I do! Thunderers hear me!"

An Iroquois of the mighty Six Nations would hold out a belt or string of wampum, make his claim, then end with the words—"This belt attests and upholds my words!"

Some Plains tribes often swore by or on the calumet. This was regarded, as other oaths, as sacred and was probably never broken. Fear of the consequences when the gods learned of the breach of faith and their vengeance of the one who betrayed was sufficient to make the oath inviolate.

Here is one dramatic form of the coup-claiming oath of a Comanche brave, whose actual coup-claiming ceremony is described below:

"Sun, Father, you saw me do it; Earth, Mother, you saw it. Let me be struck by the first lightning that lights the sky if I speak falsely!"

When a Comanche claimed coup he dramatically shouted at the top of his voice, "I claim coup!" Later, at a council fire, the leading chiefs sat in a semicircle, within a circle of lesser chiefs, and braves. A buffalo hide was spread out in front of the semicircle. Indians danced to the rhythmic beat of drums. Warriors who wished to claim coups rushed into the circle. One at a time, each drove his spear through the buffalo hide so that the spear stood upright in the earth and declared, on oath, the deed which he had performed in order to claim coup. The leading chiefs either granted or rejected each brave's claim.

The drumming stopped suddenly and there was complete silence as the braves, selected by the chiefs, counted coup, one by one.

COUNTING COUPS

There were almost as many ways of counting coups as there were ways of claiming them.

A Crow, after his claim had been allowed by the council of chiefs, stuck a long eagle feather into the ground and repeated the claim which had won the coup feather.

Other branches of the *Absaroke*—the Crow People—counted coup by driving a short, pointed stick adorned with little downy, "breath," feathers tied to the top, into the ground and then recited the reason why the coup feather had been awarded.

Counting coup was also done by striking a specially set up coup pole with a tomahawk or club and by other methods.

COUP GIVE-AWAY DANCES

Often when a young brave had counted a notable coup, a Give-Away Dance was held in his honor. As part of the ceremony, he had to solo dance and then gifts were given to his friends by his parents and relatives. A rich donor often gave fine blankets, and even horses as gifts. A game based on this ceremony will be found in Chapter 17.

TRANSFERRING PERSONAL COUPS

When counting war coups became too difficult, after the coming of the army of the white man, the Comanche thought of a way of making coup honors possible through transfer of coups, in much the same way as a Northwest Coast Indian would transfer his ownership of a dance or song. In council, the owner of a recognized coup stepped forward and told the details of the coup which he was transferring to a brave and worthy warrior. He then declared loudly, "This coup I now give to my brother, Yellow Hawk. From now, until grass grows no more, it is no longer mine. I have spoken."

The warrior named then went into the circle and said, "I now take this honor deed. Sun, Father, Moon above and Mother Earth, witness that the coup is now mine." The big drum was given a thunderous stroke and the transfer of the coup was recognized for all time. In future it could never be again transferred, inherited, traded nor sold.

MODERN COUP-CLAIMING AND AWARDS

Modern chiefs may use their own adaptations of coup-claiming, coup-counting and awards. They can be made colorful and effective, making striking additions to a ceremonial council fire. Members of Indian bands who are away from the main council fire (where their coup claims can be considered for recommendation) turn, when they feel that their achievements merit claiming coup, to their band chief. He is told in detail of the exploits so that they can be claimed, awarded, and counted at a ceremony to be held in the main council fire circle at a later date.

In Indian encampments, a modest brave who was outstanding in any way was "noticed by the chiefs" and, often to his surprise, was recommended for a coup feather award by the council of chiefs. In such cases, the claim could be made for the honored brave by a chief and immediately after the claim was honored by the chiefs in council, the proud brave to whom the award had been made was called on to count coup at the council fire. Such an award was usually considered an even greater honor than one personally claimed.

This should be kept in mind by modern chiefs in charge of encampment bands, and suggestions for these awards made to the chief of the main camp, or council of chiefs, who can decide to award the coups or reject the claims, as they see fit. Awards made in this way, especially surprise awards, make a considerable impression on modern braves of all ages and often inspire others to be deserving of being "noticed by the chiefs."

It is suggested that councils of modern chiefs adopt special coup awards for their bands and tribes. Coups can be claimed, awarded, and counted for really outstanding work in swimming, for example, woodcraft, pathfinding, star finding, special service to the band, wildlife watching, fire making, trail finding, trail making, stalking, tracking, fishing, Indian arts and crafts, racing, wrestling, archery, weather forecasting, and, last but not least, conservation, best called Wildlife Guardian coup. Grand coups should be claimed and awarded only for very special achievements along any of the above lines. Other reasons for awarding coups will occur to chiefs from time to time.

WAR PARTIES

War parties were usually organized by a chief or leading warrior for a number of purposes: to avenge an insult to the tribe, uphold tribal honor, or seek glory, for revenge or reprisal, to drive trespassing hunters of an adjoining tribe from tribal territory, and for loot, especially for horses. Young braves joined war parties for various reasons: chiefly for glory or revenge, but also for excitement and adventure, the chance to prove their bravery, impress a woman, or acquire horses and other loot. The leader of an important war party was nearly always a war chief with a fine war record built on courage and skill in his craft, which was war. The leader of an average war party, whether he was a chief or not, was shown great respect and held the power of life or death over the members of the war party. He was given the best food and even his moccasins were repaired by his comrades so that he would be entirely free to plan the coming campaign, which was a difficult matter, since often small bands attacked powerful tribes in a hit-and-run maneuver, still a part of the present-day Commando tactics.

War parties were generally well organized, and practically every detail of exactly what they were going to do from the time they left their village or encampment until the time they arrived at the enemy village was worked out well in advance and completed en route to hostile territory, as were the tentative after-attack plans up to the return to their own village. Each member of the party was assigned to the special sort of work which he did best. The leader decided whether the attack was to be one in which the strategy of silence at the outset was best or whether the shrill war cries of the band, coming from the different points to which members of the war party had been assigned, would help to demoralize the enemy or at least throw it off balance at the outset of the attack. All tribes had their war cries and battle calls and they were of a fear-inspiring, far-carrying, and piercing nature. The tribal war cry of the Sioux, for example, was *Woo-oo, hey-ah, yoo-wee-doo!* and that of the Crow, *Wh-o-o-o-o-o-o!* They also had rallying calls and distress calls, like that of the Seneca being *Go-o-o-o-weh!*, which sounded like the supposed wail of a banshee.

A war party became a secret society at its first encampment. Occasionally a boy of thirteen would be allowed to go on one of these parties, after proving himself at some time before the party was formed. Often still younger boys would, without permission and keeping out of sight if they could, follow a war party so far that they had to be taken along, or left far from their village should the leader decide not to take them as punishment for following unbidden. Often, such foolhardy followers would have only the moccasins they wore, or what was left of them, and a boy or warrior without extra moccasins was a menace to the entire party. Each brave chosen for the war party carried several pairs of moccasins, sometimes as many as ten, on such a mission. Pemmican, or jerked beef, parched corn, sweetened corn meal and other rations which were compact and easy to carry and did not spoil easily were taken along, frequently stuffed into the toes of the spare moccasins.

Since war parties were often on the move in winter, they built rough shelters or lodges in thick pine woods, covering the framework poles with pine boughs and then snow to make their daytime hide-outs practically invisible from even a very short distance. The stars usually guided such groups on their long, forced night marches. Sometimes it was so bitterly cold that a small, comparatively smokeless fire had to be lit inside these shelters.

RAIDING PARTIES

Though there was almost as much risk and chance of losing their lives on the part of the braves who joined raiding parties as if they had joined war parties, the prestige gained by a raiding party was considerably less than that accorded to a war party. Often such raiding parties were countenanced by the tribe from which they set out but had no official status. Usually such bands were headed by an older subchief or warrior, and usually less experienced braves or ones who had never before been on a raiding party went along. Practically all such raids, except in Woodland or Northwest Coast territories, had one main objective—horses. The party which succeeded in capturing mounts usually rode for one night and one day before stopping for a brief rest. This was not only wise but a necessary precaution, since a well-mounted and armed party of sixty to one hundred braves might ride out after the horse-rustling band of eight or ten. Saving face by capturing or killing the raiders and recovering the horses was important enough to the tribe raided to cause it to spare no effort to wipe out the invaders of their territory.

Quite often members of raiding bands rose to the rank of chief by using the experience gained in the raids as the first of a series of stepping stones which later led to fame and glory.

SCOUTS

The most hazardous work connected with raiding and war parties fell to the braves whom the leaders chose to form a small scouting party. Their work was to size up the situation when the raiding or war band was deep in hostile territory and close to its objective. Quite often none, or perhaps only one or two, out of a party of two to six scouts returned from such a scouting foray, despite the fact that each scout had been chosen with infinite care. This is easily understandable, because such scouts were usually captured or killed many hundreds of miles from their own territory and their presence alerted the enemy to the fact that a war party was in their territory. Little imagination is required to understand that the utmost care was taken by scouts on enemy terrain. Capture generally meant torture and death, while the safe return from a successful scouting mission usually meant coup or grand coup awards and much prestige.

These scouts, wolves, as they were generally called, were highly skilled in every ruse that might deceive the enemy. Clever camouflage and patient, stealthy movement by day, combined with the acquired ability to move like faint shadows by night helped them to escape detection—but not always. Sometimes these wolves imitated the real animal of caution and cunning, from which the scouts got their name. They painted themselves with gray clay or mud and wore complete wolf skins with the head covering the head of the scout. So disguised, from high lookout positions, they watched the groups or herds of elk and buffalo, as these animals were quick to indicate enemy movements. The wolves, especially those of the Crow and Blackfoot, were able to imitate the various calls of real wolves so well that it was impossible for the most skilled enemy to distinguish between the scout call and the wolf call. The scouts knew that wolves usually gave a high-pitched quivering, two-noted howl, but that the leaders of wolf packs used a long drawn-out unwavering call to assemble the pack. The other barks and calls of wolves—and there were many to meet many situations—

were also known to the human wolves, who knew that the wrong call at the wrong time or place might mean capture and a lingering death. In lightly wooded country, the call of a bird or birds was given as a signal, but only if the birds imitated were to be found in that immediate section of the country through which they traveled. The far-carrying call of a crow was sometimes used and the scouts knew the whole series of crow calls from the rally to danger calls. Never did a scout give more than five crow calls in a group, because they well knew—and so did the enemy scouts—that a crow never did.

SCALPS

Despite the fact that scalping has been so frequently written of as one of the practices characteristic of all Indians of all habitats, such statements are quite erroneous. Scalping was practically unknown to the great majority of Indian tribes until the American colonial government offered a bounty, ranging from ten to sixty dollars, for each Indian scalp brought in. Since both the British and American armies paid bounties on scalps, scalp hunting soon became a profitable business among some tribes. In spite of this inhuman encouragement by white men in responsible positions, many tribes never took scalps, and scalping was unknown to the Indians of the Northwest Coast. It is quite probable that the palefaces of the early days of scalp warfare took more scalps than did the red men.

COURAGE TESTS

Testing the courage of young braves or applicants for coup-counting privileges was a common practice among some Indian tribes. Many of these tests though carried out by seasoned and skillful chiefs, were of too risky a nature to be set down here.

The Comanche executed a courage test on horseback which is safe enough for modern Indians to carry out dismounted. At full speed, the Comanche galloped in an ever-tightening circle around one or several young braves who had expressed the wish to undergo the test as a proof of their readiness and fitness to join raiding or war parties. This test of courage, carried out by Comanche horsemen, who were magnificent if somewhat reckless riders, was almost as hairraising for those looking on as for those undergoing the test. It was impossible, until the tight-knit circle unwound itself, to tell whether the encircled braves had been trodden into pulp by the flying hooves of the ponies or whether they were unscathed. Certainly if they were uninjured and still unafraid, their courage was beyond question.

As a variation of this test, wedges of Comanche horsemen formed a huge circle, with the wide part of the wedges, each consisting of about four horsemen, forming the outside of the circle, each wedge of ten horses and riders narrowing until the thin end of the wedge was formed by only a single horseman. Those undergoing the courage test stood in the middle of the great circle. At a signal from the chief in command, these wedges of horsemen raced at top speed toward the center of the circle. When each horseman and wedge stopped simultaneously with sudden, lightning speed the circle was greatly reduced in size, but it was completely compact, so solid that a lance could hardly be placed between the horses forming the outer edges of any of the wedges. Certainly when the wild charge abruptly ended, those in the center of the circle could strike the noses of all of the horses forming the thin end of the wedge without stretching an arm to do so.

Modern chiefs who wish to emulate the courage test charge of the Comanche can have dismounted braves execute modified versions of the tests described. The wedge formation is *not* recommended, even for testing older braves, but something colorful and spectacular can be done with the encirclement test, if care is taken in staging it. All tests decided on should, of course, be without risk of any sort to those who ask that their courage be put to the test. The value of the test must lie in symbolism, *not* risk. Other daytime tests may be devised by modern chiefs of bands in which suggestion, imagination and implication are made as exciting throughout the courage test as the finale. Such tests are usually reserved for the time when one or more braves suddenly declare, in or out of council, that they have achieved fearlessness as the result of a quest or some other powerful medicine.

FEARLESSNESS VERSUS FOOLHARDINESS

Often, as one follows life's trails, it takes more control and courage not to act on certain occasions than to act foolhardily and regret it later. The courage displayed so very often by Indian chiefs was usually to inspire their tribes and show contempt for the enemy. On the field of battle an unarmed chief in full regalia would race on foot to touch the horse of an armed, mounted chief or brave. It required far more courage to do this than to attack armed and kill the warrior on horseback.

Such feats are on a par with the officer of a British Guard's Regiment who dribbled a soccer ball across no man's land toward the enemy trenches, followed by his charging men. The French General Pierre Bosquet summed up such deeds in his tribute to the Charge of the Light Brigade at Balaclava, "It is magnificent, but it is not war!" It is good to know that the General was wrong! Victories by land and on sea were built on such undying traditions. General Custer went down to defeat at the Battle of Little Big Horn because of the long-past coups of Indian chiefs which built up into counting grand coup during that battle.

INDIAN WEAPONS OF WAR

The Indians were adept at making weapons of all sorts, each one well adapted for its particular use. Not only were these arms effective for the chase and war, but so much artistry and skill went into their making that they were artistic and decorative as well as deadly. Feathers, strips of gaily colored cloths, skins, furs, and dyed buckskin were used to decorate various weapons, when they did not in any way interfere with the efficient use of the arms embellished in this manner. Sometimes such decorative strips helped to make a weapon more effective, as they distracted the attention of an enemy.

Some of the decorative weapons mentioned here will prove useful for beautifying council houses and dwellings, and those such as lances may be stuck in the ground outside of a tepee or other dwelling with a shield slung on each to add to the effect.

Shields

Shields were considered as potent weapons by many tribes because of their medicine designs and the magic believed to be conjured into them by medicine men and painted on them because of medicine dreams of their owner. The designs on some shields were painted to throw enemies off balance, so that they could not shoot at the bearer of the shield accurately. Some shields were thought, by their magic, to cause arrows to be deflected before even striking the shield, while others were said to render the shield-bearer invisible, or nearly so. Stepping out of the mystic realm of medicine and magic, the Comanche realists often had from four to six big medicine feathers fastened loosely on thongs around the shield. The purpose of these fluttering feathers which danced on a puff of wind or at the shake of the shield, was to disturb the aim of the enemy as he drew taut his bowstring for a fatal shot. Bear teeth painted or fastened on a shield denoted a great hunter, one as tough as a bear. Scalp locks attached or painted on a shield marked a great warrior, while horse or mule tails, actual, painted, or in miniature, on a shield indicated a clever raider.

Shields were highly treasured, as most of them were credited with "spirit power," sometimes hidden in the geometric or other designs which ornamented the shield. Braves usually acquired shield "power" in one of three different ways.

A warrior could set out on a vision quest, which took time and was not always successful; he could ask a medicine man to conjure up a suitable power design by the use of medicine or, easiest way of all, have a brother brave whose shield had great spirit power to share that medicine with the searcher for shield power.

The medicine in a shield often meant that the bearer had to observe a strict taboo or taboos. This he did, in order not to lose power, no matter how difficult these taboos were to carry out.

Lances

Lances were used by a number of Plains and Northwest Coast tribes and those who carried them did so proudly and used them effectively. Among the Comanche, the war lance ranked higher than a war bonnet as a war symbol. Only the bravest warriors carried a lance, which meant hand-to-hand fighting until the death. No retreat was ever known to have been made by a lance-carrier. These beautifully balanced and deadly weapons were *never thrown*, like a javelin, but were used with swift underhand thrusts. They were made of the toughest wood available. The shaft was 6 or 7 feet long and 1 or 2 inches in diameter. A keen, leaf-shaped blade chipped from flint or stone, 12 to 20 inches long, was lashed onto the tip of the shaft. When metal became available, later on, they tipped their lances with it. The lance was often painted with decorative stripes and usually the only other decoration was a few feathers tied together and attached near the butt of the lance.

The lance was sometimes stuck into the ground, butt down, in front of the owner's lodge.

Dog Soldier Lances

Special lances were used by the fierce Dog Soldiers of the Cheyenne and Kiowa, who were bravest among brave warriors. The Dakota who carried similar lances were known as Strong Hearts and belonged to the elite Strong

Heart Society. Two of the men in that Society, outstanding in bravery, wore sashes around the neck which hung down on one side of the body. They were known as Sash Wearers. When the Dakota took part in a fierce battle, these Sash Wearers pinned themselves to the ground by driving their lances through the sashes. They fought, with knife or tomahawk, anchored to the ground, until they were either killed or released by another Strong Heart. The special lances of these Dog Soldiers and warrior Strong Hearts were often decorated with pieces of animal skins, feathers, and tufts of dyed horsehair.

Indian Marksmen

Prior to the arrival of traders with cheap rifles, which proved most expensive for the Indians, who traded furs for them, the chief weapon of the Indian was the bow. Probably no other warriors used the bow with such skill and to such deadly effect, with the exception of some Oriental archers and the long bowmen of England. The Cheyenne, splendid bowmen though they were, could fire an arrow accurately for only about 150 yards, but the English archers frequently fired their long bow shafts effectively for distances up to 300 yards. In the skilled hands of an Indian bowman, the bow was a powerful and deadly weapon. Frequently these hunters drove their arrows entirely through the bodies of buffalo bulls. When one considers the extremely tough hide of these animals, protection by mud wallow-soaked hair, their huge size, and the fact that a buffalo bull sometimes weighed 2,300 pounds, one realizes what a deadly weapon the Indian bow was.

Indians used most of the skills and tricks used by the best bowmen of today. They contested for length-of-arrow flight, for accuracy on still and moving targets at various ranges, and in high-shooting contests. They competed to see which brave could fire the greatest number of arrows accurately in the shortest possible time. Though the Indians counted on the strength of their finely developed arms to fire arrows for almost unbelievable distances, they also knew the trick of reclining on their backs and holding the bow with their feet when they wished to send a shaft on an unusually long flight. In modern archery, as in many other things, we owe the Indians a great deal.

Bows

Many different types of bows were used by various tribes. Their bows differed greatly in the manner of construction, shape, and length, though a four-foot bow may be considered the average length. The bows of Plains Indians were short, as they were often fired from horseback. Many were cleverly made in a manner which today gives the top bow manufacturers a number of useful pointers. The *usual bow* was made from one piece of wood. The *compound bow* was made from layers of wood and bone, glued and lashed together. The *sinew-wrapped bow* was wound with sinew to protect wood which did not bend easily, like cedar, and also to give more strength and spring to bows of light, supple wood. Especially powerful bowmen not only used the toughest woods, which already necessitated a powerful pull, but also wrapped the wood tightly with strips of green rawhide, first soaked in water to cause them to practically merge with the wood. Indians used various woods for bows, such as ash, second growth hickory, Osage orange wood, dogwood, ironwood, cedar and other suitable, pliable hard woods. Bows were made also from bone and horn, and the different tribes used the various materials for bow-making which they found in their habitats.

Indians treated their bows with the same respect that modern marksmen do their rifles. The bows were usually kept unstrung and placed in artistically decorated bow cases. The Comanche treasured his bow and arrows. In wet weather he carried his thong bowstring under his armpit to keep it dry. He generally fired his valuable arrows across a flooded stream before swimming his horse over and retrieved them on the other side.

Many Indians wore a wide buckskin band on the wrist of the left arm to prevent severe bruises from the released bowstring.

Arrows

The Indians had many sorts of arrows for many purposes, ranging from the heavy shafts tipped with keen war heads to the blunt-tipped and light arrows used for bird hunting. Whatever purpose these arrows served, they were both effective and artistic. Arrows were usually made from arrowwood, a variety of dogwood and viburnum, young willow shoots, and the strong, pithy reeds and cane shoots used by some tribes. These reeds and shoots were bound into bundles to straighten them and then hung up inside a tepee or some other place to season before use. Arrows ranged from about 24 to 34 inches in length.

Arrow Points

Arrows were often tipped with the tips of antlers of various kinds, also obsidian—glassy, volcanic rock—and other sorts of chipped rock prior to the introduction of steel by white men. After that, most effective arrow tips were made from iron hoops from barrels and various other metals.

Fletching Feathers

Indian arrows were feathered with wing feathers from the same wing of a bird, usually a bird of prey, such as eagle, hawk, or owl, and tail feathers were practically never used. Though bird of prey feathers were favorite fletching feathers, some tribes used the wing feathers of wild turkeys for feathering their arrows. Indians had many beliefs and superstitions about the use of feathers for fletching arrows. For instance, they never used the feathers of a crow, as they firmly believed that crow feathers made the arrows fly in a crooked fashion. Practically all arrows were fletched with three lengths of feathers, split down the backbone and glued and lashed with thongs onto the shaft. The lengths of feathers ranged from two to five inches for the actual flight feathers. Quite often these feather lengths, which were trimmed to ⅜ to ½ inch in width, were only fastened at each end and not in the middle. Various tribes used entirely different methods of fletching their arrows. Perhaps this difference was most noticeable in the feathering of the Plains and Woodland arrows. Some of the Woodland tribes glued their arrow feathers on in a twisted style, quite different from the straight feather technique fletching of the Plains tribes. The Eskimo did not split the feathers with which they fletched their arrows.

Arrow Releases

All Indian tribes had one thing in common when it came to releasing arrows: they all held the nock of the arrow between thumb and forefinger. Some tribes used the two finger pull on the bowstring, while others used three fingers. The Eskimo, a tribe of Alaskan Indians, used what modern archers call the "Mediterranean release," which is used a great deal at the present time. Arrow release was an important factor in driving shafts forcibly and far from war and hunting bows with a pull of at least 45 pounds and frequently considerably more.

"Lightning Marks"

Some Indian tribes cut grooves, sometimes called "lightning marks," along the sides of arrows so that the blood of a wounded animal flowed out of the wound and left a trail on ground and bushes. This made it easy for a hunter to follow the wounded beast and give it the *coup de grace*.

Arrow Ownership Marks

Many Indian experts in arrow-making turned out arrows which were very much alike. As arrow identification was important, especially when two or three shafts were buried just back of a buffalo's shoulder, the Indians marked their arrows in many different ways so that ownership of arrows was easily established. Stripes, circles and dots on various parts of the shaft denoted ownership but some Indian marksmen used more elaborate markings, on feathers or shaft, which left no doubt as to who had fired the arrow.

Tomahawks

The tomahawk was a deadly weapon in the hand of an experienced warrior, even in its most primitive form, before metal-bladed tomahawks were brought into Indian country by white traders. The earlier tomahawks were often made from a piece of chipped flint or obsidian inserted into a slit in the end of a handle

of hickory or other tough, strong wood and tightly bound in position with a strip or strips of green rawhide. These weapons were frequently decorated with a few tufts of dyed hair, small feathers, or a strip of dyed deerskin or cloth. The tomahawks offered by the traders—generally for far too many valuable pelts —became more and more elaborate as they vied for the Indian trade.

The Indians used this weapon from horseback or when on foot, for close combat work and often it was used in a hand-to-hand struggle to dispatch a huge black or grizzly bear. Tomahawks were rarely thrown, unless in a real emergency, or when the chance of recovering the weapon after it was thrown was fairly certain.

War Clubs

Practically all war clubs were formidable weapons and there were many shapes, sizes, and weights in use. An owner usually fashioned a club to suit his own particular needs and these clubs were frequently artistic as well as deadly. The Iroquian club shown in the drawing is an example. Some clubs were made entirely of very heavy wood, others had insets of flint and other hard rocks, chipped to a sharp cutting edge, prior to the introduction of metals. When

steel and iron could be had, many war club wielders added knobs, points, crescent, and other forms of sharp-cutting edges to their weapons. The artistic side of the Indian nature was evidenced in their clubs. Like the tomahawk, clubs were not usually thrown and a considerable number of them had a wrist thong fastened to the end of the handle so that it would not fly out of the owner's hand or be knocked from it in battle.

Knives

Decorative as well as serviceable knives, used for both war and chase, were made from flint, obsidian, and other hard rocks before metal knives and sheath knives came into the hands of the Indians. The Indians kept their blades as keen as possible at all times, which helped when cutting the tough rawhide ropes of ponies when raiding hostile territory and when using knives in hand-to-hand combat.

4

Indian Hunters and Trappers

All of the peoples of the Northwest Coast believed that the abundance of wildlife with which they were blessed came from the spirits of the sky and ocean, and they gave constant thanks for the mercies bestowed. Children were taught to hunt and fish but they were first taught to respect wildlife and promote conservation of waters and forests. The children were present when offerings were cast into the ocean for "the ocean people" and when offerings were placed in the fire to be borne aloft in the smoke for "the sky people." The children were also taught to believe that a virtual covenant existed between man and wildlife and that the breaking or abuse of it by the Indians might lead to famine. The Nootka knew the dog salmon as "bright fish," or "bright ones," and the first caught were accorded the honors of a great chief.

SPEAR FISHING

There were a number of types of spears used by Indians of different tribes. These weapons varied greatly in weight, length, thickness and barbs, each one being made to meet the requirements of the habitat in which it was used. There were also variations caused by whether the spear was thrust or thrown and what its target was going to be. Almost as much difference existed between the various types of harpoons used by the Indians, especially the ones used by the natives of the Northwest Coast. Lightweight harpoons with detachable, barbed heads were used for spearing salmon and other big fish. Medium weight harpoons were employed for seal and walrus spearing; and massive, 14-foot long, yew-shafted harpoons were used by tribes such as the dauntless Nootka for whale hunting.

Spears of various sorts were used effectively by Indian tribes, who included many sorts of fish in their diet. This applies to some extent to tribes of the Plains and Woodlands, but more especially to the Indians of the Northwest Coast. These tribes not only used their varied and cleverly-made spears for spearing salmon but also in the chase of sea mammals. Lances were also important weapons in the equipment of the small Nootka whaling crews. Once a whale was harpooned and the sturdy whaling canoe driven alongside, daring members leaped onto the surfaced whale's back, knowing that it might submerge at any moment, and used lances to end what might otherwise be a long, drawn-out struggle. Such a feat was a grand coup among grands coups and each of those who boarded the thrashing whale was forever after euphemistically known as "He Who Has Stepped on a Whale."

Indian Fish Spears

Indian boys made light, effective fish spears, like those illustrated, without difficulty. These spears were of various sorts, the chief types being single-, double- and triple-pronged, the prongs being made of hard wood or bone, as were the barbs. The shafts of these lightweight spears ranged from 6½ to 8 feet in length and were often made from wild cherry, though grey birch or a slim, straight maple sapling were also used. This shaft tapered from about 1¼ inch in diameter at the barbed end, to around ¾ inch at the top. The barbed head was about 16 inches long, which allowed for about 4 inches, lashed onto the spear shaft, which is flattened or grooved on each side so that the head could be lashed on more firmly. The number of barbs on the inside of the spear head ranged from 3 to 6. The wedge which held the prongs apart was made of hard wood and was about 2 or 3 inches wide at the point where the prongs were fastened to the shaft. For their usual fish spearing, two prongs were sufficient but for really big fish, such as the salmon and sturgeon of the Northwest Pacific Coast, there was often a third barb set between the two outer prongs. Such prongs were either lashed to the spear shaft, at the heavier end, or attached by two small hardwood pegs driven into the shaft through two small holes, bored one above the other, which were drilled through the bone. Some spear-makers preferred lashing as the easiest way of attaching the prongs to the shaft.

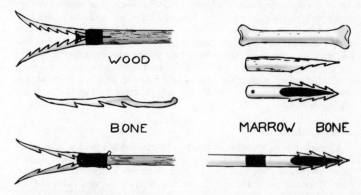

WOOD

BONE

MARROW BONE

Single Prong Spears

The single prong, for the single-pronged spears, was made in exactly the same way as the prongs for the twin-barb spearheads and it was often barbed on both sides, instead of only on one. Long bones or straight hard wood sticks were ground or filed down to make both prong and barbs. The drawing shows how a big, hollow, marrow bone was sawed off at each end and ground down to form the barbs. When finished, it was either lashed or pegged and lashed to the shaft or tightly fitted into a hole made in the exact center of the spear shaft.

The brave-to-be who succeeded in spearing and landing a fish deserved to have it for his next meal, as spearing fish was no easy task. That was not only on account of the speed and darting tactics of most fish but also because the deep water deflected the spear point before it reached the fish. An allowance had to be made for deflection in water of different depths and only practice developed expert spearsmen.

Most Indians killed the fish speared immediately with a sharp blow on the back of its head with a heavy stick or club. The Indians of the Northwest Coast had special clubs for killing salmon and halibut.

FISHING AND FISH OBSERVING FOR MODERN INDIANS

Fishing with rod and line provides good sport, and often training in qualities of patience for the modern Indian. As some chiefs in the encampment are fairly certain to be enthusiastic fishermen, a few pointers are set down here which may prove of interest to seasoned fisherman and novice alike. They are built on personal experience and have proved practical and handy on many occasions and in many encampments.

Finding Bait

Frequently standard baits such as minnows or worms seem far scarcer than fish in an encampment area. It is sad to realize that many good pan fish or even brook trout may abound in an area in which braves are equipped to fish only with bait such as minnows or worms, if they could only find some! As a rule, neither minnows nor worms are really scarce, but they may be so hard to find that even the most stout-hearted brave may become discouraged, after wading for an hour in shallow water just off the lake shore or in a stream or after turning over the twentieth rock, under each of which he had hoped to locate at least one little worm. Here are a few ways to help to secure such baits without too much loss of time.

Decoying Minnows

All that is usually needed to net a supply of minnows is a piece of soap which lathers easily and a small-mesh scoop net. Either from afoot inshore, from a canoe, or from the lake bank, work up a lather in the water with the piece of soap. When the suds settle, drag the net through the water that is lathered and you will nearly always catch some minnows which have been lured by the suds. Rinse them off immediately in the water and put them in a live bait pail for later use.

Luring Worms

Worms can often be decoyed from their underground lairs by simply stirring two heaping tablespoonsfuls of a detergent—soap powder or flakes—into each quart of warm water used. Pour some of this solution on the earth or grass where worms are thought to live and, if there, they will report on the double. Those reporting *must* be washed off right away in clear, barely tepid water or the washing powder suds will speedily kill them.

Attracting Night Crawlers

One way to bring night crawlers to the surface is to mix a solution consisting of one tablespoon of mustard to one quart of water. Pour about half a cupful of this mixture over the little mound of earth that generally marks that worm's home. At any hour of the night or day the worms will be attracted to the surface, where they may easily be picked up.

Keeping Worms

This useful bait can be kept healthy for weeks or longer by keeping it in a flat wooden box with a bed of moss covering the bottom. The worms will need to be fed occasionally. They eat cornmeal readily, but when none is handy a little powdered milk can be sprinkled on the surface instead. Hard boiled egg yolks crumbled and sprinkled on the moss are a good addition to a diet of worms which are going to be kept for a long time. The box containing the worms should be kept in the shade, in a cool place, indoors or outdoors but protected from rain. A *little* water *sprinkled* over the moss occasionally helps to keep the worms happy.

Carp Baits

Carp caught in clear, clean water make good eating. Here is an easily made bait with which to catch them. Dough mixed with cotton wool, just moist enough to mould into attractive little bait balls, will take carp. Though some fishermen chiefs may debate the following facts, they are worth trying. Sprinkle a drop or two of anise or lavender scent, if they can be obtained by trade with the pale-faces, onto the above mixture. It helps. Kernels of cooked or uncooked corn used as bait will also help to add a few carp to the basket, provided there are some in the waters fished.

Minnow Fish Decoy

Here is an easily made fish decoy which may help a brave to take home some fish to his tepee. Fill a large, clear glass jug or jar with water. Make a small hole in the cork or screw top. Place six minnows, more or less, or other small fish in the glass container. Lower it into midwater and suspend it in a likely spot

from a float or buoyant log so that the container is suspended about six feet or so below the surface. The small fish swimming in the jar, though prisoners, attract larger fish and as the latter cruise around outside the jar they are often quite ready to take a minnow or other bait that is easier to get at than the captive minnows.

Lighted Jar Fish Decoy

The use of a glass jar as described above recalls another method of attracting fish, but at night. Since this method of luring fish is somewhat similar to "jacking," in which a bright-burning torch or strong light is used to attract fish, illegally in some States, the method which follows should never be employed as a fish-taking device. It is useful and interesting, however, as a means of drawing fish at night when they can easily be watched by nature-loving braves from a canoe, seaworthy raft or, better still, from a dock of any sort which juts out into a lake where fish are found.

A flashlight is secured, switched on, then placed in a large, empty, clear glass jar, with the beam shining through the bottom of the jar. The jar is *sealed* with a *watertight* screw cover. To make sure that the cover lets no water in, one can wrap a piece of adhesive tape about an inch wide around the edge of cover and jar. A fairly heavy weight, such as a stone, is slung below the jar from a cord at each end of the container. These weights must be heavy enough to hold the jar below the surface at the depth desired. The jar is suspended on a cord, as shown in the drawing, the end of which is attached to a buoyant log, a float, or the end of a light pole held by a brave, so that the jar hangs in six or eight feet of water. Fish of all sizes will be attracted by the beam of the flashlight, and as they swim around the lighted jar they can be clearly observed by the watching braves.

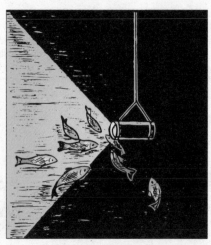

Nature's Convoy

Here is a subtle convoy which will carry a baited hook down stream under overhanging bushes to a spot where you feel sure that lurking fish lie in wait for acceptable bait. Cut a small green twig with a leaf or two on it. Pass the barb of your hook, which may be baited with a worm, or a chief may use an artificial fly, through the very edge of a leaf, as shown in the drawing, so that it may be released by the slightest twitch of the rod. Let the hook-carrying twig float

downstream until it reaches the exact spot decided on and then the slightest flick of the rod will release the hook from the floating leaf. When a worm is used, it will sink naturally down, perhaps to a waiting trout. If a fly is the lure, it can be retrieved by a series of short jerks, any one of which may get exciting results. A worm is reeled in in the usual way and may be set afloat again for another try at some practically inaccessible point downstream.

The Mud Ball Lunker Lure

Should a big, suspicious fish, such as a brown or brook trout lurk in a deep pool or hole in a stream near the encampment, it may provide your chance to claim coup. Thread a night-crawler or big, lively worm carefully onto your hook, after having mixed some wet earth and clay together to form a stiff paste. Gently mould a ball a little larger than a ping-pong ball, or still larger if the fish lies deep, around the baited hook. Now lower the hook on the end of the line into the deep pool or hole until it touches bottom. Hold the rod motionless and wait until the water and current wash the mud ball from the baited hook. Few lunkers can resist a fat, wriggling worm which has apparently come from nowhere.

Chiefs should tell their braves just how wary trout can be. Clumsy steps at the edge of a stream or pool, even in moccasined feet, or a shadow reflected in the water will alarm trout to the extent that they may not strike at any bait or lure again for several hours.

HUNTING AND TRAPPING

Indian hunters were as brave when hunting as when on the warpath and showed the same nonchalance in the path of a charging moose that they did when crouching with taut bowstring directly in the path of a charging enemy

on horseback. A hunter walked up to a big bear and, when the bear reared up
on its hind legs, killed it with a blow on the forehead with a war club or tomahawk. Sometimes the stroke of the tomahawk was delivered at the vital point
where the bear's foreleg and shoulder meet. Usually the hunter took a moment or
two of precious time, while the bear was rising up on its hind legs, to chide it
for not wanting to put up a good fight. Some Indian hunters wrapped a piece
of hide or blanket around the left forearm, which they stretched out as they
advanced with the tomahawk held ready in the right hand to attack this dangerous animal. Others did not bother with this none-too-effective shield.

. Hunters of the Northwest Coastal tribes usually fasted before and after the
chase and made special offerings to their gods before going on a hunt, whether
for land or sea mammals. The Tsimshian hunter, after killing a bear, held the
point of his hunting knife against the bear's chest and sang the mourning song
for bears. He then fasted partially for twenty days and ate no part of the killed
bear. One might say, "It would have been better for him not to have killed the
bear in the first place." This might sound logical were it not for the fact that
the band or clan to which the altruistic brave belonged was in need of food, and
bears, whether black or grizzly, made a welcome addition to their larder.

Hunting came naturally to Indians and even young boys tried to bring back
enough small game, or fish, for their family's supper.

Ownership Marks

Indians were able to claim their game and other personal property by the use
of ownership marks, which took various forms for tribal, band, and personal
identification. Painted circles, stripes, dots, or other marks at the feathered end
of an arrow, told to whom it belonged and similar marks, on an owner's stick
identified not only the brave but his family. These sticks were made of slim,
straight wands about 30 inches long, decorated in many simple or fantastic ways.
Ownership sticks were ornamented with circles, small hoops, painted disks, and
other marks, often suspended from a crossbar tied near the top of the stick.
Strips of varicolored flannel, buckskin, or other leather, feathers, or pieces of

fur were used for identification by some braves, while others used only the symbol of their animal, bird, or other personal totem, to assure the respect and safety of their property.

Hunting Taboos

Both Plains and Woodland Indians avoided eating foods that smelled strongly and would neither eat wild onions and similar plants, nor smoke, when leaving on a hunt. They believed that such odors were not only likely to betray their presence but were disliked by the animals which they were about to hunt. Hunters took sweat baths and then rubbed their bodies with sweet-smelling leaves or grass in order to remove all human scent.

Some of the tribes of the Northwest Coast had strict taboos, which governed the actions of not only the hunters but also their wives. Elaborate ceremonies were held prior to and after fishing and hunting expeditions. These applied chiefly to salmon fishing and the netting and harpooning of whales, especially by the Nootka.

Indian Trappers

Indians of all tribes excelled as trappers because they were familiar with the ways of the wild and the wildthings of air, land, lake, and ocean. They knew where the different beasts, birds, and fish lived at different seasons of the year, what they ate and how the different species of birds, beasts, and fish reacted to different situations. All of this knowledge contributed to full game bags and, most of the time, a full pot. Indians trapped animals of all sizes, and were expert at devising and improvising traps of all sorts which were ingenious as well as effective.

Trapping can be most inhuman if traps are used which catch, wound, and hold the live beasts trapped. Only with the coming of the white man did Indians learn of the hideously cruel steel spring, serrated jaw traps, which are still used extensively by white trappers throughout the "civilized" world. These traps should be banned throughout all countries which make a pretense of being highly civilized. Such instruments of legalized torture are not known in the uncivilized countries. On the other hand, live-catch traps can be used, under strict supervision, for purposes which are not only humane but necessary. Various government services, such as Fish and Wildlife Service, use traps to catch animals alive and unhurt, at points where animals of various species are too numerous, or doing damage to farmers' property. The surplus of harmless animals and damage-causing animals are taken to distant points where there is a scarcity of such animals and many of them can do good instead of harm. This is especially true in the case of beavers, as their ingenious dams and canals may cause flood trouble in some places while proving helpful in others. Thus, trapping can be carried out in the interest of scientific study, for acquiring a greater knowledge of the wonderful ways of wildthings and in furthering conservation.

Indian Traps

Live-Catch Traps. These include cage, pen, and box traps with closing doors, roofed catch-pits for animals and stake or woven net traps for fish, other aquatic creatures, and birds.

- *Injury or Kill Traps.* Snares, nooses, with or without spring pole, for animals, and gill nets for fish were among the kinds used.
- *Kill-Traps.* Deadfalls, Figure 4 and similar traps, were made, and natural-spring-release traps, which discharged an arrow or spear into the animal springing the trap were used. The Indians proved their humanity by the frequency and regularity with which they visited all their traps and trap lines. Today, many white trappers visit their traps with considerable irregularity, the visits being based on their convenience and weather conditions.

THE CAPTURE OF WILDTHINGS

It is the author's considered opinion that the "furred and feathered things," as Indians called animals and birds, should never be captured except in case of necessity, or for study purposes. This would include trapping birds or animals for food for survival, catching a wild animal which menaced the safety of the braves in an encampment, or trapping an animal, such as a skunk or raccoon, for a brief period of natural history study, after which the animals should be released as close to the spot where they were caught as possible. Very young wildthings should never be picked up, as in practically every case of fledgling birds on the ground or baby animals which appear to be lost, there is an anxious mother waiting to take care of the youngster once the intruder has gone. To take such birds or animals away from where they were first found and then bring them back to the same point, even a short time afterward, may mean their death.

Snapping Turtle Trapping

Snapping turtles devour young ducks and other species of waterfowl and a big snapper is quite ready to inflict serious injuries on a foot or hand which incautiously is thrust into its hide-out in lake or stream. The only good point about these vicious reptiles, whose savage jaws strike with the swiftness of a rattlesnake, is that they are excellent in soups and stews. How to cook them is told in Chapter 16.

Snappers are not very bright when it comes to avoiding baited traps and there are at least half a dozen humane and effective traps which can be made to catch them.

A trap for catching snappers on a large scale is illustrated here. It is built from old, long poles or straight smooth logs, the two longer ones being about 4 feet in length and all poles being about 8 inches in diameter. Old telephone or telegraph poles make a fine framework. The basket which is attached to all four poles and hangs down for a couple of feet below them is made of old chicken wire. The little ramp which leads up from the water of lake or stream to the top

of the trap can be built onto two sides of the snapper trap, instead of one. The most important thing is to have the insides of the logs bordering the basket part of the trap covered with zinc, tin, or other metal, so that once in the trap the turtles are unable to climb out. The trap is baited with fish or pieces of raw meat and some of the pieces can be enclosed in wire netting so that the first turtles trapped cannot eat all of the bait. The unfortunate part of this trap is that it catches almost all turtles which swim in the waters where the trap is set. This is not important when the chief in charge of the trap makes sure that his braves release all turtles other than snappers which are caught.

Instead of describing barrel and other traps, the author prefers to deal with only one more trap, which he evolved. It has two great advantages—it is easily made and is a sure-fire, perfectly humane method of trapping turtles. It is the author's firm belief that even when trapping the most ruthless creatures only the most humane methods possible should be used.

Snapper Trapper

An old, strong wooden box about 3 feet square and from 9 to 14 inches high is practically all that is required to make this effective trap. An oblong-shaped box will serve just as well. The wood of the box used should be about ¾ inch thick. A strong wooden frame covered with 1½-inch strong wire mesh, as illustrated, makes an excellent substitute for a wooden box. One end or one side of the box is carefully cut out to form the door of the trap, after which either the lid is nailed strongly back into place or the top of the trap is covered with strong wire mesh. The section taken for the door must be sawed smaller so that when it is hung exactly in place, the water will not cause the wood to swell so that the door jams. About 1 inch sawed from one end and the same amount sawed from the top generally serves the purpose. To insure the smooth operation of the trap door, the wood of which it is made can be soaked in water overnight, before the edges are sawed off. A one-inch square block of hard wood is nailed onto the very edge of each side of the floor of the trap, as shown in the drawing. It is all right if these two blocks project for ¼ or ⅜ inch outside of

the trap, as they must not be set further back than the very edge of the box. These blocks can be replaced by a narrow, thin strip of wood nailed across the bottom of the box, outside, so that the top of the strip comes up about half an inch higher than the foot of the door. It will be seen that the blocks or strip are simply to keep the door, which swings inward with ease, from opening outward by pressure from inside. Once the two doorstops are in place, the door is hinged at the top with two strong, oiled-leather hinges. The door has to hang centered, with the same amount of clearance all around. This completes the actual trap.

All that remains to be done is to put a strong screw eye into each corner of the top of the box. A rope of the same length is passed through each eye and a double knot tied on the end so that the rope cannot pull out of the eye. These four lengths of rope are tied together directly above the center of the top of the box, onto a large metal ring, to which the length of rope which lowers the trap into the water is attached.

Some old, heavy metal strips, when available, can be nailed onto the top of the trap, which saves weighting it down with a few large stones each time it is lowered to the bottom of a lake. Some bait, such as raw meat, fish heads or fish are placed inside the trap which is then lowered to the bottom so that it lies close to a place where snapping turtles have been seen. The surface end of the rope is tied to a float, a branch overhead or any other convenient object.

The catches one makes with this sort of trap are surprising! Turtles of all sorts, often really big ones, big fish, an occasional bull frog, and other amphibians are easily caught, several of each at times, when the trap is left in place overnight. It is the duty of the chief, after his band has had a chance to observe at close quarters the occupants of the trap, after each catch, to release all captives except snapping turtles.

Fish Traps

The Indians of tribes which were fond of fish used many different sorts of traps in which fish of all sorts and sizes were taken in large quantities. It took a lot of fish to go round when one considers that an adult Indian warrior of the Northwest Coast ate at least eight pounds of fish daily. In addition to weirs, there were traps built with long poles driven into the bottom of a river, inlet, or lake, so that the stakes almost touched, as shown in the drawing. Some tribes

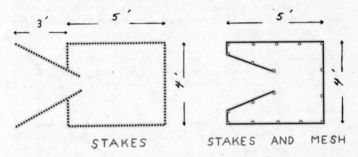

STAKES   STAKES AND   MESH

used comparatively few stakes and surrounded them with a woven net which imprisoned the fish. The V-shaped entry to these traps usually faced downstream because a greater number of fish entered the traps (which were usually square or oblong in shape) when they were set in that position. The traps were baited or unbaited, according to the techniques of the trap setters. As in all traps, whether for fish or game, exceedingly few of the creatures which found their way through the neck of the trap into it were successful in finding their way out again.

5

Safety and First Aid Measures for Pathfinders

Before one sets out on any adventure trail to meet the challenge of the unknown, the first and most important thing to do is to be quite certain that he is equipped to meet any emergencies which may occur. There may be several, only a few, or, thanks to the Great Spirit, none at all, but good fortune or luck on the trail must never be allowed to supplant ability and readiness to meet difficulties if they crop up. There are so many possibilities of unexpected things' happening to a group of young and eager braves, that it is hard to anticipate all of them. The pointers set down here do not try to do so. They merely point out some of the things which can happen and give some suggestions of how some of them may be avoided.

AVOIDING TRAIL MISHAPS

A chief should brief his entire band before setting out on a hike or adventure, whether on land or water. The braves should be told exactly what to do and how to do it before the expedition sets out.

Trail Contact

A chief will do well to keep all braves as close to him as possible at all times when on the trail, especially when new or difficult territory is being covered.

Blow Your Whistle!

The Hudson's Bay Company instructs its *Adventurers* in remote places to— "Use your whistle, when needed, to keep contact with your party. Don't shout or call—blow the whistle!"

A chief and each of his braves should carry a shrill whistle, on a lanyard to prevent its loss. A whistle should never be used except in an emergency of some sort or for assembling a band. The chief should instruct his braves to report to him immediately they hear his whistle. The chief should carry a whistle with a distinct and recognizable tone—such as boatswain's whistle, which is capable of producing several tones that may be heard for a long distance. The carrying power of a whistle or call is very important at times. The Eastern woodland resounded occasionally with the shrill call of *"Kou-ee-ee-e!"* as stray members of an Iroquoian band sought to establish contact. There is no doubting the carrying quality of this call when we know that, by a strange coincidence, the far-carrying call of the Australian bush is *"Coo-ee-ee-e!"*

Loose Rocks

Braves should be warned to take care not to dislodge loose rocks or rocks which can easily be loosened from soft ground, as such rocks can roll and cause injuries to feet. The displacement of rocks on a steep trail or when climbing or descending an embankment presents considerable risk.

Slippery Surfaces

Beware of the slippery trunks of fallen trees or logs; when damp or after rain or heavy dew, they are often as slippery as ice.

When crossing streams or rivers which are shallow enough to be easily fordable it is generally safer to wade across than to try leaping from rock to rock. Rocks can be very treacherous, especially when covered with a thin coating of loose sand, or when splashed by water. A strong pole, light enough to be handled easily, will prove helpful in crossing a stream. Flat rocks and stones may be topped not only with moss or slime but also with other rocks which sometimes appear harmless and seem to promise safe foothold but when underfoot are dangerously slippery. Moccasins and other types of footwear skid easily on such surfaces. Bare feet are, as a rule, too tender for rock jumping.

One important thing for a chief to emphasize as a great help in successful boulder to boulder leaps is that self-confidence is vital and therefore no brave should attempt a jump which he feels in advance is beyond his capacity to make surely and cleanly. Another vital point of equal importance is balance. Braves should be instructed in keeping the weight of their bodies directly above their legs as much as possible, not only when making jumps from rock to rock but also when walking on difficult and slippery surfaces. This practice makes jumping surer and walking under unfavorable conditions safer and easier.

Quicksand and Swampland

Naturally, chiefs will avoid swampland and quicksand at all times—but it is not always possible to do so, as sometimes quite innocent-looking ground is treacherous. On ground where the slightest risk is anticipated a chief must lead and test each stepping place in advance with a stout pole. Many woodsmen have saved themselves, when the ground began to give alarmingly, by instantly throwing themselves backward on the treacherous ground and rolling to safety toward the spot from which they had just come. By throwing themselves backward they broke the suction and temporarily freed their legs from the grip of the sand or swamp. The only position which offers temporary relief on such ground is a horizontal one, with legs and arms spread well out, until a rope or pole employed by a rescuer comes easily within reach of an outstretched hand. Travel over land which has been discovered to be swampy or unsafe for any reason should never be continued after sunset. It is wiser and safer to sleep out on high ground until morning light.

Beware of Darkness!

The urge to carry on until almost nightfall before setting up overnight camp has often led not only to great inconvenience but to serious injuries. The best advice regarding night travel can be given in one word—DON'T! When a band must move through the darkness of night, in case of real necessity, the chief should be a night-wise leader, and in all cases every member of his band should carry a whistle.

Leave a Message!

A chief who is forced to change his hiking plans, even if it is only a detour which covers a considerable distance, should always leave a message, where it may most easily be seen, telling of his change in plans and stating final destination. This was the rule of the Hudson's Bay *Adventurers* which always paid off.

Exhaustion Test

When a chief takes a long trail with older braves he should make certain that none of them becomes overtired. Even seasoned soldiers become exhausted on a long, forced march and hardened woodsmen are not immune from exhaustion. Here is a sure-fire test for exhaustion practiced by some outdoorsmen. Look up at the sky: if it seems to keep backing away from you—*rest!*

Feet Up!

This is important on the trail through woodland or over rock-strewn terrain. A nasty fall can be taken by letting a branch or stick get in between the legs while advancing along a wooded path. Such a needless accident can be dangerous when climbing down an embankment or hillside. The sure way to avoid such a mishap is to be constantly on the alert on the trail, using the eyes continually; do not follow another brave so closely, when moving in Indian file, that a branch across the trail cannot be seen, and lift the feet high enough to step over such obstacles. A 10-foot interval between braves in bushy country will give springy branches room to swing back into place.

Snake in the Grass!

A snake in the grass presents little hazard to braves on the trail compared with a snake which lies behind a fallen tree or log, or lurks in a hole in a stone wall which the band has to cross. Another real menace is the poisonous copperhead or a rattlesnake, taking a brief sunbath on an overhanging ledge, which the unwary hand of a brave climbing from below can touch with deadly results. Great care should be taken when stepping over logs, boulders or brush piles, especially after dusk, as it is then when most poisonous snakes are most active. Even big rattlers will usually move out of the way of a human being when they have sufficient warning to do so, but when taken by surprise they will almost invariably strike. It is important to keep constantly in mind that a rattlesnake need not, and often does not, rattle before attacking. A brave who gropes in holes or crevices in rock formations, puts his hand blindly into a hole in a tree or log, or feels for firewood in the dark is asking for trouble.

Deer Flies and Mosquitoes

Fast as a deer is this big fly with a vicious bite. Fortunately, it hesitates for an instant after alighting on the back or other part of the victim's anatomy.

This is the moment, if *she* is within sight and reach, to deal with her. Yes, like the mosquito, the male deer fly contents himself with the juices of plants. Braves on the trail in Indian file should be able to deal with this enemy when it alights on the back of the brave ahead.

Mosquitoes—because of the malaria germ they sometimes carried, in addition to germs of other diseases, such as yellow fever—plagued the armies of Julius Caesar, Alexander, Napoleon, and other well-known leaders.

The female mosquito has a preference for blue colors, something for braves to remember when they are dressing for the trail.

The bites of these insects are dealt with in the First Aid section which follows, but they are mentioned here so that the warning never to scratch such bites may be sounded. This is hard advice for some braves to follow but the result of scratching bites, especially when the hands are not clean, often means troublesome infection.

Plants and Flowers that Harm

A long dissertation on some of the many poisonous or harmful plants, flowers, and berries which often grow alongside a trail can be avoided here by giving a few simple pointers. There is little point in a chief's warning his braves not to eat the flowers or berries of such plants as hellbore, moonseed, or the poison sumac when the novice brave does not even know what these plants look like. The wise chief sternly warns his braves to eat absolutely no berry, flower, or plant found during a hike until it has been examined by the chief and declared not only harmless but edible. Should the chief not have a very good botanical knowledge, the plants and berries in question can be taken back to the encampment for proper identification or shunned entirely.

An important point often overlooked by some chiefs is that many wildflowers and plants can cause irritation to or sores on the hands, especially to braves who may be unusually allergic. Often simply picking such apparently harmless plants as the buttercup will cause the fingers to become infected, on account of offensive juices in the stems. The great danger is not caused by the infection of the hands but by the fact that too often the braves so infected will rub around their eyes with their fingers, causing badly inflamed eyes.

This rubbing with infected fingers, or even touching other parts of the

anatomy which have not been infected, is especially troublesome when the plant tampered with is *poison ivy*! This is a three-fingered, shiny plant, which is easy to identify and it should be pointed out by the chief to his band in or around the encampment. The sure way to avoid such irritation and infection is for the chief to warn his braves not to touch or scratch their faces, or rub their eyes, after touching any plant or flowers while on the trail.

Friend or Foe?

The ax or hatchet can be either to both woodland, tree, or thoughtless brave. These so-often-misused tools should always be carried sheathed when on the trail and sheaths should never be removed without permission from the chief. No brave who is unable to use an ax with some skill or has not been thoroughly briefed on the role of an ax in conservation and destruction should be allowed to carry one. A sharp ax is safer than a blunt one and an ax with the full-length handle is invariably safer than short-handled ones. This is easily understood, as when a hatchet or short-handled ax is deflected from a branch or log the blade is far more likely to enter the leg, or even body, than when a long-handled ax is used. Sheath knives can also be classed under the above heading and are often wisely replaced by large, good-quality-steel, sharp clasp knives.

Sunburn Prevention

Sunburn can be as painful as a bad burn caused by a cooking fire or campfire. How to treat sunburn is told under First Aid but the far more important thing is to prevent the necessity of treatment. Chiefs will find that the skin of some braves cannot stand even slight exposure to the sun at first and such braves should invariably wear shirts, even long-sleeved ones, and jeans until gradual exposure to the sun, at hours when its rays are least hot, insures immunity.

Blisters

As all of the pointers in this section deal with prevention against the necessity of first aid, and prevention is far better than the best cure, the treatment for blisters is given under First Aid. Blisters on the feet, which can become infected and give a lot of trouble, can be largely prevented by wearing heavyweight wool socks under the moccasins or hiking shoes, which should fit snugly but never tightly. When a blister begins to show, covering it with a sterile pad often keeps it from developing and assures comfort on the trail. A strip of adhesive tape applied over a beginning blister will prevent further rubbing of the sore spot and often this is the only treatment needed.

Beginning blisters on the hand, from paddling or chopping wood, can be greatly helped by adhesive strips placed over the sore spots. These preventive measures are used before the blisters form, otherwise the blisters usually have to be punctured with a sterilized needle or pin. Flame is an efficient sterilizer.

Insects in Ears

Quite often on the trail some misguided insect mistakes a brave's ear for its tepee. Frequently, turning the ear toward the sun will cause the insect to fly or crawl out. On sunless days, a flashlight shone into the ear from a distance of about a foot will, sometimes, have the same effect.

Heat Exhaustion Prevention

Before a brave has a reason to complain of giddiness, faintness, or nausea while on the trail on a hot day, the chief by allowing brief periods of rest in the shade can prevent his band members from developing these symptoms.

Road Accidents

With the encroachment of civilization, chiefs may have to lead their bands over and along highways. A band should then proceed to hike in Indian file on the left side of the road, facing oncoming traffic. *Never* should hikes along railroad tracks or over trestle bridges be allowed.

Bulls!

Fortunately, these animals are rarely encountered on hiking trips; they are often savage, swift, and cunning, being much more dangerous than buffalo in attack. Chiefs should be alert to this menace when bordering farm property or following streams where bulls may go for water.

Lightning!

One is inclined to treat danger from lightning rather too casually. This may be caused by the fact that a comparatively small number of living people have ever been injured by lightning and one rarely hears of friends who have been seriously inconvenienced by it. One can best appreciate the menace of lightning on learning that the estimated farm and other property losses caused by electrical storms in the United States over a period of one year reaches well over $36,000,000, not counting the enormous and irreparable loss caused by the approximately 7,000 forest fires attributed to lightning yearly. Brief newspaper items reporting the death of a few fishermen, whose boat was struck by lightning, or of a few children killed by the same source while playing on a beach, or in a park or woods, may not suggest great mortality. Because of this, it is well to remember that official figures prove that lightning kills more people in the United States than any other natural disaster, including storm and flood; and it becomes essential to know the best ways to avoid the death-dealing light shaft as it hurtles *upward* at 30,000 times the speed of a bullet. The discharge of this electric bolt carries millions of volts which are in search of a suitable target. Chiefs should take every possible precaution to protect their braves during lightning storms. Here are some helpful pointers.

• *How to Take Cover from Lightning.* Lightning generally strikes a higher point in an area and frequently one that stands alone. A brave in a canoe or any other craft is a prime target for a lightning bolt, apart from the fact that water is an excellent conductor, largely because he is the *highest* point in a vicinity where lightning may strike.

When suddenly caught outdoors and at some distance from buildings or natural shelters, braves can find comparative safety by lying flat on the ground, and especially in a depression, even though the ground be wet.

Never stand under a tree, especially an isolated one, during an electrical storm.

Assure greater safety in an electrical storm by getting rid of steel-headed axes or hatchets, steel fishing rods, and all other metal gear—*fast*.

Avoid all wire fences, metal posts, or other metal objects.

Braves who are out on the trail should seek shelter on the lowest ground close by, provided there is no cave in which they can take refuge, or a steep, overhanging cliff at the foot of which they can stand. If shelter in a nearby house is available, keep away from open windows, doors, or fireplaces until the storm is over.

Braves should get off the water in the fastest possible time if they are out in a canoe or any other small craft.

Braves should get out of the water with top speed if in swimming when the storm arrives.

- *Spotting the Approach of an Electrical Storm.* The approach of an electrical storm with its accompanying deadly lightning bolts is indicated by a build-up of dark thunderheads—thick towering clouds, called *cumulo-nimbus* clouds. Electricity discharges from cloud to cloud or from a cloud to the earth causing lightning. Rain and hail form a part of this build-up to an electrical storm.
- *Treatment for Electric Shock.* Should anyone be stunned by the shock of a distant lightning bolt, the person is treated for shock as prescribed under First Aid in this chapter and is given artificial respiration as described in Chapter 18.
- *To finish on a note of cheer.* If you see a flash of lightning, don't worry—the danger is already past.

AVOIDING MISHAPS IN THE ENCAMPMENT

Many of the accidents of the trail can take place in the encampment, too, but there are a few which are most likely to happen at times when the braves are not out on an expedition.

Poison Ivy Markers

Clumps or patches of poison ivy which seem impossible to exterminate entirely may grow in or around an encampment. Such places should be marked by a stake at least 2 feet long and 4 inches wide at the top, tapering down to a point, driven into the ground close beside the poison ivy patches. The stakes should be painted a light shade of orange, white, yellow, or light red, whichever color is most easily seen in each particular spot where the ivy grows.

Breaking Firewood

Chiefs should warn that this must never be done across the knee. Even attempts to break thin pieces of branch or wood across a knee can cause injury to the kneecap, and an injury at this point can take days or even weeks to heal. Thin pieces of dry wood should never be broken close to the face, as quite frequently a short length of the wood will fly up from the center of the piece, leaving both hands grasping an end of wood and an injury to face or eye which can easily be serious. Thin, dry sticks and branches can most safely be broken by laying them with one end on the ground and the other on top of a log. When stepped on sharply, the wood will snap and even if one end flies up it is not likely to do any damage to the cautious brave.

Lifting Logs

When a log, rock, or anything else has to be lifted by one or more braves, no attempt to raise it should be made without first bending the knees. The legs and arms should play their part when lifting anything. The additional flexibility caused by bending the knees can prevent serious strain.

Driving Stakes or Poles

Serious injury to the hands can be avoided if, when one is driving stakes or poles into the ground a small, shallow hole is first made—*not* with an axe blade—and the point of the stake placed in the hole. While being driven, the stake is held in place by a stout, supple green withe doubled around the stake as illustrated.

FIRST AID

Many accidents happen in an encampment and on the trail because the braves are living in surroundings to which they are not accustomed and doing unfamiliar things, in which they have had little or no practice. Following are some simple treatments for the most commonplace accidents which are likely to happen in an encampment.

It is most important that all chiefs bear constantly in mind the fact that first aid is often only the preliminary treatment given in an emergency prior to getting the injured brave safely to the doctor in the main encampment. Any well-meant attempt made by an inexperienced chief to go even one step beyond what is strictly first aid can result in serious injury to a patient.

Basic First Aid Kit

Having too many items in a first aid kit is almost as bad as having too few. The kit should be kept as complete and compact as possible and should always be in a place where it can be reached at a moment's notice. This necessitates a smaller, separate kit to take along on all expeditions and even on hikes.

Using the Kit. It is important that the few persons entitled to open and use the kit know just where each separate item and instrument is located in the box or case. Turning out items which must be kept sterile, onto a blanket, or anywhere else which is not sterile is contrary to every principle of efficient first aid. Hands should be made scrupulously clean before any move is made toward rendering first aid, especially in any case of bleeding.

Contents of Kit. It is much better to assemble a first aid kit—under supervision of a doctor or chief who is expert in first aid—for the special purpose for which it is intended than to buy a big, bulky kit containing much that is needless, at a cost of two or three times more than the made-to-order one. The suggested contents of a practical first aid kit, which should be carefully packed in a light metal or very strong plastic case, are as follows:

Materials

Gauze bandages in assorted sizes	Sterile cotton
Gauze compresses in assorted sizes	Adhesive tape in assorted widths
Sterile pads in assorted sizes	Adhesive bandages in assorted sizes

A few Triangular bandages

Instruments	*Medications*
One pair of scissors, good quality	Spirits of ammonia
One pair of tweezers	Ampules of 3½ per cent of tincture of
One medicine dropper	iodine
One pair of small, strong wire cutters	Rubbing alcohol
Thermometer	Hydrogen peroxide
Needles and thread	Boric acid powder
Safety pins, assorted sizes	Merthiolate
Wooden spatulas	Baby oil or olive oil
Swabs, sterile, cotton-tipped	Ointment for burns
Resuscitating tube (Airway)	Sunburn lotion and ointment
Soft rubber tube, ½ inch diameter	Insect repellent
and 24 inches long	Calomine lotion
Snake-bite kit	Green soap or other antiseptic soap
	Aspirin tablets
Note: The tweezers are for removing	Salt tablets: use with care, following
stingers and splinters; the wire cut-	directions on bottle
ters, to cut barbs from imbedded	Iodine, small bottle of 2 per cent
fishhooks; the rubber tube, for mak-	Oil of clove, small bottle, for tooth-
ing an *emergency* tourniquet.	ache

The tourniquet is a *very dangerous* instrument and should only be used in an extreme emergency when hemorrhage can be stopped in no other manner. It should only be used for short periods, then loosened, as it completely arrests circulation.

The contents of the first aid kit can be helpfully augmented by the addition of necessary items which are dictated by the kind of expeditions to be undertaken and the sort of terrain which will be covered en route. A snake-bite kit, for instance, which, most fortunately, rarely has to be used in the average encampment, is imperative in country where any venomous snakes may possibly be encountered. Equally imperative is a chief with knowledge and ability to use the snake-bite kit speedily and effectively, without chance of danger to the patient.

It is important that any chief who may have to use a snake-bite kit learn the instructions *which come with that particular kit* before he sets out with his band.

A good, *modern* first aid handbook should be kept handy, close to the first aid kit. But thorough knowledge on the part of a chief of the contents of the manual and how to use the instructions given is even more important than the handbook itself.

Sprains

Cold compresses applied frequently to the sprained part, coupled with elevation of the strained limb to reduce swelling, will give relief in the case of minor sprains. Sometimes the entire foot, when it is a case of sprained ankle, can be soaked in a cold stream or lake. Hot-water applications following the cold-water ones may be required to promote circulation in severe sprains. When conditions make it necessary for an older brave to keep advancing despite a sprained ankle, it is well to place the entire foot, with the boot or moccasin on, in a cold stream or pool. This will allow the brave to carry on until the boot can be removed and further treatment given. All sprains which continue to cause pain and trouble should be treated as suspected fractures.

Fractures

Any attempt to actually treat what appears to be even the simplest fracture is work for an experienced medical man. Even an expert first aider should *never* attempt to set an arm or leg, or any other broken bones, unless extraordinary circumstances make such a dangerous and drastic course imperative. Unfortunately, elementary first aid must be given in cases of fracture, at times. This is too bad because the best possible first aid treatment, could it be carried out, is simply to let the patient remain immobile, keeping him warm (as shock treatment) until a doctor can be brought at the earliest possible moment to the scene of the accident. When the patient must be transported back to camp or to a doctor, the fractured limb or part must be carefully splinted with padded splints, *before the patient is moved.* Moving a fractured limb, even a little bit, may cause a simple fracture to become a compound one, in addition to the probability of causing a severe hemorrhage. Splints can be improvised from straight slats of wood, straight branches, several plies of strong, heavy cardboard, or from a roll of thin wire mesh. Soft bandages or cotton wool can be used to pad any splints before they are carefully bandaged in position, the actual pressure of tying the knots in the bandage coming above and below the fracture point.

When a broken forearm has been splinted, it must be supported with a bandage. A triangular one is best, as it supports the elbow as well as the forearm while the patient is being taken to a doctor.

Cuts and Wounds

Often the most dangerous side of cuts and wounds lies in the possibility of infection. A chief should never attempt to render first aid in such cases or dress the injuries unless his hands are really clean. Washing them with medicated soap and then rinsing them with denatured alcohol is one satisfactory way of sterilizing them. Minor wounds should first be washed with an antiseptic solution; a small quantity of antiseptic salve can be lightly spread on the wounded area and then a sterile pad can be bound snugly over the injury with a gauze bandage. Use sterile pads, but never sterile cotton wool, on wounds. When the pad which directly covers the wound is tightly stuck to it, it is best to trim around the edges of the pad, without disturbing the scab, and dress with another pad over the original one.

Pressure will usually stop blood flow from nearly all cuts and most minor wounds. When the cut is on a hand or foot, elevating the injured limb will reduce the flow of blood, when necessary. When a wound has been covered with several pads and bandages, it should be uncovered gradually and carefully, lest bleeding recommence when the cut is exposed.

Swelling, redness, or pus oozing from a wound at any time is a sure sign of infection and a danger signal which warns that the patient should be taken to the nearest doctor in the quickest possible time.

Wounds caused by puncture of any sort, even though they may not bleed to any extent, should always receive competent medical treatment at the earliest possible moment.

No mention of a tourniquet has been made in connection with stopping the flow of blood because the use of one in inexperienced hands can cause very serious damage to the injured member, perhaps even the loss of the limb. This method of arresting the flow of blood should only be used by an experienced chief or used in extreme emergency, when combatting severe hemorrhage which cannot be stopped in any other way.

Infection

It is best to stress infection at this point, as it is one of the major menaces in all sorts of injuries where bleeding occurs. Stepping on a nail may cause serious infection and the injury, without prompt and adequate treatment, may mean the loss of a foot. A simple scrape on a rock, or a scratch on a dirty hand, may set up a dangerous state of infection with serious results.

Frequently a camp doctor will give an anti-tetanus injection for practically any wound, no matter how slight, whether the injured camper is in a so-called "tetanus zone" or not.

An unknown quantity to consider in infection is that some youngsters appear to be practically immune from such a condition, while others will become dangerously infected if they only scratch a finger on a pin! Because of this, an alert chief will *never* overlook the possibility of infection following even apparently slight injuries and, as soon as possible, he will have the injured brave examined by a medicine man in order to eliminate all possibility of an injurious after effect.

Fishhook Injuries

In this nasty type of injury the possibility of infection, even before the hook can be removed, is ever present. If the fishhook has just penetrated the skin, the barb can sometimes be manipulated slightly so that the hook may be backed out fairly easily. When the hook has penetrated more deeply, say in a finger or hand, the barb can be forced out through the skin, occasionally, close to where it entered. In such case, the barb must be snipped off with a good pair of wire cutters and the hook backed out of the wound.

After the removal of a hook, the wound must be washed out in a fairly strong antiseptic solution, some antiseptic salve should be spread on the wound with a wooden spatula and a sterile pad placed on the injury which is then bandaged. It is wise to have a doctor examine all such injuries as soon as possible, to prevent infection.

Should it be impossible to remove a hook by either of the first aid methods given, the best course is to cover the wound with antiseptic salve, cover it with a sterile pad and bandage it in such a way that the hook will be immobilized and enter no deeper, and then take the victim to the nearest doctor.

Eye Injury

First aid only covers the most elementary treatment for any injury to the eye. Luckily, the chief injury which usually has to be treated on the trail or in the encampment is "something in the eye." Often, tears wash out the offending matter before any sort of first aid can be used. If the victim closes the eye containing the foreign matter and winks the other eye repeatedly, the obstruction will often be gone when the injured eye is opened. Occasionally, blowing the nose will help to dislodge something in the eye.

Never should a sharp instrument of any sort be used, nor should attempts be made to roll the eyelid over a match stick in order to better carry out the search for the foreign invader.

A foreign body can often be removed from the eye by using the corner of a clean handkerchief twisted into a point and dipped lightly in oil. A piece of bandage may be used in the same manner. The foreign matter will usually adhere to the oiled point. An eye may be bathed with a 2 per cent solution of boric acid, which will generally wash out the offending matter. Amateur first aiders should never try to wash out the eye with oil. To stop possible irritation of the eye once the object has been removed, the eye should be kept closed for a few minutes.

If the simple first aid media mentioned fail to give relief and the foreign body remains lodged in the eye, a doctor's help is necessary. In the case of injury to an eye by a spark from a fire, it is best to cover the closed eye lightly with a gauze pad and bandage and take the patient to a doctor as soon as possible.

Ear Injury

Any injury of an unknown nature which causes an ear to bleed or give considerable pain for some time should be attended to by a medical man. Temporary help can be given by putting a little sterile cotton or a sterile pad in the ear to stop the flow of blood, but first the cotton should be coated lightly with antiseptic ointment to prevent its sticking to the blood.

Nosebleed

Usually bleeding from the nose is caused by a blow of some sort, though high altitude, high blood pressure, or over-exertion can start a nosebleed. Generally the bleeding comes from a small vein which has been ruptured, near the end of the nose. Slight upward pressure where nose and upper lip meet may stop the blood flow, or the nose may have to be packed with sterile cotton lightly smeared with the antiseptic ointment.

If the bleeding is rather severe or continues after pressure has been applied, the patient should be made to lie on his back with blankets or some other support under his head and shoulders to raise his head considerably. Cold compresses are applied to the back of the neck, down to shoulder level, and cold wet cloths should also be applied to the face around the nose area. The patient should be kept quiet for a little while after the bleeding has stopped and warned against blowing his nose too soon following the bleeding.

Burns

There are three degrees of burns: *first degree burns*, which only cause the skin to become red and slightly irritated; *second degree burns*, which are marked by watery blisters of varying size; and *third degree burns*, which destroy part of the flesh.

The first degree burn is taken care of by the application of a good ointment for burns, and there are a number of these such as ones containing picric acid. In an emergency where no ointment is available, salad oil, baby oil, olive oil, a strong solution of tea, or even an application of melted soap, baking powder, or flour may be used to cover the burned surface, which is then covered with a sterile pad.

A second degree burn should first be painted lightly with an antiseptic solution, after which the blisters are carefully punctured with a sterilized needle, so that the water may run out. Flame is a good sterilizer but the needle must be allowed to cool before use. The tops of the punctured blisters are a part of nature's healing process and should not be removed. The burned area should be gently covered with a good ointment for burns and then bandaged, but not too tightly.

Third degree burns should be treated by a doctor, but first they may be covered with a burn-ointment, as soon after they occur as possible, and covered with a sterile pad or pads to exclude the air.

Sunburn

Sunburn is easier to prevent than to cure. Gradual exposure to the sun should prevent the need for treatment. Sunburn can be as painful as the most painful burn. There are several good ointments especially made for the treatment of sunburn and one of them should be gently applied as soon as possible after the sunburn has occurred or, better still, while it is still in the process of development. If the burn is blistered, it should be covered with a sunburn ointment and a sterile dressing, as for a second degree burn. When a brave has badly burned shoulders or arms they should be loosely bandaged even after the healing scab has formed, to avoid its being scraped off, with infection resulting.

Insect Stings

The stingers of insects, such as bees, should be quickly removed from the flesh with the point of a sterilized needle and tweezers. The puncture should be washed with a fairly strong antiseptic solution and then covered with spirits of ammonia or calamine lotion. Cold compresses will help to relieve pain when the bites of insects such as bees, wasps and hornets occur on sensitive parts of the anatomy.

The bites of mosquitoes and similar stinging insects are treated by the application of alcohol or ammonia to the bitten parts. These are really counter-irritants which give welcome relief from the itch caused by the bites or stings. Calamine lotion is also used in the treatment of mosquito, black flies, midges, "no-see-ums" and deer flies, though a stronger counter-irritant will drive the itch out faster.

Poison Ivy Infection and Nettle Sting

The Indians had a remedy for poison ivy itch which is fully as effective as some of those on the market today. They used the juice of the Jewel Weed to combat the sting of poison ivy. For the burn and rash of nettle stings, they used the juice of big dock leaves which, through a quirk of nature, can usually be found growing close to nettle patches.

One treatment for poison ivy infection is a liberal painting of calamine lotion, after the infected clothing has been removed. The clothes should be washed in a strong solution of antiseptic soap before being worn again. Washing the affected parts with a strong solution of green or brown soap, then dabbing gently with rubbing alcohol also gives relief.

Today, there are one or two really effective preparations to combat the effects of poison ivy. One especially, in tablet form, has stood up under severe Marine and Coast Guard tests. It not only relieves but speedily cures poison ivy itch, and can be bought at any good drug store.

The effects of poison ivy infection are slight in some cases and very severe in others. Chiefs should teach their braves to recognize the plant. This is very easily done. Here again, prevention is far better than cure. The braves should be warned that if they think they have contacted poison ivy they should be most careful to touch neither around their eyes, mouth, nor any other parts of the body until they have washed their hands very thoroughly with green soap or other strong antiseptic soap.

Heat Exhaustion and Sunstroke

When heat exhaustion occurs, the victim should be placed in a reclining position in the shade and cold compresses can be applied to his head and back of neck. Plenty of water should be given the patient and a salt tablet every two or three hours will help to combat the effect of the heat exhaustion. The same treatment will help in cases of mild sunstroke.

Shock

Shock may result from a great number of injuries, such as burns, wounds, fractures, and immersion in water. The principal part of the simple treatment necessary is to keep the patient warm, with blankets, and in a reclining position. In most cases of shock a hot drink, such as chocolate or coffee, the latter being a stimulant, can safely be given.

6

Orientation and Woodcraft

The simplest interpretation of the word orientation, stripped of all technicalities, is the ability to find one's way about in little-known or unknown country. The meaning actually goes a little farther than that, because the art includes one's familiarization with and adaptation to an environment or situation. A good magnetic compass is most essential for any chief who is concerned in any way with orientation.

PLOTTING A COURSE

Before a chief sets out with a band on any kind of expedition, over any sort of country, he should prepare a map of the territory which he is going to cover. When there is a good map available, such as a U. S. Geological Survey map or a Canadian Department of Mines and Resources one, he should study it most carefully and plainly mark on it the route or routes which he intends to follow from the encampment to the objective of the expedition, and the route chosen to return from there back to the starting point. With such a map, on a scale ranging from 1 to 2 miles to an inch and on which all prominent landmarks will be shown, and at least two good compasses in the band, there should be little difficulty on the part of the chief in making the expedition a complete success.

A chief will make any expedition, especially one over terrain unknown to the band, far more interesting by going over the map with the braves and pointing out the destination, landmarks, and other points of interest which they will pass en route. The most seasoned chief will enjoy hearing an enthusiastic brave exclaim, "There's that big hill we saw on the map!" or "There's the gully where we're going to look for a cave!"

A chief with some experience in drawing even rough maps may like to try the method used by many pathfinding chiefs and leaders of raiding and exploring bands among the American Indians. This is how they did it.

The war parties of a number of tribes were carefully briefed before starting out on the unfamiliar country which they were going to traverse. The members of the war party sat in a circle on sandy or bare ground and a chief who knew the route or a well-informed scout, drew on the ground with a pointed stick the course which they would follow. All of the easily identified features were marked plainly on the map. The principal guiding features were, of course, rivers, mountains, hills, gorges, and valleys; these and all other identifiable features helpful in accurate pathfinding were carefully mapped. Water holes were most carefully noted in country which had to be traversed when there were no rivers, lakes, or streams. A distinct line was then marked from the starting point to indicate the trail to be followed up to the first night's stop. A stake marked with a single notch was driven in at that point. When questions had been asked by younger and less experienced warriors and the entire party had made a mind picture of the route and all geographical features which seemed most important to them, the route for the second day's advance was carefully marked over the territory plotted to represent accurately the ground to be covered on the second day and a stake with two notches driven in at the end of that day's journey. Indians sometimes learned such details for an expedition of four or more days, which is a tribute to their mental ability and gift of storing mind pictures for future use.

DIRECTION FINDING

The necessity of having an accurate compass in pathfinding and exploring cannot be overemphasized.

Another sure-fire way of finding one's way is by known landmarks or, of course, ones shown on a map. This method of travel from point to point is used not only by seasoned pathfinders on land but also by skilled navigators on the water. Recently, when crossing the most difficult Hecate Strait to and from the Haida islands, between Prince Rupert and Queen Charlotte City and returning from Masset to Prince Rupert, the author had the pleasure of watching a skilled pilot make as much use of islands and landmarks, fore and aft, as of the chart which, naturally, he had to depend on for depth. Travel on both land and sea by the use of known landmarks is recommended by experts both in the field of land exploration and in marine navigation.

The two "O's," orientation and observation, are very closely allied. Woodsmen have the habit of glancing back fairly frequently, in difficult country, and observing landmarks along the trail which they travel, so that the return will be easier should they have to retrace their steps.

THE COMPASS

Countless lives have been saved by the use of accurate compasses and no chief engaged in pathfinding or leading expeditions should be without a compass. Knowing how to use a compass skillfully is as important as owning one, and when an accurate compass and a good map are teamed together they are unbeatable.

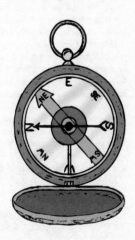

Buying a Compass

A good compass is not expensive these days. There are many stores which sell surplus goods where excellent compasses can be bought at very reasonable prices. A compass with a special, movable directional line-of-travel arrow which indicates the route being followed by the user as he advances when the magnetic needle points north, is a fine model. Should this type not be available, any good compass with a cover which closes to protect the dial and a directional arrow and marking which are easily seen and read should do a good job. A luminous dial compass is sometimes an asset, though the average chief will probably use his instrument only in daylight. Once a compass has been bought and *tested*, the next important step on the road to using a compass with complete confidence can be summed up in a motto —TRUST YOUR COMPASS!

Testing a Compass

A good compass rarely gets out of order, especially when it is kept in a dry place away from metal objects.

When the compass needle swings freely back and forth several times and then settles with the needle pointing in exactly the same direction on three or four tests, the compass can be considered in good working order.

Using a Compass

The compass is best used when placed on an absolutely flat surface, or it can be held flat on a steady hand. It should never be used close to any metal, such as axhead or knife, as such metals throw the magnetic needle off course. Since the compass is a magnetic one, the needle does not indicate true north but magnetic north, as the needle is attracted to the Magnetic Pole instead of the North Pole. This declination can make a considerable difference in direction at the end of a lengthy expedition but does not affect short trips to an appreciable extent. In any case, all good maps, especially those used in wilderness travel, plainly indicate the true and magnetic north in relation to the territory they cover, giving the difference in degrees, so that a chief can easily figure out the variation once the difference reference is found on the map. On practically all maps the top indicates the true north.

It is interesting to note that from 1831 to 1945 the Magnetic Pole was believed to be fixed on the Boothia Peninsula in Northern Canada. Since 1945, however, the true position of the Magnetic Pole has been accepted as being fixed on Prince of Wales Island, 300 miles north-northwest of the former site.

When a compass is not equipped with the additional directional needle mentioned, this is how the ordinary compass can be used to travel, for example, in an easterly direction. Place the compass so that the needle points north. Pick out a tree or prominent object in a due east direction and go to it. From this point, line up another object and continue to do so as long as due east is the objective.

Two different compass points, situated at different angles, taken from a given point, will fix a position precisely. Two distinctive or unmistakable points, such as a certain hill, island, or unusual tree, are marked on a map. With these two fixes and the point from which they were shot marked on the map, it is easy to know one's position exactly upon return to the same terrain at the point where the landmarks of the double fix can be seen.

ORIENTATION BY CONSTELLATION

At least several chapters could be written on pathfinding by the stars but the outstanding aid to celestial orientation can be set down in a paragraph or two.

Ursa Major, the so-called Big Dipper, furnishes the most accurate and easily seen guidance for seekers of the North Star. The two pointer stars are found in the end of the dipper, from which the water would flow if the dipper were tipped. Lining up these two stars with the brightest star in that section of the sky points out Polaris, the North Star, and the true north.

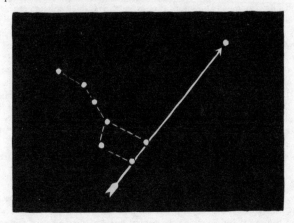

Indians said, "Stars do not lie," but one has to know the stars and their positions before their silent talk can be correctly interpreted.

A brave or band which has been unwary enough to be overtaken by darkness and has little chance of locating camp or encampment in the dark, is better off finding a nearby windbreak or temporary shelter in which to spend the night, than to travel aimlessly, and dangerously, in the dark, since a fresh start can be made with the coming of dawn. A fire should be lit and kept burning as brightly as possible throughout the night. A missing brave or band is much more likely to be located by searchers in this situation than if wandering haphazardly around in the darkness.

Pole Star Compass Check

One can infallibly check his compass direction accuracy with the help of the North Star. When the stars are visible, drive a straight staff into the ground so that its top is about four feet above ground level. Go back twelve feet and drive another pole into the ground at the exact point where on sighting over the top of both poles they line up *accurately* with the Pole Star. At sunup, sight over the pole tops and bring some distant object directly into line. Now focus the Magnetic North needle on the object, while standing at one of the sighting poles. The difference between *True North* and where the compass needle indicates *Magnetic North* will be the variation which, in short distance travel, will not prove of major importance in an area where the variation is slight. In Maine and some other States, however, the variation is about 18 degrees.

"NATURAL COMPASS" DANGERS

The modern chief is advised to be very sceptical about direction pointers which are supposed to be indicated by "nature's compasses." Such pointers usually contain such information—and misinformation as: certain plants always lean in a certain direction; certain birds nest in holes which always face east; a certain direction point is surely indicated by the "usual" way in which white pine and hemlock lean; and one nearly always finds more waterfowl on the west side of lakes and streams. Many more of these "indicators" are quoted, but there is always the chance that one is traversing a section of country where plants and trees do not always obligingly conform and a sudden move of fish to the east side of a lake also draws the waterfowl to that side, instead of the west. True, there are some natural signs of direction which are reasonably reliable, but it is better to leave pathfinding by such signs to Indians or experienced woodsmen—because, under certain conditions, even these indicators can be wrong. These "as a rule," haphazard, and often misleading "pointers" on finding one's way on unknown terrain, coupled with many other sources of false advice on orientation, can be deadly.

Wrong Direction

In the days when white men had good reason to fear the Indians—not because of what the Indians had done to the white men but because of what the white men had done to the Indians, and the natural desire of the latter for reprisals—three white men were lost in what was then Indian territory. Their rations had run out and days of wind, rain, and storm had obscured the sun. The men were unable to tell directions by the stars, even when these were briefly visible, and so, because of their lack of knowledge of orientation by means of constellations, they had not the slightest idea in which direction to travel in order to proceed north. They knew that a small army fort lay only a short distance to the north and that it provided their only hope of survival, if they could reach it in time.

Suddenly, in the far distance, they saw the tepees of a small Indian encampment. Through a battered telescope, the man acting as leader scanned the encampment and found that it was occupied by hostiles. Eagerly he told his weary companions that they were saved by what he had seen. He was supposed to be well-versed in Indian lore and when he declared that now he knew for certain in which direction to travel in order to head due north and reach the fort his companions did not doubt his word. Starving but encouraged they set out.

When the trio was accidentally found, far to the south, a few days later, two were dead and the leader was dying from exposure and thirst. He told the men who had found them that he led his party directly northward after seeing the Sioux teepees, because he then knew exactly in which direction north lay. "The doors of Indian teepees *always* face east," the dying man declared when asked on what he had based his direction of travel. Unfortunately for him and his companions, his knowledge of Indian lore was not sufficient to inform him that Indians quite often erected their teepees so that the doors faced away from the direction from which the storm wind blew. On the morning when he had seen the Sioux encampment, the doors of the teepees were all facing *west*, because of the severe storm which had been blowing toward them from the east when they had set up their lodges!

Truly, "A little knowledge is a dangerous thing."

FINDING THE WAY

As finding the way is an important part of orientation, it is well to take up this subject from the viewpoint of a person who is wandering on completely unfamiliar terrain. Direction does not interest this nearly lost wanderer, as he does not know in which direction to travel, his one idea being to contact somebody or find a habitation in the difficult, wooded area in which he finds himself. A few pointers on how to do this may prove of interest to braves who may at some time find themselves in a similar situation.

Using the Eyes

Seeing a wisp of smoke in the distance can lead to a campfire, a shack, or some other habitation.

A piece of fresh moss hung in the crotch of a tree or a wisp of hay hung from a tree branch may indicate that someone must have been there recently and a blast on a whistle may cause that person to show up.

From the vantage point of a hill or tree one may see a cabin, house or village in the distance.

A blaze, a paint or chalk mark on a tree can lead to others which point the way to a camp or habitation of some sort.

A wall or fence seen in the distance may help to set you on the road to civilization.

Fresh ruts at the edge of a wood are likely to have been made by farm carts or lumber wagons coming from an inhabited place.

Using the Ears

Listening carefully for sounds and then moving in their direction will often lead to habitation. In a lonely, unfamiliar part of the woods or forest the faint sound of a pump in the distance is an assuring noise.

The ring of an ax in the forest is as welcome as the sound of a dinner bell to an amateur woodsman who has lost his way in the North or any other woods.

The bark of a dog, the shrill crow of a rooster, the sound of a cow lowing, are all welcome sounds when searching for people who can furnish information as to the best route to take to get where one wishes to go.

The sound of a car on a distant or hidden road is a welcome sound.

The shrill whistle of a train in the distance can indicate direction.

Using the Nose

The fragrance of new-mown hay drifting from any direction into thickly wooded country where a novice brave is having trouble finding his way is a priceless scent.

The smell of a pigsty in the circumstances described above falls into the same category of welcome fragrances.

A barnyard, horse stables, chemicals, all have distinctive odors which can indicate the direction in which people are most likely to be found.

Vicious Circle

If one is unfortunate enough to have to advance in unknown country in a certain direction on a dull day, without a compass, care must be taken not to advance in a circle. This is an easy, perhaps instinctive, thing to do and the best way to avoid doing so is to learn to move in a straight line by sighting on objects straight ahead. This can be done by lining up two trees or other prominent landmarks straight ahead and then advancing from the first to the second, then looking ahead for further distant objects in a direct line so that a straight course may be held as one advances.

There is, perhaps, some sort of mechanism in even a trained woodsman's head which will cause him to circle when traversing unknown country on a dull, windless day or a starless night without a compass. It is unlikely that one outdoorsman in a million really has that vaunted "sense of direction," on which the majority pride themselves. One should never count on possessing this sense, as it may prove no more than an occasional "hunch" and a hunch can often prove a dangerous thing in the wilderness.

Deceptive Distances

The distance between points proves most deceptive at times. This is especially true when hiking in fine, clear weather in mountainous country. Mountains which appear to be close at hand, because of the crystal-clear atmosphere, are really quite far away and one becomes discouraged in trying to reach an object which seems to retreat as it is approached. A way to correct such illusions and avoid discouragement, if not fatigue, is to multiply any apparently short distances by five, and apparently long distances by ten, when travelling in such country.

Distress Signals

Calling for assistance can be done by sound or sight signals. Three short, loud whistle blasts in succession, at short intervals; three bright-burning fires, placed about three feet apart; or three columns of heavy, steady smoke, from fires covered with a layer of damp grass or leaves, and also about three feet apart, all mean the same thing—HELP! This is now an accepted International code.

A good way of calling for help by sound, when in difficulties in woods or forest, is to beat out a series of three loud strokes in succession, at short intervals, with an improvised hardwood club on a sound, dead tree, or on a live tree which best gives off the sound.

FINDING A LOST TRAIL

Indians always cast about in all directions when they lost a trail until some brave in the party picked it up again. This was a difficult task, as the trail which the Indians had lost might easily have been the almost invisible tracks of one brave, doing all in his power to throw his trailers off the scent. When modern Indians lose a trail, it is nearly always a rather faint path or narrow trail which has become so indistinct at some point that it apparently ends there. The same ending may occur when a band is following a brook or small stream which suddenly vanishes underground. The chief can assume that in both cases the trail or brook can be discovered again somewhere ahead of where it vanished.

One way to find a lost path is illustrated in the drawing. The chief leaves two or more of his band at the point where the trail has come to an end. Those who remain behind should have whistles, as should the chief, at least in the party of trail seekers. Suppose that the path they were following ran north and south and they were traveling north when the trail disappeared. The chief can start out in a northeasterly direction. The braves with him spread out in line only a few feet apart and not farther than thirty feet away from the chief. They move in the same direction and after the chief has covered a distance of about sixty yards he turns and proceeds due west, his braves moving along with him in the same formation as before.

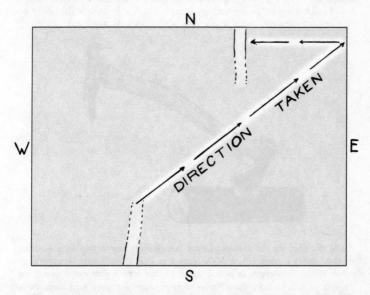

The path which they seek may lie toward the northeast, *or* toward the northwest, so after the searchers arrive in line with the braves marking the known end of the lost trail, they proceed fifty or sixty yards due northwest. In this way they are practically certain to run across the continuation of the lost trail, whether it runs toward the northeast or northwest. Once the trail has been found, the chief calls in the braves waiting for his signal and they assemble at the newly found trail.

The drawing shows that the trail was found to the northeast of the known trail, but it could have been crossed while the searchers moved in a northwesterly direction, had it not been discovered on the first leg of the search. This disciplined way of finding a lost trail is far different from letting the band spread out in all directions, running in circles until the trail is found, and possibly losing two or three braves during the search.

WOODCRAFT AND AXMANSHIP

Woodcraft is the way of the woods, how to enjoy it and understand and employ the many crafts which make a brave wood-wise. Woodcraft can be called *woodscrafts* since it embraces many of the Indian ways and becomes part of the life of the modern Indian who finds kinship in the outdoors. Axmanship is an outdoor skill of woodland and forest which should neither be learned nor perfected at the expense of nature. Woods and forests nearly always require the skillful use of hatchet, ax, and saw as an aid to conservation, but unskilled and careless use of these tools is a menace to all that conservation stands for. Chiefs should point out that "trying out" an ax on a live tree or bush is the height of stupidity and sabotage, and is a sure sign of ignorance of woodcraft.

The idea that one can acquire a better knowledge of axmanship by graduating via the hatchet is quite fallacious. A hatchet is a far more deadly weapon to its owner than a full-length ax and it is the hatchet which does more than three quarters of today's very considerable damage done outdoors with these tools.

Any effort made here to attempt to teach the correct uses of an ax or the art of felling a tree would be fruitless. Such skills are taught in the woods, not on paper. No would-be woodsman was ever graduated from a correspondence school of lumbering to a job in a lumber camp. Ax skills are best taught in the forest by an experienced chief, wise in the ways of the woods and able in the art of axmanship. An amateur knows as little about where the tree will actually fall as a beaver does as it works on a tree. Such vital details as the natural lean of the tree, extra weight of the branches on one side of the trunk, the direction of the wind, the depth and angle of the two notches, and other considerations of lesser import have to be worked out before an experienced woodsman actually knows just where the tree will fall.

Ax Don'ts and Nevers for Would-be Woodsmen

There are certain rules which should govern the use of *both* hatchet and ax and they are mostly *don'ts* and *nevers*, because few tools are abused to the same degree as an ax. Here are some of the most important rules, which should be considered laws, governing the ax and hatchet and their use. These rules should be learned and mentally accepted by all novices before an ax or hatchet finds its way into their hands.

- Never needlessly injure a tree, branch, or bush with an ax.
- Never gash nor cut down a tree, branch, or bush without permission from a chief or other responsible person.
- Never use a dull ax.
- Never drive an ax into the ground.

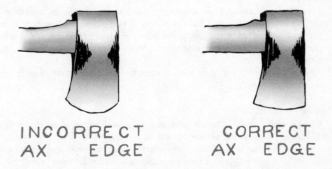

INCORRECT AX EDGE

CORRECT AX EDGE

- Don't use an ax with a rounded blade—this *tree to knee* model is untrustworthy.
- Don't "throw" an ax over a shoulder in order to carry it in that position.
- Never use an ax if the handle is even *slightly* loose.
- Never pass an ax blade-first to anyone.
- Don't leave an ax, even a sheathed one, lying carelessly on the ground.
- Don't, as a novice woodsman, use a double-bitted ax of *any* weight.
- Never swing an ax "for fun." This should never be done even while chopping down a tree unless one is absolutely sure that there is *ample* clear space *above* and *entirely around* the area the swung ax will travel. An overhead vine is a most dangerous chopping hazard.
- Never cut through a knot—chop around it.
- Don't drive an ax into a log by striking it on the head with another ax.
- Don't use a cold ax on a cold day without first warming its head.
- Never throw a hatchet nor an ax at any tree, nor at anything else, at any time, in any place.
- Never place an ax close to a fire and never burn a broken shaft out of an ax by putting the ax head directly into a fire.

Do's and Musts for Would-be-Woodsmen

Let's break away from a partial list of nevers and don'ts and take a look at some *do's* and *musts*.

- Always carry an ax sheathed.
- Always remember that it is the weight of the ax, though lightweight, that makes it cut, *not* brute force; and endeavor to develop a rhythmic swing when chopping.
- Always make sure that the ax lines up correctly, with the cutting edge exactly in line with the center of the handle.
- Always keep an eye on the chopping objective, *not* on the ax.
- Always chop at an angle of close to 50 degrees.
- When splitting blocks or cutting sticks, always use a big, tough chopping block, or a big, fallen tree of the right height, with the top of the trunk flattened.
- Always trim branches from a fallen tree by lopping from the underside of the branch, working from butt to crown. Never chop into the crotch, and always lop branches from the opposite side of the trunk from the side at which one stands, unless for some good reason this may prove to be virtually impossible.
- Always split logs by using wedges of metal or ironwood, driven in by a hardwood maul.

Conservation by Ax

Conservation-conscious braves who may fear that they will never get practical experience in actual axmanship will be encouraged to learn that there are practically no forest or woodland areas which cannot be greatly improved by the *judicious* use of ax and saw. There are countless good-sized "weed" trees, "wolf" trees, and deformed and diseased trees which can be cut down to great advantage. There are mature and defective trees choking the growth of eager young trees, which are unable to develop until a sympathetic ax removes the offending older trees. After a survey of a number of wooded areas, one realizes the truth of the saying that "Forestry begins with the ax." Because nature dislikes parting with her tree children, the majority of natural stands of timber are too thickly wooded to be healthy and productive. The natural thinning process favored by nature is not fast enough to get results and save young trees from destruction. An ax knowingly employed by a forest-wise chief and willing braves under his supervision may, sometime in the future, make up to some extent for the ruthless mutilation and destruction of healthy wooded areas by today's unskilled and unsupervised novices.

≋ CONSERVE-DESERVE! ≋

Choosing an Ax

The author prefers the Hudson's Bay type of ax with a full-length, 36-inch handle, and a blade weighing 3¾ lbs. Older braves will find it easier and safer to swing a full-length ax, but with a blade weighing 2½ lbs. The three-quarter-length ax, with a 28-inch handle and a 2- or 2½-lb. head, is contemptuously referred to as a "boy's" ax in the North woods. Though this sort of ax is a favorite with some junior groups for use on canoe cruises and in pack trail camping, the author does not recommend it because it can prove almost as dangerous to the user as a hatchet, chiefly as the result of a chopping miss. A really good ax is more expensive than a fairly good one because the ax blade is made of finer steel, assuring a fine tempered ax bit and a well-hung handle of straight-grained hickory, but the difference in price is merited. So many good axes are spoiled by the attempts of novices to sharpen them that it is safest to carry out this rather delicate task under the supervision of a chief versed in axmanship.

SAWS

Saws of almost all sorts, including cross-cut, buck, Swedish, and pruning saws, prove almost as useful in forestry work as axes. Saws have the advantage of being considerably easier to use than axes and, even in the hands of amateurs, do a much cleaner job. This especially applies to the work of trimming branches, pruning trees, and cutting logs into suitable lengths for firewood. Considerable skill is required to use the various sorts of saws really well, as chiefs who have used cross-cuts and buck saws on tough logs are aware.

There is less romance in the sighing sound of a saw than in the resounding ring of an ax and the loud "Huh!" from the open mouth of a lumberjack each time the bright bit of his poleax bites into the hardwood trunk, but both tools have their places in even an Indian encampment. Chiefs should encourage the introduction and skillful handling of the various saws which have many uses in forestry and other fields.

LOG ROLLING

This handy and easy way of moving big logs saves a lot of strain and needless pulling and hauling by an entire band. The work can be done by two older braves, instead of six or eight. The drawback to this way of moving logs is that they cannot be rolled on terrain which presents obstacles such as tree stumps or rocks. The only equipment needed is a length of stout rope ½ to ¾ inches in diameter and from 30 to 40 feet long and a stout, round stake about 12 inches long and 2½ inches in diameter, tapering to a point.

The stake is driven into the ground at a fairly acute angle, slanting away from the log, and from 6 to 10 feet away from it. The center of the rope is placed around the stake, as shown in the drawing, and the two ends taken to the log. The two braves raise one end of the log very slightly, slip one end of the rope under and then over the log and then do the same thing at the other end.

By each brave's pulling on one end of the rope, the log will be made to roll along behind them toward the stake. When the log reaches the stake, the stake is pulled out and driven in again about 8 feet away. The rope is then adjusted as before and the log rolled on the next leg of its course.

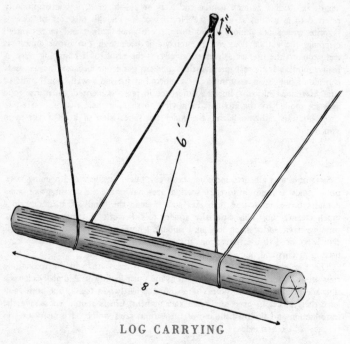

LOG CARRYING

Few encampments may own a log carrier such as those used by lumberjacks for moving heavy timber. In such cases, when a log cannot be rolled because of rough terrain, it will have to be carried, provided it is not too heavy and there are some older braves available to do the carrying. One way to carry logs is to take four stout saplings, each 6 or 7 feet long, and slide them under the log to be carried so that there is a pole close to each end of the log and two poles, evenly spaced, under the rest of the log. The log is lashed onto the center of each pole. A brave at each end of the poles does the carrying with the arm hanging down at the side, in a natural position. Three carrying poles can be used on lighter logs, at the discretion of the chief.

LOG CRADLE

Another way to carry logs, especially long ones which are not too heavy, is to take two long, strong poles, each about 10 feet long, and form a sort of cradle by passing a strong rope around and back and forward between the two carrying poles until a cradle about 2 feet deep is formed between and almost from end to end of the two poles. One pole, roped and ready to go, is slid under the log. Then both carrying poles are manned by three or four braves walking on each side of the log. In this way the log is transported on its carrying cradle. This log-moving method is especially useful when there is only a narrow trail over which to travel.

Chiefs will remember that the knees should always be bent when lifting anything heavy and realize that when logs have to be carried, it should only be for comparatively short distances at a time.

SNAKING LOGS

Logs which are not too heavy can be slid for short distances over favorable ground by snaking. This is done by fastening one end of a 12-foot length of strong rope about 6 inches from the butt end of a log, using the Timber Hitch described in Chapter 20. From two to four braves pull on the rope, rather close to the end of the log, raising its end when it runs into roots or similar obstructions which would stop its progress.

Of course, long logs can also be rolled on short lengths of smooth, easy rolling logs. These rollers should be about 3 feet long, and two or three of them are slid under the log to be moved, which is pushed forward, butt first, to the desired position, the rollers being replaced as they roll out from under the end of the long log. This is a rather laborious, though effective, method of moving logs into position.

7

Trailcraft and Outpostcraft

Bivouacs and outposts are the same type of encampment. The word bivouac will be used fairly frequently in this section to stress the fact that such an encampment is usually an overnight one or, at the most, one involving a few days' stay. Because of the temporary nature of this type of outpost there is no need for some of the refinements which are found in many of the more permanent encampments. Despite this, it is vital that the water supply be good, the sanitary arrangements adequate and the meals for the braves well balanced and appetizing.

The simplicity of a bivouac can be modified when it is used by bands once a week during a summer season. In such cases, and provided the site is on private property, owned or rented by the main camp, any reasonable amount of work and improvement put into the site by each band using it will be all to the good. The kitchen facilities can be added to—an inconspicuous, improvised cupboard and a stone fireplace or two, a stone water cooler built in a nearby stream, a food cache, a waste disposal pit and other near-necessities of a real encampment are in order. A correctly located and sanitarily installed pole latrine, instead of a straddle one, is another worthwhile addition.

PACK TRAIL KNOW-HOW

All modern Indians should be able to pack and carry all of their own personal gear needed for the trail and an overnight bivouac—or one for several nights—without difficulty. In addition, the bigger braves should be able to help the chief to transport some part of the lightweight general equipment required by the band on the expedition. Such extras should be light, and they may not amount to more than a square or oblong of lightweight but completely waterproof material to form part of a lean-to or some part of the food required for the band. True, each brave can carry his own rations for the entire expedition, when the menus have been carefully worked out by the chief in advance; but meals cooked for the entire band under the supervision of a chief can assure a better deal all around. Such mass meals also eliminate the possible danger from fire, ever present when each brave makes his own cooking fire somewhere near the bivouac.

The chief can carry a sharp, lightweight, full-length ax, sheathed. The Hudson Bay model is handy and efficient, and the fact that the chief carries a serviceable ax makes it unnecessary for the braves to carry one. The chief can also tote the waterproof ground cloths required for the two shelters, some of the food supplies, and what little general cook-out gear is absolutely essential.

All gear should go in the packs, and the belts of braves should not be festooned with canteens, cups, and similar gear. The general equipment carried, as well as the personal belongings for each brave, may vary with each expedition. Just what must be taken along on each trip is decided by the chief and based on the duration of the expedition, the terrain covered en route and conditions at the bivouac site which is the goal. It is wise to make all decisions concerning gear and supplies several days in advance of the departure. The following list is merely suggestive of the essentials for an average two-night bivouac.

Suggested Equipment for a Band of Eight Braves

• Ample lightweight but waterproof canvas or shelter cloth to completely cover two sapling-frame shelters
• Two or more waterproof ground cloths to completely cover the ground of each shelter (waterproof ponchos can be used for this purpose, should the chief so decide)
• Two cooking pots and one or two canvas pails
• Dishcloths and soap—floating

Well-chosen rations, ample, nourishing, compact, tasty, and easily packed, should be taken along for the period required. Emergency rations should also be taken along in case of unforeseen delays and a too-long stretch between two meals. Carrying boiled, but never powdered, eggs, powdered potatoes, dehydrated vegetables, soups, and other convenient and compact rations will reduce the number of cooking pots needed. A few sheets of stout tin foil will help to eliminate nearly all cooking utensils, especially when combined with skewer, hot stone, and ember cookery, as described in Chapter 16.

WHEN INDIANS ATE

The main meals of most Indian tribes were a substantial breakfast and a hearty supper in the evening, but hot food was usually available in a village throughout the entire day, the braves helping themselves from a huge, simmering pot which the women of the tribe kept full and hot. The noon meal was often one of packed, dry rations, as the men were frequently on the trail or in the forest, scouting, exploring or hunting during the greater part of the day.

PROVISION BAGS

Bags of various convenient sizes for the transport of food can be made from strong cloth, such as sailcloth, waterproofed by ironing paraffin wax into them. These are useful on the trail and in the encampment. To doubly assure dry rations and insulate the contents of each ration bag, a small, odorless plastic bag can be used inside the cloth containers.

KNAPSACK, PACK BOARD OR PACK FRAME, OR PACK BASKET?

The chief, who may have to carry the lion's share of the general gear and food, will have to make his own decision regarding the controversial topic of packs.

All four types of back-packs mentioned are serviceable, practical, and efficient when properly packed. A chief will make the best (and frequently lifetime) choice by experimenting with all four types before coming to a decision. Whichever type of pack is decided on, it can be encased in lightweight, tough waterproof material to keep out rain or damp. So much good and varied plastic material for all purposes is available these days that there is no excuse for wet packs, whether on land or water trails.

TUMPLINES

Although Indians used this headband-assist method of carrying heavy duffle and all sorts of gear over portage and other trails, *it is not a practice to be recommended for young, modern Indians.* Indians have frequently carried loads of 350 pounds by tumpline over rough trails three miles long, without making one stop en route. A tumpline is a strong, soft leather headband ranging from 2 to 3 inches in width with two narrow but strong leather lines from 6 to 8 feet long fastened one on each side of the headband. The headband of the tumpline is placed high on the forehead and the duffle carried on the back, attached by the two leather thongs. Sometimes tumpline users pack with only the tumplines, while others attach these two lines high on the pack and also use the shoulder straps of the pack to carry the load.

The person using the tumpline walks in a slightly bent forward position. Though there is much less strain on the body when using this method of carry, since the neck is surprisingly strong and supports a great deal of the total load, one has to become accustomed to the tumpline carry before deciding whether its use is advantageous or not. The chief danger of the tumpline lies in the fact that if one stumbles on the edge of a river or stream while making a portage, the line can easily slip down around the neck, when the weight of the pack being carried drags the bearer into the water. The same danger is ever present when crossing improvised bridges, perhaps made of a single tree trunk, and once the headband or a thong is around the neck, it is almost impossible to remove it when in the water, struggling under the weight of a heavy pack.

Sometimes Indians and trappers improvised tumplines by using a strip of soft leather, canvas, or other strong cloth for the headband and thin, strong ropes or rawhide cords for the two lines.

THE ART OF PACKING

A pack which is comfortable to carry can be assured by practical packing, and such a pack is essential. Good packing cannot be done if the pack is too small. After making sure that the pack is as light as possible when packed, the next points of major importance are that the pack should feel comfortable and sit well on the back. Balance is important. Smaller loads can be carried higher on the back but heavier loads should ride lower, for comfort and easy carrying. The softest clothing and articles in the pack should be against the bearer's back, even if a blanket has to be used as padding. Hard objects and gear with sharp corners should never be packed so that they can press on any part of the back. The carrying straps on all packing gear must be wide enough to assure complete comfort for the shoulders at all points. Nowadays, foam rubber is the answer to problems concerning straps which cut into the shoulders or packs which ride hard against the back. The heavier things should go in the bottom of the pack. A spare pair of moccasins or hiking shoes can be packed one on either side of the mess kit and clothing bag, which is best placed in the center portion of the pack. The cup belonging to the mess kit should be carried conveniently toward the top of the pack. The blankets usually top the pack, unless they are tied or strapped around the pack, outside, in horseshoe fashion.

Packs, especially rather heavy ones, should not be wrestled onto the back. They should be lifted, by the top corners, or "ears," onto the right knee, the right arm is slipped through its strap, the left hand grasps the strap for the left arm and the pack is hoisted onto the back without strain or the danger of a broken strap. Should there be a convenient stump or a tree trunk of about the right height, the pack can be lifted onto it and the arms then slipped through the carrying straps without difficulty.

It is suggested that all chiefs point out the sad fact that *all* packs feel at least twice the weight they actually are after a few hours on the trail.

Suggested General and Personal Equipment for Each Chief

- First Aid Kit—and Snake-bite Kit, if traversing venomous snake country
- Compass, a good and tested one
- Map, topographical or any other good, large-scale map of country to be covered
- Water purification tablets: Halazone, Chlorine, Zonite, iodine, or other tablets or liquids
- Watch, an accurate and sturdy one
- Flashlight, powerful, with new spare batteries and bulb
- Ax, a full-length, sharp, light, Hudson Bay or other type
- Trenching tool, of the small, lightweight, folding type
- Sheath knife, a sharp, serviceable one, and/or a large, sharp pocket knife
- Matches and case—waterproof match case containing a supply of waterproofed matches, paraffin-dipped
- A few short, thick candles for emergencies, and a candle holder
- Ground cloths, waterproof, for shelters (ones which the braves did not carry)
- Tarp or canvas sections for shelter construction, which the braves did not pack

- Food which braves did not tote
- Rope, good, strong, lightweight, 30-foot length
- Cord or string, strong, 30-foot length
- Wire, strong, tough, thin, 20-foot length
- Insect repellent
- Toilet paper
- Fishing tackle, if desired
- Camera and photographic equipment, if desired
- Clothing: this corresponds very much with list given for braves. A Sou'wester-style *oilskin* with rain hat to match is far better and stronger than any plastic raincoat
- Toilet Kit—Mess Kit, with stainless steel utensils—Sewing Kit

Suggested Personal Equipment for Each Brave

- Clothing: sweater or windbreaker
  trousers or jeans, spare pair, tight weave, longs
  socks, extra pair, heavy wool
  moccasins or hiking shoes, extra pair, hard soles
  poncho and colored handkerchiefs
- Toilet kit, with floating soap
- Mess kit, compact and containing only essential utensils of stainless steel
- Sheath knife or, better and safer, a large, sharp, good quality pocket knife
- Compass, if available

ON THE TRAIL

Though the record for a mile walk is about 6 minutes and 20 seconds, a chief should remember that an easy hiking pace is 4 miles an hour on good terrain and considerably less when the going is rough. When climbing hills or mountain trails a band may not average more than 2 miles an hour. About one mile per hour can be taken as a close estimate for easy climbs and this allowance should be doubled for steep climbs.

A chief knows that the pace is dictated by the slowest hiker in the band and that he should not force the pace unless it becomes a necessity.

The braves will hike further and with less fatigue if the feet are placed almost flat on the ground but with the toes just touching first and pointing almost straight ahead, Indian fashion.

To stimulate energy quickly one can suck a hard candy or a piece of lump sugar while on the move.

Selecting an Ideal Bivouac Site

To select a really fine bivouac site requires practice, good judgment, and often considerable time but, fortunately, it is not quite so difficult a task as choosing a site for an encampment because of the brief periods for which the bivouac site is generally used. Despite this, it must be kept in mind that some of the essentials of a good bivouac site do not differ from those required for a long-term encampment. High, suitable ground, with a good source of water supply and firewood close by stand at the top of the list. In principle, springs on forested hillsides, and springs coming out of the rock are usually safe. If cattle are grazing on the hillside where the spring is or if there is even one habitation on the hill, it is wisest to consider the water polluted. Boiling such water for not less than 20 minutes will make it safe to cook with and also safe to drink.

A site where there is the slightest danger from rockslides, falling rocks, or falling trees or branches should be carefully avoided. A site where there is any possibility of flood from rising waters of a river or lake should not be considered. Floods and flooding usually arise in the hills, perhaps far distant, where a sudden, heavy rain causes a flash flood or sudden rush of water which may reach and submerge the bivouac site in the dead of night.

When a suitable, well-situated bivouac site is found, it does not take very long to do the ground-clearing necessary and set up simple shelters. Despite this, it is always wise to reach the terrain where one plans on bivouacking well in advance of darkness. A minimum of two hours is not too much and at least one hour more should be allowed if the band is inexperienced.

BIVOUAC SHELTERS

There are a number of good, waterproof, temporary shelters which can be set up for bivouacking without much trouble when tents are not used. Shelters made entirely from wildwood material, which are spoken of in Chapter 2, are not recommended for a number of reasons, the chief one being that they are hard to build so that they are really weatherproof. Making them really waterproof borders on the impossible without spending considerable time on the job and the wind is hard to keep out on a raw, windy night. For these reasons alone, apart from the ruthless destruction of saplings, branches and bushes which trying to build these entirely wildwood shelters sometimes brings about, it is suggested that bivouac shelters be built of other, more practical, materials. The shelters described in this section require a framework of light saplings, which a wood-craft-wise chief can cut from overcrowded stands, helping rather than hindering true conservation. When there are no trees on a spot chosen for a bivouac site, chiefs have to resort to rope supports for shelters or have the braves carry light-weight, but strong, poles which can be carried in sections by using ferrules so that different lengths of poles can be fitted together to secure the length required.

Tarp Shelters

There are several types of these practical shelters the materials for which can be easily carried and set up with the minimum of trouble. Though the first shelter described is often called a "tarp" shelter or lean-to, nowadays, with so much choice of tough, lightweight, waterproof materials, there is no reason to make them of tarpaulin. In this or any other shelter mentioned, the chiefs will make the choice of either lightweight, waterproof canvas, heavy, waterproofed cotton, or one of the few suitable plastic materials available. One big drawback in using most forms of nylon or plastic sheets for building shelters is that the shelters become terribly hot in sunny weather, even though the front is entirely uncovered, as in an Adirondack type shelter. REINFORCEMENT of all stress lines and points where guy lines are fastened to the material is of major importance in setting up *all* tarp, duck, canvas, or other shelters. For instance, a horizontal guy line running fore and aft and securely sewn onto the fabric will offset stress.

When there are some quite small trees, even three or four inches in diameter, growing ten or twelve feet apart in convenient positions and on suitable ground for erecting shelters on the bivouac site, they can be used to advantage. Though shelters can be set up on the fringes of woods or on lightly wooded areas, it is wise to avoid the possible hazards of falling branches or lightning by not bivouacking inside a wood or forest, unless there is a big, suitable clearing available. When any two trees are conveniently spaced, the ridgepole can be lashed to them at the desired height. Five feet is ample for smaller braves. The ridgepole can be made from a straight, lightweight sapling about 3 inches in diameter and long enough to reach between two trees and extend 3 or 4 inches beyond each tree. The pole should be lashed, not nailed, in position. Four or six saplings, all of about the same length and thickness, and considerably lighter than the ridgepole, are used as a framework to support and hold in place the material which covers the entire back of the shelter; *but* instead of lashing these at even intervals to the ridgepole, so that the bottoms of the poles rest directly on the ground, there is a far better and more comfortable way of constructing the shelter. Drive two stout, pointed poles, each 20 inches long, 8 inches into the ground at the rear of the shelter, one at each end of the ridgepole and about 5 feet, more or less, out from it. A straight, lightweight sapling is lashed across the top of these two short poles.

This forms the simple framework of the all-important wall, which adds very greatly to the comfort and utility of a shelter or tent. It makes the same difference in shelters of this type as that between the very superior wall tent and the pup tent. This shelter wall can be made any height, from 12 to 24 inches and the higher it is the more upright room there will be along the back of the shelter. Even the 12-inch wall described allows the occupants of the shelter to lie with their heads close to the wall with little risk of touching the shelter material above their heads. This adds to shelter comfort as practically all materials will let rain leak through as soon as the material is touched on the inside. Chiefs will realize that the over-all height and size of a shelter and the height of the wall are based on the amount of material which a band can afford to buy, but a few extra yards, to assure a reasonably roomy shelter, with a projecting awning, will prove a worthwhile investment.

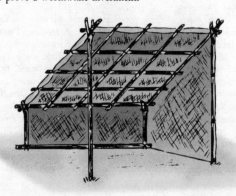

The drawing of this shelter shows both the shelter and the slant-roof framework of light saplings which supports the material cover and also strengthens the structure greatly. Once the size of the shelter has been decided, the cover can be tied securely onto the framework with strong tapes or cords sewn onto the material. The author favors grommets set into the edge of the material, about 8 inches apart and with the hole big enough to allow a half-inch rope to pass through. A side cover can be cut to size and tied onto one end of the shelter, as illustrated, or a side cover can be used at each end, thus converting the shelter into a sort of canvas Adirondack type shelter. This is added comfort which is not really required, especially when the weather is good. One added comfort which is well worthwhile is an awning of canvas or other material, from which the shelter is made, extending beyond the front of the shelter to any distance desired. From 24 to 40 inches is suggested but the further it projects the more protection from rain and sun it affords. This awning can be a continuation of the canvas cover forming the roof. The cover for a shelter can be made big enough to form a ground cloth also, which is brought into the shelter under the bottom bar of the wall framework. A shelter which has separate ground cloths spread on the ground is comfortable, but these do not afford the same protection from wind that the combined shelter cover and ground cloth does.

Chiefs know that this type of tarp shelter can be set up a little more quickly and easily by simply having the framework over which the covering is stretched reach from the ridgepole directly to the ground, thus eliminating the wall. In such cases, the shelter will be a little more comfortable if the ridgepole is a foot or so higher and the framework poles longer, reaching the ground in a considerably less acute angle than if shorter poles were used.

As will be seen from the drawings, this type of shelter can also be supported on a ridgepole lashed between two trees or mounted on poles forked at the top and driven very solidly into the ground. Another, more solid, form of end

supports for the ridgepole can be made by driving two strong, lightweight saplings or poles into the ground in such a way that they can be lashed in the shape of an inverted V, as illustrated. There should be a 6-inch fork left at the top ends of each V, into which the ridgepole is lashed.

Wedge Shelters

The two wedge-shape shelters shown in the drawings are self-explanatory and need little if any descriptive details. The chief requirement is a stout rope to support the waterproof cover, which goes over the rope, though the smaller of the two models can be tied onto the rope with half a dozen strong tapes sewn

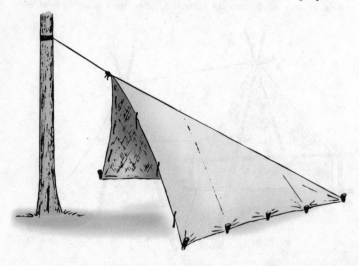

securely onto the top of the material, if desired. Such a shelter can be made in one piece, though there may be several sections sewn together to make that piece, necessitated on account of the original width of the material. The larger wedge shelter can be made in two sections, as illustrated, one half overlapping the other at the top and being laced in position by a strong cord running through grommets set into the edges of both sections, at equal intervals.

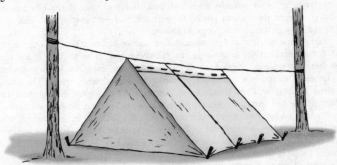

All of the shelters shown can be adapted to some extent by chiefs to suit the need of their bands, the materials at their disposal and the terrain on which they bivouac. The solidity of the frameworks used or the decision not to use a framework at all, will depend on whether the shelters are constructed chiefly for overnight use or will be used again in the course of the summer. Bad colds and worse can result from a band's being caught in a rainstorm in an overnight shelter which is not rainproof. For this reason, alert chiefs take a dim view of makeshift shelters, hastily set up with the thought in mind that, after all, the bivouac is for only one night.

BEDS

Few bands can be expected to take the time and trouble to build any sort of temporary bed for an overnight bivouac, nor may they take the time to set up an encampment loom with which to weave sleeping mats. It is a different matter

when a bivouac is used for several nights in succession or where the site will be used a number of times throughout the summer. Even then, beds such as the one illustrated—though made about 6 feet long and 2½ feet wide, inside measurements—take up a lot of room. This bed is made from a piece of strong canvas or heavy sacking folded exactly in half, lengthwise, the two sides then being sewn securely together. This improvised mattress is then stuffed with dry grass, dry leaves or other suitable wildwood material found around the bivouac. A strong, straight pole is then pushed through the mattress cover at each side and pegged onto two supporting logs, as shown.

Perhaps the quickest and most convenient type of bed to make, yet one which is not uncomfortable, is made in the following way. The ground inside the shelter is completely cleared of all twigs, roots, and even the smallest stones. This done, each brave sets about preparing his own sleeping space. The place where his head will rest should be at least as high, or slightly higher than the foot of the bed space. He lies on his bed-to-be and after a little measurement, and check on measurement, scoops out two shallow hollows in the ground, one at the place where his shoulder will rest and the other hollow to accommodate his hip. A fair-sized hollow will assure greater comfort, as the brave will move around a little while asleep. The hollows and the rest of the ground which will be the bed are then carefully covered with the softest wildwood material available—sedge, soft grass, or soft ferns, if the scent of crushed fern frondes proves pleasant. This material is then covered with the waterproof ground cloth or poncho. Trying to tuck the edges of the ground cloth under the wildwood material generally proves a waste of time: it will not stay under for long.

A mass mattress can be made by strewing the ground thickly, after it has been cleared and prepared, with soft wildwood material and then covering the material with one large ground cloth or ground sheet—a waterproof one, of course. In this type of mattress, the shoulder and hip hollows are not made.

Individual mattresses can be improvised by each brave's carrying a mattress cover of some sort (such as unbleached muslin, which is lightweight and satisfactory) and stuffing it at the bivouac site with the best wildwood material available to assure a night of comfort. Whatever type of wildwood material is used, it is essential that it be covered with a waterproof ground cloth so that no damp can reach the sleeper from the material used to stuff the mattress.

Browse Beds may be all right for the North Woods but are neither recommended nor described here because of the considerable amount of wildwood material required to make even one individual bed.

Jungle Hammocks

Though the Indians of North America never slept in hammocks, some tribes of South America made use of this comfortable form of bed, which they wove from lianas and vine tendrils. Jungle hammocks, as they are usually called here, can be bought cheaply at some surplus stores. Certain types of these hammocks, protected by individual waterproof canopies, are waterproof and warm, with blankets under and over the sleeper. When suitable trees or saplings from which the hammocks can be hung are suitably located, braves may find this novel sleep-out way comfortable and intriguing. Tenderfeet are advised to sling their hammocks low, to begin with, as they are likely to be thrown out a few times before they gain mastery of their hammocks and learn how to sling and use them correctly. A chief should experiment with one prior to deciding on their practicability for his band.

BEDDING

This is a topic which can fill many chapters, so only essentials are dealt with.

Sleeping Bags

A really good sleeping bag is expensive, and a luxury for the average bivouacking brave. Inexpensive sleeping bags are not to be recommended as they are usually filled with kapok or cotton substances which mat easily, are heavy and difficult to air properly. An important point to remember is that all really good sleeping bags can be zipped entirely down one side and along the foot. This allows them to be opened out flat and aired in the sun. Generally, the run-of-the-mill sleeping bag can be advantageously replaced with blankets or improvised bed rolls, covered with water-repellent material.

Blankets

The brave who does not carry a sleeping bag will find that two good blankets, preferably wool, and a waterproof ground cloth of textured vinylite or rubber-coated cotton are usually sufficient for summer nights. Wool blankets are far superior to any others, but they are costly. The next best thing to assure sufficient warmth on cool nights is to have blankets with as much wool content as possible. Blankets may be kept clean by making a loose sleeping bag of strong khaki duck or similar soft material, for use inside the blankets.

Pillows

Though pillows may be smiled at by novice braves, experienced outdoorsmen know that a pillow of some sort, especially a really comfortable one, provides much additional comfort when sleeping in the open. This, of course, only applies to those who use pillows. Pioneers and woodsmen used boots, covered with soft clothing, as pillows. Cowboys used saddles for pillows and there are many other sorts of improvised pillows which add to a sleeper's comfort. Modern braves can carry a smooth pillowcase which can be filled with soft grass or, best of all, soft, dry clothing. Care should be taken never to fill a pillowcase with any wildwood material which has an unpleasant odor.

Bedtime Pointers

To keep warm, it is necessary to have at least as much covering underneath as on top. Being wrapped up *tightly* in one or two blankets does not assure so much warmth on cool nights as being wrapped *loosely* in one or two blankets, provided the blankets are correctly used to keep the cool air out. A chief should instruct his band members in making one or two of the simple forms of the so-called envelope bed, which can be made with one, two, or three blankets, on top of the protective ground cloth. A brave tucked into a simple blanket arrangement, such as that shown in the drawing, should sleep warmly and comfortably. The envelope shown in the sketch has fold-overs about six inches wide, held in place by large, blanket type, safety pins.

Real outdoorsmen never suffer discomfort needlessly and chiefs should impress that fact on braves who seem to seek discomfort at times in order to show what hardy woodsmen they are.

Once bed rolls and blankets have been thoroughly aired, they should be kept rolled up until bedtime.

When turning in for the night, it is best to remove *all* daytime clothing and change into clean night clothes of some sort. Dry underwear, a clean shirt and shorts, or pajamas, assure real comfort. All night clothing must be loose in order to be comfortable.

Never sleep in damp clothing or under damp blankets.

A close check for ticks, leeches, mites or other insects which may have been picked up in the course of the day is a wise nightly precaution.

FOOD STORAGE

The illustration shows one good reason for hanging food storage containers out of the reach of prowling animals, which often take over when an encampment is off the beaten track and the braves are sleeping under the black blanket of night. Raccoons, opossums, skunks, squirrels, chipmunks, rats, mice and other animals are eager to get at many sorts of food, especially when they detect an appetizing odor which appeals to them. The animals mentioned are dawn and dusk foragers as well as actual night prowlers.

Suspending the food out of reach and where even intrepid climbers cannot secure a foothold is one sure way of keeping marauding creatures from the food. It cannot be correctly said that such storage method is a food cache, as food caches are actually hidden stores of food buried underground, or hidden away inside a tree or other place where it is out of sight of man and beast. Foods cached in such places must be in metal or other containers which are impervious to insect attack.

Another type of food guard is made by stringing a strong wire between two convenient trees or poles and suspending the food sack or box hung from another wire strung from the middle of the length stretched between the two trees, so that the container is about seven feet above ground level.

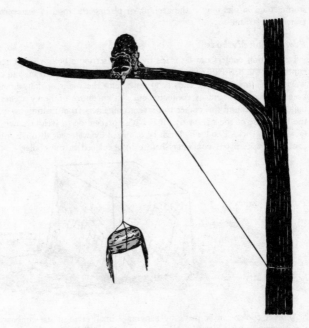

A big funnel, made of any light, pliable metal or other suitable material, attached to a pole or sapling, as shown in the drawing, is another good way to prevent intruders, especially rats and squirrels, from reaching supplies. Lightweight cupboards made from orange crates or light, strong slats of wood can be suspended from branches by wire, with the assurance that the contents are safe from raiders.

Food Coolers

There are a number of practical ways of keeping food fresh and cool in summer. The chief methods for outdoor use are evaporations, storing food in pits dug in the ground, or placing the food in waterproof containers in a stream.

Evaporation Methods

Evaporation coolers can be made by simply setting a box or other receptacle containing the perishable foodstuff on a few flat stones in a stream and covering it with a cloth so that the ends hang down into the water, soaking up water to keep the container and its contents cool. An enclosure of heavy stones can be built loosely around this cooler to prevent containers from floating away, should the wind arise or the stream rise. It is a wise precaution to weight down all containers with rocks. Food which can be damaged by water, or damp, is, of course, packed in waterproof containers before being placed in the cooler.

Another cooler can be made by hanging a small crate or slat-cupboard under a pail suspended from the branch of a tree. The pail is filled with water, and a large cloth covering it is made to sink to the bottom of the pail by placing a heavy stone in its center. The ends of the cloth are draped down over the edges of the pail and down over the food container beneath, which is kept cool by evaporation, aided by any breeze which is blowing.

Pit Coolers

Dig a hole 2 feet square and 3 feet deep in the ground, in the shade and conveniently located. The sides of the pit should be shored up with thin boards or wide, thin stakes. The hole is then about half filled with gravel from a stream bed or small stones of any sort. Once or twice a day two or three buckets full of water are poured onto the stones and the food in cans or other containers is placed on top of them. The top of this storage pit should be carefully covered with wet sacking, burlap or other heavy cloth, covered by wet newspapers and then another wet cloth to exclude all above-ground warmth. A cooler of this sort can have a temperature of as much as 20 degrees lower than the outside air temperature.

Fly Menace

The greatest care should be taken to screen and cover all receptacles containing food of any sort so that it is protected against the menace of flies, especially bluebottles and other blowflies. These filthy insects not only carry disease on their feet but also lay their eggs in meat and other foods. Chiefs should regard all such flying things as a *very serious menace* to health.

SANITATION AND HEALTH

These two necessities for happy bivouacking go hand in hand, since good health in the encampment depends on good sanitation. Fortunately, it is not difficult to insure not only adequate but satisfactory sanitary conditions in even a temporary encampment. The things of greatest importance along these lines follow.

Water

Pure water, whether it be naturally pure or purified by the use of chemicals, is of the utmost importance. Water means life, and sometimes death! Polluted water has probably caused as many deaths in the world as deadly disease. It is therefore one of the first duties of a chief to be certain that the water which his braves drink is not contaminated. Sometimes even the most isolated and, apparently pure, sparkling stream or brook may be infected with tularemia germs. Though this disease is generally blamed on rabbits, it can be carried by dogs and other domestic animals. Other deadly diseases such as typhoid and dysentry may lurk in deceptively clear water—whereas yellowish, brackish water which looks unfit to drink may be free from germs.

Naturally, a chief has no certain means of establishing whether a source of water is pure enough to be safe or not. He can, however, take the simple and necessary precautions to assure its being safe before it is used either for cooking or drinking. Among the many simple methods of doing so are: boiling the water at a rolling boil continuously for at least twenty minutes; and the use of some of the many water purification tablets or liquids. One drop of 7 per cent iodine to each quart of water will purify the water, but iodine should not be used if a member of the band is a victim of hyperthyriodism. Halazone and some other prepared tablets which assure the purification of water may be bought at most drugstores and the detailed instructions with each package must be followed exactly to get the desired results. Zonite, calcium hypochlorite, and several bleaches are also used for purifying water but those using them must be most careful regarding the quantity used and the time which must elapse before the treated water is safe to use.

Apart from the aeration method of making boiled water taste less flat mentioned in Chapter 16, following the making of an Indian well, there are several other satisfactory ways. The addition of a little lemon or lime juice to the water, or even a little vanilla extract or table salt, makes a great improvement in the taste of otherwise flat and generally unpalatable drinking water.

Garbage Disposal

Sanitary disposal of all trash, which includes empty cans, dirty cloths and wastepaper, is another bivouac must. As much of the garbage as possible should be burned, which necessitates a good fire. All empty cans should be flattened, burned to sterilize them inside and then buried. Waste paper which is being burned should first be squeezed into compact balls, which will not blow out·

of the fire and start a much bigger one some distance away. For garbage which cannot be completely destroyed by burning, a pit about 3 feet square and 3 feet deep should be dug some distance away from the bivouac and a little earth thrown on top of each new layer of garbage thrown into the hole. This pit should be entirely filled when leaving the bivouac for the last time in the season. In grassy areas it is good conservation to cut sod patches when digging all pits, water the patches and replace them carefully when leaving.

Dishwater Disposal Pits

Water used for washing dishes should never be thrown onto the ground around the bivouac, since it will attract flies and eventually cause a disagreeable odor. Throwing such water, and even food remains, into a stream will eventually contaminate it, making the water unsafe to drink. There are two ways of disposing of dishwater, the best one being to dig a waste-water disposal pit about 2 feet square and 4 feet deep. The foot of this hole should be covered with about one foot of loose sand, if available, and if not, fine gravel. The next foot is filled with gravel or small stones. Since all food plates should be scraped to remove any remaining food before the dishes are washed, the dishwashing water should contain no solids. The top of the pit should have a fire lit on it every day to burn off the grease and keep it sanitary.

Another, less satisfactory way to get rid of dishwater is to pour it into a short trench 3 feet deep, situated at least one hundred feet away from the kitchen and let the water seep into the ground. Burning out the trench every day will help keep it clean.

Latrines

There are two sorts of latrines suitable for bivouac use, the simple, straddle, trench type or the pole type, which is a modification of the former. Constructing a latrine is an easy job. Figuring out just where is the best place for the latrine is the most difficult and important part of this vital sanitary installation, because it should be in a secluded spot fifty to sixty yards from the actual bivouac and below the point of water supply. Such a site prevents contamination of water used for drinking and cooking. The old idea that water purifies itself by filtering through sand and gravel, or flowing over a sand bar has been proved a myth. The bacteria still live.

Straddle Trench Latrine. For a bivouac site with only one or two bands bivouacking, a trench about 3 feet long, 3 feet deep and 18 inches wide will prove ample. The earth or sand dug out of the hole should be piled at one end of the trench and a wooden or strong bark scoop stuck upright in it. Each time the latrine is used, some of the earth should be scooped back into the trench, at the strategic spot. The trench should be burned out with fire every few days and always at the end of a bivouac period, before being filled in, if the site is not going to be used again that season.

Pole Type Latrine. A refinement of the above latrine, suitable for younger braves, as balance is a necessity in such a situation, is the addition of a few poles to assure seating and security. Two peeled saplings 3½ feet long and about 4 inches in diameter are set at a proper angle and height over the trench, one to serve as a seat and one as a backrest. These poles rest on two stout, round, pointed poles driven into the ground, in scissors fashion, straddling the trench at each end, and then being lashed together where they cross. Two of these supporting poles should be about 18 inches longer than the other two poles, since they support the single-pole backrest. The two shorter poles only project about one inch beyond the seat pole, which is lashed onto the crotch formed where the support poles cross above the trench.

These latrines can easily be screened, on both sides at least, by hanging sacking or similar material on a light but tough pole framework, set up on each side of the trench and about 3 feet away from it.

Keeping the Bivouac Site Clean

Possibly a cleaner site results when a chief details different braves daily to the various tasks which must be done around an outpost. This procedure assigns and distributes responsibilities, which no real brave tries to shirk. This proves a fair way of getting the necessary work done well without imposing on the most willing braves. The personal supervision of a chief and a daily informal but thorough inspection, with the right words of commendation or criticism, will assure good sanitation, good order, and the resulting good health.

8

Exploring Like Indians

One of the first and most important tasks which confront a chief before even brief exploration trips are undertaken is to concentrate on removing the inherent FEAR OF THE UNKNOWN from the minds of his novice braves. Such very real fear has had devastating effects on the minds of strong men. Primordial fears cannot be dismissed from the mind of a brave who is alarmed by a mysterious noise after dark by merely saying, "That was nothing, certainly nothing to be afraid of." In darkness, which has caused man to fear from the beginning of time, the vivid imagination of a novice brave can run riot.

NOISES OF THE NIGHT

There are countless strange and mysterious sounds in the dark night which prove alarming to a *cheechako*, though to an experienced woodsman they are easily explainable. The wild cry of a loon, the quavering call of a lynx, the rasp of branches in the wind, the hoot of some species of owl, a sudden loud rustling in the leaves, strange calls which might be made by either bird or beast, a stone rolling down a bank, a sudden splash close at hand, all these, and many more, are normal sounds of the night which one soon becomes accustomed to, perhaps even able to interpret correctly. There are very few dangers to be met with in woodland and forest from the animal inhabitants. Man is the most dangerous predator afoot and the one most likely to cause damage and trouble.

FOREST EXPEDITIONS

A band which is unused to traveling through a well-wooded forest will find it both impressive and interesting. In some places the forest will be dim-lighted by what light or sunlight filters down through the boughs and leafy canopies high overhead, and the occasional sunlit glade is a thing of beauty and wonder.

What does a chief look for to make forest trips doubly interesting? There are many facets which will command interest. The forest floor alone is worth more than a casual glance. Whether it be carpeted with evergreen needles, moss, or humus, it is a world apart and a universe which teems with countless things which fascinate and interest. Slender shoots which, at the foot of a beech tree, appear to be beech shoots are actually beechdrop parasites which have tapped the roots of a beech tree to feed at its expense. Miniature moss gardens may be seen in places, and a powerful magnifying glass will reveal the infinite wonders of the structures of the miniature mosses.

Multicolored plants which look like fantastic mushrooms can be seen in shady glades. Puffballs grow beside and from decaying stumps and an occasional Indian Pipe shows up like a "Ghost Flower," as the Indians named it, against a dark background of the fallen log from which it grows. Fungi of many other sorts, including the interesting "bracket fungi," which form woody shelves on trees, await discovery. A clump of poisonous Jack-O'-Lantern mushrooms may be seen. A wood-wise chief will not only tell his band that they are luminous by night but, by covering the fungi with a thick, opaque cloth of some sort, will prove it. The braves who put their heads under the cloth will see, when their eyes become accustomed to the obscurity, the soft, greenish glow which emanates from under the mushrooms' caps. In a forest's depths, slime molds of many sorts may be observed, many as beautiful as they are interesting. Miniature forests of lichens grow upward from bark or logs or encrust the sides and tops of rocks. Lichens are dealt with as survival food in Chapter 16.

Keen eyes will, perhaps, spot a wolf spider, a funnel-web spider, or a hunting centipede on the prowl. Not to be outdone by a lesser-legged relative, a millipede on the march shows up for a moment alongside a flattened clump of matted leaves. Unlike the centipede, he is not a hunter but a vegetarian, feasting on decaying plant tissues. The millipede can exude an evil-smelling fluid and is best manipulated with a twig. Various species of ants, snails, termites, and beetles roam the forest floor and its logs and stumps. Frequently a red-backed salamander may be discovered under a stone or log.

WOODLAND EXPLORATION

Pathfinding in even lightly wooded country can be made as interesting and exciting as traveling through a forest. There are many secluded glades and fair-sized clearings in wooded areas where birds and beasts can be seen, as each glade and clearing has fringe areas which attract the wildthings. Traveling through woodlands offers good cover for a band moving under the direction of a wood-wise chief, so birds and beasts are sometimes caught off guard and can be observed from cover for some time before they take alarm.

Rivulets, streamlets and miniature marshes may be encountered on a woodland trek, and a little mirror-like pond reflecting the azure of the sky may await discovery in some hidden hollow. What can be found in brooks and ponds? Crawfish, trout, turtles, and perhaps water cress are among the many things which may be found there. Answering such questions by actual exploration as wooded country is covered by the band adds interest and fascination to woodland travel.

In woodland expeditions, a chief should lead his band rather leisurely, and every ten or fifteen minutes the last brave in the Indian file should move up directly behind the chief so that he has a chance to learn just how the chief plots the course and leads the expedition. A chief can also have a brave move up just ahead of him, so that each one can say that he actually led the band for a part of the exploratory trip. The leader of such an expedition will discover that there is a considerable amount of know-how required in order to lead his band safely through the most interesting and best tracts of woodland and make the trek attractive throughout.

There are fallen logs to examine, cautiously, to discover whether there is a furred or feathered thing taking cover there. An empty nest is discovered in a thicket which illustrates the wonderful workmanship of some feathered friend. Holes of various sizes and shapes may be seen at varying heights in tree trunks which offer the puzzle of who did or does live in these trees. Was the rustle which a keen-eared brave just heard caused by a mouse or a shrew? What wild-flower is it which makes that brilliant patch of color on the edge of a woodland glade? There are, as in forest exploration, strange insects and creatures to be found under stones and logs as well as aquatic ones awaiting discovery in ponds and rivulets. There is much to make such excursions interesting, exciting, and instructive.

HILL DISCOVERY

In wooded country, "discovering" hills is not always easy unless the hill is a high one. Once it has been discovered there may still be some other interesting discoveries to make regarding it. Each side of the hill may offer something of interest, provided the hill is a fairly large one and not uniformly cone-shaped. One side may present interesting depressions, cup-shaped or otherwise, which may offer good places for concealment in some game at a later date. A spring may be discovered bubbling out of the lower slope of a hill and sometimes a miniature pond may be found in a depression halfway or more up the slope. Wild flowers and interesting plants can often be found when exploring a hill, and not infre-quently some forms of wildlife may be seen on its slopes.

One slope of the hill may be smooth and sandy, or grassy, offering a fine place to toboggan down on a summer sled, which is described in Chapter 17. When a hill is steep, good practice in elementary climbing can be had in scaling it from different slopes. Rappelling exercises may be carried out on the steepest and most difficult face of the hill, provided no danger is involved.

An ideal site for a small council fire or cooking fire may be found on some hills, where such fires can be lit safely and enjoyed in unique surroundings. A hill is an ideal place on which to light a signal fire, where its message of flame or smoke can be seen for a considerable distance. A hill with a suitable flat surface and background can also be used advantageously for signalling with arms or blanket, when the messages are being read from a certain direction. A sunrise or sunset can be watched from the top of a hill and chiefs will find many other ways in which hills will provide exercise, enjoyment, and instruction for the braves in their bands.

WEATHER

Despite the enormous accumulation of weather-wise data, the millions of dollars expended on scientific instruments for weather forecasting and the far flung, strategically plotted web of weather stations, as one weighs radio and newspaper weather "forecasts" he is amazed. The amazement arises because one wonders how, in the circumstances, it is possible for so many weather reports to be so wrong in their predictions! The chief who is able to read and interpret nature's own weather signs is able to avoid much inconvenience and uncertainty. In the face of so much information, and misinformation regarding weather, the author undertakes the very difficult task of doing a little weather forecasting based on his own experience, in the hope that it will be of some service to modern chiefs.

There should always be a chief in a band which goes on canoe expeditions, overnight trips, or on exploration trips of a few days duration, who has a general acquaintance with what is known as "weather wisdom." There are many weather warning signs, not given by radio but sponsored by The Great Architect of the Universe, which will save a leader with some weather knowledge from many of the discomforts and difficulties which can be caused by rain, thunderstorms, and squalls which come up all too quickly on lakes and over open country.

Weather is made in the West, so it is wise to keep a weather-eye in that general direction when trying to figure out what sort of weather to expect. A chief will do well to find out from someone on the spot, from what direction the local good, and bad, weather comes. A game warden, forest ranger, farmer, or fisherman usually knows.

A chief knows that an east wind is one that blows *from* the East, not toward the East. A wind vane is so balanced that its arrow always points *into* the wind.

So many frequently "dependable" signs used in weather forecasting are prefaced by the cautionary word "usually" that the weather-wise chief realizes that there is always a certain amount of calculated risk involved when deciding on setting out on an expedition in doubtful weather. Even calculated risk must be reduced to an absolute minimum when planning to set out on a lengthy canoe trip.

Good Weather Signs

So many signs of good weather to come are heralded in the sky, by clouds and colors, that a weather-wise chief will frequently turn his weather eye skyward.

Sky, Sky Colors and Clouds. Evening sunset skies often tell the weather story for the next few days.

A rose or crimson-colored sky generally predicts fine weather for next day.

A light mauve evening sky also foretells fair weather for the following day.

A gray evening sky, when shot with yellowish streaks, forecasts good weather for the next day.

Cloud formations are helpful in judging what weather conditions are going to be. They forecast the weather and the winds deliver it. The following are some of the different sorts of clouds on which to base predictions.

Cirrus. This is the scientific Latin name for the "mares' tails" clouds. They are fleecy, feathery, whitish clouds, and while their wind-blown arrival often announces the end of a fair-weather spell, good weather can still be expected for at least thirty hours before rain falls.

Cirro-stratus. This high, thin, delicate, web-like formation of clouds is a combination which forms a layer blanketing the sun, and it warns of rain in about six hours' time.

Cirro-cumulus. This fish-scale-appearing combination of clouds forms what is called a "mackerel" sky. They are generally fair-weather clouds, though sometimes showers are ushered in by such cloud formations.

Cumulus. These clouds look like flocks of big, woolly sheep in the sky. They are serene summer clouds until they swell in size to such an extent that they reach the bloated, dome-shaped, or global, *cumulo-nimbus* stage and the *thunderhead* so formed is most likely to cause a sudden downpour or squall, or both. Fortunately the change is made apparent by a darkening gray cloud wall behind these clouds, making their identification easy.

Nimbus. As their name implies, these black clouds assure rain.

Alto. Higher cloud formations, such as *alto-cumulus*, announce fair weather as they float high above, in white or grayish masses, in the summer sky.

A happy note should be added here regarding high-riding clouds. Such clouds will not rain on you, as it is the lowering and low-riding clouds that cause rainfall.

Cirrus and Stratus. During summer months, a hot sun may disperse these clouds and chiefs will have to fall back on other signs, given later on, such as wind, or various sounds, or the behaviour of birds and animals, to forecast the weather.

Winds. A major factor to remember when using wind to forecast weather is that all changes in the weather come with the wind. When there is no wind there will be no change in the prevailing weather.

As a general rule, winds from the Northwest, West, and Southwest bring good weather. Winds from the other compass points often bring bad weather.

Wind swings often indicate whether stormy or clearing weather may be expected. For instance, when the wind swings clockwise—that is from north to east—and so on around the compass, it is likely to bring good weather.

When wind springs up before a sudden shower, it will most likely die down when the rain stops.

A golden-yellow sky usually foretells coming wind, rather than rain.

When clouds tinged with red float high overhead at sundown, wind is coming soon.

Rainbow. A rainbow in the evening indicates that good weather is on its way and that the next morning will likely be bright and fair.

Haze, Mist, and Fog. Summer evening mist, over lakes and low-lying land, which clears as the morning sun rises, tells of fine, warm weather for the rest of the day.

One says that the sun "burns off" the mist, but the sun may take several hours to do so when the mist is heavy.

Light fog in the early morning is generally a sign of a rainless and, often, sun-lit day.

Dew. Grass wet with dew on a summer night almost invariably proclaims fine weather for the following day.

Stars. A few bright stars in a pale sky indicate a continuance of good weather.

Miscellaneous Good Weather Signs

When a rainy morning and forenoon begins to clear between eleven and one o'clock, there is a good chance for a fine afternoon.

When the sun sinks in a flaming ball of fire, the next day should prove fair.

When the first fingers of dawn show low in the eastern horizon, the day will be fair.

Smoke rising straight upward foretells good weather.

Wildfowl generally fly unusually high in good weather.

When swallows and other insect-eating birds fly high, it is a sign of good weather.

One very old sign, often accepted by country people versed in weather lore, is that when chickens and other domestic fowl are feeding outdoors, they will scurry for shelter when it begins to rain only when the shower will be brief.

Bad Weather Signs

The sky is an important factor in forecasting bad weather. Rain, storms, squalls, and other bad weather to come are all usually written overhead.

Sky, Sky Colors and Clouds. When the eastern sky is a dull coppery-red before sunrise, rain may be expected.

A sunset sky of dull coppery-red usually foretells rain coming shortly, and perhaps high wind.

A light yellow sky at sunset usually warns of a rainy day to come.

A grayish sunset and red sunrise indicate bad weather close at hand.

Small, gray-black clouds, usually in a gray-blue sky, warn that rain is not far away.

Winds. When it begins to blow while it is raining, the wind will most likely increase and continue even after the rain stops.

When the wind "backs up" and travels counter-clockwise—from east to north, for example—a storm is usually on its way.

Winds from the Northeast, East, and South usually bring bad weather.

The first sign of even far-distant wind clouds approaching indicates the speedy arrival of wind. Such clouds are always dark and threatening in appearance. For instance, when ragged-looking, wind-tossed clouds, though high in air, are seen it is time to "Hold onto your headdress!"

Haze, Mist and Fog. When the sun shines through a moist haze in the afternoon, it will nearly always rain that night.

A heavy mist which is not burned off by the obscured morning and forenoon sun is likely to cause poor visibility for the rest of the day.

Rainbow. A rainbow in the morning generally warns of coming rain, when it forms in the west.

Halos. When the sun sets with a tinted halo around it, rain is not far distant.

Rain is on the way when the moon is encircled by a halo, especially when the halo is at some distance from the moon.

Heat Lightning. When these flashes light up the sky they indicate the presence of a thunderstorm in the distance. The wind will help you to decide whether the storm is headed your way or not.

Thunderheads (Cumulo-nimbus.) It is when these clouds begin to bloat and their centers spread and darken, while the top flattens, that one has to look out! When the thunderhead outgrows itself it becomes the alarming *cumulo-nimbus,* the technical name for thunderhead.

Dew. An almost certain sign of rain next day is foretold by grass which is dry to the touch on a summer night.

Stars. A black sky filled with stars, and with the Milky Way unusually visible, is a sign that rain is due soon.

Miscellaneous Bad Weather Signs

A number of the following signs were well-known to weather-wise Indians as a part of their woodlore.

When crows stunt and roll in the air, high winds are on their way.

Birds have the habit of perching more before stormy weather takes over, as low-pressure air makes it less easy for them to fly.

When field sparrows, which can be identified by their pinkish bills, splash around in puddles, rain is not far away.

When swallows and martins fly low, rain is not far off.

When smoke is prevented from rising straight up, because of lowering atmospheric pressure, rain is not far off.

When distant objects which generally do not appear clearly stand out distinctly, rain and a change in the direction of the wind are most likely.

When distant noises sound loud and hollow, they are echoing off the lower cloud ceiling and warn of rain on the way.

Whistles of any sort sound louder and clearer before rain.

Odors of most sorts are more noticeable shortly before rain.

Leaves turn their backs before rain, as a change of wind turns them over.

When a rainy forenoon does not clear up by noon, and especially if it is still raining at one o'clock, there is not much chance of the rain's ceasing until late in the afternoon or evening, if then.

Wind Direction

There are a number of ways for a chief to tell with certainty from which direction the wind is blowing. It is important to have this information in order to make accurate weather forecasts. Such knowledge is also useful when stalking animals for observation purposes.

Indians threw a little fine dust, sand, dry grass, or a fluffy feather into the air in order to learn the exact direction in which the wind blew.

A *Voyageur* stuck a forefinger into his mouth for a moment or two until it was moist and warm. Then the finger was taken from the mouth and held up above the head. Even a very slight breeze told him from which direction the wind came by blowing cold on one side of the finger. Sailors use this same trick today.

Special Weather Signs for the Voyageur Chief

When out on a lake, look to windward, the side *from* which the wind is blowing, for tell-tale streaks on the water. They warn that you will be safer close to a projecting point or some other part of the shoreline, or island, which will protect from the force of wind and wave. The shelter chosen should be as close to your canoe as possible because wind-driven waves grow in size according to the distance they travel.

As the wind circle blows counter-clockwise in this hemisphere, face the wind and the storm will be on your right.

When a rain squall or thunderstorm follows wind, look for calm weather when the rain stops.

When one is in a canoe on a lake, lightning in the West or Northwest usually forms part of a storm which will reach the craft. The storms to the South or East pass.

Wind Lore for the Fisherman Chief

General beliefs about fishing winds, which seem to be substantiated by results in some sections of the country, are:

Wind from the south means good fishing.

Wind from the west is often favorable for fishing.

Winds from the north and east often mean poor fishing.

Estimating Wind Velocity

The Indians had no Beaufort Scale of Wind Force but they did know a great deal about the vagaries of wind, how hard it was blowing, and how long it was likely to continue blowing at that velocity. This was necessary knowledge for hunters and for those about to set out on long canoe trips on vast lakes or on the ocean. Here again, accurate forecasting could often avert disaster and death.

Such knowledge is equally precious to modern Indians and may save their canoemen from upsets and far worse difficulties. A few facts and signs which can be seen by modern Indians (though some of them were unknown to the Indians of yesterday) follow:

Wind—Miles per Hour	Indicated by
1-3 m.p.h.	The light air can scarcely be felt. Only smoke drift indicates direction of breeze.
4-7 m.p.h.	Light breeze felt on face; leaves rustle gently.
8-12 m.p.h.	Keeps leaves and twigs in constant motion and small flags flying horizontally.
13-18 m.p.h.	Blows sand and dust and loose paper about. Small branches sway. Though classed as a "moderate breeze," it warns and demands caution.
19-24 m.p.h.	Sways small leafy saplings and raises a good-sized swell on lakes. This so-called "fresh breeze" is actually a wind which makes *canoeing dangerous* and made hunting very difficult for the Indians, because an arrow was only effective at this wind speed when fired from a strong bow at fairly close quarters.

9

Adventuring Like Indians

Expeditions into all kinds of territory, and especially into marshland areas, can prove very interesting and revealing in many ways; but they always entail some risks, which the chief leading the party should be ready to counter.

MARSHLAND EXPEDITIONS

Exploring swampland can be dangerous to some degree, even when the explorers are equipped with canoes and boats, and is not recommended except for small groups of well-equipped older boys with a competent and swamp-wise chief in command. Comparatively small marshes, up to a mile or two in extent, slightly wooded in places, with tufts of grass and sedge showing and little islands and dry points of higher ground in the marsh area, are often conveniently situated and may be explored, after permission has been obtained from the owner. He generally knows whether the marshland is treacherous or not and which parts of it should be avoided.

Marshland expeditions should never be made up of more than six to eight older boys under a seasoned chief—*carrying an accurate compass.*

Equipment

Suitable equipment to carry should comprise: a stout 8-foot pole for each member of the party; two 30-foot lengths of strong rope, not less than ½ inch in diameter; at least four 6- or 8-foot lengths of strong, lightweight plank; and half a dozen straight, strong but lightweight sticks each about 4 feet long. A breechclout, shorts, old moccasins or sneakers, are suitable and comfortable wear for marsh exploration. The chiefs should select as members of such expeditions only braves who know how to obey orders quickly and co-operate speedily in emergencies.

First Phases of Exploration

The first step in exploring marshy terrain is cautiously to follow the edge of the swamp, circling the entire marshy area when possible. Sometimes this cannot be done because of stretches of water, which may be deep or shallow, or streams of various widths and depths which run into or out of the marsh. The leader, who should be first in the Indian file party, may have to retrace his steps when only a quarter of the way around the area and start out in the opposite direction from the first starting point. Before actually entering the marsh, the chief should mention what they are likely to find in the stretch of mysterious, unexplored terrain. Braves may make suggestions as to what wildlife they expect to flush, and quite a lot of them may prove to be accurate. Wildfowl and other birds, including bittern and heron, rats, perhaps muskrats, rabbits, maybe marsh rabbits, mice, hawks, marsh hawks, blackbirds, marsh hen, plover, a majestic blue heron, and even a deer may be flushed from a bed in the reeds, close to the mainland. Wildlife varies according to the location and size of the swamp.

Cattails and rushes for weaving encampment beds may grow in the swamp and there are often a number of interesting and perhaps useful plants and flowers to be seen in a stretch of average marshland. There are few swamps that fail to reveal something of real interest if the exploring braves use their eyes and ears.

Entering the Marsh

The marsh is best entered at the driest point, discovered in the preliminary phase of exploration. Chiefs leading their bands should find out whether the rise and fall of marsh surface water is affected by tides of any sort, whether they are close to the sea or tidal rivers and creeks. Once the driest point of entry is found, good use must be made of the drier patches of grass, sedge and tufts which appear to be able to support the marsh adventurers. Often the drier spots, weight-supporting tufts and clumps of rushes, and other spots which seem to offer fairly dry foothold and support are discovered by the trial and error method, but errors can be offset by care. Pressure with the ends of the long balance poles, then cautious follow-up foot work will reveal vantage points for further advances. The planks taken along may be used to bridge small pools and creeks, provided there are safe supporting places on which the planks will rest. One or two of the long sticks driven into the ground on either side of the improvised footbridge will help to hold it steady and in place. Any loose brush or dead branches which can be found near the point of operations can be used to lay over wet spots and for building miniature corduroy roads over the marsh in places. No crossing should be attempted at any points where the water appears deep around half-submerged reeds and grass tufts, and constant care on the part of the chief is required so that no brave takes chances in any way. Ropes may rarely prove necessary, if route caution is observed at all times, but ropes are always handy things to take along. A member of the band who volunteers to pathfind over what appears to be rather uncertain terrain should be roped to the leader when he is standing on firm ground, and the studied use of balance pole and planks will assure safer reconnoitering. Marker flags or cloth streamer markers should be set up at intervals and with assured visibility to indicate the exact route followed into the swamp, unless the trail left can be plainly seen and followed without the use of flag markers. Few things are easier in the way of outdoor misadventure than to work one's way with fair ease and dispatch into the middle of a marshland. The very great difficulty may come when an endeavor is made to find a way, any way, out of the marsh! In some cases one can neither proceed nor retreat and an advance well into the marsh which may only have occupied one hour of fairly easy going, may be followed by several hours of search for a way out. Chiefs engaged in marshland exploration must remember that sometimes dusk seems to rise with surprising speed and that dusk is one of the marsh explorer's worst enemies, with the arch enemy, darkness, following close in its wake.

It should be carefully noted that some safe stepping places in marshes often become wetter and wetter as the tufts of swamp grass, sedge, or rushes are pushed down by a number of persons treading on them, assuring at least wet feet for the last few braves in line. With due precautions, there is no reason why marsh expeditions should not be carried out in complete safety, wet legs and feet being the only inconvenience of a well-planned exploration trip.

The object of marsh expeditions may be to reach an island somewhere toward the middle of the marsh, and then either return to the starting point or endeavor to continue to another side of the marsh by a new route. Such trips may have varied objectives as there are always a number of reasons for such exciting, off-the-beaten-track adventures, such as the *challenge of the unknown*.

Marsh Ladders, Skiis and Marsh Shoes

The author has led bands in the exploration of vast swamps which proved so fascinating that a number of expeditions were made into the same swamp. For one such expedition, the band prepared some special equipment, such as long light ladders made by nailing strong, lightweight slats about 5 inches wide and 2 feet long onto long poles. These ladders were laid flat over the swampiest places, which could not have been negotiated without them. Marsh "snowshoes," like the ones

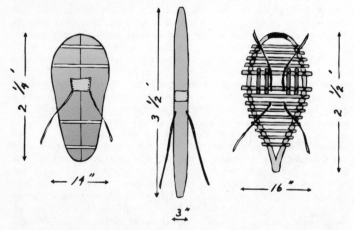

shown in the illustrations, also proved useful at times and the ski type were easily made from lightweight barrel staves. The rounded "bear paw" type snowshoes were made from strong willow or other resilient branches, bent into an oval shape and then "webbed" with strong, rigid branches, cut into rods and lashed securely across the frame, as illustrated. Another sort of snowshoe was made by joining two shaped, light pieces of board together with tough crosspieces, as shown in the drawing. The thongs with which both types of snowshoes, or rather marsh shoes, were attached to the feet were made of short lengths of lamp wick, heavy cloth webbing, or leather strips. With a little care and some practice, one learns to use the shoes quite effectively and they can prove to be very useful in marsh exploration. The chief danger in their use arises from the fact that when a little skill is developed one tends to use them with over-confidence! Chiefs must keep in mind the fact that these marsh shoes are *not* water skis and that some solid or semi-solid marsh, though soft and wet, must be under them in order to support the wearer!

No band engaged in marsh exploration should ever number less than three or four and they should always explore under the supervision of a mature and marsh-wise chief.

At least one excellent, accurate compass is a *must* on all such exploration.

Whistles have not been mentioned throughout marsh exploration for the good reason that the chief should *never* lose sight of even one of his braves, for one minute, during such expeditions, and all braves should keep within sight of each other at all times.

ROCK, CLIFF AND CAVE DISCOVERY

Searches for big rocks, hidden cliffs, and, still more, hidden caverns can be an exciting and useful project. Here again, if there are two mature, wood-wise chiefs available, a band of eight can be divided into two groups or in the case of only one chief, the band can travel in a spread-out formation. Whistles are a *must*. It is surprising how many imposing rocks and even cliffs are sometimes hidden away in a small, wooded area. When found, some can be used as rallying points and landmarks, especially after being decorated with some Indian pictographs or a band totem. A big rock may be found which is ideal for a council rock or for out-of-encampment pow-wows. A cliff, even if it is a small one, is an even more exciting discovery and its best use can be decided by its location, height, shape, and the amount of ground covered by the formation. Perhaps it can serve as a lookout point or as an ideal spot for staging an ambush.

Discovering a cave, even if signs indicate that it has been used before by some unknown hunters or perhaps real Indians, is a major event and one which is usually kept a close secret by its discoverers. A cave has many exciting possibilities—after it has been explored with the very greatest care to make certain that a bear, porcupine, or even a wild cat, does not consider the cave its personal domain. A cave can be used as a hide-out in a number of games. It can be used for band secret society pow-wows or initiations. Who can forget an initiation carried out by torchlight in the mysterious depths of a cave? It can be used as an overnight retreat for a "power quest." A cave can be used as a place for story telling, or meditation. Other ideas will occur to modern chiefs.

Caves are often very tricky places to locate and there are literally hundreds of them waiting to be found in the most unexpected places. A novice cave-hunter will meet with the best chance of success when searching along the high banks of a stream, river, or cliff, in the side of a gorge or on the side of a jagged hill.

Some of these caves may prove to be man-made but others will be natural and, perhaps, even unexplored. There is an ever present danger from a number of sources when exploring a deep or dark cave. Perhaps it has an animal or human occupant who may resent visitors. Perhaps there are deep shafts into which one can fall.

Yes, this is clearly a time to DARE WITH CARE! It is possible to unintentionally dislodge loose stones in the side of a cave which may form a rock slide. The cave may be large enough to get dangerously lost in, unless one has been thoughtful and wise enough to explore while holding a long cord or rope which has been securely tied to a stake driven firmly into the ground just inside the opening of the cave. A powerful flashlight with fresh batteries, and one or two spare batteries on hand, is a *must* for cave exploration. It is a wise precaution to fasten a short length of strong cord to the flashlight and tie the other end of the cord around the wrist—just in case!

Enormous caverns and caves of all sizes have been found in the United States, Canada, France and throughout the rest of the world during the past year or two, the entries to which have been small, hole-like openings, hidden behind bushes or under displaced rocks.

DARE · WITH · CARE

No attempt should be made to explore a cave of any apparent depth or size, or with side passages, unless there are at least two or three older braves and a chief together; and they should be armed with good flashlights, a long, strong rope and at least one or two shorter ones, and a ball of strong cord, the length of which will decide the depth or length of their exploration. An ax or a prospector's pick, and one or two long, light, strong poles should be regarded as the minimum equipment for cave adventuring. Braves should mark the place where they discover an entry to a cave and then find their chief before attempting exploration under his guidance.

CLIMBING

There is no better place where the slogan DARE WITH CARE can be reiterated.

Safety is such a very important factor in encampments and on the trail that any sort of climbing which involves real risk on the part of the braves will be carefully avoided by chiefs.

Tree Climbing

There are certain precautions which can be taken when older braves wish to climb trees, even trees that appear to present few climbing obstacles. An important thing to consider is that it will hurt the climber just as much to fall from a height of forty feet out of a tree which looks easy to climb, as it would if he fell the same distance from a problem tree. When older braves climb, it is well to instruct them to grasp the branches as close to the tree trunk as possible, to assure maximum security. The closer the grip is to the trunk, the less likely it is that a branch will suddenly snap off.

Even an amateur knows that climbing down from a tree is usually more difficult and risky than the upward climb. Feeling with a foot for a necessary branch which does not seem to be there is one of those hair-raising experiences met with in tree climbing! A very careful test of branches, thick and thin, should be made before trusting the weight of the body to them. A brave should be as careful about hand holds as he should be about foot holds; the risk is equally great when a branch snaps.

Carrying a 20-foot length of stout rope wound around the waist while tree climbing is a wise precaution.

When it is actually necessary to climb up into a high tree—in order to check a position, for instance—either the chief or an older brave who is used to climbing trees should be the climber. Often an improvised rope ladder, or a ladder made from two stout saplings with crosspieces lashed firmly on, proves necessary in order to reach the lower branches of a tree with a thick trunk and high lower branches, from which point the real climb begins. How to make a rope ladder is told in Chapter 20.

Cliff and Mountain Climbing

When obstacles such as cliffs and high hills or mountains rise in front of a band on a cross-country expedition, the chief must know of a way to circumvent them. The best way would have been to plot the route on a large-scale map the day before, so that difficult climbing could be avoided. Failing that, climbing can frequently be avoided in mountainous country by following valleys, ridges, or animal trails around the natural obstacles. A few climbing hints may prove helpful in what is known as "balance climbing."

Whenever possible, choose the route for ascent and descent where climbing up or down can be done with the least possible risk.

Climb as steadily as possible to avoid putting unnecessary strain on either the braves, footholds, or handholds. Only one foot or hand should be moved at a time.

Test each handhold and foothold before trusting your weight on it. A needless second of strain on a weak hold may cause an accident.

When climbing up or down a steep cliff or slope, always face it, keeping the weight of the body as close to the slope as is comfortably possible, turning feet sideways when necessary.

Never climb among loose stones or rocks unless it cannot be avoided. The risk of starting a landslide in such circumstances is always present.

Remove all loose stones or small rocks from your climbing path so that they won't fall or roll down on you or those who may be below you.

Never set rocks in motion while climbing up or coming down a steep, rocky hillside.

When footing is bad or uncertain, distribute your weight as much as possible by spreading your feet apart so that all of the strain is not placed on one point.

Rappelling

This method of coming down or climbing up certain sections of sloping cliffs or steep banks is by far the safest and best and has the advantage that it may be used safely by one person—though lone climbing, like lone swimming, is a foolhardy and dangerous business! Rappelling is the way to brake yourself down a steep incline by means of a stout, strong rope. The drawing shows just how rappelling is carried out.

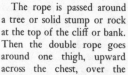

The rope is passed around a tree or solid stump or rock at the top of the cliff or bank. Then the double rope goes around one thigh, upward across the chest, over the shoulder, then down across the back. The rope is grasped by one hand while the other hand holds the rope on the opposite side of the body from the rope-encircled thigh. The body should be held in line with the cliff, the feet should be spread apart and pressed against the projections on the cliff face, whenever the chance arises. In this way, the body is eased down the cliff face by slightly relaxing the grip on the ropes with the hands. The rate of descent can be slowed down and checked at will by simply tightening the grip on the rope. Heavy clothing should be worn or soft sacks can be used as padding where the rope presses hardest on the body, at the shoulders, back, and thigh, as a protection against chafing and possible rope burns. All rope used for climbing should be tested and strong enough to stand any strain which may be put on it.

A handy feature of rappelling is that one may pull the doubled rope clear of the tree or stump when one reaches the bottom of the cliff, by merely pulling on one end of the rope, provided one does not wish to use it for a climb back to the top of the cliff again.

A heavy, single rope about one inch in diameter can be used for rappelling in the case where the rope is left in a fixed place for some time and does not need to be pulled down after the last climber has made the descent.

It is the job of a chief or older brave who has some skill in climbing, to be the first to climb the cliff and set the rope for the others who follow him.

Though the once hard and fast rule, "Never climb up what you can't climb down!" has been modified to some extent by the art of rappelling, it is still a sound precept.

Before touching on another form of climbing it is well to mention that perhaps the three most important requirements for mountaineering—besides good judgment and a steady head and nerves—are balance, friction, and traction. The word balance is self-explanatory, friction is what makes climbing up and down chimneys in the mountain possible, and traction is what a climber lacks when he steps on particles of sand on smooth rock.

In uphill work it is safer, better, and less tiring to have the weight of the body balance on the ball of the foot, with heel unsupported, on a level surface than to have the weight resting on the entire foot supported on a sloping surface.

A novice climber will benefit greatly by a little mountain climbing practice in the backyard before tackling the nearest mountain. By setting a strong, long ladder at a fairly steep angle against a wall or building, and securing it there, he can learn some useful lessons in balance and the best angle to climb steep slopes. He will feel more secure, and there is less danger of cramping the muscles, when his body is held some distance away from the ladder rather than almost lying against it.

Rope Climbing

This form of mountain climbing is becoming increasingly popular. There is no magic in the rope itself, but when used skillfully it does make climbing safer. A rope is usually 120 feet long and approximately ½ inch thick. Nylon ropes have almost completely replaced even the finest ropes of silk and linen which were formerly used. Two of the advantages of nylon rope, apart from its strength, are that it is resilient and rot-resistant.

A rope is more safely employed when it is used by two or, at the most, three climbers, the third bowlined into the middle of the length of rope. Each climber on the rope above three adds immeasurably to the risks of rope climbing. The two-climber team uses a bowline to tie a climber in at each end of the rope. The most experienced climber leads. When he has reached a favorable position he winds a turn of the slack rope around a safe projection of rock, takes up the slack and waits for the second climber to reach him. Should there be no rock knob conveniently located, the climber in the lead braces the rope over his shoulders or behind his hips, according to his position. When the second climber reaches him, he now has the belay position and pays out the rope as the lead climber needs it, keeping the rope reasonably taut. A great number of handbooks on mountain climbing are available, so these few pointers on the subject are merely meant to help beginners on easy slopes.

REMEMBER: In every form of mountain climbing, one split second of inattention or the slightest carelessness can mean death or disaster, so—DARE WITH CARE!

RIVER AND STREAM EXPLORATION HIKES

Interesting exploration of rivers and streams can be made on foot by younger braves. Even older braves may have to do their adventuring on foot when the waterways are either not navigable or situated too far from the encampment to make convenient transport of any water craft possible. A river or stream can be explored from almost any point at which it is first reached, provided that it does not run through private or posted property at that point. Permission can generally be obtained to follow a watercourse through posted property or, in some cases, the posted property can be skirted or a detour made to reach the river or stream above or below the posted area.

Upstream or Downstream?

When a band reaches a section of the watercourse which the chief has decided to follow and explore, the stream may be rushing between steep, rocky cliffs or flowing placidly through a marsh. Some exploration is then required to decide where an accessible edge of the stream can be most easily located. When a good map of that section of the country is available, it is easy to decide whether a hike upstream, toward its source, or downstream, toward its mouth, will prove more interesting or present the greater challenge.

One thrill of river and stream exploration on foot lies in the sudden discovery of a deep gorge, perhaps with a waterfall or a mysterious cave on one side of the cliff. A wide, clear pool may make its appearance where lurking fish, crayfish or turtle may be seen by a cautious approach and keen, observant eyes. Birds and beasts along the water's edge, especially when reeds or bushes border the stream, are another interesting feature of stream exploration. Sometimes the majestic blue heron, bittern, duck, kingfisher, crow, blackbird, and an occasional hawk are among the birds to be seen when a band moves silently, in Indian file, up or down stream. Animals such as deer, muskrat, or raccoon may be spotted at times in daylight during one of these exploration hikes in more remote country.

There is no reason why a chief should not divide his band into two groups when following a stream, provided there is a sub-chief or trustworthy older brave who can take charge of the second section of the divided band. When a band follows a watercourse in two sections, one on either bank, there is often the problem of finding a safe and suitable place where the crossing can be made, and the excitement of discovering just where the two sections can unite again, after some miles of exploration along a river which is unknown to the chief and band. When divided band exploration is undertaken, a chief should give strict orders that both groups advance at the same pace, and abreast, as far as possible. This prevents a section from advancing ahead of the other one and alarming birds or beasts so that they take off before the section in the rear reaches a vantage point from which the wildthings can be best observed.

A challenge awaits the chief who finds that the stream or river which his band is following branches into two distinct watercourses, the distance apparently widening between them, as they flow into the distance. A pow-wow may be held to decide which branch should be followed and perhaps a scouting party may have to be sent out, under a reliable leader, along each arm for a mile or so to decide which one offers more interest and excitement.

One advantage of this stream-following cross-country exploration is that it is practically impossible to lose the way on the return hike to the encampment.

Getting Personal Gear across a Stream, River, or Narrow Lake

This practice is to keep clothing, foodstuffs, and other supplies from getting wet when a stream or river which proves safe for fording, in one way or another, is encountered on a cross-country expedition.

Indians used to pull or push their scant clothing, bows, arrows and other gear which they wished to keep dry, across streams and rivers, on a small raft, rough-built from suitable wildwood material such as small logs, branches, bark and rushes, which they found close to the spot from which they set out to swim across. As a rule, the Indians towed such rafts behind them. When a river was fairly deep, but fordable without swimming, the bundles of belongings were tied on top of the head or shoulders by some braves, while others still preferred rafting their things across, while they waded. Often the head and shoulders carriers were sorry when they suddenly went over their heads in deep holes in the bed of the river. The braves of some tribes made a habit of shooting their arrows across the stream before they set out to swim it, each with his bow securely tied on the back of his head.

Fording or Swimming a River or Lake

Chiefs realize that extreme care is necessary when even older braves set out to ford or swim a river which is unknown to the band. A chief and one or two of the older braves should first of all endeavor to ford the stream at what is apparently the most favorable point, before any other member of the band enters the water. If the current is at all swift, it is a wise precaution for the chief to rope himself and his one or two fellow adventurers together, as in mountain climbing, because a stream can be crossed safer in this way. As an added precaution, one end of the rope to which the chief and braves are attached should be paid out by one or two older braves stationed on the bank of the river. Braves crossing the stream or river should be equipped with a strong, lightweight balance pole 6 to 8 feet long. Such a pole is a useful aid not only in preserving balance but also for probing the bottom of the stream in order to locate deep holes and find rocks which may jut upward from the stream bed. These poles can also replace ropes in an emergency, the ends of the poles being held by the stream forders, one brave in front and one behind on each pole. Even when the stream proves to be fairly easy to ford and not deep, the chief and his one or two sub-chiefs should wade back into the water again, after having crossed to the far side, and take up stations at intervals across the stream at the point where the remainder of the band will follow in their footsteps while making the crossing. In these positions the leaders not only serve as markers but can extend a helping pole when a brave stumbles and loses footing for a moment. Of course, all chiefs and senior braves should be able to swim strongly and know the standard methods of lifesaving in case of emergencies. When braves swim across a narrow lake, escorted, naturally, only those who have passed adequate swimming tests should be allowed to make the attempt. Even when the best swimmers undertake the crossing they should be accompanied by a boat, raft, or canoe, rowed or paddled by experienced watermen equipped with a long pole and lifelines. Those swimming across the lake should do so by two's, in close proximity to the craft escorting them. When these two swimmers have crossed, the boatmen row back for two more and continue this ferrying until all of the band has crossed in safety.

Another way of getting the band and equipment across a body of water is to load the gear onto a light, buoyant raft made from wildwood material, and have two good swimmers push or pull it across. After this, one of them, as raftsman, with an improvised paddle or pole, navigates the raft back empty for more gear, or for two swimmers who swim alongside the raft and can hold onto it when necessary in order to rest. The size and buoyancy of the raft will determine how many braves can safely hitch onto it at one time, should they become tired during the crossing.

Chiefs can devise other safe methods of getting braves and gear across streams, such as using a strong rope doubled and joined securely at the ends, to make an endless cable, tying the gear to the top strand, and pulling it across. This is most effective for the transport of gear only when the banks of the stream are high enough to use the cable without danger of the gear's dipping in the water on the way across stream. Even with this cable practically touching the water or actually doing so, the braves of the band can swim or ford the stream by using it for support, when it is operated by two strong, older braves on opposite banks at each end of the doubled rope. Naturally, a tree conveniently situated on one or either bank of the stream can be used to considerable advantage to help take the strain. It is understood that the chief has first of all forded and investigated the bed of the stream at the point used for the crossing. Before the last two warriors of the band, those who have been operating the endless cable transport, cross, the doubled rope is passed over a stout, round pole, strong stake, firmly driven into the ground or, better still, the convenient tree on the bank of the stream. When a tree is used, unless it has served throughout the operation, the cable rope will have to be unknotted and fastened around the tree before the last two braves cross. When they have made the cable support crossing safely, the two ends of the cable are pulled across to the side on which the band has assembled. The chief unfastens them and pulls the rope across the stream, ending the operation.

10

Watercraft and Voyaging

The pointers which follow, a number of which are original, deal chiefly with adventuring and voyaging by canoes and other craft on lake, stream, and river. There are always chiefs and braves expert enough in the use of the paddle to make such voyages safe and possible.

CANOES

Although the author has a sentimental preference for the well-made wood-and-canvas canoe—though it weighs more than twice as much as the occasional birch-bark craft encountered in the Canadian woods today—the aluminum canoe has some important points in its favor, which help to offset the fact that it can be noisy and offers the wind a better target than many wood-and-canvas models. The aluminum canoe has stability and is lightweight, the latter quality being appreciated in long portages, and will right itself automatically in case of upset. The aluminum canoe is not easily damaged by floating logs and the average rounded rock encountered in a lake or river, so instead of being holed in such mishaps, it usually suffers only a dent or two, which can be beaten out fairly easily with a club. Those who have had to frequently repair holes, or even cracks, in wood-and-canvas canoes, without suitable repair material and tools on hand, can appreciate the ease of repairing aluminum craft. Setting sentimentality aside, there is little doubt that in some ways the metal craft is superior, especially for use by younger braves, to the wood-and-canvas canoe.

EMBARKING AND DISEMBARKING FROM CANOES

Perhaps the greatest strain and damage suffered by canoes comes when inexperienced canoemen embark or disembark, despite the simplicity of these operations. First of all, the canoe is carried to the water's edge and placed right side up, stern first, on the shore of the lake or river, one canoeman handling the craft on each side of the center thwart. The stern is lifted carefully into the water and the rest of the canoe is then slid hand-over-hand, with the grip on the gunwales, into the water. The bow paddler now steadies the bow of the canoe between his legs while the stern paddler embarks, aft of the center thwart, and walks cautiously down the middle of the canoe to the stern, facing the stern and holding onto the gunwales as he advances. He sits down carefully in the position from which he will paddle. This raises the bow of the canoe so that the bow man can climb into the craft. The reverse of this method of launching is carried out when disembarking. Even greater care must be taken when it is necessary to embark in a canoe from a rocky shore, where the craft must be held parallel to the bank while going aboard.

LOADING CANOES

More than half of the difficulties encountered by canoe crews while voyaging are caused by the failure to trim their loads and to load back of center. A canoe should maintain perfect balance, from side to side, and this is one sign of a well-trimmed load. Though a canoe rides better if the weight of its load is just back of center, the craft should be loaded in such a way that *both* the bow and stern ride reasonably high. This is accomplished by loading as little heavy duffle as possible directly in the stern. The gear in every packsack or bundle should be enclosed in a really waterproof bag and most packs will store easily under the thwarts. Lashed in that position, they will add buoyancy to a canoe which upsets in rough water. The canoe load should never be higher than the gunwale. There is always danger in lashing heavy, unprotected duffle in a canoe, since it may cause the craft to sink in case of upset. Careful loading of carefully packed duffle should make the possibility of an upset nearly impossible unless under the most hazardous conditions.

TOWING CANOES

Before describing methods of towing canoes, it is well to say that towing canoes in *any* manner is not a safe practice for braves who are amateur watermen. If circumstances necessitate towing, all of the braves should voyage in the leading (towing) canoe provided it is not overloaded by an additional one or two passengers.

Perhaps the best method of towing two canoes is one behind the other, unless rough water makes the side-by-side tow advisable for seaworthiness.

To tow one canoe behind another a simple rope harness has to be used. One end, approximately 8 feet long, of this 24-foot long "bridle" of rope is hitched around and tied to one end of the forward gunwale or seat, continued across the canoe and hitched and tied around the other end of the gunwale or seat. What is left of this end is brought forward and down and tied, with a bowline, to the longer towing rope close under the curve of the bow, just above water level, as shown in the drawing. This method of bridle attachment puts the towing strain low on

BRIDLE

the canoe and the craft, loaded or unloaded, tows more easily and without the bow's sinking low in the water. The canoe being towed can ride anywhere from 8 to 12 feet behind the towing canoe, the distance being based on conditions of wind and water. The end of the tow line is fastened in the stern of the towing canoe.

TRANSPORTATION BY DOUBLE CANOES

Modern Indians can call this method Catamaran Canoe Transport and it is also a form of towing if the paddlers are in one canoe and the other is empty or wisely loaded. A great advantage of this form of transportation is that it is extremely seaworthy in bad weather. Canoes in this side-by-side position can be paddled easily and form an excellent means of transporting long tepee poles, planks, and other lengthy and cumbersome gear. Additional poles can be lashed crosswise, between the two poles which hold the canoes together and apart, to make a flat platform on which the equipment can be carried. This is how the two canoes are lashed into position. A strong, light pole is laid across the two canoes and lashed securely to a forward thwart in each canoe. The pole must be long enough to allow the bows of the canoes to ride three feet apart, and must overlap for about a foot on each outside gunwale. A second pole is lashed across the two canoes just forward of the stern seats, holding the canoes four feet apart. The distance between the canoes is absolutely necessary to prevent the water from splashing into the craft and the slightly increasing distance from bow to stern is helpful in letting the water which piles up between the two canoes, run off easily astern, especially when they are running before the wind. Without the difference allowed, there would be a heavy backwash of water.

MAKING A SEA ANCHOR

Such an anchor is easily improvised and proves a blessing in a strong, following sea. Braves can use it when their craft is running before a strong wind. The popular idea that in such circumstances one can "take it easy" is a bad mistake. Steering in fast-following water is very difficult unless the canoe can be kept going forward faster than the following water is moving, and to slow down too much means shipping water over the stern. Using a sea anchor of some sort is the way out of such a difficult situation. It is easily made with a pail with a wire handle,

to which a length of strong rope ten to twenty feet long is attached. The author has frequently used a folding canvas bucket instead of a metal pail and found that it worked just as well. The rope holding the anchor must be fastened low down to the stern of the canoe and, since few canoes have a place to which the end of the rope can be fastened at that point, it is best to make a rope bridle to which the line of the sea anchor can be attached. When the anchor line is attached, the pail is thrown overboard, fills with water, and drags behind the canoe just below the surface, holding the canoe on a straight course. In a really heavy sea, it is well to crouch forward and paddle a little farther away from the stern, since this will help to raise it a little higher out of the wash.

TRACKING CANOES

Tracking in this case has nothing to do with trailing, but describes the art of leading a canoe, from dry land, along a lakeshore or bank of a stream or river by the use of two lines. These tracking lines should be about 50 feet long for real tracking, though they can be considerably shorter when tracking conditions are favorable. These lines can be either thin, lightweight but strong rope or, better still, heavy sash cord. One of these cords is fastened to the bow and the other to the stern of the canoe, as far forward and aft as it is possible to firmly attach the ends of the cords to the gunwales or other convenient points. It is interesting and, at first, surprising as one practices this art along the treeless shoreline of a lake, to note that the canoe runs forward on its own accord and that it can easily be headed out or toward shore by simple manipulation of the lines. A slight pull on the bow line or a tug on the line attached to the stern, does the trick. When one has mastered the easy art of tracking a canoe along a lakeshore, it is time to try tracking along the bank of a slow-flowing river. Of course, the banks of a stream which is comparatively free from trees and tall rocks close to the water's edge make for ideal tracking. When one is tracking upstream, a pull on the line fastened to the stern will turn the bow out into the stream, while this works in reverse when tracking downstream.

At times, the author has had to use ropes even longer than 50 feet in order to have enough spare cord to guide canoes around rocks cropping up some distance from the shore, in cases where the canoe had to be tracked around the outside of such rocks rather than on the shoreward side. Tracking can be done either from

the same level as the canoe or from the bank of a stream situated high above the stream. A slight pull on one line while letting out on the other, works wonders while steering the obedient craft around obstacles. One of the pleasantest tracking experiences comes when taking a canoe along a long stretch of sea or ocean just off a sandy beach. The tracker can wade along in the water a few feet from shore and run his canoe ahead of him, as fast or as slowly as he wishes, perhaps digging up an occasional scallop with his toes so that, as he holds the shellfish in his hand, he may admire the rows of bright blue eyes as they look out from a partially opened shell in order to see what is going on outside.

Two canoemen can track a canoe, instead of one, one man on the bow line and the other handling the stern line, but it is surprising how well the work can be done single-handed.

ANCHORS

Anchors play an important part in canoeing when it is not desirable to beach the craft, but the carrying of this extra gear is not always an easy problem to solve. Lightweight anchors are more like grappling irons and the most effective type has three arms armed with flukes and stock through shank. The disadvantages of such anchors are that they occupy a certain amount of storage space among the duffle in a canoe, they have to be transported while portaging, they are fairly expensive, and they can become wedged on the bottom in certain lakes and streams, sometimes so securely that they have to be cut loose and abandoned. Before one resorts to the latter, however, the lodged anchor should be pulled on from all points of the compass, as well as straight up, so that all angles of possible release will have been tried and found ineffective. Abandoning an anchor can generally be avoided when there is a skin diver in the crew and the waters permit safe underwater exploration.

An anchor can be improvised when there are fairly heavy rocks to be found on shore or beach, the difficulty being to find a rock with convenient bulges which assure the rope's being held securely in place. A canoe adrift can prove serious in certain circumstances. Fortunately, there are usually plenty of small rocks of varied shape and small stones to be found. They solve the anchorage problem. A net can be improvised from lengths of strong, oil-soaked, heavyweight twine or light rope. It need not be a real, woven net but merely one oblong in shape, with the meshes sufficiently small to hold in the odd shaped stones which are used to fill it. The opening at the top of this improvised "net" is tied together with a strong piece of rope. A small loop is made in it, to which the anchor rope is fastened. Such a net-anchor case can be made to hold up to 30 pounds of small rocks or stones, providing ample weight to hold a canoe in place while moored where the current is not too strong. When this anchor has served its purpose at one mooring site, the stones can be emptied from it and the case carried along for use at the next stopping place.

Another form of portable anchor can be made more easily than the net type. All that is required is a stout sack, such as a potato sack, a sailor's needle or any other heavy needle, a length of strong, oiled twine, a short length of lightweight rope, and a piece of stout canvas about 2 feet square. The top of the sack is doubled back like a cuff all around until it reaches the bottom of the sack, where it is sewn all around. The piece of canvas is pushed down into the sack to rein-

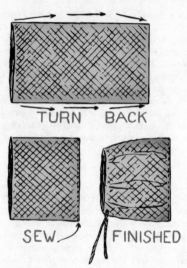

TURN   BACK

SEW   FINISHED

force its bottom. It need not be sewn into place as the stones or rocks will hold it in position. A small hole is made through one thickness of the sack, about one inch from the top. A length of oiled rope is threaded all around between the two thicknesses of sacking. About six inches of each' end of the rope are left protruding through the hole at the mouth of the sack. After the sack has been filled with stones or pebbles, the two ends of rope at the mouth of the sack are pulled tight, knotted, and a small loop made so that the end of the anchor rope can easily be fastened to it. If a heavier anchor is needed, the sack is turned down only part way and a larger piece of canvas used to reinforce it. Of course such an anchor used in strong tidal waters or where there is a strong current running will wear through the canvas after some use. Despite this, the anchor will fill its purpose when there is no other suitable anchoring device available.

MOORING POSTS

When fairly long, strong poles are available they can replace anchors. One way to use this sort of mooring is to allow two poles for each craft to be moored. The length of the poles is decided by the depth of the water in which they are to be used. One end of each pole is pointed and the poles are driven firmly into the bottom of the lake or river, allowing about three feet of clearance, fore and aft, between the poles and the bow and stern. Painters are attached to the craft fore and aft, and the ends of these ropes are fastened securely to the poles, allowing the canoe to ride easily and securely between them. One main mooring post with three other poles evenly spaced within a quarter circle and about 26 feet distant from the main post permits three craft to be moored with three poles instead of six. Additional poles will moor more craft, still using the one main mooring post.

BUILDING RAFTS

This type of improvised craft has great importance in the field of water transportation, as it has many uses. Rafts are made in many sizes, from the small raft used by the Indians for carrying clothing and personal gear across water to the huge craft large enough to transport up to a dozen or more persons safely.

The logs of all larger rafts should be strongly lashed together and one or two stout poles fastened diagonally across the raft logs, as shown in the drawing, to prevent the raft from telescoping when in use. When beginners build a raft they are usually greatly surprised by the number of logs required to support even one person. This is particularly true when suitable wildwood material is not available and oddly assorted logs or wet and green logs have to be used.

This is how a band of braves can construct a raft, under the directions of a chief. The details for this larger raft will serve for rafts of all sizes insofar as the arrangement of the logs is concerned. The smaller the raft, the thinner and shorter are the logs used. The rafts may be either nailed or lashed together, or both, but sufficient lashing correctly done should serve the purpose very well. When nails are used, the logs should be notched where the crosspieces cross, so that shorter nails can be used effectively. Raft materials recommended are white pine, or other pine logs, balsam, fir or cedar, sawn from the butts of *dead* trees which can generally be found in wood and forest. These logs should be dry, about 8 or 10 feet long and from 6 to 12 inches wide. The logs need not be uniform in thickness but a raft made from logs of about the same thickness looks better and is, perhaps, better for good rafting.

The logs are rolled to the edge of the water, laid parallel and lashed together with two stout green poles, as shown in the drawing. The two diagonal poles,

RAFT

important for holding the raft firmly together, are green, and diagonally lashed, as illustrated. They may also be lashed in the middle, where they cross, in addition to the end lashings shown. Thin rope, or strong sash cord, oiled, should be used for fastening the logs and poles together. The more suitable the logs used in the construction of the raft, the more buoyant it will be.

All amateur built and navigated rafts are best used when the rafters are either wearing breechclouts or bathing suits and seated on the raft, but clothing and other gear which should be kept dry can be set on top of a pile of brush, which is placed on the raft. Though much extra buoyancy can be assured by lashing small or big metal cans or drums onto the frame of the raft, or building them into the raft by holding them against the raft logs with a retaining woodwork frame, suitable drums are not always available when wanted and there is always some danger that they will be punctured while in use, thus losing buoyancy.

A strong, slim pole, from 8 to 12 feet long, is used for poling and "paddling," though improvised paddles can be cut from suitable slats of wood to help drive the raft forward.

Catamaran Raft

This type of raft, though not used by the Indians of North America, is very safe and good, and is used by some tribes of other habitats. The chief point in its favor is that it is exceptionally stable and almost impossible to upset. The double outrigger, instead of the single one, assures balance and seaworthiness.

CATAMARAN   RAFT

The drawing shows a small raft made with three buoyant logs, held together by crosspieces and the planking in the center, on which the rafters sit and gear is carried. Braves using the raft can sit with their feet and legs in the water, when the cross planking is narrow. The two outside logs are the outrigger balance logs and nobody rides on them.

Raft Adventuring

Rafting downstream is thrilling fun provided the rafters are all good swimmers and a water-wise chief accompanies each raft. The rafts used should be thoroughly seaworthy and the streams and rivers navigated comparatively free from rocks and entirely free from rapids. Sluggish streams should be used by the rafting braves for their early adventures and they should not be graduated to swifter waters until they have not only confidence in themselves and their craft but a good knowledge of rafting, acquired by practice. Rafts can also be tracked downstream, with only the gear aboard.

MARKING WATER TRAILS

There are a number of ways of marking trails which lead over lakes and up and down rivers. Some Indian tribes drove a stake into the ground at the water's edge to show that they had embarked for a known destination by canoe. The braves who saw this sign knew where the party in canoes was heading and required no further sign. When the destination or even direction in which the water trail would lead was unknown to those who should follow, two sticks or poles were driven in at the water's edge, one indicating the starting point and the other, sticking out of the water at a few yards distance away from the embarkation stick, indicated the direction in which the canoes would travel (see diagram in Chapter 11). Further "pole" trails of poles driven into the bottom of the lake in shallow spots guided the water trail followers to the final sign, a disembarkation pole driven into the lake shore at the point where the party had left their canoe or canoes—which would be cleverly concealed in the woods or forest upon disembarkation. Similar poles driven into the bed of a stream at points where the river divided into two channels clearly indicated which branch of the stream had been taken. The direction in which the tops of these water-trail guide posts slanted pointed the route to be followed. A withe hoop tied to the top of a pole or stake by a party at point of embarkation meant, "Destination unknown."

Modern Indians can use the streamer trail-marking method to point out the route followed up a branching river or among scattered islands on a lake. A bright yellow streamer dangling from a tree branch or a tree overhanging the lake tells clearly that the advance party, or first canoe, passed that way.

The author has also used to advantage, on unfrequented rivers, streams, and lakes, small, anchored floats made of pine blocks painted in bright colors to show the direction in which the canoe traveled among islands dotted over shallow lakes or up and down streams where the current was not fast enough to cause the floats to drag their anchors.

VOYAGING ON LAKE, RIVER AND STREAM

The condensed pointers which follow deal only with the usual craft used in connection with an Indian camp or encampment, canoes and improvised rafts.

Lake Voyaging

Cruising on big lakes should be done reasonably close to the shoreline. This course is by far the safest as the bands can paddle for shelter upon the first distant appearance of a storm.

Voyages on lakes, or on any other waters, should never be undertaken unless at least one water-wise and weather-wise chief is in command.

Even simple navigation on lakes and rivers is not quite so easy as pathfinding on land. There is nothing easier than to lose one's way on a chain of lakes studded with islands or on a river with several arms, especially when the lake or waterway is unknown to the chief. A good chart, when available, and an accurate compass will serve to keep the navigator or lead canoe on course and with some water-trail marking, as detailed elsewhere in this chapter, a chief who is more at home in the trackless forest will soon be just as much at home on the trackless waters.

Swimming should be considered one of the major skills associated with watermanship. The ability to swim confidently and well is a great asset to a brave. It may mean the difference between life and death on some unexpected occasion. A good knowledge of the elementary lifesaving skills is essential.

Braves should not be encouraged to believe that launching, handling, loading, and disembarking from canoes is an easy accomplishment. It takes skillful instruction and much practice in elementary canoe and navigation skills before a real canoeist emerges, ready for canoe trail camping and the many emergencies which can arise en route.

On a big lake, there are many miles of shoreline, and lengthy voyages can be made along the shoreline in two directions from the encampment without risking a lake crossing which might be interrupted by a storm. Such trips may take several hours in each direction and a noon meal can be cooked en route. Lake trips of this sort should not be hurried. The *voyageurs* should be able to land and explore an interesting-looking cove or waterway which runs inland from the lake. There are shore and waterbirds to be seen, and perhaps animals on the bank or in the water which should not be overlooked. The chief can allow a brave who first notices something of real interest to claim coup. This keeps all braves on the lookout and greatly increases the interest of the voyage. Sometimes piles of logs and driftwood can be found in some sheltered bay where storm winds and waves have carried them. This gives a band a fine chance to build a good raft which, perhaps, may be navigated back to the encampment in easy stages by a trustworthy crew of two or three braves, under close escort of one or two canoes manned by good swimmers.

Lake voyages are made more interesting when one or more fair-sized islands are within a mile or so off shore. Such islands form an objective and a place where a cook-out meal may be enjoyed. One difficulty in navigating on large, island-studded lakes is to distinguish between large islands and mainland peninsulas. Sometimes there may be a chain of lakes where older braves, who have been well-schooled in canoe craft may enjoy voyages of several days' duration, under the command of a seasoned chief. The *voyageurs* camp each night, going ashore at a suitable spot well before dark.

The band carries the necessary rations, tarps or lightweight tents, blankets or sleeping bags, and other supplies needed for the days spent away from the encampment. Often, for such adventure trips, a capable sub-chief goes along to help the chief in charge of the expedition. Pointers for packing and carrying provisions and gear are given in Chapter 3.

Participating in canoe trail camping should be considered a great honor and the older and more skilled braves should be encouraged to contest and excel in canoe and camping skills in order to merit plying a paddle on such trips. Land expeditions undertaken by Indians were carefully plotted and prepared but not more so than canoe voyages of several days' duration, whether by lake or river. Pre-voyage preparation was carried out under the supervision of skilled chiefs and each brave knew exactly what to take and what to do from the time the band left the encampment until the braves returned. Similar briefing should be carried out for all canoe trail camping voyages undertaken by modern Indians. Only disciplined braves, who can obey an order as quick as a loon dives and think fast in an emergency, should make up the party.

Voyages of this sort can offer unique opportunities for firsthand nature study, and chiefs should plan to make good use of the opportunities which arise en route.

The average lake offers wonderful opportunities for chiefs to develop canoe skills, under favorable conditions, among the braves of their bands. There is plenty of sea room, few bothersome currents and no rocks protruding from swift waters to snag the unwary canoe. Chiefs can evolve a simple system of canoe skill coups and grand coups which will keep the braves interested, keen, and eager to develop advanced canoe skills.

Adventuring on River and Stream

Canoe expeditions on rivers and streams are entirely different from those undertaken on lakes. Such voyages are strictly limited by the width, length, currents, known and possible obstructions to navigation, and conceivable dangers of the rivers or streams to be navigated. Some wide, placid rivers and streams offer conditions not too different from those encountered on a lake, especially fairly close to the mouth of the river. Other waterways are swift and difficult to navigate, and offer so many hazards that wise chiefs will not even consider them as possibilities for canoe travel. Should a main camp be well equipped with motor transport of some sort so that the braves and canoes can be taken upstream for a number of miles and then voyage downstream, such a voyage can be safe, interesting, and thrilling. It is suggested that chiefs in charge of such voyages should make it a point of covering in a canoe exactly the same waters which they will traverse later with the braves. Ability to make portages, if necessary, should be seriously considered before undertaking any lengthy river trip. Obstructions to canoe travel, shipping of any sort which might be encountered on the voyage, and all other possible hazards should be well known to the chiefs in charge of river canoe trail camping projects and also the chief responsible for the main camp and over-all activities. No alert chief will consider undertaking any trip by water which presents any danger to his *voyageurs*. DARE WITH CARE! is especially worthy of insertion at this point.

11

Tracks and Trailing

So many writers on outdoor subjects have written casually about cutting blazes in trees, that one may forget at times that one is needlessly wounding a living thing with ax strokes which are unnecessary. It is understandable that a woodsman who is lost in a forest may resort to gashing live trees with his ax in an endeavor to mark out a trail. It is quite another thing when chiefs in encampments where paint is available start out on a tree-hacking campaign in order to mark the various trails which braves may have to follow between several points in the wooded encampment area. The ax should be used as an instrument of conservation, not as a weapon of sabotage and destruction. No brave should be allowed to possess an ax in the Twentieth Century until he has either reached the age of fourteen and been instructed in the necessity of conservation, or reached an age of maturity and understanding which has caused him to take the conservationists' oath, which he sincerely intends to keep. All youngsters should be well educated in both conservation and axmanship *before* being allowed to carry either hatchet or ax. The ruthless use of an ax should be outlawed.

MAKING AND MARKING TRAILS

Being able to mark trails skillfully is as important to the woodsman and modern Indian as being able to follow trails. A well-marked trail can point the way to an encampment, a food cache, or a cabin when often it would be next to impossible to locate them without markings. Frequently, the author has avoided being more or less lost, or bogged, by following his own trail markings out of a swamp area, or densely wooded area, back to the starting point—the point is that the markings were made on the way *into* the difficult areas.

WAYS OF MARKING TRAILS WHICH SHOULD NEVER BE USED TODAY ARE: lop sticks, in which many of the lower branches on an evergreen are lopped off to call attention to the easily seen top, which serves as a landmark; blazes cut in trees with an ax, even though they only debark the trees; or breaking off branches as trail markers, or leaving broken branches hanging from trees to mark a trail. Bending young trees to mark a trail should never be done. Many dwarfed and badly deformed trees are found in woods and forests today, where thoughtless trail blazers left their mark in times long past. With these trail-marking methods ruled out, a modern Indian may ask what other methods exist which can be recommended. Here are some of them.

Cloth Streamer Markers

The use of small colored streamers of some lightweight cloth has already been suggested as trail markers. Tied onto tree branches or bushes at the most conspicuous points, they make excellent trail guides and will remain in position throughout a period of several months without being replaced. Different colored streamers can mark different trails, one series leading through the woods to an encampment, and perhaps another set marking the way to a council ring or other site.

The colored cloth strips used to mark trails can measure from 4 to 6 inches in length and 2 inches in width. They can be cut in pennant shape, if desired, and such markers made from dyed parachute silk will be found on trees for two years or more after they have been tied onto branches, especially if the thin, strong twine used to tie them on has been soaked in oil before use. An advantage of this type of trail marking is that the markers can be removed easily, once the braves have learned the various trails, and this streamer type marking of trails can be used when experimental trails are being laid out, while paint blazes may be desired after the routes have been established.

Chalk Marks

Chalk marks on trees, rocks, or cliffs are good ways to mark trails, and chalk of different colors can be used to indicate special trails. If the spots for the chalk mark blazes are well chosen, so that a rainstorm cannot wash them out, and the point of the chalk is wet before making a solid mark, such markings as squares or circles will remain visible for quite a long time.

Tufts of Grass and Sticks

Tufts of grass, sedge, or moss can be stuck into the forked branches of low trees or bushes, or into split sticks of various lengths, pushed into the ground at points where they will be most easily seen.

A stick or pole driven into the ground with the end pointing in the direction to be followed will keep braves on the right track. Such a trail is especially useful over marsh stretches as the poles indicate a firm pathway which, if followed carefully, will keep moccasins dry.

Tree "Blazing"

Round or oblong patches of orange or white paint marked about shoulder high on suitable trees will leave a plainly marked trail which will point the way for at least several seasons. Apart from conservation practiced in paint blazing, there is also the advantage of being able to mark each trail by a different color blaze so that a brave knows whether it will take him to a cook-out, pow-wow, or other area which he wishes to reach. Such a paint-blaze trail can also be marked on rocks, cliffs or big stones in treeless sections of the route.

Rock, Stone, and Grass Markers

Rock, stone, and grass-twist trail markers were commonly used by Indian tribes to indicate trails to be followed. Indian rock and stone "trail-talk" was used a great deal in rocky and mountainous country, where small rocks and stones were by far the most plentiful material for making trail signs.

Disk Markers

One other excellent way of marking a trail is by cutting a number of blazes from thin plywood or a sheet of hardwood and nailing them to the trees by one

1½-inch thin nail driven through the center of each blaze. One great advantage of such trail signs is that they can be used to mark even secret trails. For instance, a square blaze may mean one thing to the band or tribe using it, a circle has a different meaning, while an oval or oblong marking has still some other meaning. These cutout blazes can be about 3 inches wide for circles or for square blazes. They should be painted in highly visible colors, except in the case of secret trails. Special code markings, in different colors or shapes can be painted onto the blaze to leave messages which only the band or tribe can read. The drawings of various standard trail signs in this chapter show how they are made and there are also some drawings of special code blazes which can mean whatever the chief and his band decide they should. A chief, for instance, instead of using the standard blaze of *one* square or circle to indicate the trail *from* the encampment and *two* squares or circle blazes to mark the trail *to* the encampment, can use a *white* blaze to mark the trail toward camp and a *yellow* blaze to mark the trail away from camp.

SECRET TRAILS AND HIDING PLACES

Frequently the lives of lone braves and entire bands of Indians depended on secret trails. Sometimes these trails were natural so that those who knew and used them did so with extreme care and left neither tracks nor trail to be discovered by keen-eyed pursuers or searchers. These secret trails crossed rocky plateaus, valleys and other terrain and were often spoken of as blind trails. Combined with "blind" spots, when the trails had to cross less favorable country, they provided a fair margin of safety for their users. Such trails were largely followed by some inconspicuous landmarks in the distance or more or less along the trail which, to the initiated, indicated the way. Quite often, the extraordinary Indian sense of direction also aided them in following these practically invisible trails.

Hidden Hide-outs

Some of these secret trails were hidden in the beds of shallow streams, others lay over stony ground and ran through rocky caves, which were often connected. The narrow entrances to such caves were so frequently hidden by bushes, rocky overhangs and natural tree, bush, or rock screens that one had to practically fall into an opening before realizing that such a cave, or chain of caves, existed. Sometimes concealed openings in sheer cliffs led from the bank of a swift-running stream into caves, which led on and on, at times into hidden canyons or valleys. Large bands of Indians, with their horses, often lived for weeks and months in such hidden valleys and canyons while troops of cavalry and at times renegade Indian scouts sought in vain for the whereabouts of the Indian bands which had "disappeared." History often records this.

Indians sometimes used animal trails which they knew, as secret trails, because even the best enemy trailers had great difficulty in following the almost imperceptible prints of moccasins on such trails. Secret trails across difficult terrain were at times marked with thin, short twigs or tiny stones, placed fairly far apart, and in such a way that they would be unnoticed, even by the keen eyes of hostile trackers. Indian boys of the tribes using such trails were trained to

ROCKS OR STONES	THIS IS THE TRAIL	TURN RIGHT	WARNING! OR CACHE
DISKS ON TREES	TURN LEFT	TO	FROM
TUFTS OF GRASS	THIS IS THE TRAIL	TURN RIGHT	WARNING! OR CACHE
CLOTH STREAMERS	THIS MARKS THE TRAIL		
LAKE AND RIVER MARKERS	EMBARKED HERE	DIRECTION TAKEN	UNKNOWN DESTINATION
SPECIAL CODE BLAZES	MEANINGS DEVISED BY TRAIL BLAZERS		

observe everything, no matter how small, and they were taught that being highly observant could save their lives when engaged in perilous quests or raids.

Evasion

Indians whose scalps were being hunted by enemy warriors were often forced by encircling scouts to escape from unfavorable ground, where even their light tracks could be read as an open book by their enemies, to terrain where their moccasins would leave no tell-tale tracks. They did this in many clever ways. At times, when the chance occurred, they would approach a tree with wide-spreading branches which overhung rock-strewn ground, where their tracks would not show. They would then pull themselves up into the tree, by jumping for a low-hanging branch on the side of approach, wriggle along that branch or another which extended even further over rocky or hard ground where a track would be least visible, and then drop lightly onto such ground when the branch became too thin to support their weight. They knew that some time would probably be lost by the trackers when they arrived at the tree. They must look well into the tree to make certain that their quarry had not found a hiding place in a well-leaved nest of branches instead of dropping out of it when it had served its purpose. Causing the pursuers to lose time often meant life to the pursued, especially when they were racing against time until darkness shrouded their tracks from even the keenest eyes, or were nearing a band of their tribe which they knew to be not far distant. For the trackers to follow the trail by torchlight was something done only in yarns, with little foundation on fact. Similarly, covering up tracks by walking backward and brushing away the tell-tale tracks with an improvised branch-broom was seldom done by the Indians, though the ruse has frequently been played up in tales. It was difficult to really obliterate the tracks without leaving other tell-tale marks in their place.

Indians of various tribes sometimes used boots made from the feet and part of the legs of larger animals, such as bear or elk. These boots were worn by an Indian to throw his pursuers off his trail, or while scouting around an enemy encampment after dark. The bear track boots were the ones used most successfully, as the tracks left when the Indian wore the feet of other big animals rarely threw an expert tracker off the scent.

Another stratagem used for throwing pursuers off the trail was to leap from the ground onto a convenient flat rock or rocky outcropping and leave that rocky patch at a point where tracks would be less visible.

A similar ruse was resorted to when Indians were following the bed of a stream or shallow river which flowed through sandy or grassy country, and felt certain that their enemies were following along the stream not far behind them. When a convenient stretch of rocks, or a natural causeway of rocks, extended up onto the shore they would leave the stream by that point and trust to the favorable ground to conceal their tracks as they moved over the rock patch away from the stream. Of course, they had to feel fairly sure that they were far enough ahead of their pursuers to give their wet moccasin prints on the rocks time to dry before the trackers reached that point. Such ruses generally caused the pursuers to lose valuable time, if not the trail, which they often did until they were able to circle and pick it up again. Sometimes darkness fell before the lost trail could be rediscovered, and by then those who were being pursued had a start which often discouraged the trailers, who were forced to drop the newly discovered trail as soon as darkness covered the land and tracks.

Making a Secret Trail

Modern Indians can make secret trails by traveling through woods or forests to a secret camp or meeting place in ones or twos, instead of all together. In this way, so little trail is left that it is most unlikely that it could be followed by a modern tracker of a rival band. Of course, very great care has to be exercised by the chiefs of the makers of the secret trail that nobody gets lost, which is quite an easy thing for novice braves to do in heavily wooded country. Each brave should carry a loud, shrill whistle to sound if and when he runs into difficulties. An even better precaution is for the compass-equipped chiefs to travel, with all caution, by compass toward the goal while the braves travel by twos or threes within sight of their leaders, though still carrying their whistles. After a number of trips over the terrain, en route to the secret encampment, most or all of the warriors should be able, by noting prominent or distinctive landmarks, to know the direction in which to travel. Naturally, the band should have keen-eyed scouts on the lookout for Indians from rival bands who may be spying or following in order to find the location of the secret encampment or camp.

Trackless Travel

Modern Indians should learn to slide their feet through grass, instead of trampling it down, in order to make their trail difficult to follow. They can also lay deceptive trails which are hard to follow, by heading for rocky ground which goes in the general direction in which they wish to travel, traveling on it as far as possible and then radiating from the place where the rocks end so that no heavy trail, left by the massed members of the band, is left to help possible trailers. When the ground of the forest was covered with leaves or the ground was hard and unfavorable for any trackers who might try to follow, small bands of Indians sometimes moved in Indian file, with a wily leader, who knew how to take advantage of every piece of favorable ground, moving at the head of the file.

Another good way to reach secret encampments without leaving a tell-tale trail is for the modern Indians to walk in the bed of a shallow stream, which winds in the general direction toward their goal. Again, scouts of the cautious band are on the lookout for hostiles and signal when the band wading in the stream should take cover under the bank, or on a willow-covered island, until the questing spies have disappeared. At times, the rocky bank above a stream may have to be followed when the banks are too steep to climb, at some points.

Up a Tree

Though Indians sometimes climbed into a leafy tree in an attempt to have those on their trail pass them by, they knew that it was a risky trick. It was generally used as a last resort or close to nightfall by a dog-tired fugitive, who climbed some distance up the tree and, supported by a crotch, clung to the tree trunk so that his body would not be silhouetted against what light was left in the sky and seen by his pursuers, who might look upward when they came to that tree. Concealment in a tree had disadvantages even in the darkness, as it was practically impossible, except in storybooks, for even the most supple and strongest brave to wriggle and swing from tree to tree by means of the branches, without making considerable noise, and even the slightest rustle of leaves was enough to bring lynx-eared pursuers swiftly to the spot.

If the trackers suspected that their quarry was up a tree on which leafy branches were so thick and the foliage so dense that he could not be spotted from the ground, from any angle, they posted a few guards around the foot of the tree while the main body scouted in a widening circle around the tree searching for tracks. When the braves guarding the base of the tree were tired, instead of climbing up into the branches, they usually waited on the ground to hear if leaves, a small, dead branch, a piece of tell-tale bark or nuts would fall from the tree, indicating that their quarry was most likely hidden in the branches overhead. With such encouragement, one or two coup-hunting warriors would climb the trunk and start a search among the branches. This was always a risky task, well meriting a coup, especially if the pursued had an arrow fitted to his bow thong ready to send faint-whistling death from his place of concealment. Sometimes the guards at the foot of the tree lit a smudge fire under a tree in which they believed their prey was hidden. Even the most stoic Indian found it almost impossible to keep from gasping or coughing when the smoke eventually enveloped the tree branches.

Misleading Sounds

The act of throwing a walnut or a short piece of a heavy branch—provided one was loose and handy—from one's hiding place in the tree, in order to attract attention of listening trackers to another tree, is also a ruse born in fiction. It was a risky ruse even when carried out from behind a clump of bushes on the ground and doubly so when executed from a leafy tree, where the chances of the object thrown rebounding from a hidden branch of the tree in which the pursued was hidden was always present. Indians only took chances of this sort when the situation was so desperate that any ruse could do little harm and might do some good.

Bird and Animal Informers

Hiding in the branches of the leafiest tree was often a dangerous business in daylight. Pursuing Indians were quick to note it when a woodpecker or jay suddenly changed its mind about alighting in a certain tree and then went winging off with loud protests about what could only be a two-legged intruder

trespassing on his domain—and they were at the foot of that tree swift as a loon dives. Squirrels, and they were plentiful in the early days, were also ready to greet a stranger in any of their favorite trees with the loud *chir-r-r-r* of anger and alarm which told the wood-wise searchers to take a look up that particular tree.

How Indians Hid

When Indians on foot were surrounded, or their trail was being followed over ground too favorable for the pursuers, who were perhaps mounted, the pursued had an uncanny way of speedily disappearing from sight. Often they vanished like foxes into a clump of natural cover and worked their way out of it unseen, moving as silently as wisps of wind-blown smoke from point to point without leaving a trail. They took advantage of every inch of uneven ground, patch of weeds, or grass on the way out. On the desert or when traveling over sandy ground, with a favorable wind blowing to cover their tracks, when pursuers drew too close, the hunted Indian sometimes scooped a hole in the sand, crouched inside it and then covered himself and the hole with his skin robe or blanket. Quite often, when the pursuers were not too close, this ruse escaped attention, as those who followed could see nothing on the flat expanse of sand which afforded cover.

An Indian sometimes hid from pursuers by lying under water, beneath logs, breathing through a hollow reed, the tip of which barely showed above the surface. At other times Indians swam under a projecting bank until they found a spot where they could come to the surface and still be hidden by the edge of the bank.

The storybook trick of hiding on a moment's notice inside fallen, hollow logs or in hollow, upright trees, was little used by the Indians except in cases of extreme emergency. Not only were there, as a rule, far too many spiders, centipedes, termites, ants, and other stinging things in such hide-outs for even the most stoic Indian, but the trailers regarded such logs and trees as suspicious and rarely passed them by without inspection.

Another well-known, tall-tale ruse tells of turning a well-defined trail into one which cannot be followed by walking backward on the visible tracks, which lead forward, then jumping onto a rocky ridge and disappearing into thin air. The twice-used trail actually hides no secret from a skillful trailer following it. He knows instantly, from even faint indentations, that his quarry has walked backward on that part of the trail because the heel marks, even should the pursued be wearing soft soled moccasins, are more pronounced when one has walked backward than when he has walked forward. Also, strides or steps are shorter when a person walks backward.

Despite the apparent advantages on the side of a clever tracker, following the trail of a person who has good reason to cover his tracks and knows a number of ways of doing so is an extremely difficult job for a good tracker and an impossible task for an unskilled one.

Betrayed by the Sun

The sun has proved the undoing of many secret trails, when the trackers sought its aid and had the skill to use what it revealed. Tracks which are invisible to a tracker with his back to the sun become highly visible when looked at with the sun behind them. The minute marks, when examined by the tracker with the tracks between himself and the sun, become clearly discernible indentations, sometimes sufficiently raised to leave tiny but distinct shadows.

Tracks *can* tell interesting and often dramatic stories but it is only on snow, or the most favorable ground, that other than a truly skilled tracker has the skill to interpret them.

INDIAN TRACKERS

A thorough knowledge of tracks, trails, and trailing was considered a very important part of the education of Indian boys. So well did they listen to their instructors and apply themselves to the task that many of them developed into trackers whose unerring skill seemed to border on the miraculous. The eyes of these trackers saw, and their minds analyzed, everything as they followed a trail. Nothing escaped their keen scrutiny: a minute mark in the dust, a crushed blade of grass, a displaced pebble, pieces of loosened moss or stones, and flattened patches of moss or lichen on rocks, where the one being trailed did not watch quite closely enough where he placed his feet. These trackers would, when on a difficult trail, crouch, peer, ponder, then set off on the trail again at surprising speed.

LANDMARKS AND MIND

Landmarks and good trailing often went hand-in-hand. Carefully noting the position of distinctive landmarks along the trail helped greatly when the trail was lost and the trailer had to cast back in order to try to pick up the trail again. When the trail left was so faint that it was impossible to follow more than in the general direction, a tracker was often reassured that he was on the right trail by noting tracks which indicated that startled animals had left that immediate area in alarm. Birds taking flight suddenly at a point some distance beyond the tracker, in wooded country, was also a sign that someone was on the move, and usually the lost trail was picked up again a little further on.

A skilled trailer, who usually had good powers of deduction, also gained time at various points on the trail followed by figuring where the pursued person would most likely go as he advanced from point to point. Since the quarry, when crossing open country, would try to keep boulders, patches of scrub or occasional trees and bushes between himself and the direction from which he most feared pursuit, the tracker took advantage of such facts and often moved rapidly from point to point on such terrain. He only stopped from time to time to make certain that the tracks of his quarry were visible at times, so that the trailer knew that he was on the right trail.

Tracking is actually a game of wits, and when the tracker can outthink his quarry, he wins.

PALEFACE TRACKERS

Tracking is a skill which does not come naturally to a white man. Fortunately, it can be taught and developed; but even if a modern brave does not become a skillful tracker, he can at least learn how to use his eyes to advantage when in the woods or on a trail. As his powers of observation develop, he will find life in the open more fascinating than ever before and his newly acquired ability to observe will stand him in good stead even when he is in a city.

Tracking and trailing do not mean just the skill to note and follow minute signs on the ground; the real skill in tracking is best described by one word—observation. Another precious part of tracking is the art of *interpreting* what is seen on the trail. This is not an easy part of the work and can be developed only with considerable actual practice and on the basis of trial and error in the early stages. Even on the most favorable tracking terrain, such as virgin snow and smooth, fairly firm sand, it is not always an easy task to interpret the signs found.

Novice on a Tricky Trail

Let us take a look at the difficulties which can confront a novice tracker even on favorable ground.

The tracks of a barefooted person, perhaps a man, are found skirting a sandy shore bordering the sea. Almost covering them in places, then apparently falling far behind, but apparently going in the same direction, are the big tracks of, presumably, another man wearing sneakers or rubber-soled boots.

The amateur tracker asks himself, "Is there any connection between these two sets of tracks? Is the person wearing sneakers *with* the barefooted person, or *following* slowly behind, or chasing him?" This train of thought poses still another question: "Are the tracks made by people who are running or walking?"

Somewhere the amateur tracker has read that the footprints of a person who is running are farther apart than those of one who is walking, and that the toes of a runner leave a deeper indentation than the heels. The fine stretch of smooth sand gives him a good chance to try these means of identification for himself. Yes, he finds that when he runs his tracks look exactly like those pictured in the book. He examines the two sets of footprints with new interest. He finds that the barefoot tracks are far spaced, which seems to indicate that the person was running—but the toes do not dig into the sand as they are supposed to. Why not? The sneaker-track footprints seem to be far enough apart to indicate that they were also made by a person running, yet the toes do not appear to dig into the firm sand and the heels leave only slight drag marks. How about that?

The tracker is determined to get to the bottom of the mystery. He decides to follow the tracks until he catches up with those who made them, and he sets off, on the run, on the trail. After trotting along for about half a mile, he suddenly sees to his surprise that the tracks no longer indicate a couple. Another set of tracks shows that they are now a trio. A little dog has mysteriously joined them! Where did *it* come from? The trailer's eyes scan the sand to the ocean and search the sand dunes in the direction of the woods which border the beach, but without success.

Then tragedy seemed to add itself to mystery. The larger footprints point directly out to sea and the tracks show, this time unmistakably, that the one who made them was running at top speed. The smaller footprints and the paw marks follow the tracks of the runner as far as the line where the breakers crash on the beach; then the dog tracks vanish, but the others continue diagonally and, the tracks plainly show, at full speed along the shore in the direction of the little town which lies some distance ahead. He must be running for help, thinks the novice tracker as he follows the trail on the double.

Now, other footprints begin to crisscross the ones he is following. A board-walk appears on his left, leading to a casino ahead. He realizes that he must hurry or he will lose his quarry, should the latter decide to take one of the narrow boardwalks which will soon lead from the beach to the promenade. They do, and the tracker is foiled—the tracks are hopelessly lost.

His mind conjures up this picture as he speeds toward the town. Two men, who did not know each other, must have been hiking along the beach, one behind the other but at different times, so that the barefoot man did not know that he was being followed. Most likely the second man had been close enough to see the man ahead race toward the line of breakers bordering the angry sea. As the second man pursued the one who seemed intent in ending it all in the seething sea, no doubt he had yelled "Stop! Stop!" but he had been too far behind to catch up and his shouts had gone unheeded. This seems a logical way of interpreting what should have been tell-tale tracks—but the dog? The dog which came from nowhere had apparently vanished in the surf!

Had the frustrated tracker been on the trail an hour earlier, he would have seen what actually happened, and the supposed mystery would have been solved.

A tall young man hiked along the beach with a long, springy stride. He was barefoot and wore a bathing suit. Some distance behind the man his wife ran after him. She was wearing a sport shirt and shorts, and her not-too-dainty feet sported red sneakers. She carried her husband's bathrobe. In front of her capered a little fox terrier. Suddenly it gave a little yelp and held up a paw. Apparently the sand was bothering it, so the woman picked the dog up and carried it. As she gained on her husband she whistled shrilly. He turned and waited for her. Unfortunately, this was about fifty yards before the novice tracker picked up the trail, because after they met they walked briskly along with a swinging, outdoor **stride**, the husband leading the way. The wife, interested in the beach and shells, dropped the dog on the beach, and sometimes walked considerably behind and to one side of her husband. Suddenly, she heard a shout from her husband and saw him sprinting toward the surf. She raced after him but before she could catch up he had reached deep water and was swimming strongly and easily, despite rough water, parallel with the beach. She knew that a strong, favorable current ran close to shore from there to the town. She snatched up the dog and ran swiftly in order to meet her husband as he came ashore close to the casino. The little dog, held firmly by one hand on the runner's shoulder, seemed to enjoy the chase. The wife arrived as her husband was making his way through a group of bathers to join her on one of the boardwalks that led up to the promenade. She handed him his beach robe and they went to have a cup of coffee at a snack bar. From there on, their tracks were lost.

In the circumstances, it is easy to see why the amateur tracker made so many wrong deductions as he "read" the trail. Had he thought to backtrack for 50 yards or so when he decided to follow the trail he would at least have solved the mystery of the dog, because when a dog's trail appears and then disappears, it is easier to guess what has happened to it than when it suddenly materializes, apparently out of nowhere. Yes, tracks can be most misleading!

Tracking

When following tracks, one must never walk on them but alongside, so that the record is there for further reference if needed. Crossing from one side of the trail to the other is sometimes helpful, as indentations may show up better from one side than another, especially if the sun is on one side of the tracks.

Under unfavorable tracking conditions, which include hard ground, a sunless day, a handy stream for the pursued, outcroppings of rock and other baffling aids for one who does not wish his trail to be followed, tracking is a difficult art. Even when the quarry wears tracking irons, which are supposed to leave at least a followable deer trail for the benefit of the trackers, following the trail is no easy business. The trouble usually is that once the trail is lost, it is often too difficult for amateur trailers to circle and pick it up again.

Laying a Trail

The old track-laying standby, a rather heavy log about 2 feet long, with about 12 inches of one end studded with long, protruding nails and the other equipped with a stout rope by which the log is dragged along the ground, lays the trail easiest to follow for amateur trackers. Even the rather obvious track left by this means of marking a trail is not always easy to follow and, unless carefully and thoughtfully used, it can tear up ground which should not be disturbed—or at least a farmer or camp owner may think so.

Tracking Terrain

The best way to teach tracking is to carry out the work on a specially prepared stretch of soft earth, measuring about 30 by 20 feet. This is large enough to offer the necessary scope for beginners in the art of tracking but the ground must be kept well-raked and smooth so that the various kinds of imprints made on it are plainly visible, if not always easy to interpret. It must be constantly remembered that successful tracking is based on careful, painstaking observation and deduction, assuming that the would-be tracker has good eyesight.

The Tracks that Vanished

We have seen how a dog can "disappear" when being trailed by an amateur tracker. Let us look at a case which puzzled experts for a long time.

In the Grand Canyon area of Arizona, explorers, engineers, and trackers were mystified by lizard tracks which disappeared, apparently into thin air. Their footprints were quite apparent in the soft sand where the lizards had climbed up one side of towering sand and clay formations. But, when the tracks reached the top and arrived at the edge on the far side, they vanished. Although nobody had actually seen the lizards climb to the top of the dunes and then, apparently, became air borne, that seemed the only solution to the mystery. Soon the tall tales of the flying lizards spread until one day a young scientist decided to find out what really happened to the lizards when they reached the top of the sandy formations. As the easiest way to do so, he put half a dozen lizards into a light carrying case and set out in the late afternoon for the nearest group of sand formations. After starting the lizards up a steep slope, which was not an easy task, he took up a point of vantage from which he could watch what they did when they arrived at the edge on the far side of the top of the high formation. It was at just such a spot that the lizards were either supposed to take to the air or vanish. After waiting patiently for some time, the scientist was rewarded by the sight of the lizards' reaching the edge on the far side of the narrow plateau, high above the valley. There the mystery was quickly solved. The lizards, having had their full of the plodding climb, simply lay down on their bellies at the edge of the steep slope, tucked their legs backward, so that they would not interfere, and then tobogganed down the steep incline, leaving an almost invisible trail as they sped downward, and one which would quickly be filled with the loose sand blown by even a light breeze.

Animal and Bird Signs

When a brave sets out on the difficult task of trying to track animals or birds, he should choose an easy starting point. This may be along the banks of a river or a stream with a sandy or muddy shore line, or the edge of a lake or pond, where tracks of any sort are more easily visible. A small pool or depression half filled with water, where animals like to wallow, may provide a clue to the whereabouts of animals, as may scratch marks on a tree or a little tuft of animal hair caught under a piece of rough bark. A knowledge of what sort of tracks the different animals in that part of the country make is essential to a tracker.

Snake Signs

A snake's trail is a hard one to follow, though it does leave a trail which can, most of the time, be followed by a good tracker. The direction in which the grass leans or in which fine sand or dust is flattened shows where the reptile is heading. It is interesting to be able to judge the girth of a snake when its tracks are found on favorable ground. One way to establish this is to measure the width of its tracks at three points and divide the result by three, or measure at four points and divide by four. Now multiply the result by three, in the first case, and four in the second case, and you will have the approximate circumference of the snake. Naturally, the width of the track will vary somewhat according to the terrain on which the measurements are made—whether there is deep, soft sand, or the firmer sand of a lake shore, for instance.

In some countries, Africa and India, for example, it is not difficult to tell by the tracks whether the snake is poisonous or harmless. There, a venomous snake wriggles over the ground in a series of curves, while the non-venomous snakes move forward in a much straighter line. A good example of this, in the United States, is to compare the tracks of a blacksnake with those of a sidewinder.

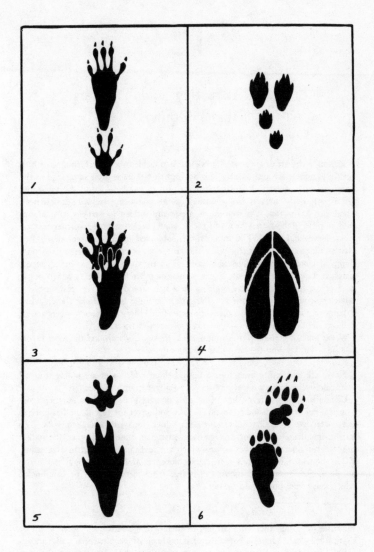

The above tracks are imprints made by:

1 Grey Squirrel   2 Cottontail Rabbit
3 Raccoon   4 Whitetailed Deer
5 Muskrat   6 Skunk

12

Stalking, Attracting, and Watching
the Wildthings

Stalking is the art of approaching as close as possible to a person, animal, or bird stealthily, noiselessly and unseen. It is obvious that there is little advantage in the ability to move quietly if a brusque movement of the head, hand, or any other part of the body attracts the attention of the one being stalked. Experienced woodsmen know that it is movement, especially sudden movement, that alarms wild animals. Stalking is a heel and toe business, heel first on grass, toes first on rocks, leaves and twigs. The toes, clad in soft-soled moccasins, served the Red Men as additional eyes. Often, while the keen eyes of an Indian were fixed on a clump of cover ahead which could conceal an enemy, his toes, as he advanced, searched the ground for twigs, leaves, stones, or other loose objects which might snap, crack, roll, or make any slight noise which would betray his presence.

Background into which one's clothing blends should be carefully chosen when stalking or hiding. There are many times in field, forest or woods when a wise stalker fears his own shadow—it betrays so much at times.

Never look *over* the top of a stump, rock, or log. Look *around* the most favorable side of it, keeping the head close to the ground.

Keep head and body close to the earth when moving over rising ground.

Never pull the entire branch of a bush, behind which you are hiding, toward you: cautiously displace a leaf or two with a finger in order to see out.

Camouflage such as ferns, leafy branches, or long grasses can be fastened from a neutral-colored headband to shield the face and cover the top of the head, when one is stalking or hiding on terrain with which such camouflage merges. Too much camouflage of this sort may prove worse than none at all when the stalker festoons too liberally or uses colors which are revealing rather than concealing.

The best stalking dress is soft, dark-colored clothing which will not brush noisily against bushes and rocks, and is free from metal buttons or belt buckle which can shine, jingle, and betray.

WARY WOODCHUCKS

Farmers consider these animals one of their worst enemies and shoot them on sight, if they can! Hunters know that ground hogs are very hard to stalk successfully. Their dens are usually found on sunny, grassy hillsides and sometimes on rock-strewn slopes. Occasionally, they may be taken off guard some distance from their burrows, but they are seldom far enough from their holes to be unable to reach them in safety before the fleetest brave can outrun them. Top strategy, cover when available, patience and considerable stalking skill are required to cut a "whistle pig" off from his burrow. Braves who succeed in doing so certainly merit claiming coup. Few warriors will be able to withstand the strangely swift charge of the 'chuck as he comes full-tilt, grunting, whistling, and challenging toward his burrow to hole up!

PAINTED TURTLES

Though most turtles like to bask or just sit on logs, the painted species offers the greatest stalking challenge. They are surprisingly sensitive to vibrations, observant, and quick to slide or plunge from the log when they sense danger, which is often even before they see or hear it. Chiefs who know the location of "turtle logs" in lakes or streams can have their braves spread out and, only two or three at a time, try to get as close to one or more turtles on a log as possible without alarming them.

Indians knew that if the backs of the turtles on a log were dry, nothing had passed close enough to alarm them for some time. A modern chief can estimate that they have been out of the water for at least twenty minutes, unless the sun is unusually hot. On sunless days, dry backs will mean that the turtles have been out of the water for a considerably longer period. Chiefs have every reason to wish their braves "Good stalking!" when they take the turtle trail.

BIRD STALK

A good stalking test for a brave is to try to approach one of the larger species of birds as closely as possible without alarming it. A great blue heron, goose, egret, duck, or bittern—if this near-invisible bird can be spotted in the first place. Stealth is a prime requisite for a close stalk, but occasionally a seasoned brave will catch them off guard. Two such times are: when they are preoccupied with feeding or when they are attending to their toilet. Most birds are unbelievably meticulous about their toilet, which is, perhaps, why the beautiful great blue heron carries a special comb on his foot for his lovely plumage. Most birds spend more than half of their waking hours preening and oiling their feathers. Perfect feathers assure perfect flight. When sun bathing, birds are also easier to stalk than when they are not, and the same applies to birds taking dust baths.

DEER STALK

Chiefs and older braves who are fortunate enough to camp in deer country and ambitious enough to try to stalk these alert animals should know that when deer enter a thicket or brush clump to rest, they face their back trail. The best way to approach really close to deer is to make a wide circle and enter the thicket from the rear or a little to one side of the deer, watching wind direction during a cautious advance. Sometimes the tired deer will circle immediately after entering the covert but usually they end up facing the direction from which they came.

WHERE?

When a brave is stalking a bird or beast on the edge of a grassy area, wood, or thicket and the creature suddenly disappears into the cover, he should walk quietly, quickly, and directly to the spot where the quarry appeared to enter the covert and drop some piece of bright-colored cloth, or a handkerchief, at that spot as a marker. With this point as the center of his search the brave has much more chance to come upon the bird or beast which is taking cover in the grass or bushes. Without a marker, it is surprising how far one can wander from the search center without knowing it.

SNAKE STALKING

Stalking these vibration-conscious reptiles offers a very real challenge. Even to stalk them visually from a distance, when the terrain is favorable, is a difficult feat. The moment a brave takes his eyes off the snake it appears to vanish.

STALKING POSITIONS

There are three principal positions for advancing in daylight when stalking.

An *upright*, half-crouching position is a speedy way to advance when distance or some handy cover helps to screen the movement.

Crawling, which is not creeping, is a slow and rather tiring method of progressing but proves useful when approaching a person or animal on the lookout. To advance by crawling, lie flat on the ground, put your hands on the ground about eight inches in front of your head, with both elbows down but spread outward. Push your body forward with either leg, keeping your heels as flat as possible and, above all, with hindquarters as much in line with the waist as possible. Stomach and chest must be on the ground throughout these movements. When some cover is available, progression is faster when the forearms support part of the body weight.

Creeping is a hard and irksome way of moving forward, but less tiring than the crawling position. It can only be used when low cover is available, such as when advancing along a shallow ditch, low wall, or tree trunks. The body rests on the lower legs, elbows, and forearms. With chest and stomach just off the ground, the body is forced forward by pulling with alternate arms, aided by slight pushes with the knees when they are in a position to help. A knee must never come directly under or ahead of the hindquarters, as this raises the hips into a very visible position. Muscles for crawling and creeping can only be developed by practice, and it takes a good deal of that before one can cover distances greater than 50 yards without becoming tired.

The *Bear Crawl*, used to advantage at night, is a quieter and somewhat more comfortable position for covering ground than the two preceding methods. The cover of night is helpful in concealing figure and movement and progression is much more silent than in crawling and creeping. This advance is made on hands and knees with alternate hands feeling ahead and clearing a spot free from twigs, leaves, or anything else that may rustle, hurt, or betray the stalker. When one hand has cleared a place, the knee on that side moves forward and is placed in position, and the other hand and knee are advanced, ready for further forward movement.

The *Prone Crawl* is a very hard, though useful, stalking position. It is sometimes called the *Belly Crawl* and is only used for an approach of not more than 40 yards or so. The body is prone on the ground with its weight supported on the elbows and toes. The body is lifted on elbows and toes and is pulled and pushed forward, without letting the stomach or chest drag on the ground. At the end of each elbow-pull and toe-push, the body will automatically be lowered so that the advancing movement can be repeated.

There is considerable difference between stalking in daylight and practicing the same skill at night. The cover of darkness offers advantages and disadvantages to the stalker. These points are dealt with in Chapter 13.

ANIMAL STALKERS

Instinct, perhaps aided by heredity and evolution, helps the polar bear as he silently stalks, on his hairy-soled feet, the seals of the snowclad wastes of his bleak habitat. When he sees that the seals begin to show signs of restlessness, because of his nearness, he continues his noiseless advance, keeping his dark eyes turned to the ground and, when he pauses for a moment, covering his black nose with a paw. At such times he is nearly invisible because of his protective coloring.

The varying hare, better known as the snowshoe rabbit, displays none of the polar bear's intelligence nor instinct. Believing, perhaps, that he is next to invisible, in his winter coat, this rabbit sits motionless in the snow, often allowing one to approach within a foot or two of him, not realizing that his dark eyes, which are highly visible, betray him.

Among the most skillful animal stalkers of North America are the big carnivora of the cat family, cougar, lynx, and wildcat. Not only do natural stealth, silence of movement, and cunning aid these animals as they stalk their unsuspecting prey, but the manner in which they take advantage of every possible bit of cover as they approach contributes greatly to their success as hunters. It will be seen that successful animal stalkers use very much the same technique as those used by coup-worthy braves who excel in the same exciting craft.

DON'TS FOR STALKERS

Braves on a stalk have some handicaps to contend with that animal stalkers do not have. Here are two of the worst and how to overcome them, with luck.

Don't Sneeze

This may seem easier to say than do—but it isn't. To stop a sneeze, when it is on its way, press the side of your forefinger against the point where nose and upper lip meet and press fairly hard, with an upward movement. While this pointer will not prove effective if you don't catch the need to sneeze in time, this little gesture has saved so many lives that it is well worth trying.

Don't Cough

To stop a casual cough, press lightly against your Adam's apple with thumb and forefinger, applying a slight pinching pressure. You may have to try this a few times to find out how much pressure is required, as too much may increase, rather than stop, coughing.

WAYS OF ATTRACTING BIRDS AND ANIMALS

To attract birds and animals by imitating their calls or whistles takes a certain skill which can only be developed by considerable practice. Many birds and animals are equipped by the Creator to make strange sounds and calls which signal their presence. For a human being, the difficulty of reproducing these sounds makes it wise to commence with the easiest imitations, those made almost entirely with lips and breath, after which imitative sounds made by voice can be attempted.

Calls of the wild which have to be imitated by using the palate and vocal cords are far more difficult to perfect. Though some birds and animals appear to respond to some ill-made calls of this sort, which the optimistic if inexperienced caller thinks are fairly close to the real thing, experienced outdoorsmen are of the opinion that the animals' or birds' interests are aroused by sheer curiosity and perhaps the desire to see anyone or anything capable of producing such strange sounds.

Bird Calls and Whistles

An expert caller knows that intonation, grouping, and phrasing have to be just right to really deceive animals or birds and attract and lure them. A barred owl, for instance, knows that the mimicry of an owl is not an owl of his own species unless emphasis is placed on the last, drawn-out *whoo* of each group of four. The amateur caller who hopes to lure the blue goose, or snow or wavey goose with the well-imitated *Ker honk! Ker honk!* of a Canada goose will be disappointed. The call notes of the geese he hoped to attract are loud, resonant, and musical ones of three syllables—*Kouk! Kouk! Kouk!*, quite unlike the two-syllable honking of the larger Canada goose. Crows, and many other birds, have a set series of distinct, meaningful calls, as one will discover if he gives the crow alarm call instead of the four distinct notes of the rally call when he is trying to stalk within rifle range!

Here are a few of the bird calls which are fairly easy to imitate well. The two noted whistle of the bob white—*bob-white, bob-white*, is easy to copy but it must be noted that the first note of each two notes is rather long and without pause, while the second note is staccato and accented. The whistled *teacher-teacher-teacher* comes rather easily. A kitten-like mew may attract a catbird but it should be remembered that the catbird is a magnificent mimic which can give dozens of entirely different calls.

It should be borne in mind when searching for the right words to help memorize a bird whistle or call that almost no two listeners will write down the same words or syllables for the call heard. Some bird watchers hear the blue jay shrill *jay! jay!, or jay! jay! jay!*, while others declare that the bird called *thief! thief!* With this in mind, the would-be bird caller should establish his own interpretation of bird calls, recording as exactly as possible just what the bird said to his ears and how the call was spaced and accented.

The call of the kildeer is easy to mimic. *Kill-dee kill-dee* are the notes usually heard because they are the alarm notes given as the bird flies away when someone comes too close to him. Around the breeding ground his calls are a series of gentle trills. The prettily marked chickadee is named for his best known call—*chick-a-dee-dee chick-a-dee-dee-dee*, though he also has a number of plaintive, soft, single and double notes, such as *phee* and *dee-dee*, in his repertoire. The sedately clad phoebe is another of a number of birds which name themselves. This little bird is most easily identified by its call—which is true of many birds, though they may remain unseen—and a second means of identification is its strange ability to flick its tail up and down as well as sideways. Its sweet, soft-whistled call of *phee-be phee-be* adds music to wild areas and the banks of streams.

The vibratory whistles of some birds can most easily be mimicked by the combined use of tongue and lips. This produces a fluttery whistle, such as the *cheerily cheerily* of a robin.

Animal Calls

Animal calls are much more difficult to imitate accurately, especially when made by voice. A number of calls require some mechanical aid, such as the birch-bark horn for calling moose and a horn used by some Indians for attracting elk, the call of which sounds like a musical, bugle note and, in the far distance, has an almost birdlike quality. The high, wailing note of a wolf is also a difficult one to mimic really well and it can be done more easily and realistically by forcing the head back while making the howl.

A number of animals such as deer, marmot, and woodchuck, whistle, especially when startled, while the bustling little cony of the Rocky Mountains and other habitats is so very curious that a sudden, soft whistle will nearly always bring him out for a look or freeze him in his tracks as he scampers along, usually with a wisp of grass in his mouth. A shrill, single whistle will often cause a woodchuck or marmot to sit up at the mouth of its burrow, or even when further afield.

Curiosity Calls

The curiosity of practically all living things often allows animals to be lured into showing themselves by their desire to know what is going on. Here are some ways of playing on the inquisitive streak in wildthings.

Rapping with a hardwood stick on the trunk of a den tree will often bring a squirrel, a sleepy-eyed owl, or other birds, or even a raccoon, to one of the doors or windows to see if someone "so unkindly knocked, or no."

Tapping gently on the gunwale of a canoe with a stick or paddle will frequently cause a beaver or otter to surface for a moment or two to see what caused the noise.

Tapping two pebbles lightly together will attract chipmunks, squirrels, and often rabbits.

The author brought a big black bear, getting ready to den up for the winter, out of a cave by rapping on the rock outside with the handle of an ax. Since that time, he does not recommend trying a bear's curiosity in this way!

Squeaking and Clucking

A wide blade of grass held and kept tightly stretched between the two thumbs, as illustrated, with the edge of the grass to the front, can be made to squeak enticingly when the lips are placed so that they touch both thumbs and a sharp current of air is blown through the hollow space between the thumbs. This simple squeaker will stop chipmunks, squirrels, and other animals in their tracks, excite curiosity in birds, and often cause heads to be poked out of trees.

Making a sucking noise with the lips on the back of the hand also incites interest among a number of smaller animals and a clucking noise, made with the lips, is usually equally successful.

Mechanical Decoys

In recent years, a number of fairly effective decoys for attracting animals and birds have appeared on the market. Bird whistles and duck and geese calls, which used to be standard lures, have been added to, and new sound makers and horns have been devised which are said to attract almost any wildthing from deer and wolves to fish. A fair number of these decoys do work very well, but most of them require a considerable amount of practice before they really intrigue the animals they are meant to attract.

WHEN, HOW AND WHERE TO OBSERVE THE FURRED AND FEATHERED THINGS

Several things besides patience are required by the watcher who wishes to observe the birds and animals in their natural haunts. Most birds and animals live secretly, now that they are hunted so ruthlessly. Nowadays one is forced to write in generalities when suggesting the best hours to watch for the different species of animals. Many of the animals which one wishes to observe are most active around dawn and dusk and throughout the night. Despite this, the habits of animals are more or less based on the habitats in which they are found and are often decided by the amount of movement in and the safety of such areas. Raccoon, skunk, opossum, beaver, porcupine, and muskrat—which may rightly be classed as nocturnal animals—are often to be found feeding, playing, or resting in daylight hours in national parks.

Often when canoeing on the Bow River and adjoining streams in Alberta, Canada, in the late afternoon or late in the morning, the author has had to stop paddling to allow two or more log-propelling beavers to cross just in front of the bow of his canoe; and many of the so-called nocturnal animals are to be seen in broad daylight in the Canadian national parks. Almost complete protection in these habitats causes the animal inhabitants to become fearless.

In forested or wooded areas around camps for young folk, a number of animals will be found on the prowl in daylight, provided they are not illegally hunted or chased by dogs in these sections. The birds and beasts which the modern Indians see will be decided by the location of their encampment.

Observing birds and beasts successfully often means early rising but, provided some are likely to be seen, it is well worthwhile. Around 4:30 A.M., where daylight-saving time is observed, is a good time either to set out along a country path or trail or to be concealed in a favorable position overlooking an area where animals either cross or come out into an open stretch in the early morning hours. All observing is better done with the sun behind one's back. With the sun in that position, one can see the coloring and markings of the various birds and beasts instead of seeing them as dark shadows. Groups of four or five watchers make a good number for such activities and larger parties should be grouped in this way and travel with a chief in charge of each band. The sky as well as the ground bushes and tree tops should be scanned frequently, as birds and animals so frequently sit or move in such screened and stealthy ways, and are so aided by their protective coloring, that the first thing seen by the would-be observer is the sudden flight of the bird or animal he had hoped to watch.

There are two ways of trying to observe sitting birds. The first is to "freeze" the moment one sees the bird sought and try to focus a field glass on it, without any jerky movements of hands, head, or arms. The second method applies especially to observers who have no field glasses and when the bird is spotted at fairly long range. The thing to do then is to stroll slowly in the general direction of the bird or birds, as in this way one has a better chance of getting a close-up view than if he lost time in trying a stealthy stalk, the success of which cannot be assured in advance. Needless whispering or low-voiced talk should be avoided unless in case of sheer necessity. Even though most birds hear such sounds rather poorly, there is always the possibility that some keen-eared animal, up wind, can hear the observers before he sees or smells them and give the alarm. As though to make up for their hearing handicaps, birds usually have much keener eyes than most animals. Eagles and hawks are armed with the keenest eyes in the world.

Dawn and Dusk Animal Observation. Both dawn and dusk are excellent times for observing animals, as animals of both day and night may be found roaming around at those mystic moments. The daylight wildthings are thinking about their homes and bed, in burrows, banks, and den trees, while the wildthings of the night are abroad, ready to start prowling in the coming darkness.

Daylight Wildlife. The following animals are daylight prowlers, though a few of them may also be found on the move at night: moose, deer of various species, bear, fox of various species, marmot, fisher, otter, marten, catamount, mink, weasel, muskrat, porcupine, woodchuck, rabbit, chipmunk, squirrel, and other animals, according to habitat.

Night Wildlife. Under cover of darkness, wildcat, lynx, catamount, beaver, raccoon, opossum, flying squirrel, skunk, porcupine, and deer like to roam. Among the smaller creatures, rat, shrew, and the white-footed mouse are often on the prowl.

These partial lists give some idea of what to expect when adventuring in wildwood and forest at varying hours. It should be remembered that some animals, of different species, do not remain true to type in their habits. Nocturnal animals may decide to take a stroll in daylight and animals that one expects to find only during daylight hours are seized with a sudden impulse for exploration in darkness. Such unpredictable impulses make animal observation a constant source of wonder for modern Indians, and even for experienced woodsmen whose lives are lived off the beaten track.

"FRINGE" HABITATS

The novice outdoorsman usually believes that if he wishes to flush many birds and beasts he only requires to get deep into a wood, forest, field, or marsh to do so. The experienced woodsman knows that exactly the opposite is the case. One can flush from six to ten times more game from the fringes of fields, woodlots, forest, woodland, hedgerows, brushpiles, the banks of ditches, and thickets. Though much-hunted animals may be forced to take refuge deep in a wood or forest at times, their more natural habitat is, for example, the border of woodland next to a field of corn, wheat, or other grain. The fringe of any cropland often offers sufficient cover from hunters, especially inexperienced ones, and such cover is close to something good to eat.

Little patches of trees, marsh, and scrub in flat, grassy country also house a surprising number of wildthings. Of course they will lie low, very low in some cases, almost letting you step on them before making a break from their hideouts. Waterfowl will rise from very small ponds and patches of marsh, proportionately many more than may be found around one big pond or lake. It is good to note that both wildfowl and mammal wildlife often take over one end of a lake or pond for their habitat and practically shun the rest of the lake or pond.

Ferns and bracken offer wonderful hiding places for many wildthings, both furred and feathered. The light that filters through the feathery fronds is most deceptive. The shadows cast often help to conceal a crouching fawn or a family of quail chicks from their enemies.

In Chapter 14 some simple suggestions are given for developing "living edges" for wildlife.

Modern Indians should keep in mind the fact that many animals and birds do not change their fixed habitats greatly unless driven to do so by some very good reason, such as fire, exhausted food supply, predators moving in, or being bothered too often by guns, slings, sticks, or stones. A rabbit will generally run in almost a circle, when flushed, as too many wood-wise hunters know for the cottontails' good. The rabbit's simple tactic is carried out for the very good reason that he does not wish to get too far away from the terrain which he knows best and which offers the best chance of survival because of that habitat knowledge.

RENDEZVOUS WITH FURRED AND FEATHERED FRIENDS

Such rendezvous are not easily arranged because of the fact that nearly all animals and birds live secretly. Because of this secrecy one must learn to move like a real Indian. The slightest noise, any quick movement which triggers wood-land folk into instant flight or makes them take cover with unbelievable speed, must be avoided. One must be prepared to "freeze" instantly as soon as the lift of a head or the impatient switch of a tail warns that the wildthing under observation senses that it is being watched. A modern Indian is less likely to be spotted if he stands beside a tree trunk, or looks around the side of a stump. Infinite patience must be developed while waiting or watching. The Forest Folk are far more likely to watch you, without being seen, than you are to even catch a glimpse of them. Animals found in field areas usually move along low walls and fences and keep close to patches of natural cover. Forest animals, when suspicious or alarmed, usually move alongside fallen trees, logs, brushpiles and shelter behind such cover, and the trunks of standing trees.

Beaver, muskrat, raccoon, and water rats will generally keep close to the overhanging banks of lakes and waterways. Look for the tracks and worn trails of these animals and you are fairly certain to find these trails leading down to the water's edge, where the trails made by field and forest animals as they seek the edge of stream or lake to drink will also be found.

FLUSHING WILDLIFE

An effective way of flushing birds and animals from a field or marshland firm enough to offer sure footing is for two modern Indians to drag a strong cord or thin rope, 60 to 80 feet long, between them over grassy or reedy terrain, so that as much as possible of the rope drags along the ground. It is flipped over low stumps or bushes by the hunter at each end of the rope. Sometimes this drag proves more successful when a rounded piece of hardwood is fastened to the middle of the cord.

FISH WATCHING

Fish may best be watched from the cover of clumps of willows or other trees along the bank of a stream or pool. They are more easily seen when one has the sun behind him but care must be taken to avoid letting any shadow fall on the water or, especially in the case of trout or other game fish, letting vibrations from the bank reach the sensitive fish. Fish face upstream when feeding or idling, so that they are headed into the current. When stalking fish in the water, one must take care to approach them slowly and cautiously from behind. The feet should be slid gently along the bottom to avoid splashing.

CATCHING ANIMALS AND BIRDS
OFF GUARD

One of the easiest ways to approach animals or birds is from behind the sort of shield used by Indian hunters in the arctic for approaching seals and other animals unobserved. All that is required to make the screen is two sticks, about 3 feet 6 inches long and around ¾ inch in diameter, placed one on top of the other in the form of an X held together with a diagonal lashing and lashed onto a lightweight, near-triangular frame, as illustrated. This frame is covered with heavy unbleached muslin or strong cotton, dyed olive-green or a buff color, based on the general color of the countryside where the stalking is being done. While all animals are said to be color blind, and it has been proved that a great number are, they are keenly sensitive to degrees of color intensity. Any light-colored object moving against a dark background, for instance, will almost instantly spook animals into flight. A slit 2 or 3 inches long by about ¾ inch in width, or a peephole, should be cut in the screen at the point found most convenient for observation when in a lying or crouching position. Some of the Eskimo hunters both observe and shoot the seals from around one side of the shield while others watch and shoot through the slit.

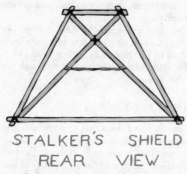

STALKER'S SHIELD
REAR VIEW

Another effective way to observe animals when they are off guard is to do so from a height of at least 15 feet. Strangely enough, few animals look upward for danger though they will look on either side and back along their trail frequently for possible enemies. With the wind in a favorable quarter for the watcher, that is, blowing toward him from the direction in which the animal approaches, a deer will often pass under a tree in which an observer is sitting without camouflage on a lower branch, because a deer rarely looks upward as it moves along.

The platform of a water tower, the roof of a shed or house, or the safe branch of a tree with a view, make good observation points.

Braves seated on a hillside and looking down into a valley will frequently be able to watch the movements of unsuspecting animals which leisurely pursue their ways of life, ignorant of the fact that keen eyes are watching them.

PORTABLE OBSERVATION BLINDS

One of the easiest and most effective ways to observe both birds and animals is from the concealment of a blind. The drawing shows a very good blind which is not only light in weight but which can easily be set up. Light bamboo rods are ideal for this type of blind but any straight, light sticks can be used. This blind can be made any width and height by simply using longer or shorter rods for the framework. The round top-piece, into which the top ends of the rods are thrust, can be made from a piece of pine about a foot in diameter and 2 inches thick. The bottom rod of the blind, which holds the upright rods in place, is made of a long, springy stick. Either the feet of the upright rods are tied to it or each one is slipped through a string loop before the end is pushed a short distance into the ground. From 8 to 10 upright rods will make a good blind frame. The cloth cover for the blind is made of strong, unbleached muslin or similar material, dyed to blend with the background. Forest green or olive green is suitable for a blind set up in woodland or forest. The door of the blind is formed by a vertical slit about 3 feet long, the ends of which overlap at the foot of the blind as illustrated. Slits are cut on four sides of the blind for observation and photography, the apertures being cut in the cloth where no upright rods obstruct the view.

A blind of the sort described may be set over a shallow circular pit about 2 feet deep, and the ends of the upright rods are forced into the ground either just outside of, or inside, the pit. Less cloth is used in making this blind and, of course, the roof is lower.

A circular blind, quite similar to the ones described, can easily be made by using an old beach or garden umbrella, with the end of the pole driven securely into the ground. This forms the roof of the blind and the side screen is made by sewing the cloth onto the edge of the umbrella. The door and peepholes are cut in the side curtain, as in the other blinds described.

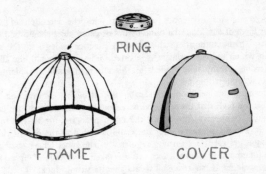

RING

FRAME   COVER

ANIMAL OBSERVATION CIRCLES

Such circles are easy to make and help greatly in the study of naturecraft. In a remote part of the woodland or forest of an encampment, mark a circle about 30 feet in diameter and cover it with sand or a mixture of earth and sand when sand is scarce. Moisten the ground within the circle in the evening, rake it smooth and leave some tidbits for the animals known to be in the vicinity, in the middle of the circle before darkness sets in. Next morning early, just after dawn, before the sun has had time to dry up the dew which makes all spoor doubly visible, visit the circle. Examine the ground carefully to see which tracks are visible and try to identify the animals or birds which have made them. The strange sets of pairs of tiny twin paw marks are surely those of a weasel, whose rear feet fit into the prints left by the forefeet.

These observation circles should be located close to trees, or an old shed with a solid roof, if possible, from which night observation, with fixed flashlights or a spotlight, can be carried out later on when the nocturnal visitors have become accustomed to the tasty handouts provided by the keeper of the circle.

Night Illumination

A number of animals, such as skunks and raccoons, which are attracted to an observation circle will feast there at night under the beam of a 200-watt electric light bulb, suspended from a tree branch, without showing either fear or discomfort because of the illumination. Even the addition of a metal reflector which throws the light directly downward from the bulb does not appear to bother these and other animals. It is best to turn on the lights as soon as food has been placed in the observation circle and the watchers have taken cover, but quite often the wildthings show no alarm when the area in which they are feeding is suddenly flooded with light after they have started their snack.

An observation spot can also be laid out in the form of a half circle on the bank of a stream or lake. Sometimes a place covered with fine sand is conveniently located, sometimes even under an overhanging bank from which observation will be easy and rewarding, provided a good spot is chosen for the baited area.

Warning!

Before setting out any foods whatsoever with the intention of attracting animals or birds of any kind, the camp owner or camp chief should find out from the fish and game authorities whether such practice is legal in the state and locality in which the encampment is situated. The chief should also discourage regular feeding of any wild animals as this mistaken kindness undermines animals' natural food-getting instincts.

The encampment chief should also forbid the setting out of any food for wild-things when he feels that the situation may be taken advantage of by unscrupulous "hunters" who may sneak onto the camp property for an easy off-season shoot, or invade the property after the camp is closed at the end of the season. Animals soon get used to returning regularly to the spots where tasty handouts are to be found and it is such habits that are taken advantage of by poor sports, who, masquerading as "sportsmen," would shoot a sitting duck.

Food Lures

When a state permits the use of food lures to attract animals to certain spots, as an aid to nature study, the following foods may be set out at the place where a watching post or an observation circle has been established:

Animals	Tidbits
Raccoon Opossum Skunk	Pieces of bread spread with fish oil of some kind Honey-covered raw vegetables, fish (canned salmon, canned sardines, dried salted herring), crisp bacon or meat fats, hard-boiled eggs
Rabbit	Cabbage, sweet potatoes, lettuce, Brussels sprouts
Woodchuck	Sweet potatoes, carrots, lettuce, peas, sweet corn, fresh string beans, corn cob
Muskrat	Sweet apples, parsnips, carrots
Weasel Mink	Fish, fresh liver, chicken entrails, chicken heads, fish oil scents
Squirrel Chipmunk	Cereals, breakfast foods, various grains, sunflower seeds, cookies, unroasted peanuts, salted potato chips, uncooked oatmeal mixed with peanut butter
Rat Mouse	Cheese spread on bread, sunflower seeds, crisp bacon or meat fat, oatmeal mixed with peanut butter, potato chips, peanut butter liberally spread on cookies or bread, grains of corn
Snake	Small eggs, raw and whole
Snapping turtle	Tainted raw meat or liver

A good all-around decoy mixture—chiefly for all rodents, though it frequently attracts other animals—is made from the following ingredients: cooked or raw bacon, cut into small pieces; raisins, whole or chopped; and oily peanut butter, all blended in rolled oats so that it is like rather soft clay. This mixture will keep for months in an airtight jar or can.

Rolled oats forms a part of almost all standard bait mixtures for rodents.

13

Using Eyes and Ears in the Night

It is a pity that the average modern man has allowed himself to become almost a complete prisoner of darkness. The night has so much beauty and there are so many fascinating things to be heard, smelt and seen, when one has developed his night eyes, sense of hearing, and smell, that all of these woodsman's senses are well worth training and cultivating.

PITCH BLACK NIGHT?

Though one often hears of a night "black as the pit," such a night is exceedingly rare. There is always a glow from left-over twilight, during the summer months. From the stars and a waning or growing moon one also gets a low, luminous light when one has developed night eyes. This can be tested in a darkened cabin on a dark night. Look toward the window and a dim light will be seen showing through. This light is brightness itself to nature's children of the wild, blessed with eyes that see in the night. Another test of the luminosity of even a very dark night is to have a companion walk past you at varying distances while you lie flat on the ground. His silhouette will dispel the idea of "pitch darkness."

It may seem strange to read of "getting one's night eyes." It sounds somewhat like one getting his sea legs. Yet the actual process, apart from anatomical difference, is very much the same. Both have to be developed by experience and practice. Indians had eyes which were well adapted to the darkness. When his eyes have become used to darkness, any modern Indian with normal vision can see the flame of a single match at a distance of several miles on a dark night. This sounds like a catch, but it isn't, because nature takes over in such situations. The pupil of the eye becomes larger and the retina adjusts itself to the point where the eyesight of a modern Indian is nearly as good as that of a white-footed mouse, an owl, and other night roamers. When one realizes this, he loses his fear of being overwhelmed by darkness and is eager to begin adventuring in a new world, the world of night.

In addition to the fear of not being able to find one's way in the darkness, there is man's fear, which was old when the sabre-toothed cat was young, the fear of the dark. This sort of fear has come down through the ages and still lurks in the back of the minds of many a modern Indian. Fear of this sort is often more potent than mere words and is best expelled from a young mind by showing that there is nothing to be feared in the darkest night except man's own city-bred inability to meet its challenge. One "showing" method is for the night-fearful member of a band to be left with a few other members of the band while a chief, or some senior night-seasoned member of the group goes off into the darkness alone and as nonchalantly as a real Indian. This invader of night indicates his position in the distance by imitating night calls of the forest, or by whistle signals, from time to time. Upon his return he tells the others, including the novice, that it is a perfect night, just the sort of night dear to the hearts of Indians when they were engaged on a raid or surprise attack. He points out that once the eyes have been trained to serve in the darkness *nothing* remains to be feared. There are strange animal noises and some startling night bird calls, of course, but apart from that there is nothing to startle or menace the adventurers in darkness. The fearful one may not believe all of this in a night or two but after he has gone out on night expeditions with only a night-wise brave as his companion, gradually the fear of darkness will die and he who has lost it will be encouraged to further daring and allowed to count coup in celebration of his very real conquest. The surest way to *increase* a novice brave's fear of darkness is to abandon him, even for a few minutes, on one of his first few adventures into the darkness. An alert chief realizes that such tactics are as unwise as trying to teach a water-fearing non-swimmer to swim by throwing him into deep water.

NIGHT TRAINING

To run out into the night from a lighted room or to start, with or without training, to play *Will-o'-the-Wisp* or any similar so-called "night game" is the height of folly. Most night games which require speed, especially in wooded country or where trees, fences, stumps or other obstacles are dotted over the field, never graduate from the dangerous class and modern chiefs will do well to remember this.

Training in developing night eyes is best done by taking a small flashlight-equipped group outdoors after spending at least half an hour in darkness indoors.

It should be a reasonably dark night and the braves should remain without much motion, close to the chief, until their eyes become accustomed to the darkness. Eyes become used to the dark as the rods within them fill up with a sort of mauve dye. When these rods are "charged" the eyes will see rather dimly at first, but never in color. That is not the rods' business. It is the function of the cones for daylight vision to provide color vision. The author, when first showing films to natives in Africa, was astonished to find that even the most primitive natives of the African jungle knew the difference between night and daylight sight. When shown a black and white film they would say that it was "taken at night" but when a color film was shown they remarked that the pictures were "taken in the sunlight."

Here are a number of ways in which one can see more easily in the dark when normal observation fails.

Angle Vision

If you look a little to one side of an object of which you have lost sight in dim light you can see it more clearly than if you look directly at where you believe it is. This involves the tiny rods in the eyes which help to assure night vision. This army trick will help you to see more plainly in the circumstances given. Practicing it will help to develop the rods in your eyes in the same way that push-up exercises help to stimulate the muscles in your arms.

Owl Eye Vision

Night vision can be increased by cupping a hand around each eye, with thumbs touching the nose. This position increases your ability to focus clearly on the area which you are scanning, as it controls the area of vision.

Blur

Eyes can become blurred from peering for too long a time into the darkness. The best way to bring back normal night vision is to close the eyes slowly, keep them shut for several seconds, then open them slowly. One can also blink the eyes five or six times after closing them for the duration of twenty counts. If they are still even slightly blurred, try focusing the eyes on objects situated at different positions until the eyes are normal again.

Vitamin A for Night Vision

Airmen have discovered that certain foods—those containing Vitamin A—were helpful in promoting night vision. Such foods include milk, green vegetables, carrots, eggs, fish oils, and liver.

ADVENTURES IN DARKNESS

When the members of the exploratory band find that they are beginning to see certain features of their surroundings, such as trees, bushes, buildings, and similar objects they can be taken on short, slow-paced hikes with a chief leading the way over *known* ground. Similar forays taken several nights in succession will help greatly to develop night vision and the braves who prove better equipped for night adventuring than others can be taken, with care, further afield. Some braves make faster progress when these sorties are begun just before nightfall and carried on into deeper darkness. This method appears to help their coming night vision by gradual adjustment. Speaking of night*fall* brings to mind the fact that Indians knew that night does *not fall*—it actually rises. When one stands on a hilltop or higher ground and looks over the countryside at twilight the night can be seen rising from the valleys and lower ground until the higher ground and hills are engulfed in its rising darkness.

NIGHT AND STAR SILHOUETTES

Braves of the advanced night-sight bands can be shown that things in the night can be seen more easily by using the silhouette observation method. That is, by focusing objects directly against the low skyline of the horizon or against the comparatively luminous night-glow of a large lake or wide river. Trees, men, and large animals will stand out blackly against such luminous backdrops and the direction in which they move will be clearly seen.

Indians often used the star-silhouette technique. Flat on the ground, with his keen eyes fixed on a low-hung star, a brave would see the star disappear from time to time, which told him that men, perhaps enemies, were moving through his territory. Usually, by keeping careful watch (and most anybody will keep careful watch when perhaps his life depends on doing so) he could estimate how many men were in the roving band. The moon provides even a better background for shadow counting, and a modern Indian who, through field glasses, has watched flocks of geese and ducks fly with the moon behind them has seen a wonderful sight. Such a sight can be seen for many moonlit nights in spring and fall as the "wings-of-the-air," as the Indians called them, return from the south and leave for the north. For general observation, the moon should be *behind* the observer.

Chiefs should give their bands practice in lying in a hollow, or on low ground, while night-wise leaders stalk them as silently as possible. This gives the braves the chance to detect creeping shadows silhouetted against a luminous sky and increase their belief in night-sight. It takes considerable time and practice to develop really useful night vision but it can be done more easily by some than by others.

Let us take a look at the very special equipment of beasts and birds that hunt in the night. Insects also hunt and stunt shrouded in the cloak of darkness.

REFLECTED EYESHINE

Many of the wildthings have eyes which defeat darkness. The eyes of deer, bear, wildcat, owl, moth and other night-flying insects, and also spiders—which well-informed braves know are not insects—have a sort of miniature mirror set in behind the sensitive cells in their eyes. This provides such eyes with the power to reflect eyeshine, which human eyes are incapable of doing. These mirror-like additions provide all wildthings so equipped with a second chance to see in the darkness, once when the very faint illumination of night registers on the super-sensitive retina of the eye and again as it is reflected back. The prismatic reflectors, such as one sees fastened to posts and trees along a road for the convenience of motorists, illustrate the reflected light principle.

It is interesting to develop the subject of reflecting eyeshine a little further. A chief may shine the beam of his flashlight on an insect, say a moth, since they are easier to focus on because there are many of them to be picked up in the beam of a flashlight. The brilliant reflection from the eyes of an insect or animal, which flashes back in response to the bright beam operates somewhat on the principle of the reflection returned by the moon to the rays of the sun. Often the eyeshine of an animal or insect reflected from the sudden beam of a flashlight reveals a wildthing which would otherwise be completely invisible. The eyes of some night-flying moths shine and glow in a way that would do credit to much larger creatures. The eyes of some moths have a wonderful dark pigment in them to control sunshine. By drawing this pigment below the built-in mirrors or using it as a filter or screen, the moth can make its eyes reflect or not reflect, at will. This most useful arrangement adapts the moth for both darkness and daylight exploration.

There still prevails the entirely erroneous belief that the eyes of a human being reflect light. They do not! When one reads in books for adults that Daniel Boone would have shot his wife, mistaking her for a deer, had he not seen her eyes reflected by the light of his torch, or that the eyes of the Indian in ambush "gleamed bright" in the flame of some white man's campfire, it is not hard to deduct that such yarns are spun by an indoors outdoors man, who uses a vivid outdoor imagination to replace first-hand outdoor knowledge.

LIGHTS IN THE NIGHT

Many lights other than moonlight and starlight can be seen in the night. Sometimes modern Indians enjoy a dazzling display of the so-called Northern Lights or the modest glow of phosphorescent fire, so often noticeable in the woods and forests. On marshy land will-o'-the-wisp can often be seen, and at other times a damp, rotten log attracts attention by what is known as "fox fire."

EARS IN THE NIGHT

One trouble which besets the modern Indian adventuring in the dark is the fact that he, unlike the real American Indian, depends too much on untrained eyes and fails to make use of the other senses which play so great a part in the night foray field: sound, smell, and touch. These senses can be highly developed by those who come to grips with night. Sounds carry far on the still air, especially on damp nights, but our ears, like our eyes, have to be trained for effective night exploration.

By listening carefully and often, we can train our ears first to detect even the more minute sounds and later to analyze them like the Indians. The ability to know what makes the sounds is often quite as important as actually hearing them. Many Indians saved their lives, and those of members of their tribes, by that ability. The rustle of the wings of a dragon fly in its daylight flight is an easily audible sound for novice listeners, but to listening Indians it sounded more like the beating of the wings of a humming bird. The almost inaudible *whirr* of a moth's silken wings, the wing beats of other night-flying insects, the slightest rustle in the underbrush, the flutter of a moving leaf, or the drip of dew were all quite audible and identifiable sounds to the super-sensitive ears of Indians.

The ears of Indians were trained and developed from early boyhood. City-dulled ears cannot react in a week or two to the many minute, mysterious, and mystic sounds of the countryside and forest which are born in the night. Modern Indians must alert and encourage their ears to pick up and interpret the sounds of the wild, because a new world of intense interest is opened up to those who dare adventure in the great outdoors after dark.

Hearing Open-Mouthed

This method of detecting low sounds deserves special mention, as one can hear much more distinctly with the mouth partially open. Hearing with one ear pressed against the ground generally helps to intensify sounds such as hoof beats or the thud of heavily booted feet but does not help to magnify other sounds.

In addition to audible sounds, the night is full of imperceptible noises which the average human ear is, unfortunately, neither keen enough nor attuned to detect. A listener in the night must never overlook the fact that many birds and animals have a keen sense of hearing and an uncanny ability to detect vibration. An incautious movement or even a whisper may still many of the notes and noises of the night.

NATURE'S NOCTURNAL VENTRILOQUISTS

Even the modern Indian who has developed a good sense of hearing for night work will be astonished to discover how difficult it is to place with any accuracy the direction from which night sounds actually come. He can be encouraged by the thought that it is almost as hard to locate the tree or bush on which a cicada sings, even in daylight. The *ventriloqual* qualities of the notes and voices of many birds, animals, and insects throw the listener off. Try to locate the position of a tree toad or a cricket at night!

Animals far excel humans in locating sounds, as they are equipped with a central sound-locating device which tells them exactly where sounds come from. It is fortunate for deer and other hunted animals of the wild that they have these wonderful directional sound finders to give them accurate warning of the direction from which sounds from afar are approaching.

Few mammals are as well equipped with sound-locating mechanism as the bat. Bats guide themselves in flight by echo-location and those who have studied bats and their flight know that their amazing sonar installation permits them to avoid even a hair strung before them while in flight. Bats, by the way, have never learned to soar because there are too few thermals at night to make soaring worthwhile. Modern Indians may be surprised to learn that bats, with rather indifferent night-sight, locate moths, mosquitoes, and the tiniest gnats by radar location echoes. The low, precision-length squeaks which the bat gives as it flies are given at exactly spaced intervals so that the echo tells the bat exactly where and how far ahead its prey is flying. Once a bat bounces its radar rays on the minute behind of the fastest-flying gnat, that gnat has had it!

SCENTS IN THE NIGHT

Night, and especially a summer night, greatly increases scents and smells for our guidance. A keen sense of smell and the acquired ability to analyze what one scents can be a great asset in finding one's way in the darkness and enjoying another treat which night provides. Some night scents are harsh and unmistakable, while many others are evanescent and mysterious. An untrained night-nose will have difficulty at first in doing more than dividing odors into a few categories. Fragrance includes flowers, night-blooming flowers, climbing plants, water, and some trees. Smells include the mousey, musky, and other unpleasant odors.

Heat and odors work together. Flower, plant, and practically all scents are far more marked on a warm night, and less so on cool nights. Night breezes also play their part in spreading and dispelling fragrance and odors. The absence of rising air currents holds odors in place in hollows but even slight upward currents of air, aided by the breeze, will waft smells here and there at ground level. The faint odor of an aroused skunk in the distance may mingle with the fragrance of pine but, to a trained nose, the sweet perfume of partly closed but never quite dormant honeysuckle blossoms makes itself felt, despite the other mingling smells. Jasmine is another flowering plant which adds its sweet, seductive fragrance to the night's wonder-world of perfumes. Often an outdoorsman with a keenly developed sense of smell can tell his exact position in the woods around his camp by a sudden whiff of violet or honeysuckle, or the far less pleasant odor of a patch of toadstools which, in daylight, he had noted just to the south of his campsite.

FEELING THE WAY AT NIGHT

Touch is another useful sense to develop for pathfinding at night. It is used in the darkness by animals with excellent night-sight, including the domestic cat. Some animals use their long, super-sensitive whiskers to help them in night prowling. Our fingers are poor substitutes for the finer sense of touch mechanisms of animals. Yet, as our fingertips touch a tree close to a pond or stream and a piece of bark peels off easily, we can be fairly certain that we stand beside the trunk of a sycamore, provided we have felt a piece of bark of a paper birch and compared its thickness and texture with that of a sycamore. With some practice we soon learn to distinguish by touch a number of trees in the darkness by either their very smooth bark, their rough bark, or peculiarities in the barks of different species. When one knows the approximate distance from the camp site and the direction from it that clumps of certain trees grow, the finger identification of trees helps to determine one's position on the darkest night. *Remember*, when one *must* literally feel the way at night, it is done with a moccasin toe and out-stretched arm, *fingers relaxed*.

Modern Indians who try hard to develop the four night-senses mentioned—sight, hearing, smell, and touch—will be well rewarded by the extra sense of pleasure and assurance they will experience while adventuring by night.

STALKING BY NIGHT

Skill in stealthy movement and the ability to take cover silently must be developed by modern Indians who seek to outwit the wildthings of the night.

Walking must become stalking in order to move silently at night. This is how it is done. The pace must be slow at first, and each foot and knee raised high as one advances to avoid noise-producing friction against tall grass and other ground plants. As each foot is brought slowly to the ground, the toes feel the ground cautiously to make sure that the foot can be set down silently. The knee of the advancing leg is bent forward slightly in order to reach further forward. When the searching toes encounter twigs or grass that may rustle under the weight of the body these must be pushed quietly aside before setting the foot down. When the leading foot is securely in position the other foot is brought forward, the weight of the body resting constantly on the rear leg. *Balance* is an important factor in this form of progress, as in all methods of silent progression.

Lying Down Quietly

When it is necessary to drop to the ground quickly at night, certain precautions must be taken or the noise made will scare off the wildlife that one wished to observe, or reveal one's position to an enemy during a scouting game. One must crouch quietly, at the same time feeling for the ground with one hand. When the hand has found a place free of twigs, or cleared a place, the weight of the body is lowered onto the arm and hand on the ground and the leg on that side is moved carefully backward. The other leg is then placed alongside the one on the ground and the entire body is lowered gently into a prone position. Practice is needed in order to carry out these motions silently and quickly.

Flashlight Exploration

As was mentioned earlier, the eyes of some insects throw off strange reflections which are apparently far too big for the insect spotlighted by the flashlight. Some spiders also have eyes which reflect strangely and an hour or so can be spent in an interesting way, on a dark night, if the chief and one or two older braves will arm themselves with powerful flashlights and take the band on a flashlight exploration adventure. Even the casual shining of a flashlight into a clump of bushes at random may, at times, reveal a small nocturnal animal in search of food or the reflected flash of the eyes of an insect in hiding. A sight of great beauty, such as a Luna Moth in flight, may be picked up in the beam of light and quite often myriads of small winged insects such as moths, dancers of the dusk, are caught and held in the brilliant beam.

To decoy insects into close range, a blue light is the most attractive to moths and many other insects and a piece of light blue tissue paper or gelatine tied over the light of a powerful flashlight will toll far more curious insects than a white beam. Red is the least attractive light to insects and yellow comes a close second in the repulsing category. Flashlight exploration trips should not be carried out until the braves of a band feel that their night-sight has become reasonably well developed. It is then time to use a flashlight to help the night eyes to discover some of the beauties of the night which remain hidden from them without artificial aid. Using the flashlight occasionally will also give night eyes a chance to adjust to light and then readjust to darkness. For practice, try stalking a firefly.

Close quietly in on one when it alights on the grass or a bush. Its mysterious white light will dim but you can locate it by keeping its position in the beam of light. Shut off the beam and approach to within a foot or two of where you know the firefly to be. Now flash your light again on a harmless little gun-metal colored beetle. Pick it up gently and examine it carefully under the flashlight beam. Its wing covers are beautifully bordered in yellow but it is the wonderful shield over and protecting its bullet-shaped head and eyes that will draw your attention more than anything else. Its gossamer wings are shielded by tough, strong, protective wing covers which slide aside when the wings are being readied to take flight. A little yellowish-white spot at the end of the abdomen, close to the tail, is its luminous fluid lamp, which the firefly can flash on and off at will. If you blow on the lamp very gently it will glow with a greenish-yellow fire. After the examination, replace the firefly gently on the grass so that you may have the satisfaction of knowing that it will still shine as one of nature's lovely adornments.

Some modern Indians may believe that only the male firefly carries a torch. This is not so. Only the male has wings but the female too is equipped with a torch, which she shines from her tip-end, from the tip-top of a blade of grass or a leaf on a low bush in order to lure the airborne male to make a landing alongside her.

Among some of the many things which may surprise flashlight explorers of the wonders of night is to learn that on a certain trail, or in an off-trail woodland glade, the same butterflies and tired moths may be found asleep under the same log or in a hollow in the rough bark of a tree, night after night. Most of these insects choose the same sleeping place each night and raise quite a midget rumpus if some outsider takes a fancy to it. If one had time to explore further, he would find that moths which are crepuscular or nocturnal in their flight take off on a regular time schedule very much like flights of airplanes from an airfield. There is an excellent reason for this flight schedule. Were it not so, moths would all take off in one vast flight with very little hope of the various distinct species' meeting, mating, and reproducing.

Moths, with their astonishing sense of smell, can detect another moth of the same species at a distance of over five miles. When the female moth releases her fragrance in the night, males wing their way at top speed in a race to be the first to reach her. This is especially true of the larger moths, such as the lovely Luna, the Promethia, and the biggest of our moths, the Cecropia.

How to Attract Moths

The easiest way for would-be observers to interrupt the moth parade for a while, in order that the braves may see some interesting specimens at close quarters, requires only a white sheet and one or more flashlights. In front of the sheet, suspended from a branch or hung on poles, a powerful flashlight with a good reflector is set up. It should be placed directly in front of the sheet and the beam shone upward at an angle of about 45 degrees, facing away from the sheet. Another beam may be directed onto the center of the sheet. The edge of a wood is a good spot on which to erect the screen. Scientists and naturalists use a mercury vapor lamp to attract moths. It has a very long range of attraction and, for moths, such a lamp has an extraordinary brilliance which, though not apparent to human eyes, the night flyers cannot resist. Not only moths but many other insects will respond to the lure of the illuminated sheet. The most interesting specimens can then be examined without hurt and, inspection over, released to again set out on their exploration of the enchanted night.

Sugaring

Another sure way to attract moths, and frequently butterflies by day, is sugaring. The mixture used to smear the trees can be made in different ways. A pulp is made of either ripe bananas, peaches or plums and it should be allowed to stand in a warm place for two or three days so that it may ferment. Enough brown or white sugar is then stirred into the pulp to sweeten it. This pulp is painted in 3- or 4-inch circles, about shoulder high, on the sheltered side of trees standing about 20 paces apart. It can also be painted on posts when trees are scarce. The best place to carry out sugaring is either on the side of a wood, a clearing close to the edge of a wood, or in an orchard, and the sugared trail works best when it is either circular or oval. Warm, humid evenings and nights are best for this sort of decoy. As in the case of the illuminated sheet, the moths will arrive at different times, some species arriving early and others later.

SAFE NIGHT GAMES

Safety should be the first consideration of a chief when planning games and other activities to be played in the dark. Accidents can happen swiftly at night and every precaution should be taken to circumvent the possibility of their occurrence.

Will-o'-the-Wisp "Games"

All games of this type, which involve running in the dark in rough country are best when *not* played. Even when such games are played in what appear to be open fields, there is always a chance of running foul of strands of barbed wire of rabbit and woodchuck holes which make the game dangerous, and when played in even lightly wooded country it is always hazardous and can prove disastrous.

Cricket

This game is played by posting six or eight braves about six paces apart, along the edge of a wood or forest in the vicinity of the encampment. Each brave should carry a whistle, for use in emergency only. A chief who carries both whistle and effective flashlight, goes past the braves into the wood until he is about thirty yards distant from them. He then crouches, or takes cover behind a tree or bush and snaps a metal noise-maker known as a "cricket" three or four times in succession, then pauses while he counts to twenty before sounding off with the cricket again. The braves should be warned, before the game starts, to work their way slowly and cautiously, making as little noise as possible, toward the sounds, as speed of arrival beside the chief does not count. The main points in this simple game are to demonstrate the difficulty in locating exactly where sounds come from in the night and to encourage the braves to move as silently as a Redskin on the warpath. The game can continue until all of the braves have located the chief, or until the chief decides he had better terminate the activity by blowing a series of shrill blasts on his whistle. This makes it easy for "lost" braves to join the chief on their own account. Should the chief wish, he can also shine his flashlight as well as blow his whistle in order to help the novice brave to reach him more easily.

All braves who take part in night activities should be taught the wise use of a whistle and also how and when to use and when not to use a flashlight.

What Is That?

In this game, little groups of braves are taken into a wood or forest or along-side a stream or lake by a night-wise chief. The members of the band then compete in identifying the cries, whistles, squeaks, grunts, chirps, rustles, splashes, and some of the many other mysterious sounds which make night in the outdoors so fascinating. The brave who recognizes the greatest number of sounds correctly counts coup.

Landmarks by Night

This is a pathfinding game, played by little groups of six or eight braves in the charge of a night-wise chief who carries a compass and flashlight. Each brave carries a whistle and, if the chief so decides, a flashlight. The idea of this game is to set out across country, aiming for some nearby landmark which is well-known to the braves by daylight. The chief in charge should know the exact compass direction in which the encampment lies from the objective and have no qualms about being able to take his band to the objective and then back to the encampment. The flashlight should be used as little as possible throughout the activity and great care should be exercised if the route includes rocky or stone-strewn ground in places or if streams have to be forded. The chief should always travel in the lead, but when the band formation moves in Indian file a different brave should walk immediately behind the chief from time to time in order to share the responsibility of pathfinding by night. The discretion and maturity of the· chief will be tested in the selection of the route to be followed and the distance to be covered. This, of course, will be based on the age, ability and experience of the group and the distance and difficulty of the expeditions can be increased as the bands become more experienced in night travel.

Disks at Dusk

This is an activity for developing night-sight which will help to evaluate the actual night vision of each brave and indicate the increase in its efficiency, as the training progresses, from dusk through the various degrees of darkness.

The chief prepares a number of disks, ranging from 4 to 6 inches in diameter, allowing four disks for each brave contesting. These disks can be cut from heavy brown paper or, better still, cardboard of various shades ranging from light buff to dark brown. These disks are spread out on the ground over an area about 30 yards square or inside a circle 30 yards in diameter. There should be about 10 feet between disks and they should be placed on ground which blends best with the disk color. The area of the search should be clearly defined by the chief before search begins. A few white streamers mounted on poles is a good way to indicate the boundaries of the terrain or squares of white cardboard placed on the ground will serve the same purpose. When the disks are all in position, the chief has the braves form a single line around the square or circle and on the "Go!" signal they advance into the area and move in any direction they wish in search of the disks. Each brave keeps the disks which he finds and the one with the most disks counts coup at the end of five or ten minutes.

This test can also be carried out by the chief's concealing from ten to fourteen disks in the same area and having the braves, one at a time, search for the disks for a period of five minutes. The brave finding the most disks within the time limit set by the chief counts coup.

As the tests progress and are carried out in increasing darkness, braves may be allowed to move on hands and knees but blind groping in the hope of touching a disk should be discouraged as the tests are for searching eyes, not questing fingers. Braves should be encouraged to use their eyes, at any range, instead of feet, hands, and knees, to discover the disks.

Find the Raiders

The idea behind this game is to train the braves to use their eyes in the dark and to be able to take advantage of natural cover in the darkness. First, a band of six braves is sent out in charge of a night-wise chief, armed with a flashlight and a whistle, into a clearly defined area, which may be lightly wooded or simply a rough field dotted with clumps of bushes and long grass. This area should not, at first, be much more than 50 yards square. In this game each brave should carry a whistle for use in emergencies only. The first band is sent into this area and is given five or ten minutes to take cover. Then a second band, of six or eight braves in the charge of a chief, sets out to discover and capture the members of the first party, who must remain in the cover which they chose and not endeavor to dash to another place of concealment as the searchers come closer. They are captured by merely being touched by a searcher. They remain in place until, after a period of about 10 minutes, the chief in charge of the search party blows his whistle. All of the hidden braves who have been captured by touch report to him but the braves who have escaped the eyes of the searchers stand up, are noted by the chiefs and count coup. If their cover is so good that the chiefs cannot spot them easily, they may blow their whistles to attract attention. The searchers who failed to locate them then go over to where they were hidden in order to learn why they failed to discover the concealed braves.

Chiefs should instruct all participants in night activities to wear old clothes and also tell them the best sort of clothing to wear in order to be more "invisible."

Encampment Raiding

This is the most difficult activity, because it requires practice in moving quietly and surely in the darkness and self-confidence on the part of the braves taking part. Again, the raiding braves should carry whistles and also, for this game, flashlights, to be used in case of emergency. The Indian encampment defenders should carry whistles. This game can be made more difficult, or easier, by the choice of terrain on which it is contested. Lack of bushes, trees, and other suitable cover makes it difficult for the raiders to approach the site chosen for the encampment unseen, despite stealthy movement and cautious advance. This condition makes the work of the defenders more easy, just as well-wooded terrain and depressions in the ground surrounding the encampment make the work of defense harder.

This game can be played in a number of ways to suit the various situations caused by the difference in encampment sites and it is the work of a council of chiefs to make very definite rules which govern the raid. The attack is best when made unexpectedly, or partially so. The defenders of the encampment may be alerted in advance so that they know that the attack will come on a certain night between the hours of 8 and 9:30. This partial knowledge of the coming raid causes excitement and anticipation among the defenders, creating a stimulating and suitable atmosphere. Of course, scouting parties or individual scouts from the main attacking war party may attempt to spy on the encampment at any time throughout the afternoon or evening, try to locate where the guards are likely to be posted, and take suggestions for attack back to the main party. The defenders have been warned by their chief that the enemy may spy on them during the afternoon or evening prior to the raid. This form of play adds interest and tenseness to the activity as it keeps the encampment in a state of alert throughout the afternoon and evening prior to the attack. The council of chiefs may decide that any enemy spy coming too close to the encampment may be taken prisoner and held until after the attack, keeping in mind that Indians were usually courteous and even kind to their captives. Each chief and his assistants of the rival bands work out their plans for attack and defense.

When the attack comes, the raiders may work in groups of one's, two's, or three's, and the raid may be carried out on all sides of the camp simultaneously or take the form of a main attack from a favorable direction with one or more groups diverting the encampment guards from the main body of attackers. Again, the attack may be staged intermittently, with small or large groups raiding at 15- or 20-minute intervals from any direction. Sometimes this form of raid works well and at others it fails to be effective, largely depending on the skill, alertness, and strategy of the defenders. Chiefs on both sides should impress on their braves that the whole idea and purpose of the raid is to use real Indian tactics of stealth and silence and that an attack and defense where the night air is shattered with war whoops and commotion is futile. An attempt to rush the encampment is dangerous and any attacking party attempting to do so loses by default. All raiders must be caught, not just tagged, and the raid usually works out most smoothly when the defenders cannot be captured by the raiders except in special circumstances, such as when a guard is posted too far forward from the encampment and is captured by one of the groups of raiders.

The chief or chiefs leading the defense of the encampment, decide which sections require most guarding, with the thought in mind that the attackers may choose the most difficult points to infiltrate, surmising that such places will be less guarded.

There should be an understanding between the chiefs of both defenders and raiders that no advance guards of the defenders will be posted more than 15 yards, *more or less*, outside of the advance ring of guards of the actual encampment. All raiders captured should be put on their honor not to try to escape, nor to help their brother raiders in any way, but to remain perfectly quiet beside their captor or captors until a chief visiting his guards can take the prisoners back with him to the center of the encampment. Another necessary rule is that a raider who sucessfully penetrates the innermost ring of guards should blow three shrill blasts on his whistle to prove that he is entitled to count coup. He must take no further part in the raid and waits until a chief takes him to the center of the encampment. In fairness to such successful raiders, the innermost guards should not be posted closer than 30 feet from the center of the encampment.

At the time decided for the termination of the raid the encampment chief and the leaders of the raiding party blow a series of short whistle blasts to warn all participants that the raid is ended. All raiders who are outside the rings of camp guards must then blow soft blasts on their whistles and enter the encampment flashing the beams of their flashlights on the ground. This prevents last minute evasion of the guards when they are off guard because of the termination of the raid. The number of raiders who entered the encampment without being captured and the number of prisoners taken, compared to the total number of raiders, will help to decide which band is entitled to count coup.

Before any other activities take place, a strict roll call of *both* attackers and defenders must be taken in order to be certain that there are no stragglers. Should there be any, they must be guided into the encampment by whistle calls and flashlight beams until every brave has been accounted for.

Dark Walk[1]

Many Indians could really find their way in the dark by the use of that intangible thing known as "an instinctive sense of direction." It is a quality which many modern woodsmen flatter themselves they possess, though actually they do not. Here is the way to prove, in daylight, the modern Indian's ability to find his way in the dark. The only equipment required is two blindfolds and a clean handkerchief to hang on a stick as a marker.

The stick is driven into the ground about 40 or 50 paces from where the walkers in the dark will begin the test. The handkerchief is placed on top of the stick. A chief or older brave can take the place of the stick. Now, one by one, the walkers are blindfolded, after protecting their eyes from possible infection by covering them with small pads of cotton wool or sterile facial tissue. When the chief says "Walk!" the first blindfolded walker, who knows that he is directly facing the marker, sets out at a medium pace, never fast nor at a run,

---

[1] Condensed from *Book of American Indian Games*, by Allan A. Macfarlan (New York: Association Press, 1958).

toward the distant marker. The chief will either shout "Stop!" or blow one blast on his whistle as a signal for the walker to stop. The chief gives the order at any time he wishes, except on the rare occasion when the walker is in direct line with the marker and about to knock it over. Then to assure safety, the chief halts the walker with a whistle blast.

This test offers amusement to the watching braves as, quite frequently, the walker ends up many yards to the left or right of the marker and not infrequently, strange as it may seem, somewhere behind where he started out on his walk. At times, clever walkers take advantage of even a slight breeze blowing as a directional help, which is why alert chiefs usually carry out this test on a windless day.

When there are a number of would-be walkers and time is limited, this activity can be speeded up considerably by having the walker who has just finished the test return to the group by a round-about route, so that the next walker may be started out at the moment the walker before him begins his return.

14

Indian Conservation and Woodlore

Without giving it much thought one might say, "Conservation? What did the Indians know about that?" In the face of such a question, it is sad to state, though factual, that the average Indian of any period, including the twentieth century, has been a far better conservationist than the average white man.

HOW INDIANS ENFORCED CONSERVATION

The Indians of America realized that conservation was a matter of life and death to them, their future generations, and their way of life, and they took extreme care that the practice of conservation was strictly observed. A culprit responsible for a prairie or woodland fire, or found guilty of stream, river, or lake pollution was frequently executed as one who endangered civilization. Had the white man, when he ousted the Indians from their fertile lands, continued to exact the same severe penalties throughout the years for breach of conservation laws, America would be a green, clean-rivered, flourishing land today with few, if any, urgent problems of depleted natural resources menacing it.

With this thought in mind, modern white Indians should adopt the slogan, CONSERVE . . . DESERVE!—and be considerate and careful in the use of what is left of the great outdoors and the greatly depleted wildlife of all sorts which still fights for existence. The white man constantly tries to make his surroundings fit him rather than making the effort to fit himself into his surroundings. He invariably causes trouble for himself and those who will come after him by stupidly and ruthlessly upsetting the balance in nature, and then much effort must be spent in trying to find ways of offsetting the damage he has done. The Indians were far wiser than the white man about such things. They did nothing to upset natural habitats and moved from one to another, leaving wildlife relatively undisturbed, thus assuring a continuing supply of game.

THE WEB OF LIFE

It is of great importance that modern chiefs explain to their bands the wonders of balance in nature, which is also referred to as "the web of life." There is a marvelous relationship constantly at work in nature between all things, twenty-four hours a day, in every part of the world where life goes on. There is a subtle chain reaction which must be carefully studied before man starts to "promote" or destroy any one of these vital connecting links. Today, man has become inextricably involved in the web of life and this is ironic when one considers the indisputable fact that it is man who upsets the balance of nature far more than any other factor in that vast and far-flung association. True, nature too can be ruthless as well as kind when establishing some balance which might become temporarily out of hand but she uses weapons which have been forged in her own workshop, which is why they are so effective and well-fitted for their many different purposes.

HOW MODERN INDIANS CAN PRACTICE CONSERVATION

When modern Indians are made to realize how important conservation is they, like the earlier American Indians, will be eager to help. This brings up the important question—what practical steps can they take to help? The answer is PLENTY! It will be realized that apart from giving top priority to fire prevention and preventing water pollution and erosion, other steps cannot be listed in order of importance to meet the needs of all Indian encampments, as the most pressing needs will be decided by their habitat and its condition.

PREVENTING FIRES

Fire is one of the most deadly enemies of nature. All her children, birds, beasts, fish, insects, woodland, fertile soil, and water are ravaged by fire. The tragedy is that the great majority of the most destructive fires which have burned out millions of acres of forest, prairie, and woodland and mercilessly destroyed all

of the wildthings which made their homes in them, were caused by carelessness. A burning or smoldering match or cigarette butt, thrown carelessly on the ground, or a cooking fire or campfire left burning, can cause devastation over a vast area and death and suffering to man and beast. There is a saying that "One tree will make a million matches, but it takes only one match to burn a million trees." A few simple rules, strictly enforced, will help prevent some of the fire ravage often caused by criminal carelessness on the part of campers.

- Only chiefs or senior band leaders should be allowed to carry matches.
- Always break a match in two, holding both ends while doing so, before throwing the match away.
- Never break a bottle or other glass object outdoors. Curved pieces of glass can and do act as "burning" glasses and start disastrous fires.
- Put out your fire—*then make sure that it is really out.*
- Never light a fire in forest or woodland during a hot, dry spell, even when you find a sandy or gravel spot which appears to be perfectly safe. It is *not*, if there are trees overhead. Sparks fly upward and can travel far!
- Never light your fire against a tree, stump, or fallen log.
- Never light your fire on leaf-strewn, mossy ground or peat soil; scrape or dig away the topsoil until you reach mineral soil, before laying your fire. This prevents roots or peat from catching alight and carrying fire underground. Some states require a fire pit to be dug for all fires lit in or near forest areas.
- Never carry lighted sticks or branches from the fire outside of the actual fire area.

Remember that the aftereffect of a fire is frequently erosion, in sections where that scourge never before existed.

FIGHTING BRUSH AND GRASS FIRES

The best equipment for fighting brush fires is the usual type of camp broom made from green twigs, or wet sacks tied to short, stout poles. A shovel, when there is one around, makes a good fire-fighting weapon not only to beat out the flames but also to shovel loose earth or sand onto the fire. Fighting forest fires is the work of men and only experienced fire fighters with modern equipment and a knowledge of "back-firing" and other strategies are fitted to cope with such blazes successfully. The elimination of all fire hazards and extreme vigilance will prevent fires.

PREVENTING WATER POLLUTION

Indians considered water sacred and tribes of the Northwest Coast appointed River Guardians and Lake Guardians who had power to execute those whom they found polluting a stream or lake in any way. Modern chiefs in charge of bands should make absolutely certain that the latrines are so situated (at least 50 yards away from and below the source of water supply) that there can be absolutely no seepage into water which is used for either cooking or drinking. The braves should not wash their dishes into a stream or little river, as dirty dishwater will eventually contaminate the water. The chief in charge of Indian encampments will do well to have samples of the drinking water which the braves will drink when camp is opened laboratory tested to assure that the water is pure.

PREVENTING EROSION

Preventing erosion is much easier than curing it. Some of the simpler ways modern Indians can help outwit the erosion which devours mountains, hills, and valleys and feeds on the valuable topsoil, which is the life blood of a country, are suggested here.

Steps, Stairs, and Spirals

Useful steps in the direction of practical conservation are taken when modern Indians build wooden steps or stairs up a bank or grassy slope which they have to climb up and down frequently. The steps may be made of pieces of logs or ordinary wood and they will prevent the bank from becoming worn away into a trench, which would gradually develop into a gully. Rain water would gush down this gully and erosion's next step would be to wash away a large part or all of the bank in that immediate area.

When there is a lot of movement up and down a gradual grassy slope, care should be taken to travel in a spiral because if the braves all travel in a straight path over the ground, erosion will develop, just as in the higher bank.

Stone and Rock Paths

These paths laid over much-travelled ground inside the encampment area will prevent erosion. Naturally, such paths can be built only for a short distance, here and there, because of the amount of work involved in paving long stretches but there are often short distances where these trails are necessary. They are built by placing lightweight slabs of flat rock on the ground which is marked out as a path. The soil should be dug to a depth of only an inch or so, according to the thickness of the rocks, and each slab set in. This provides a foundation for the path which will hold the rocks in place and they will sink in deeper with use. Rock trails need not be wider than 18 inches, in most cases, as the braves can walk in Indian file when crossing them. Smooth stones can be used instead of rocks. They need not be very large and they can be laid in a shallow trench, about 18 inches wide, running across the ground to be paved. Mother Nature will soon take a hand and grass or weeds will grow up around and between the stones. Paths of this sort in an encampment should be built only when necessary to fight erosion, and in many sites they are a must, in order to keep conservation a jump ahead of its many enemies.

Edging Banks

When rain water flows over the edge of a bank, destroying soil and perhaps flooding a path of wild flower patches below, the flow can be deflected in this simple way. Straight logs or tree trunks from 8 to 18 inches in diameter, according to the depth and strength of overflow, can be sunk partially into a shallow, straight, tight-fitting trench along the entire top of the bank or at the part where the overflow occurs. These logs are laid in such a way that they direct the surplus rain water into a ditch, natural channel, or specially dug drainage ditch which can carry the water off with the least damage to surrounding soil. If it is possible to give the logs used for the edging a coat of creosote or other preservative, they will last for a very much longer time without being replaced.

PLANTING TO FIGHT EROSION

So many trees, bushes, vines, plants, and flowers can be planted to prevent and check erosion that a number of them deserve to be grouped in separate categories.

Trees

Setting out young trees as a wind screen, to break the force of the wind in places where it is responsible for erosion, serves a double purpose. The roots of the trees will hold the soil in place where the trees are set out and the trees will prevent valuable top soil from blowing away at some other point.

Planting willow cuttings, which will soon become little willow trees, along the banks of streams and lakes will not only hold banks which have a tendency to slip down into the water, but will beautify the borders as well. The willow shoot of last year's growth, about ¼ inch in diameter, is cut from a tree with a slanting stroke of a sharp knife. They are best planted 2 or 3 feet apart, and will usually grow when merely stuck into the moist soil; but to assure a plentiful water supply, the end of the shoot can be pushed down until it reaches water level. Spring or fall plantings yield best results. The growth of such willow cuttings prevents silt from clogging the stream and in a comparatively short time assures shade and better fishing.

The best time for setting out young trees is often either during the month of May or in August and September, though hardy conifers or most trees should grow any time, provided they are carefully planted, with a large ball of earth around the roots, and well watered for the first few weeks following their transplanting. The State Conservation Department is always glad to give complete details regarding not only the best months for planting certain trees and plants but also as to which plants and trees will grow best in various sections of the country.

Dangerous trees around the encampment should be cut down and all dead branches trimmed from standing trees. An ax can be used to great advantage to thin out stands of trees where obvious overcrowding is hurting the growth of all of the trees. Axes can be used to cut out dead undergrowth and perform other tasks which are helpful to nature and encampment alike. Lumbermen say

"A muzzled ax doesn't bite," and braves likely to misuse an ax should not carry one or should carry a muzzled ax, removing the sheath only under strict supervision.

Many of the dead trees and big dead stumps of trees which are in no danger of toppling over are thoughtlessly cut down or uprooted, though they provide comfortable homes for both birds and beasts. Den trees can provide first-class shelter for a family of raccoons, foxes, skunks, squirrels, porcupines, opossums, flying squirrels, screech owls, woodpeckers, nuthatches, flickers, martins, wrens, wood ducks, and other birds. True, too many of these trees are unsightly in well-kept woods, but a few left here and there are helpful to wildlife in general.

Vines and Creepers

Another important way to fight erosion is to plant vine-type ground covering which will help to hold up the banks of streams and bind loose soil in place. Many creepers and vines available will grow well and quickly in poor, and sometimes even in sandy soil. A number of these vines are mentioned under the heading, *Brush Shelters for Wildthings*, as these plants not only furnish cover for the furred and feathered things but often the fruits form an important part of their food.

Plants and Flowers

Many plants, small bushes, ferns, and flowers can be planted in and around the encampment which will not only beautify but also serve as cover for birds and beasts. During a half day's hike on the encampment and surrounding property, which is not off limits, plants and flower seeds which will take root easily can be planted in suitable places. Whole plants can often be transplanted, such as bracken, ferns, cardinal and other flowers which will be things of beauty in years to come.

Living Fences

Modern chiefs and braves of encampments, especially in the eastern states, can make a splendid contribution to conservation by making close-spaced plantings of rosa multiflore hedges on suitable places in the encampment areas. These hedges need not be longer than 12 feet, though they can be made much longer. Such hedges grow and flower quickly and in addition to adding beauty to the sites where they flourish, they provide wonderful homes and food for many species of birds and beasts. Among wildthings which will find protection in these living fences are rabbits, cardinals, robins, towhees, indigo buntings, and other birds and beasts. Insects helpful to nature will also move in when these shelters are ready. Rosa multiflore hedges are favorite haunts of those interesting insects called preying mantis, known for their ability to devour harmful insects.

Other living fences, planted chiefly for their loveliness, can be ones of honeysuckle, hydrangea, wisteria, morning glory, Virginia creeper, and ivy of various kinds. A light pole fence made from brushwood can be set up to train these plants, and soon, as they spread and flourish, they will form an almost solid fence. Bushes which grow into fine hedge rows, without a supporting framework, are privet of various sorts, Japanese barberry, bush honeysuckle, arrowwood, which is multi-stemmed and grows to a height of 15 feet, and the harmless sumacs and shadbush. A number of hedge rows can be grown from cuttings but when the hedges are begun with bushes 2 or 3 feet high and already in leaf, results are achieved much sooner.

DESTROYING HARMFUL INSECTS
AND THEIR HOMES

When braves have learned from their chiefs what harmful insects are in the area of their encampment, what these pests look like, what signs they leave indicating their presence, and what their nests or homes look like, these warriors are ready to take the war trail. Such parasites should be ruthlessly destroyed by all safe means. The "tents" of tent caterpillars seen on tree branches and bushes, and the immature caterpillars which they contain, can be burned with torches or sprayed. Not all insect pests are as visible as tent caterpillars. The homes of wasps and yellow jackets are found not only inside fallen logs but also just below the surface of the ground. The coming and going of these insects usually betray the locations of their nests. When the nest is in an open field, a chief or mature brave can pour a little inflammable fluid into the entry hole to the nest and build a little smudge fire on top of it. This usually suffocates the insects in the nest and discourages those who were absent when the smudge was lit, from trying to set up housekeeping again in the same nest. When the homes of wasps and yellow jackets are discovered in hollow logs on the ground they should be smoked, or even burned, out—when there is absolutely no danger of the fire's spreading. The chief risk, apart from fire, in such operations is to the braves in case of attack from these winged poisoned arrows. Care must be taken by the chief when a wasp nest in a hollow log is wiped out that *all* exits from the log be discovered before smudge fires are set alight at these entrances. Should a small smudge fire be lit at the entrance to both ends of a hollow log, other entrances can be carefully covered with earth or sand before the fires are started. Once the fires burn, the smoke from them can be fanned so that it penetrates into the main hollow and its branches.

BRUSH SHELTERS FOR WILDTHINGS

On first thought, it may seem that to conserve brushpiles would not be good conservation. Such piles, when distributed haphazardly, can become fire hazards, and when they are conspicuous because of lack of good camouflage they are unsightly. Despite these drawbacks, it is good business in an encampment where naturecraft is studied and wildlife encouraged not only to leave brushpiles in odd corners but to add new ones, in out-of-the-way places, whenever possible.

Such shelters make admirable homes for many species of birds and animals. These shelters are easily thrown together by rolling a few logs and branches of various thickness into a pile, then climbing onto it to help it settle into position. The best places to build these brushy homes for wildlife are alongside hedge rows or close to the edge of woodland or forest, as animals do not like to use shelters where open ground has to be crossed in going to and coming from the brushpile. Birds, especially game birds, feel the same way about these shelters. The very best place for brushpile shelters is in the middle of a briar patch and such locations are the most popular with both bird and beast, as their surroundings provide double protection. These shelters help to provide something which all wildlife requires almost as much as food—that is, cover. One or two of these man-made wildlife homes, built on the *edge* of woodland, will speedily attract a number of home-hunting animals and birds, which will make good encampment neighbors.

These brushpiles can be made decorative, while providing still better cover for the wildthings, and more solid by planting vines and plants at the base of the pile and letting nature do the rest. Among the best vines and creepers to bind and climb are honeysuckle, the vine species, Virginia creeper, morning glory, the seeds of which are a favorite with most game birds, periwinkle (also known as myrtle), trumpet vine, and a number of others. It is surprising how many suitable vines and shrubs can be found around completely deserted farm houses. Such plants will grow wonderfully when transplanted.

For watchers of wildthings these shelters supply a sure-fire terrain where the furred and feathered things can be seen most easily. Watching is not done by peering into the pile or shaking branches in order to try to scare some of the brush pile occupants into view. The correct method of observation is to take cover at a spot down-wind and fairly close to the brush shelter where its wildthings can be seen as they forage around for food in the adjacent woodland or nearby field.

BRUSH SHELTERS FOR FISH

Brush shelters are fish havens dropped onto lake bottoms to help and attract fish. For quite a long time, even professional conservationists could not evaluate the worth of these shelters. Now, it is known that they are far more helpful to the fish population of a lake than was ever dreamed. As a means of attracting big fish they are unequaled. Today, Florida is busily building artificial reefs offshore, based on the brush shelter idea. The Floridian cities involved in the task are spending thousands of dollars in building these fish shelters and the price is high because they are being built with old automobiles, averaging thirty dollars each, with which to form the reefs. Mother Nature's contribution of sand, coral, barnacles and sea weeds completes the task. The fishing is phenomenal in the direct vicinity of these man- and nature-made reefs almost immediately after they have been completed.

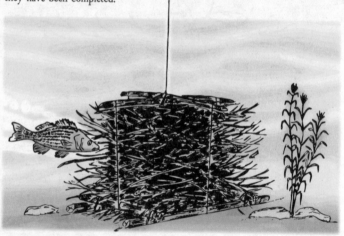

These brush shelters are easy to build and prove especially helpful to the fish population of lakes which have little natural vegetation on the bottom and clear lakes with sandy or rocky bottoms and few weed patches. This is how a good-sized brush shelter can be made. Small or large shelters can easily be constructed by using the same method of construction. Other sizes can be either 6 feet by 4 feet or 4 feet by 3 feet, which is the smallest pile that will prove of service. Commence with two hardwood poles, such as maple or oak, each about 8 feet long and 4 inches in diameter, and two more straight poles, each 6 feet long and 3 inches in diameter. Lash these four poles together at the ends with strong, soft wire to form a sort of oblong raft. Cover this framework with long, thin, newly cut brush sticks, piling them onto a height of nearly 6 feet. Place two long, springy poles in the form of an X on top of the brush and fasten the ends of these poles to the framework beneath. Pieces of brush which are not held down well may be kept in place with pieces of wire. Saw or snip off all pieces of brush which stick out at sides or ends. This shelter is now loaded onto a boat, or towed on a raft, to the place selected for it to rest on the lake bottom. Before the shelter is dropped overboard, a heavy, improvised anchor, such as a standard concrete block, or large flat rock, should be wired securely to each of the four corners of the shelter, so that the poles on the foot of it will rest on the lake bed. A rope which has been soaked in oil, or well-greased, and is long enough to reach the surface, should be securely tied to a top corner of the brush shelter. A foot-square block of pine, painted white or yellow, is now fastened to the surface end of the rope to mark the position of the brush pile.

The work involved in making the shelter and placing it in position is well worthwhile, when you consider that the chiefs and braves will enjoy much better fishing as a result. Water snails and all sorts of underwater grubs soon form on the branches of the brushpile, providing a continual banquet for the fish which enjoy the hospitality of these shelters. Small, and then larger fish, will begin to take over on short notice, deserting other parts of the lake for the food and haven provided by the brush shelter. The really big fish, not too happy in cramped quarters, hang around just outside the shelters, waiting for their meals-to-be to venture out. Sooner or later they will do so, but perhaps by that time the big fellow will have been caught by some young brave who knew just where the big lunkers hunted.

HELPING FISH IN TROUBLE

There is a way to help conservation by making some easy catches without the help of rod and line. Quite often, brooks and streams which run through or close to camp land, partially dry up in the summer months. At such times it is not unusual to see even fair-sized fish splashing in the shallows, unable to flop their way to a pool where they will be reasonably safe. When hiking along stream or river banks modern Indians should catch these fish, big and little, with hands or net, and release them in deeper reaches of the stream. When fish have to be carried even a short distance, it is best to transport them in a water-filled container, such as a canvas water bucket, to their new hide-outs.

ROCK SHELTERS FOR WILDTHINGS

When the braves in an encampment pick up large stones and small rocks which often lie around, they are not catering solely to tender feet. If they will pile the rocks gathered in a heap on some rough, unused ground somewhere in the encampment they will be paving the way to provide welcome homes for some small animals which may have been left homeless by the tearing down of loose stone walls and the encroachment of civilization.

Such shelters will attract a number of small animals who will gladly set up housekeeping in the home so conveniently provided. Among the possible tenants will be mice, ground squirrels, rabbits, chipmunks, and even skunks, according to the size and location of the rock pile. These rock shelters are made by piling up, loosely, large and small rocks on the edge of a wood or at other likely spots where the presence of wildlife has been noticed. The rocks and stones will soon settle down into a more compact pile. These piles look better when built off the beaten track, though they will not remain unsightly for long, as nature will almost immediately take a hand in growing a garden of vines, creepers and other plants to cover much of the shelter. Braves can help by planting some of the plants suggested under *Brush Shelters*.

ROCK SHELTERS FOR FISH

Rock shelters for fish prove as helpful to the fish population as brush shelters. Dropping fairly large rocks in the deeper parts of a river or stream bed, in a sort of dam formation across a small part of the stream, provides a fish shelter.

The fish, especially the larger ones, enjoy its advantages and, a little later on, the braves of the encampment will enjoy better fishing around such spots.

Dropping a boatload or two of fair-sized rocks onto the bottom of a lake, in the same spot, will have the same effect as a rock shelter formed in the bed of a stream. Such rock shelters will attract the natural food of fish, including little fish for big fish, and it takes only a day or two for fish to find this out.

KINSHIP OF THE WILD

Brief mention has been made, earlier in this chapter, of the remarkable relationship in nature of all living things which make up her family. Perhaps some condensed explanation of this vast kinship will prove useful. Plants and animals depend on each other and their dependence is demonstrated even in the lower scales of nature by the fact that insects depend on wildflowers and wildflowers depend on insects. Man is inevitably involved in the wonderful web of nature, even where the insect world is concerned, for without having useful insects constantly working for him, he could barely exist.

One who is close to nature always senses the presence, wonder, purpose, and infinite wisdom of a hand which unceasingly labors to benefit the wildthings and their habitats. A man has to be really close to nature to know that when the snowy owl flies south it will be a season in the northland when credit will have to be extended to the Indian and Eskimo, but Hudson's Bay members in the Canadian Northwest Territories are aware of the fact. They realize that the southbound migration of the snowy owl is forced by the scarcity of lemming, mouse-like rodents with short tails and furry feet, and this shortage warns that the Arctic foxes, which depend largely on the lemming for food, will be very scarce. Since these foxes supply the chief means of trade of the Indians and Eskimo of the far north, it is not hard to deduct—once the chain reaction has been followed link by link—that these trappers and hunters will require credit to exist.

The example above, among hundreds, shows how a lack of balance in the kinship of the wild can start a chain of events which may prove disastrous for some section of society. Nature has to control some citizens of her far-flung empire by ruthless extermination, from time to time. Such is the case with the lemming, which multiply faster than guinea pigs and pay for their prolificacy by "the march of death" as a climax of their fourth-year production cycle. All living things have enemies of some sort to keep their numbers down and it is fortunate for mankind that this state exists, for if a single pair of rotifers, a group of microscopic water animals, were allowed to breed without nature's stern control they would entirely fill the known universe with a solid mass of rotifers within one year!

Food Chains

All animal life depends on plants. Among living things, only vegetation can produce its own food, by absorbing necessary elements from air, water, and soil. Green plants are the basic group in all plant-animal communities, as most animals get the necessary food by eating plants. Some animals eat both plants and animals, while others, the *carnivores*, are meat eaters, though much of the prey of these animals—of foxes, for example, which feed largely on rabbits and field mice—eat smaller animals, which in turn live on plants. Plant-animal communities can be divided into separate food chains, which are a series of living things linked to each other directly by what they eat. Most of these food chains have several links but generally fewer than five. The acorn-mouse-owl and the grass-mouse-fox chains are good examples.

Modern chiefs who explore with open mind and eyes can discover wonderful things regarding food chains. They will find plants, such as the thistle, which protect the food which they give against certain insects, yet make things easy for other insects to assure that they will be well fed. It is easy to deduct that the insects which are fed so willingly by various plants must give something in return. They all do. Chiefs may discover why the evening primrose does not open its exquisite little flower hearts to beauteous butterflies in the daytime. Only at dusk will one of its buds open its fragrant, delicate, yellowish-white petals, in hope of a *rendezvous*—and it has not long to wait! Almost at once, a lovely rose-pink sphinx moth settles on the newly opened primrose, yellow-bordered wings quivering, as its long tongue searches deep in the flower's heart for nectar. The moth has not come to this primrose without a gift. While it sips the nectar, some of the sticky yellow pollen which it has brought from another evening primrose brushes off on the pistil of the flower on which it has settled. The blossom is fertilized and will produce seed.

Tomorrow morning will see the evening primrose corolla, at which the moth supped, wilted and lying on the ground and the entire plant looking limp and lifeless; but as darkness rises that evening at least another of its buds will open to lure another sphinx moth, big or little, from the fragrant dusk to an even more fragrant flower. Suppose that no moth comes. What then? When you seek and find the answer to this question you will marvel at a wonder of nature which enables a plant to step out of character to assure fertilization. This is only one of nature's miracles which makes all others seem not only possible but probable!

Balance in Nature

Each species of creature has been carefully adjusted by nature to some specific way of life. If a creature's environment is changed, a natural law affecting the cause-and-effect relationship may be shattered, with astounding consequences. The way of life of the creature affected is so upset that almost anything can happen before it can settle down again to a rearranged life in its new surroundings. Let us glance at a few examples where man has set out in a misguided attempt to help nature or promote its interest, with the usual topsy-turvy results.

After the ruinous results of introducing rabbits into Australia, Australians had another bright idea. "Let's exterminate the 'Bushman's Alarm Clock,'" they said. The harsh cry of the kookaburra, especially in the early morning hours, disturbed the Australians' slumber and made them eager to get rid of that troublesome bird. It was not protected by law and soon farmers, "sportsmen," and others went systematically about the work of destruction of that big, kingfisher-like bird. They worked with a will and got surprising results! Soon, kookaburra did not "sit on the old gum tree." Then farmers lost about thirty percent of their livestock and many people lost their lives because of the unprecedented increase in the poisonous snake population. Tardy investigation showed that each kookaburra had killed, on an average, 25 snakes daily. Since then, these birds have been strictly protected.

Starlings killed so many harmful grubs and insects in England, where they are known as the "Farmers' friend," that New Zealanders imported a considerable number of these useful birds to protect their fruit crop from the ravages of insects. New Zealand soon had good cause to regret the arrival of these birds on their enchanted islands. Almost immediately, the starlings raised five broods of young each year, instead of two as they had done in England; and to add to the New Zealanders' woes, the starlings promptly discontinued their grub and insect diet of the Old Country and hungrily devoured the fruit which they had been brought to protect.

As a final example, among hundreds, let us see what happens when nature is forced to lend man a hand. Rats arriving in freight ships at Jamaica, B. W. I., went ashore over hawsers and lines which moored the ships to the docks. The rodents enjoyed their new living quarters so much that they promptly settled down, raised large families, soon overran the island, and almost ate the natives out of house and home. All means of exterminating these terrible invaders failed and the rat population increased with alarming rapidity. Then some bright men thought of a sure means of ridding Jamaica of rats. Mongooses! Six of these living rodent traps were imported from India. After some time they justified the foresight of the sponsors of the scheme. The rats were wiped out. Man had triumphed over nature—or had he? While killing off the rats, the prolific mongooses had, under ideal conditions, increased from six to over ten thousand. With the rats gone, a change of mongoose diet became necessary and the mongooses fell upon chickens, ducks, geese, kittens, and even dogs. Man had as little luck in exterminating the mongooses, as he had when he tried to cope with the rats.

Then, doubtless with a wry smile, Mother Nature took over. She decided that the best solution to her man-made problem was ticks. Not only did the plague of ticks decimate the mongoose population but it left the few survivors so weak that they were again forced to change their diet. They had to switch from bird and animal fare to one of insects and caterpillars.

Nature's Clock

The distinct rhythm not only of plant-animal communities but in the life of all God's creatures causes them to function in many different ways and at many different times. Night and day, for instance, mark two distinct divisions in nature's clock. In daylight hours, many birds, beasts, and insects are busy. They eat—and are eaten. Butterflies sip the juices from flowers and are eaten by birds. At nightfall, most of the daylight denizens go to sleep and other food chains come into operation. Bats eat moths and owls devour mice. Observation, when dusk rises over the land, reveals how the moth and insect parade progresses. They, too, are scheduled to fly and work during certain periods of the night so that, comparatively, only small numbers of night-flying creatures are on the prowl at the same time. Habitat plays its part as to where certain species of moths and other insects that fly by night are chiefly to be found. Were it not for nature's timing and distribution of species, in a dusk full of millions of beating wings, there would be little chance of distinct species' meeting, mating, and reproducing. Were it not for the control of nature's clock, countless thousands of insects of the night would become airborne at the same time, and there simply would not be enough room for them all to go about their business in such a drove.

Plants alone cannot take cover in daylight but they do change their rhythm, having one for day and one for night. Many plants close their flowers at night while others, like the night-blooming cereus, and evening primrose, open their flowers at dusk. Though many of the changes in plant life cannot be observed because of darkness, it is known that green plants only make sugar by daylight. During the night hours the sugar which has been manufactured during the hours of daylight is taken from the leaf areas and stored in lower sections of the plants.

In the night-blooming cereus modern Indians have an opportunity to *see* one of the most remarkable things in nature—rhythm. To anyone other than instrument-equipped scientists the rhythm of nature must be accepted on faith, except in rare instances such as the night-blooming cereus. It is a magic moment watching a bud of this strange cactus plant open into flower. The long-stemmed bud sways so gently at first that the movement is almost imperceptible. Then the tempo gradually increases, the pulsating bud swinging like a pendulum until it is in full flower. The fragrant, white, lily-like blossom is almost luminous in darkness, so it can be seen in action without much use of a flashlight, which the plant appears to resent. Too much light causes the fragile flower to close.

Such wonders come upon us at unexpected times and in unexpected places. The author remembers the sudden wonderland of sheen and color that flashed before his eyes one day when he was investigating a hole in a steep, rather sandy, treeless bank close to a stream. Several feet of the bank had slid downward but the hole still continued. A fairyland shone and scintillated in the beam of a powerful flashlight which illuminated a four-inch chamber at the end of the burrow. It had been the nest of a kingfisher, probably for many seasons, and the nest-chamber floor was covered with a shining carpet of infinitely small fish bones, which shone and twinkled in the strong light like a translucent web of precious threads of silver, gold, crimson, blue, mauve and green. The babies had dined well in that nest!

INDIAN WOODLORE

The chiefs who instructed boys and braves in nature lore were skilled observers who gained their great knowledge of woodcraft, naturecraft and wildwood ways by years of observation and study on forest trails and by woodland lakes. The greater part of the nature lore and woodlore which they taught was of practical use in informing the braves of nature's warning signals and what the sounds and actions of animals and birds revealed to the warrior and hunter. These instructors were also well-versed in many things of interest concerning the furred and feathered things. Some of their knowledge is set down here so that modern chiefs can use some of the material in question form to test the skill of their braves in things concerning the realm of the wild.

Blue jays, which the Indians knew as the "Bird of Voices," never flashed like a blue flame from a tree or thicket, with warning screams, without a good reason. Something, or someone, perhaps an enemy, caused the bird's alarm.

Turtles were nearly always alarmed when they splashed from a log or bank into a lake or stream, and their sudden dive usually indicated the presence of an enemy.

When deer suddenly bounded away from where they had been grazing or resting, it indicated the presence of a possible foe. Naturally, the Indian who saw or heard the wildthing take off in alarm was sufficiently versed in the way of the wild to know whether he, or some other person or thing, caused the alarm.

All members of the animal, bird, and reptile kingdoms are intuitive time keepers, and insects as well as flowers have a strict sense of time and season. By using them as Nature's Clock, Indians could tell the passing of time not only by seasons and months but by weeks and hours.

By watching the birds and animals it was possible to tell what the weather would be. Wildthings have a foreknowledge of weather which a woodsman would be glad to possess. Some tribes called the plover "rain bird" because of its habit of scolding before rain. Iroquois said that the whistling of quail indicated that rain would come soon. They also said that much chirping of tree frogs told of wet weather on the way. Iroquoian weather-wise instructors knew that when geese flew high the good weather could be expected to continue. Their weather lore teachings taught that thunder in early spring meant that winter was finished, and that unusually bright Northern Lights in later summer told that cold weather would shortly follow. They knew that webs on the grass in the early morning were a sign of a hot sun at midday and believed that the little explosions and puffs in a hardwood fire were signs that rain would soon come. Leaving the Iroquois, with mention of their wise saying that "When the whip-poor-will calls it is bedtime for children," we return to the instructors of many tribes.

THE INDIAN INSTRUCTORS KNEW THAT:

Deer rarely look up into trees but focus their attention on things on, or close to, the ground, though they often look back in the direction from which they came.

Squirrels will not open a nut that is bad inside.

Old cobwebs across the hole of an animal burrow meant "nobody home."

Owing to the top-heavy head of the kingfisher, the Great Spirit caused that brilliant bird to jerk its tail always in a downward direction. If its tail-flirt were upward, the poor bird would almost certainly topple forward with each upward jerk of its stumpy tail.

A flight formation of geese had not one but many leaders as the birds flew onward. This can be seen when the arrowhead-like formation is watched closely, as there is an almost constant change in the point of the V.

In migrating, the males of the red-winged blackbird travel together and leave a few weeks ahead of the females.

The male cowbird was the only black bird with a brown head throughout Indian territory; today this applies throughout the United States.

Lynx scream often but, by comparison, catamount hardly ever do so.

Mink carry their young by the scruff of the neck on land and pick-a-back in the water.

A porcupine can be picked up safely by the loose skin under its chin, but the young braves were advised not to pick one up unless it was very young.

Flying squirrels do not really fly but soar or glide.

Bats are the only mammals that have real wings and can fly.

Chipmunks sing a cheery, chirping song of greeting to spring and a farewell song to summer in the fall.

A squirrel's eyes are so keen and so well able to measure distances, that it never misjudges its jump as it soars from limb to limb of trees. The Indian instructors believed that its ability came from the fact that the Great Spirit made both of its eyes to look straight forward. Since then, science has supplied additional information for modern Indian chiefs to pass on to their bands. Not only are the squirrel's eyes hawk-keen, but they are also stereoscopic, which enables them to estimate distances with complete accuracy.

A black bear mother often carries its very young cubs, one at a time, by putting the cub's head inside her mouth.

When a turtle dives under water it ceases to breathe until it surfaces again.

No *striped* snake in Indian territory was poisonous. This rule applies today to all snakes native of the United States.

To a young brave, a snake seemed to travel at a great speed, but in reality even a very young brave could outrun a snake easily. We know this is true because few, if any, snakes in the United States travel at more than five miles an hour.

A rattlesnake will practically never attack a man unless startled or provoked into doing so, because it tries to conserve its poison for killing food. Frequently a rattler does not give what is sometimes called a "warning" rattle before striking.

Snakes sleep with their eyes open, because they have no eyelids.

The old skin of a snake, which is shed when replaced by the new skin, is always inside out when found. This is because the old skin has been rolled off by the snake's wriggling through the fork of a branch on a bush or between two strong, upright stalks of plants or bushes. The Indians taught that a snake is very quick tempered at that time and may be blind for a day or so until the disk which protects its eyes loses the opaque quality present at the change of skin.

SPARE - SHARE!

15

Indian Quests

From boyhood through manhood Indians of all tribes devoted considerable time to quests. These quests were of many kinds: power quest; dream quest; medicine bundle quest; medicine power quest; medicine shield quest; medicine herb quest; medicine bow quest; medicine arrow quest, and many other kinds of personal quests. This chapter tells how many of these quests were carried out and how modern Indians may go on their own varied quests.

PERSONAL POWER QUESTS

The only sort of quest of which the objective cannot be told, though imagined, is the personal power quest, in which a brave seeks some secret power or goal of which he tells nobody, not even his war trail companion. These interesting quests have been in vogue since prehistoric man set out on them and, today, many modern men, in woods or forests or behind the closed doors of their offices, are ardently engaged in various personal quests of some specific kind. A modern medicine man, known as a doctor, may be engaged in a personal quest which will greatly benefit mankind. Such truly secret quests go on every minute of the day and night.

The modern brave should resolve to have some useful personal quest when living in camp. The quest can be kept secret or shared with a fellow brave or chief. The quest may be one to develop determination or to lose one of man's many fears, such as fear of the dark, of the water, of lightning, or of snakes. It is a fortunate thing that every modern brave carries the power along with him to be successful in such quests, for such power comes from within, and from the Great Spirit. Such power is stimulated by determination and founded on the chief source—guts. True, such powers must be developed and sometimes a chief or close friend can help in their development.

The Indians suffered greatly on many of their quests, none of which were easy. Some of their sufferings were caused by self-imposed privations which they believed would help to win success. They endured thirst, hunger, exhaustion, and suffering to a degree which is seldom borne by a white man. They ignored bodily hurt from sore and infected feet when the quest trail was long, and braved attacks by wild beasts. Yet when such a quest failed, the brave prepared himself for still another one, to accomplish what he had failed to do on the unsuccessful one. Determination was one of the most powerful "medicines" of the Indian, as well as his best weapon, and the modern Indian can equip himself with exactly the same medicine—if he tries hard enough.

POWER QUESTS

The first and foremost quest of boys and men of nearly all nations and tribes of the Indians of North America was the quest for power. Indian boys ranging in age from twelve to fourteen years, which was close to manhood for many of them, went on special quests for power, often medicine power. They prepared themselves for their dream fast by correct thinking so that they could undertake the quest with "a clean heart." Dream and power fasts lasted from dark to sunrise or for as long as four days and four nights, sometimes longer, when that amount of time was necessary before the eagerly awaited dream came, or the fast ended with some favorable sign. Sometimes when a boy was in an isolated spot in dangerous country, unprotected, hungry, and perhaps cold and alone, a vision or dream would come to him in the form of an animal, bird, tree, flower, star, or some other form, usually a natural one. From then on, the object he saw was his personal medicine, totem, guide, and friend for the rest of his life.

Often, the Indians had good cause to believe in the medicine power of their totems. A brave on foot to whom a buffalo had come in a vision was saved from death by a huge herd of buffalo coming unexpectedly between him and a band of his enemies, mounted on fleet ponies. A brave who had adopted a raven as his personal totem because of a dream was warned of a hostile ambush by a big raven which was about to alight on an outcropping of rocks, but took off instead with shrill croaks of protest. Another young warrior was forced by the circumstances of a quest for power dream to adopt a yellow jacket as his totem. He was saved from ambush and capture by a raiding party of braves from another tribe, when yellow jackets from a nest in a log beside which the band had tethered its horses savagely attacked and stampeded the mounts of the raiders. He of the Yellow Jacket Totem was well mounted and able to bring a war party from his village in time to deal with the hostiles before they were able to catch their horses.

As a rule, the dream and vision revelations were kept a secret. At times, and in special circumstances, such as when two braves who were good friends were on a war party or dangerous raid trail, one warrior might mention his secrets to the other. Close relations or members of the same family guessed or were sometimes told what the totem was and they guarded the secret, at times with their lives.

Can a modern Indian go on a power quest? Yes, in this way. He tells his chief that he has an urge to undergo a power quest. The quest may take the form of wanting to arrive at an important decision which will affect his life in some way, or to think out whether a "yes" or "no" is the best answer to a personal problem. He may seek power to resist certain temptations, or greater courage to meet emergencies with Indian-like fortitude. The brave should actually believe according to his particular faith, as did countless Indian boys according to theirs, that he will gain some strength or power, or perhaps have a dream, which will have some bearing on his problems or future. In such circumstances, no chief will be inclined to put obstacles in the brave's path, though he may see that the quest seeker takes all precautions to ward against damp and cold and that he returns from the place of quest not later than "when the sun is at its highest point" next day. The chief helps the quester to decide on the best point to await the dream or revelation, even though it come from within—which is very good medicine. The top of a high hill, or the top of a great rock in a nearby wood or forest, may be the place chosen. A chief, his plan known or unknown to the quester, may sleep within earshot of the place that night; or two or three mature braves, who themselves wish to go on a quest at a later date, can sleep fairly close to the place-which-must-not-be-approached even by their chief, their presence unsuspected by the brave on quest, until the quester has left the place by noon the next day. The chief or unseen helpers may take food and warm drinks along but must not light a fire nor talk except in case of emergency, and then not above a whisper.

When the quester returns to the encampment next day he, and the unseen helpers, whose mission was unknown to the quester, will all be a little older, a little wiser, and a good deal braver as a direct result of the quest.

MEDICINE BAG QUESTS

A quest to find suitable and powerful medicine objects for a medicine bag is perhaps the easiest one to start with, since the objects required are small and can be found without too great difficulty somewhere fairly close to the encampment. A medicine bag is a small pouch, like the one illustrated here, and should not be confused with a medicine bundle. Time, skill and care can be spent in making a medicine bag, even though it may be hidden away from all eyes except those of the owner. The secrecy shrouding the actual medicine bag is decided by its owner. It does not need to be hidden and secret—it can even be worn openly on a belt—but its contents should be, or else they lose their power. The quest is to find small things which the owner considers worth carrying always in his medicine pouch.

Because an Indian had faith in the power of the finds which he decided on for carrying in his medicine bag, each was an object of magic, power, and medicine capable of helping him when he called on it in emergencies. If it failed to help him, the owner did not blame the medicine object, nor discard it for another

one; he philosophically thought that the gods had not come to his aid on that occasion because, for some reason unknown to him, he was unworthy of their help. The fault, he decided, was in himself and he took a sweat bath and burned sweet grass to purify himself and become more worthy of a favorable response from the magic objects in his medicine bag.

When an Indian was fortunate enough to find a "buffalo stone," he believed that the Great Spirit, or some lesser god, favored him above all men. The finder took the stone respectfully and fearfully to the forest or his tepee and in prayer and seclusion covered the medicine stone with a little buckskin covering, artistically painted or beaded with all his skill. He never forgot to make a small hole in the leather covering through which the stone could see. There must always be such a hole if the stone were to prove powerful medicine. Such stones were placed in both medicine bags and medicine bundles whenever they were found. Now, many of the stones regarded by the Indians as buffalo stones were not really so. They were actually especially strange-appearing stones which the Indians picked up where buffalo roamed, close to such places, or even much further afield. Because of their faith, the Indians derived just as much medicine power from the non-buffalo stone as they did from the real stones which came from the buffaloes' stomachs. This knowledge is encouraging to modern Indians because if a stone strange enough or beautiful enough is found near the encampment or on the trail, whether it be by plain, forest, wood, lake, or sea, it may be a buffalo stone, or at least so like one that it possesses the same medicine power.

Let's stop a moment on the trail at this point to consider a problem which modern chiefs can encounter with some modern, matter-of-fact brave who asks the question, "Isn't it foolish for intelligent people to believe in lucky charms in this modern age?" For a moment one is blocked by a wall of realism, but suddenly the memory is flooded with kings, princes, knights, warriors, great Indian chiefs, and others who believed so completely in talismans of various kinds that they would not go into battle or council without wearing them or carrying them in a secret place on their persons. But that was long ago, so let's think again. Of course! We know or have heard of many ultra-modern people who too carry their lucky charms wherever they go. Such people may be athletes, soldiers, sailors, explorers, artists, or even motorists who carry, or hang up in their cars, some lucky charm. Some of these persons may declare to some very matter-of-fact questioner, "Of course, I am not really quite convinced of my lucky charm's power, but, just the same, I feel better when I have it with me." Now, let's get back to suitable medicine objects for our medicine bags.

Indians got inspiration for suitable objects to put into their medicine bags from dreams, looking into the flames of a fire, seeing something strange in the sky, hearing a strange and unusual noise in the forest, listening to the song of a stream, and from many other sources which are still available to modern Indians.

There is no reason whatsoever why any small, strange-looking stone, be it red, white, black or brown, round, oval, or square, should not serve as a buffalo stone and be placed as a medicine object in the medicine bag. Other things to put into the bag can be small feathers; a piece of hair or fur found around animal dens or a raccoon tree; down from a bird; a strange or beautiful shell; small pieces of strangely-shaped roots; a flower, attractive weeds, or grasses; a piece of bark from a strange-looking tree; or some gaily colored beads. Modern chiefs will think of many other suitable objects, such as a strip of white buckskin, a small bag of sand or earth of varied colors, a small mirror—before white traders came the Indians used mirrors made of mica—a miniature arrow, or a small turtle carved from wood or bone. The Indians used all of these and also grizzly bear claws, elk teeth, and many other things.

Finding the desired objects for the medicine bags of modern Indians may have taken several and not too easy quests, but once found, the quest of an Indian was only half over. For *each* article placed in the "conjuring pouch" many Indians composed and sang a short, suitable song; otherwise the object had no medicine value to the owner of the medicine bag. The song was usually composed and sung in secret. A bear song was sung for a bear's claw, a bird song for a bird's feather or down, a water song for a medicine pebble or shell taken from a stream or sea, and many other special songs which seemed suitable to the owner of the pouch. The contents of these medicine bags were loooked at in secret once a week, once each moon, or perhaps only once each year, when the first lightning was seen, or the first snow fell, or the first flower bloomed on the prairie. Modern Indian medicine bag owners must make their own decisions regarding such important things.

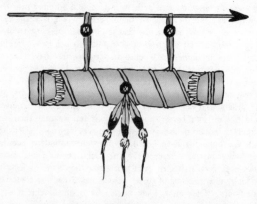

MEDICINE BUNDLE QUESTS

These quests are of much the same nature as the medicine bag quests, only on a larger scale. A Medicine Bundle may be the special secret property of only one brave, or it may be made up of medicine objects collected and placed in the bundle by members of a band or tribe and may belong to them. The keeper of the sacred bundle, in council with the medicine men, decided which of the objects offered merited a place in the bundle. These bundles varied greatly in size, contents, and wrappings, according to ownership and habitat of the tribes to whom the bundles belonged. Many sacred and elaborate ceremonies were connected with them and bands and tribes sometimes went on the warpath, and warriors died fighting for a collective medicine bundle belonging to their band or tribe.

Sacred bundles were often carried into battle to insure victory for the band which owned them and most of the bundles were never allowed to touch the ground. This applied not only to the earth but also to the backs of horses. When a mounted tribe carried even a very large medicine bundle into battle, it was always lashed onto the back of the bearer of the sacred bundle, medicine man or chief, in such a way that it never rested on the back of the bearer's horse. Usually there was a special tepee in which the medicine bundle was hung. Some tribes considered it safe to lay the sacred bundle on a decorated buffalo or elk hide or on a colorful blanket spread on the ground. Medicine men who dared to open the bundle never did so abruptly or in one movement. Usually they raised their arms skyward in supplication first, then made several feints in the direction of the bundle, drawing back in fear a number of times before again raising their arms to the Great Spirit and then kneeling to undo the rawhide bindings which held the bundle together. Opening a sacred bundle was a very serious and cere-monial affair, rarely undertaken more than once a year, and some tribes never opened their bundles until faced with some crisis, such as flood, famine, or prairie or forest fire.

The contents of a medicine bundle might include such things as an otter, sea otter, or weasel skin, or the entire stuffed animals. The dried skin and feathers of a bird, such as an eagle, horned owl, loon, woodpecker, or the entire stuffed bird, an arrow, an ear of corn, a turtle shell, a calumet, and some *kinnikinick* made worthwhile and symbolic additions. The much sought buffalo stone might be considered the most powerful medicine in the sacred bundles of the prairie tribes, while the skin of a sea otter, Dentalium shells, or a miniature "copper" might hold the place of honor in the minds of those tribes whose habitat was in or close to the far-flung habitat of the Northwest Coast. With few exceptions, the remainder of the contents of the sacred bundles were much the same as those mentioned in the medicine bag section.

The fact that the ends of such bundles usually have to be folded over, *par-fleche* manner, and tied securely in order to prevent any of the sacred objects from falling out, must be taken into consideration by modern Indians when making a bundle cover. It can be made in any size from 3 to 5 feet long and from 2 to 3 feet wide, and these sizes will serve whether the wrapping is used for the cover or inside of the bundle. When it is used as an inside wrapping, it is generally wrapped outside with strips of strong cloth, or leather, which in their turn are lashed securely onto the bundle with rawhide thongs or leather straps. Heavy canvas is a good material to use for a wrapping and it can be dyed any color—turkey red or crimson, for instance—or colored to resemble white or yellow buckskin. Plains or other symbols, depending on the tribe or band to which the bundle belongs, can be painted on the top, bottom, and sides of the bundle, or a more elaborate painting can cover the top of the roll only. Leather thongs or dyed tape fastenings can be sewn onto the bottom of the wrapping, one a few inches from each end and one at the middle so that the bundle may be tied securely when all of the objects have been ceremoniously placed inside. Nothing must fall out when the bundle is being carried as that would be very bad medicine, and to prevent such a happening an extra thong may be sewn onto the bottom of the *parfleche* so that a thong can be brought up around each end of the carefully packed case and tied securely on top of the bundle. Soft leather, any big animal skin, with the hair outside, and similar material can be used to make a more elaborate wrapping for the bundle. No matter what material is used in making the *parfleche*, additional decorations, such as feathers and gaily colored strips of cloth can be sewn onto the outside of the covering, so that they will show to advantage when the bundle is assembled and tied. When the bundles were carried on a ceremonial march they were carried either by thongs, attached to each side of them, or on a pole painted red. Other tribes passed red sticks through the thongs of the bundle and carried it by the sticks. Only specially chosen medicine men and chiefs were allowed to carry the sacred bundles.

It would require several long chapters to even partially describe some of the many Medicine Bundle Ceremonies of various tribes, such as the Pawnee. They held two sacred bundle ceremonies each year: one in the spring at the time when the first thunder was heard, as that was believed to be a sign that the gods, who withdrew from earth during the winter months, had returned; and the second ceremony during the summer or fall. The main part of the ceremony consisted of declarations by medicine men and priests restating the acts of the supernatural beings, with the dual purpose of directing the attention of the gods toward the people and reminding the people of how much the gods had done for them. The ritual also pointed out that the original sacred bundles had been given to the villages by these deities. A usual part of such ceremonies were elaborate displays of conjuring, magic, and hypnotism by the medicine men to convince the people of their medicine powers.

Opening-a-Sacred-Bundle Ceremony

A gaily colored blanket is spread out on the ground, ready to receive the sacred bundle and its contents. If there are many objects in the bundle, a second blanket will be necessary, as neither the bundle nor the objects inside it must be allowed to touch the ground. A chief and a medicine man stand beside the blanket, awaiting the arrival of the sacred bundle. The braves are seated in a big circle surrounding the blankets. About three paces away from the blanket a drummer beats a rhythm in four-four time while one or two braves, each with one or two rattles, keep time to the drum.

The keeper of the sacred medicine bundle now enters, walking behind two braves in full regalia. They carry the Bundle slung from a red pole which rests on their right shoulders. They halt beside the blanket and the medicine man steps forward and helps the keeper of the bundle to unsling it from the pole and gently lower it onto the blanket. The two bearers retire to the background and the medicine man and keeper of the sacred bundle stand to one side of the bundle and close to the chief. The medicine man raises his arms skyward and remains in that position for a few moments. The drum beat is very soft at that point and the *whirr* of the rattles becomes almost inaudible. The medicine man says, "My children, I am about to open our sacred pack. It has been good to us in the moons which have passed. Truly, the pack looks out for you. Live things are in our sacred pack. It is long since they have seen the light. Let our song be sung as I prepare to open the pack."

At this point, one or more braves can sing a tribal or band song, to the accompaniment of the drum and rattles. The braves do not ordinarily hum, as that is

practically always done by the women of the tribe, when they are allowed to watch a bundle-opening ceremony. The medicine man kneels before the bundle and, as the song is nearly ending he begins to undo the four thongs which hold the bundle together, reaching toward the bundle three times and withdrawing quickly each time before he touches the first thong. Shortly after the song has ended, the thongs lie beside the pack, on the blanket, and the bundle is ready to be unrolled.

The Medicine Man says, "Now, as I burn this sweet grass as an offering to the Great Spirit in thanks for the protection which our sacred pack has given us, let the Dance of the Opening of the Sacred Pack be given." He then burns a bunch of dried grass and anywhere from two to eight braves in full regalia perform a dance which has been developed with the help of their chiefs. It should be slow and solemn at the start, as is the accompanying music, and can imitate the bringing in of the bundle and the placing of it on the blanket. The dance can then proceed solemnly for a few minutes, with slow, conventional steps being used, after which the dancers stand with arms lifted toward the sky, while the drum and rattles stop. The dance begins again. Slow steps are danced to groups of four drum beats, and then the tempo quickens until drum and rattles speak in fast time. The dancers dance in that rhythm, the music growing faster and faster until, after one loud drum beat, it suddenly stops and the dancers drop into a low crouch. After a moment in that position, they rise and file outside the circle of watchers, to a slow accompaniment of drum and rattles.

As the medicine man and keeper of the sacred medicine bundle now kneel beside the bundle and unroll it slowly to the soft, slow hum of rattles, the chief can perform the calumet ceremony. When the bundle covering lies flat on the blanket, the objects are taken slowly and carefully, one by one, by the medicine man and placed on the blanket beside the bundle cover. The medicine man now stands and raises his arms skyward for a few moments, then burns a wisp of sweet grass. If the chief performs the calumet ceremony to the four world quarters (wind, cloud, lightning, and thunder) he can empty the tobacco from the pipe onto the little sweet-grass fire lit by the medicine man.

One or more medicine men can perform some magic at this point, such as sleight of hand tricks, or the braves can sing another Indian song. When it is finished, the medicine man kneels and begins replacing the objects, one by one, onto the bundle cover. It is then rolled and closed with all objects inside, and to the fast, rhythmic beat of the drum and rattles, the thongs are tied firmly in place. Then the medicine man and keeper of the sacred medicine bundle stand one at either end of it, holding up the loop in the thongs at each end, through which the pole will be passed when the bearers arrive.

They enter the circle to the slow beat of the drum, pass one end of the pole to the medicine man and the other to the keeper of the sacred bundle and stand one behind the other so that the pole may be rested easily on their right shoulders when the medicine bundle has been slung onto it. When this is done, they march slowly around the circle twice and then out of it, the bundle hanging from the pole between them and the keeper of the sacred medicine bundle following closely behind. The medicine man stands with uplifted arms until the bundle bearers and the keeper leave the circle and then takes his place alongside the chief. The ceremony can end at this point, or another dance or song may end the ceremony.

What the white man called sacred bundles can be better translated into English by using the term sacred pack. Among the many tribes using medicine bundles were the Sioux, Omaha, Osage, Sauk, Fox, and Winnebago; and the majority of their bundles were covered by an oblong piece of buffalo hide, usually with the hair outside, measuring about 4 feet long and 2½ feet wide. When the sacred objects were placed on the hide it was rolled up into a more or less oblong bundle and fastened with rawhide thongs which passed around it and were knotted securely.

A modern Indian chief may wonder what is the best disposition of sacred bundles when the encampment closes for the season. It is evident that bundles which have been assembled with considerable work, thought, and care cannot just be left lying around. One solution is that the bundles may be left hanging up in a weatherproof building, being deposited there with due ceremony, until the Berries-Ripe Moon, as the Blackfoot say, of the following season. Another good and impressive way to dispose of the bundles is for the owners who are willing, to offer them to the winds, the sun, or the lightning. The bundles are then placed with considerable ceremony on a bright, flaming fire, so that the covering and contents of the bundles are completely consumed. It is bad medicine to allow the braves or bands to carry their bundles away with them when the encampment closes, though if they wish, they may take along their personal medicine pouches.

Medicine Shields

If the band is one in which the Indian warriors formerly carried shields, then each modern brave of that band is entitled to make and carry a shield on special and ceremonial occasion. In fair weather, when the shields are not carried, they may be hung from poles, or encampment-made lances, driven into the ground either in front of the tepees or in front of the central meeting place of the village. Shields are round and vary in diameter from about 14 to 20 inches. They can most easily be made from a piece of strong, white canvas, cut 2 or 3 inches larger than the actual size of the frame on which the canvas is to be mounted. This margin is folded to the back of the shield, all around, and a strong cord is criss-crossed through it to hold the decorated shield front well stretched. A green willow withe or a suitable branch of any other pliable wood forms the frame onto which the canvas is stretched. The ends of the shoot or branch used must overlap 2 or 3 inches when it is then bent into a circle so that a hoop is formed. Though less "Indian," a circle of tough cardboard or very thin plywood can replace the withe to advantage for several reasons. With such a frame the shield will be perfectly circular and it will hold its shape far better than when a green withe is used, as the latter are liable to warp even when they are dried before use. The overlap of canvas at the back of the shield can be made a little wider all around when cardboard is used for the shield frame, and the circle of cardboard which shows at the back can be painted or dyed the same color as the cloth on the front of the shield. This makes the cardboard or plywood almost unnoticeable. A hand-grip, made of a strip of leather or heavy cloth, is securely fastened to the back of the shield and it may be held either by the hand or wrist or by passing the forearm through the grip.

Of course, the face of the shield can be covered with buckskin or other soft, pliable leather if it is available and not too costly. Considerable thought should be given to the design which a brave paints on his shield. The design must be one in use in the area from which the band originates: Plains designs for prairie warriors, Northwest Coast designs for bands from that region, and so on. The motif can be painted directly onto the white canvas or the canvas may be dyed in some way first. As simple a dye as a strong infusion of tea leaves will give the cloth a nice buff, buckskin color and it should be allowed to dry thoroughly before a design is painted on it. Other suitable designs for shields are found in Chapter 3.

Special ceremonies can be carried out during the shield making, such as having a medicine man in full regalia "make medicine" over the shield and its maker, or over the entire band of makers of shields as they work.

Cases of lightweight canvas or other cloth can be made to cover the shields when they are not in use or on display. These cases are usually round and the cloth can be dyed a buckskin or other color. Though soaking the cloth in strong solution of coffee will give it a buckskin color, it will be found that the cloth smells of coffee afterwards and the color fades out more easily than when tea is used. Some Indians painted the same design on the cover as on the shield but this is not necessary and any suitable device or none may be used to decorate the shield cover.

MEDICINE SHIELD QUESTS

Should a band be awarded a shield as a trophy for special Indiancraft efficiency or some other good reason, instead of holding a formal presentation ceremony of the shield, it can be well hidden in wood or forest with two or three morning or afternoon hours being granted the band to locate the shield and bring it back in triumph to the encampment. Such a quest develops keen observation on the part of the braves in the band and also helps to test their powers of deduction and woodcraft in thinking of suitable hiding places for the shield within a well-defined area of, say, one-half or one square mile. The shield may have a camouflage cover over its protective cover and it should be hidden by a wood-wise chief where it will be difficult but not impossible to find. The shield may be hung from a not-too-high branch on a leafy tree, stood upright in long grass, or placed against a background which blends so well with the camouflaged cover that it is practically invisible unless seen from a certain angle. Of course, the age and ability of the searchers must be considered when hiding the trophy. The tribal chief should have wide-spaced patrols of braves, who are well-versed in woodcraft and know the section of the country where the shield is hidden, on the lookout for younger braves who may have lost their way. Alert chiefs know that, despite platitudes which are meant to be heartening, braves as well as tepees get lost at times!

Searches for hidden shields may also be undertaken as training for all braves of different bands, each band contesting against the other. The time allowed for the search can range from one to two hours and the terrain, shield camouflage, and place of concealment should be based on the age, ability, and experience of the questers.

Again, all precautions should be taken to prevent any brave from experiencing that demoralizing "lost" feeling. The unfortunate psychological effect on a brave of believing that he is lost must be given serious consideration and everything done to try to prevent such a feeling from arising or, if it does, to nip it in the bud at the soonest possible moment. One of the best means of doing so is by having him "found" by one of the patrolling braves at the first blast or two of the novice's whistle. Like a beginning swimmer who has had a bad experience in the water and tries to avoid it for some time afterward, the "lost" brave, though he may experience that rather terrifying adventure almost next door to civilization, will show no great keenness for a return to the forest even in the company of his band brothers.

MEDICINE ARROW QUEST

When an Indian brave wished to make a medicine arrow, either in miniature for his medicine bundle or to keep, for its medicine value, in his quiver, he went alone on a secret quest to find the necessary materials with which to make the arrow.

After much searching and choosing he found suitable wood for the shaft, perhaps a willow shoot. Then he quested in search of appropriate feathers for fletching the arrow in a decorative and distinctive way. The arrowhead was chipped from flint, obsidian, bone, or horn, and then the arrow was devised and assembled in some secret place, so that it would not be seen by others until it was entirely finished, if then. Sometimes the maker of the arrow was content with it as it was. Other arrow makers had a medicine man impart some special magic to the shaft, so that what medicine it had would become still more powerful.

MEDICINE ROCK QUEST

The Crow and other Plains Tribes often had a medicine rock to which they offered gifts for the sacred ones. Such natural rocks were chosen from among many because they had some special feature which appealed to the medicine man and chiefs. Some of the bigger stones looked like bears or buffalo, some were shaped like the head of a wolf or other animal, while others were naturally colored and shaped in various ways which denoted some medicine quality.

Tobacco, beads, feathers, and other offerings were made at such rocks and when they had natural projections which suggested ears or horns gifts were hung on them as well as being placed on the ground at the foot of the rock.

Modern Indian bands who wish to make a medicine quest for such a rock should try to locate one in as wild or out-of-the-way a place as possible. Once a medicine rock has been selected, the chief leads his band in conducting a suitable discovery ceremony, either when the rock is found or at a later date. After the ceremony, a gift from the entire band, perhaps an artifact on which all members of the band have worked, is left at the base of the medicine rock. As part of the ceremony, all members of the band should promise not to reveal the position of the rock to any Indian of a different band.

When a modern Indian leaves a feather, a few beads, or a strip of gaily colored cloth at the base of the medicine rock, he can wish for something worth while which he wants very much. Then, as the Indians who first used such rocks used to do, the modern brave should work hard toward helping the wishing rock to fulfill his desire, lest the spirits should deem him unworthy.

16

Cooking Like Indians

The way of life of American Indian tribes compelled them to be food gatherers. When food was plentiful and the hunting season good, the Indians dined well and abundantly. During months when food was scarce—and March was too often not the only "hunger moon" for Indian tribes—they adopted many wily hunting and trapping tricks in order to bring a little food into their lodges. When even these ruses failed, the Indians existed on the so-called "survival foods," such as lichen, called *tripe de roche* (rock tripe) by the French *Coureurs du Bois*, roots of water lilies, the almost tasteless bearberry, and various forms of cactus. Aspen buds were chewed as survival food and proved sustaining. The Indians showed that practically every living wildthing can be eaten when man's survival is at stake, and mice were considered rare delicacies on many a survival menu until something more substantial was procurable.

The women and boys of the tribes did their share as food providers and, since many of them were not experts with a bow, they used strategy instead of bows. Sometimes they were able to scare an owl from its kill, and put the latter into their game bags. With sticks as weapons, they attacked eagles and hawks and drove them from their captured prey, which was easier when the big birds had difficulty in taking flight with their kill. Thus a rabbit, hare, partridge, and other game were often added to the Indians' meager store. Some of the Indian methods of trapping were as simple as they were ingenious. The women and boys caught geese and swans in ditches. They dug them about two-and-a-half to three feet wide and three-and-a-half feet deep and baited the entrances with wild grain. The big birds proved easy prey as, once in the ditches, they could not spread their wings for flight nor jump out of the ditches when pounced upon by the trappers, who lay hidden nearby.

INDIAN FIRECRAFT

There are things braves should know about firecraft even before the search for tinder and firewood is begun.

- *Never* build a fire against a standing or fallen tree, nor on mossy ground.
- A fire needs air: oxygen is more important to fires than added sticks in the early lighting stages.
- Choose tinder and fire-starting fuel carefully.
- Have a good supply of kindling and assorted firewood ready before starting a fire.
- Start with a small fire and add fuel as required.

- Add fuel sparingly, *above* the flames, because fire climbs.
- Split wood burns much faster and better than uncut, small logs.
- Get dead branches from standing trees, preferably evergreens. Dead, dry branches break with a snap.

Fires lit by amateur woodsmen generally go out shortly after they have been lit because heavy sticks were put on the fire too soon. Fires must be carefully fed sticks which increase gradually in size until the flames have really taken hold.

Tinders

Tinders for lighting fires quickly and surely include: dry evergreen needles; dry cedar bark; dry grass or moss; dry fuzz from pussy willows or down from milkweed, dandelions, or fireweed, among others; or fluff from cattails or cotton grass. Birchbark should be spared whenever possible, but in an emergency, when some bark may be required to light a fire in a hurry, enough loose bark is generally found on the trunk of a canoe birch. It should be taken from the tree carefully with the fingers.

Kindling

Among the best kindling for a fire are shavings or chips from a dead, dry pine, and the roots of most dead pines, especially white pine. They ignite easily and burn brightly because of the pitch in them. The small dry branches which are found on live pines make good twig-kindling which starts a fire going quickly.

Firewood

There are two kinds of wood suitable for use in an encampment, fuel for cooking and fuel for the campfire. Dry poplar is among the best woods for cooking. It gives off a lot of heat and is very clean to work with. It cuts easily and almost splits itself. Birch is also a good wood for the cooking fire, but it, too, must be dry in order to burn. Windfalls are usually a poor source of wood supply, as the wood is usually wet from lying on the ground or it has rotted and such wood is of no use whatsoever for a good fire. White pine and jack pine burn well enough but they burn smokily and—because of the pitch in them —give off considerable soot compared with poplar or birch. Alders, aspen, and cottonwood, when procurable, are good woods for the cook fire.

Though the "best" sorts of firewood always head a list, such woods may not be available in many areas and braves in search of firewood may have to be content with a second or third choice. Sometimes they are fortunate if they find even that, but a knowledge of firecraft also means making the most of what woods you can find in and around the encampment. The best firewood is, perhaps, hickory, because of the amount of heat which it generates and its long-burning quality. Hickory is scarce and growing scarcer. For burning quality, it is followed by oak, beech, ash, elm, maples, birch, pine, chestnut, poplar, and basswood. To keep the fire burning, green birch, poplar, and dry white or jack pine make good firewood, and they throw few sparks, which is often important. Woods such as cedar, hemlock, tamarack, green pines, and spruce throw sparks and should be used little unless they are the only wood available.

Firewood by Categories

Fast and Flaming	*Long-lasting Coals*
poplar—yellow birch—white birch—	locust—white ash—hickory—beech—
black birch—hard maple—pine—	rock elm—oak—ironwood—cotton-
basswood—	wood—

Log Cabin Fire Framework and Back Logs

red maple—chestnut—red oak—elm—hickory—ironwood—

It is unfortunate that framework and back logs should be green in order to give the best and longest burning service. However, in many encampments tree have to be felled from time to time in the main camp to make room for a building going up or to increase play space, so that such woods become available without needless destruction of good standing timber. National and state parks usually stack logs for the use of campers and the kinds named above can often be taken for the purposes set down.

Whether for campfire or cooking, braves should, whenever possible, without destroying living trees, mix dry and green woods to get the best results, as such fires will burn longer and give better service.

INDIAN COOKING FIRES

The Indians showed good sense in building fires of various sorts to suit the conditions under which the cooking had to be done. In time of drought, when

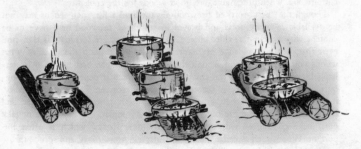

there was danger of prairie or forest fires, they often cooked on a fire built in a narrow trench, when they could not find a patch of bare earth, rock, or sand on which to light the fire.

Oblong fires were often used so that several cooks could prepare a meal at the same time, but the average cooking fire used by individual cooks was simply a *small* fire, round, square, or oblong in shape. The smallness of these fires is stressed, as the paleface tendency is to build much too big a fire for cooking. For good individual cooking the fire must be small, hot, and concentrated, not spread out with a few burning sticks trying to cope with the cooking.

Some Indians did build rock fireplaces and built fires between two green logs at times, in addition to using tripods of green saplings on which to hang kettles over a pyramid-type fire which concentrated heat at its apex.

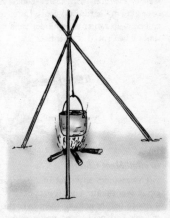

Stone boiling, cooking in improvised pots and pans made from the paunches of cattle, or in bark kettles, is not recommended for modern Indians. Paunches and patience are scarcer these days, so it is well to assume that the modern Indian encampments, through trade with the palefaces, have come into possession of metal pots and pans. An ultra-modern chief may well ask why they have not acquired some aluminum foil as well. Sooner or later they will certainly do so, but this part of the chapter deals only with the less modern methods of Indian cookery, including cooking food on skewers, directly over the fire, baking and broiling in hot embers, hot stone cooking, and other forms of non-utensil cookery. Not only will the food cooked by these methods prove tasty but members of the bands will have the chance to cook their own meals, and from time to time the meal for the entire band. Let's start with one of the most primitive cooking methods.

SKEWER COOKERY

All sticks used for broiling, baking, and toasting should be sharpened at one end and made from green hard wood. They should be as straight as possible, not too flexible, and of sweet wood, such as sugar maple, cherry birch (also known as sweet birch), wild plum, or apple. Quite a number of trees and bushes, such as evergreen and some nut trees will give an unpleasant flavor to whatever is impaled on or twisted around them. Laurel, sumac, and poison oak should *never* be used for skewer sticks.

WIRE   WOOD   WOOD

Skewer sticks can either be single or forked, as illustrated, and cutting a slight barb into each sharpened prong, by making a little notch on each of two sides, close to the sharpened point, helps to hold the thing being cooked firmly on the skewer. The modern chief should take note that if some thin, metal rods or some paleface coat hangers, from which good skewers and toasting forks can easily be made, are found around the encampment, he is faced with the choice between the more romantic form of cooking and the more practical one. It is sad but true that once an Indian cook had a trade metal toaster in hand, the former wooden skewer toasters were used for some other purpose and the near-smile on the Indian's face showed satisfaction with the shift from tradition to modernism.

Before listing some of the foods which are easiest to cook on skewers it is well to mention that skewer cookery, like most outdoor cooking, is best done over glowing hardwood coals. Little tongues of flame reaching upward from the embers help rather than hinder such cookery and are an aid in speeding it up at times when speed is essential.

Broiled Meat Chunks

This includes any kind of meat, game, or fowl broiled on a skewer by holding it over the fire until it is cooked to suit the owner's taste. Such meats are best seasoned before holding them over the embers, as they are more appetizing when the salt and pepper, or onion powder and salt, have been cooked into them. Small thick steaks can also be grilled nicely on a skewer.

Mixed Broils

Many tasty and interesting broils can be made kabob style, on a skewer. Small cubes of steak, kidneys, liver, veal, or lamb, bacon squares, onion slices or cubes, eggplant, green peppers, mushrooms, tomatoes, apples and other meats, vegetables or fruits can be impaled on a skewer, first a piece of meat and then a piece of vegetable, and so on, slices of meat and vegetable being skewered alternately. The skewer-load is seasoned before broiling and the blending of meat and vegetable juices makes these broils very tasty.

Frankfurters may be available, after a raid on a paleface larder, and they can be "done to a turn" on a skewer when grilled, as always in skewer cookery, over red hot coals and embers. Frankfurters with skins on can be cooked more easily, as the skinless sort require more care to keep them grilling on the skewer until ready. A frankfurter can be impaled either lengthwise or crosswise on a skewer. It will stay on better when a straight skewer is inserted lengthwise, but when a forked skewer-stick is used, there is less danger of the frankfurter's biting the dust.

Skewer Broiled Fish

Insert a well-pointed skewer well into the cleaned fish, just above the backbone, as shown in the drawing. Hold the fish fairly close to the red embers of a fire, turning it for the first few minutes, so that it broils evenly. The fish cooks quickly and becomes quite soft as it reaches the nearly done stage; but the skewer, if correctly pushed into the fish, will remain in place until the tasty morsel is ready to butter and eat.

Roasted Corn Cob

Cut the ear off directly at the stalk end so that the pith shows. Leave the husk but remove the silk. Now force the pointed skewer up into the pith at the thick end of the ear. The ear, kept revolving a few inches above the fire of glowing coal and embers, should cook in a few minutes. Butter and salt the cob only when it is ready to eat.

Twists

This is an easily made sort of bread. Once the dough has been prepared, it can be twisted around a sweet stick and baked over the embers. To 2 cups of flour, add 4 teaspoonfuls of cream of tartar, baking powder, ½ teaspoon of salt, 1 tablespoonful of sugar *if desired*, and mix these ingredients thoroughly. Mixing such ingredients with a clean knife blade does a thorough job. Stir 1 cup of evaporated milk, straight or diluted, into the mixture. The dough can be rolled out with a bottle or improvised wooden rolling pin, and then shaped into foot-long strips, each about one inch wide and about ½ inch thick. Wrap this strip in a spiral around about 12 to 15 inches of the top of a 3-foot skewer, leaving at least a one-inch space between each twist around the stick. Hold the twist about 6 or 8 inches above a bed of red coals, turning the stick slowly so that the twist has a chance to bake equally on all sides.

Stick Broiled Apples

Had the Indians of yesterday big apples instead of crab apples, they would have broiled them on a skewer stick.

HOT STONE COOKERY

For stones on which to bake, Indians often used soapstone, a rock formation of talc. On the banks and beds of streams, on rock-strewn lake shores and at the seaside, large, almost perfectly flat stones ranging in thickness from 1 to 2 inches can usually be found. Many of these make excellent griddles which retain the heat and do not crack or splinter when a hot fire is lit under them. Sandstone, or stones of a similar texture, generally serve the purpose very well. When a suitable piece of stone is found, it should be washed and then set up on four big stones of the same height, from 8 to 12 inches, one stone underneath each corner of the flat stone. Another good way of supporting the flat stone is to drive a length of iron pipe into the ground at each corner of the cooking stone and then placing it on top of the supports so that it is level. A hot, steady fire kept burning under a stone of this sort will cook most things tastily, evenly, and well. Some Indian tribes which used stones greased and polished them for days before they were used for the first time. The stones which cooked best were kept oiled and polished and served for many moons.

A double-tier version of this flat stone griddle not only cooks meats and other foods more quickly than the single-tier type, but also serves as a warming plate. On top of the single stone cooker, at each corner, put a rather small, flat stone about 3 inches high. On top of these four stones place a second flat stone of about the same size as the lower stone, or a little larger. There will be sufficient space between the two stones to put meat, vegetables and other things to be cooked and the extra heat kept in and absorbed by the top stone speeds up the cooking. The top flat stone is soon hot enough to serve as a hot plate to keep things warm. The size of the flat stones can range from 12 to 30 inches square, according to the amount of cooking which has to be done.

COAL AND ASH COOKERY

One elementary mode of cooking was passed down from the prehistoric Indians to their descendents in all habitats, that of cooking directly on the hot coals and embers of a fire. This simple, non-utensil form of cooking, broiled meats tastily and proved equally good for baking some vegetables. Here are a few simple recipes for live ember and hot ash cookery, best done on the glowing bed of coals produced by a criss-cross fire.

Broiled Meat

Meat of any sort can be well and tastily broiled on the hot embers of a fire. Rake the ashes from the top of the coals, then fan the fire with a piece of bark for a moment. This leaves the top of the red coals hot, clean, and ready for broiling. Place the steak or other meat to be cooked directly on the embers and cook for two or three minutes on each side. A green skewer stick or fork is needed to turn the meat on the embers and remove it when cooked. Fish, cleaned but with scales or skin on, can be cooked in the same way but it is more difficult to handle as it is delicate and liable to break into small pieces if not lifted on a flat lifter.

Corn Ears

Corn cobs can be broiled on embers by removing the silk and keeping the husk on while cooking. The ear is dipped in water and then placed on the hot coals for a few minutes, being turned once while broiling.

Potatoes

The potatoes may be placed directly on the embers or may be put in the hot ashes and covered with more of the same until a sharpened stick tells that they are ready to be eaten. Potatoes can also be baked in clay and, as in all clay baking, the clay covering the potato should be allowed to dry before the fire. Then the potato is placed on the fire and covered with embers.

Squash

The Woodland Indians baked whole squash in the hot ashes of a fire. Place the squash in the glowing ashes and pile more hot ashes around and over the squash until the vegetable is covered all over. Test the squash with a pointed stick after it has been on the fire for 10 minutes or so and continue to test at short intervals until the stick indicates that the squash is tender and ready to eat, after seasoning.

BAKING IN CLAY

Some tribes baked whole, small animals in clay, thus saving themselves quite a lot of work. Waterfowl and other birds did not need to be plucked, nor fish scaled, skinned, nor even cleaned. The feathers, fish scales, skin or fins came off in the baking clay, when the food was ready to be eaten. This is how Indians prepared game baked in clay.

First, the Indians found suitable clay, of a blue-gray color and rather hard to find in some areas. Other clays, such as reddish-colored ones, which are workable, will serve. Occasionally, mud was used when clay was not available, but it proves far less satisfactory unless it contains a fair amount of clay as a binder. The Indians covered the bird or beast to be baked with a coating of clay about two fingers (approximately 1½ inches) thick, after the game was cleaned and drawn and the head and feet were removed. The clay was flattened out into a sheet and was then molded around the game until it was completely wrapped. The clay was then allowed to dry in front of the fire, after which the bird or beast was placed in a bed of hot coals and embers built around and over it.

The time required for thorough baking depended on the heat of the fire, the continuity of the steady heat, and the size of the game being baked. The cooking time ranged from about 20 to 40 minutes for fish and from 1 to 2 hours for birds and small beasts.

MEALS FOR THE BRAVES

Considering the handicaps involved in primitive cooking, Indian women were good cooks; and the men, too, could prepare a tasty meal when necessary. The Indians of the Plains were great meat eaters. Most braves could eat at least four pounds of buffalo or other meats in a day. The fishers of the Northwest Coast ate an even greater amount of the meat of sea mammals, such as the whale, and Indians of the other habitats found plenty of meat on elk, moose, deer, antelope, bear, and other animals, not to mention beaver and *musquash*, as the Algonquinian tribes called the muskrat. The following are some of the simple dishes that the American Indians enjoyed.

Soups and Stews

Vegetables and fruits were cubed and little squares of meat were added and the mixture boiled in not too much water, so that a thick soup was the result. Some Indian cooks kept what we know as "stock" on hand so that really nourishing soups and stews were cooked in meat bouillon instead of water.

The warlike Winnebago made rice soup by boiling plenty of wild rice and blueberries together, with or without meat being added, often sweetening the soup. It should be remembered that although we use little sweetened soup, such soups were not only popular among the Indians but were also in favor in Europe. Fruit soups, in which one finds cherries and plums, among other fruits, often appear on European menus.

A favorite Chippewayan dish was made from wild rice, wild onions, dried corn, and fish of various sorts. After the vegetables had been nearly cooked, in a broth of almost any sort, the fish was added and the mixture allowed to cook for 5 to 10 minutes longer. Sometimes this dish was thin enough to eat as soup and at others it was thick enough to be called a stew. Modern Indian cooks can decide whether they prefer the thick or thin version of this dish.

Pueblo Succotash

Some of the Pueblo People cooked small squares of meat of any sort, usually deer or rabbit, with young green corn in a broth. The Zuni added green string beans and sunflower seeds and the mixture was simmered until it made a thick, rich, tasty soup.

Corn Chowder

The corn used can be fresh, cooked corn kernels or cans of cream style corn, if the palefaces are in a trading mood. Three cups of milk are used for each cup of corn; the chowder-to-be is seasoned and brought to a slow boil. After about 10 minutes of gentle simmering, it is ready to be eaten.

Potato Soup

This is easily made by merely stirring one cup of mashed potatoes into one cup of very hot milk, seasoning and allowing to simmer for about 10 or 15 minutes. The addition of ½ teaspoonful of onion powder, a little sugar, and a tablespoonful of butter or margarine, added when the soup is beginning to simmer, helps. The proportions given will help in making this soup for any number of braves and it can be made thicker or thinner as desired.

Fish Soups

The Indians of several habitat groups and especially those of the Northwest Coast, made rich, nourishing soups by boiling various sorts of fish into a thick, tasty soup. Sometimes wild vegetables such as baked, sun-dried blue-flowered camas roots were cut into pieces, boiled separately, and then added to the fish soup, making a fish-vegetable broth.

Waterfowl Soups

Many tribes plucked and cleaned waterfowl, such as ducks or geese, which were then cut into pieces, placed in boiling water, and simmered into a tasty broth. The Indians drank the broth and ate the pieces of fowl which they found in liberal quantities in their bowls. At times wild vegetables and roots were cooked along with the fowl, the mixture being boiled down into a thick, stew-like soup.

Porcupine Soup

Porky was not classed as a survival food by the Montagnais, who regarded porcupine as a staple food. The flesh of the porcupine was cut into small squares and boiled in water or a broth, along with wild vegetables of various sorts, into a thick, nourishing soup.

Snapper Soup

Prepare the turtles for cooking in the way described under *Meats and Fish*, in the section following.

Pour the pot-liquor which formed when simmering the turtle through a strainer of some sort, into another pot. Pick the meat from the bones and put it in with the pot-liquor. Add cooked vegetables and simmer the mixture for fifteen minutes or so. To thicken the broth, mix a dessert spoon of flour in cold water and stir it into the soup. A cup of mashed potatoes will serve as a thickener if no flour is available.

Snapper and Fish Chowder

This Indian dish can be made thicker or thinner and eaten as either soup or stew. Any undercooked, flaked fish can be added to hot turtle broth. Season and heat together without boiling for about 10 minutes. Add cooked, diced potatoes and cooked onion slices. If raw fish is used, it must be boiled in the broth until cooked.

MEATS AND FISH

Here are a few new meat and fish recipes for modern Indian cooks to try.

Woodchuck

Ground-hogs, to use their other name, are very good eating. The fact that their food is largely clover helps to assure their tastiness. The gray 'chucks are tastier than the reddish-colored ones, but both are good. This is how to prepare them. Skin, clean, and draw the woodchuck—and cut out the little red kernels which are found at the back of their forelegs, as these are very bitter. Boil the ground-hog for about 30 minutes in fast-boiling water; then throw out the water, in which the gamey flavor remains. Then, cut the meat into convenient sections, season and broil in sizzling fat in a pan, turning and basting the pieces until tender. It may be well to point out here that the term "pan broiled" is used when meats and fish of various sorts are placed in a very hot pan, instead of being fried in a pan which is not so hot.

The woodchuck, when cooked as described above, will prove a tasty dish, well worth the effort of catching and preparing.

Snapping Turtle

Preparing the turtle for the pot requires some work but it will be found easy after the first one has been dealt with. Kill the turtle by cutting off its head with a sharp ax or sharp, heavy knife. Hang the snapper up by the tail for fifteen minutes or so to drain off the blood. Drop the turtle, shell and all, into a big pot of fast-boiling water for 15 minutes. The upper and lower shells will now come apart easily. Separate flesh, with skin attached, from upper shell. Cut off and throw away the entrails and claws; also throw out the water in which the turtle has been boiled. Cut off the neck, legs, and tail from the rest of the snapper. Skin them. Season these parts and the rest of the meat and put them in a covered stew pot, covering them well with water, and simmer until the meat falls off the bones and the skin is soft and jelly-like. The skin makes good eating too. Simmering may take well over two hours and the water which evaporates should be replaced when necessary.

Crayfish

Remove the extreme end of tail with a sharp tug and the entrails will come out along with the tail. Drop the crayfish into rapidly boiling, salted water and cook until the crayfish turn red. Peel the crayfish and eat as though they were lobsters, dipping them into a melted butter sauce, butter and lemon juice mixed, or some specially concocted sauce devised by a chief with some culinary know-how. How to catch these swift backward darters is told in Chapter 20.

VEGETABLES

Vegetable cookery is not difficult, as many vegetables, such as potatoes, carrots, cabbage, pumpkin, and squash can be boiled and served in pieces or mashed.

Potato Cakes

Peel and grate 3 medium-sized potatoes, add ¼ teaspoonful of salt, beat one egg and mix it thoroughly with the grated potatoes. Either fry in one piece, like a large potato pancake or form into small, flat cakes and fry in hot fat until they are golden brown on both sides.

Boiling Ears of Corn

There are two *must* rules when boiling ears of *fresh* corn in order to assure perfect results. Remove the husks and silk from the ears just before cooking. The water into which the ears are dropped must be *unsalted* and boiling merrily. The ears should be *boiled*, with the pot *uncovered*, for exactly *3 minutes*, no longer. Every minute that really fresh corn ears boil longer than three only makes them tougher.

Corn Fritters

Scrape green corn from the cob and pound it into little round or square cakes about ½ inch thick. These cakes can be fried in a little fat in a pan or baked in the ashes, in a couple of green corn husks which serve as the cooking utensil.

Broiled Tomatoes

Fairly green, or any not-too-ripe tomatoes, can be cut in medium thick slices, seasoned, and broiled for a few moments on each side in hot fat of any sort. As a variation, corn meal can be sifted onto each side of the tomato slices before broiling.

DESSERTS

Fruits were, of course, the most common Indian desserts, and are always tasty additions to Indian menus.

Broiled Apples

Modern Indians can enjoy real apples, instead of crab apples, and here is an easy way to prepare them. Cut the apples in fairly thin slices, without peeling them, core the center slices and broil in hot fat, adding 2 or 3 tablespoons of water after a few moments. Continue cooking until apples are fairly soft, sprinkle well with brown sugar, and serve.

Stewed Apples

This is one of the easiest and tastiest ways of cooking almost any kind of ripe apple. Cut in half, then peel, slice, and core the apples. Place them in a pan and pour in just enough water to cover them, no more. Sprinkle them with brown or white sugar, the amount used depending on the sweetness of the apples. After water boils, cook the slices on one side for 2 or 3 minutes, then turn slices over and cook the other side for the same length of time. The apples will become yellowish and fairly soft when they are ready. If they are over-cooked they will quickly turn into near applesauce.

Stewed Fruit and Berries

Many domestic and wild fruits can be stewed to add to the menu of modern Indians. The sweeter fruits, such as strawberries, blackberries, and raspberries, need comparatively little sugar but the fruits which are less sweet, such as plums and cherries, require about one cup of sugar to each quart of fruit, the sugar being added to the water which just covers the fruit being stewed.

BANNOCKS, BREADS, BATTERS

Breads were a basic part of the Indian diet, and modern Indians will find some of the following recipes well worth trying.

Indian Bannocks

The following way of baking bannocks was demonstrated for the author by a Chippewa. This recipe is followed exactly by many of the expert bannock bakers of the North Woods, Indian and white man. Indians find the bannocks tasty, nourishing, and easy to pack when on the move. When the chance arises, the Indians add to the bannock diet, fish, fowl, game of other sorts, and jerked beef but often an Indian family of six or seven persons will travel nearly continuously for twelve or fourteen days and during that time will live almost entirely on bannocks. Forty pounds of flour, a small bag of lard, and some baking powder, will nourish the whole family, even without any additional food, for the entire period. Here is the recipe, which changes slightly from band to band only because the Indian bannock bakers do not worry about exact quantities of any of the ingredients. The sameness of the finished bannocks shows that a little more or less of any or all ingredients apparently makes little noticeable difference in the finished product. The time spent in cooking these delicacies of the North also varies, from 20 minutes to one hour being the range of cooking time—but, here again, the taste and texture of the finished bannocks are almost exactly alike. The author has found that 20 to 30 minutes of baking should do if a good ember cooking fire is used. The recipe given will make one good-sized bannock, which should satisfy four modern Indians.

Pour one pound of white flour into a mixing bowl and stir ½ teaspoonful of salt and 2 or 3 teaspoonfuls of baking powder into it. Make a hollow in the middle of the flour and pour in one tablespoon of melted lard and about ½ pint of fairly hot water, but not hot enough to activate the baking powder. These are mixed thoroughly into the dough, which is kneaded, pounded flat, and then kneaded thoroughly again. Indians and old timers always use their hands for kneading and mixing, but it can also be done with a fork, spoon, or improvised wooden roller. The lump of dough should now, when flattened out, be pressed into a well-greased, hot frying pan, so that it touches the edges of the pan all around. The dough should be about ½ inch thick. The unusual part of the Indian bannock is apparent at this point, because he does not bake the bottom of the bannock first but props the frying pan up, about eight inches away from the glowing ember fire, so that the top of the bannock cooks a little first. He turns the bannock three or four times, basting it each time with lard so that the bannock forms a thick, browned, crust. At the end of 20 or 30 minutes, depending on the heat of the fire, the bannock will have risen to a thickness of about two inches and, when turned out of the pan, looks like a big, brown baking powder biscuit. Though the Indian eats his bannock dipped in melted lard, the modern Indian may enjoy his even better when it is spread with butter or margarine.

Bannocks can also be baked on a hot stone, or even in the well-prepared ash bed of a cooking fire.

Hopi Piki-Bread

In the Southwest, the tribes made a wafer-thin corn bread cake which they cooked on large, flat stones, heated by a fire underneath. The baking is a one-sided affair, done in this way. A thin batter is made by mixing corn meal with hot water and a *thicker* batter is *then* mixed using cold water. A big spoonful of the hot mixture, the *thin* mixture, is poured onto the hot rock, followed instantly by a similar spoonful of the cold batter poured over the first spoonful of hot batter. The cakes bake in just a little over 30 seconds so they are ready to lift from the baking stone just as soon as the two batters have merged on it.

Indian Corn Bread

Indians made this very simply by merely mixing the corn meal with enough water to form a stiff dough. This mixture was salted and the dough shaped into thick cakes which were baked on the embers. Modern Indians can fry these little corn loaves in a slightly greased frying pan.

Corn Bread Cakes

The Indians ground corn into meal and then mixed it with water until a thick dough was formed. They added salt and formed thick cakes of dough, which they baked in the ashes or on hot coals. Today these cakes can be fried in a little fat in a frying pan.

Cornmeal Fritters

These differ somewhat from the last recipe because the corn meal is blended with white flour. To 2 cups of corn meal, add one cup of white flour, ½ teaspoon salt, and one cup of hot water. Mix into a stiff dough, leave it for half an hour, then pat it into thin, small pancakes. Brown both sides of them in a greased frying pan.

Flour Batter

Modern Indians can enjoy many easily made biscuits and pancakes by using one of the various prepared mixes. A more Indian mixture, used as a base for tasty fruit batters, is prepared in this way. Measure one cup of flour, add one or 2 teaspoons of baking powder, the cream of tartar (*not* the alum content kind), one tablespoon of sugar and ½ teaspoon of salt. Mix in enough water to make a rather sticky batter. These measurements are merely given as an idea of the proportions of each ingredient, since at least three or four times this quantity will be needed for a dessert base for a hungry band of modern Indians.

This batter is useful for many dishes. Potato slices, for instance, can be dipped thoroughly in it and then fried in shortening, such as vegetable or other fat. The sugar in the batter should be left out for vegetable cookery.

Elderberry Blossom Batter Biscuits

A big bowl of elderberry blossoms, dipped in the batter described above and broiled in very hot shortening until the batter is golden brown, will be found tasty. The batter-covered flowers can be cut into individual squares or broiled in one big piece.

Berry Batter Biscuits

Berries of many sorts, such as elderberry, cranberry, blueberry, and blackberry, can be added to the flour batter described above in liberal quantity before broiling.

INDIAN BEVERAGES

Indians made many beverages by boiling various fruits, leaves, twigs, small branches, and roots in water. In the interest of conservation, no drinks made from roots are mentioned here. The strength and flavor of the fruit and similar drinks are decided by the amount of fruit, stalks, twigs, flowers, or leaves used to each quart of water, and the length of time they are boiled or allowed to steep in boiling water. It is always good medicine to make a strong infusion and then, as needed, add more water to thin the beverage.

Wild Fruit Beverages

Among the many fruits used by the Indians of various habitats in making drinks were: cherries, elderberries, grapes, mulberries, raspberries, strawberries, and the *red* fruits of *staghorn* and *dwarf* sumac. As there is also *poison* sumac, here is how to identify the harmless plants with complete certainty: the harmless sumacs, which are generally found on *dry* ground, have leaves with *serrated edges* and the flowers are *red*, all of the characteristics being different from those of poison sumac. It is always wise not to make beverages from any fruits or plant parts until a chief who is well versed in botany has examined them and decided that they are harmless.

Sumac Fruit Lemonade

This can be made by boiling quite a large quantity of the red fruit of either staghorn or dwarf sumac, then straining off the fruit and adding sufficient sugar to sweeten the liquid, which is allowed to cool before use. Adding a few tablespoonfuls of sugar to the mixture while it is boiling helps to draw out the maximum lemon-like flavor.

Rose Hip Tea

Some Indian tribes were very fond of this beverage though it may not become very popular as a drink with modern Indians. Though rose hips can be used at any time after the rose petals have fallen, they are at their best after the first frost. The easiest way to make them into tea is to remove their stems, cut hips into thin slices and then boil them for about 10 minutes. A tablespoonful or so of sugar added to the water in which they are boiling helps to draw out the juice and make a stronger infusion. Strain the hip pulp from the infusion before using and add the extra sugar necessary to make the drink more palatable, as rose hip tea needs a lot of sweetening.

Other Beverages

Elder Flower Beverage. By steeping elder flowers in boiling water for a few minutes and then straining off the flowers, one can make another of the beverages enjoyed by the Indians.

Mints. All mints make a pleasant-flavored drink when the leaves and stalks are boiled for five minutes or so in water and the beverage strained and allowed to cool.

Persimmon. These leaves boiled in water and sweetened, then strained, make an Indian drink.

Wintergreen. The leaves of this plant, when boiled in water and strained, make a piquant drink.

Oswego Tea. Indians used this plant of several other names—such as wild bergamot, horsemint and beebalm—from which to make a mint-flavored tea, by boiling an infusion of its leaves and then straining them from the beverage.

Iroquian "Coffee." The Woodland Indians made this beverage by boiling the shells of roasted sunflower seeds for a few minutes. The strength of this drink is decided by the amount of water and quantity of shells used in making the infusion. This drink does not taste like real coffee but proves to be quite pleasant, when sugared. The Iroquois also made coffee from ember-roasted corn kernels, pounded into a rough powder and then boiled in water for a few minutes.

Black Birch. The dried leaves of this tree, also the buds and tips of twigs, make an infusion which tastes like wintergreen when boiled in water, or even when steeped in very hot water for half an hour and then cooled.

Sweet Birch. The tips of the twigs of this tree, which is also known as cherry birch, when boiled in water make a refreshing drink.

Wild Strawberry Beverage. The leaves of these plants, when young, make a tasty drink when boiled in water for a few minutes.

THIRST QUENCHERS AND WATER SUPPLY

Thirst can be torture, especially on a hot day, and it is useful to know how to offset it to some extent until drinking water is found. When one is fortunate enough to discover any wild fruit or berries which are edible, the immediacy of finding water is lessened.

Holding a smooth, clean stone in the mouth is one way of forming saliva and making thirst less acute.

An even more effective way, provided one has an onion in his pack or can find a wild onion, is to hold a small slice in the mouth.

A lemon or lime, carried in the pack for emergencies, will prove most useful when one is thirsty.

Rinsing out the mouth with rain water, perhaps found in a hollow tree, provides great relief from thirst but care should be taken not to swallow any suspect water, even if it has to be used as a mouth rinse in emergencies.

Rain water, caught in a clean container as it falls from the sky, is, of course, pure and acceptable as drinking water without treatment of any kind.

Water from Vines

One can get good drinking water from wild grape vines by the following method. Cut a deep notch almost all the way through, high up on the vine; *then* cut the vine through several feet below the notch. Good drinking water will drain out. If the vine is cut at the bottom before the notch is cut, practically all of the water will flow upward and be lost.

The Indian Well

When one has to cover terrain which has neither river, lake, nor brook, finding water suitable for drinking becomes a major problem. The best way out of this difficulty is to find a marsh, swamp, or small pool, which need not appear clean on the surface. Dig a hole about 15 inches in diameter and about 3 feet deep six or seven paces away from the edge of the swamp or pool. Scoop the water out of the hole as soon as it begins to fill up, let it fill again, twice, bailing it out each time. When it fills again, the water should be clear. Such water in virgin country would be as pure as filtered water but so little really wild and uncontaminated terrain remains accessible today that it is necessary to boil the water from the "well" continuously for at least 20 minutes before using it for cooking. Before drinking such water it is much safer, despite boiling, to use a purification tablet in the water, as suggested in Chapter 7.

To get rid of the unpleasant flat taste which boiling causes in drinking water, pour the boiled water back and forth from one clean container into another, keeping the containers as far apart as practicable, and once the air is back in the water it will taste much better.

Man has been, and is, the chief cause of water pollution. He has been so thorough in this deadly work that practically all streams, ponds, and lakes in the United States have been contaminated and made unsafe as a supply of drinking water, without chemical treatment.

The dangerous idea that running water purifies itself by flowing over fine gravel, or sandbars, or that seepage from a toilet is decontaminated by the process of "filtering" through sand and earth before entering a stream or lake, is wrong.

Water flowing from a spring in rocky ground is about the only natural water left which can be drunk with comparative safety.

KITCHEN GEAR FOR MODERN INDIAN COOKS

Were these pointers for use in a regular camp or even for outpost use, they would fill an entire chapter, but the few hints given here will prove useful for resourceful chiefs and braves, who know how to get along with little gear and improvise when the occasion demands.

Cooking Pots

Wide-bottomed pots cook faster and better, because they present more surface to the heat. This type of pot cooks more evenly than pots with bottoms narrower than the tops, which should be avoided. All pots should be low-slung, broad of beam, with covers, but without knobs, spouts, or handles, other than a wire handle by which the pot is lifted or hung over the fire. Pots should be seamless and of strong, light metal, such as aluminum, tin, or—when lightweight and comparatively inexpensive—stainless steel. Pots which nest easily are preferable. Enamel cooking utensils are most unsatisfactory for outdoor cooking.

Tin Can Cookery

This cooking fad was not adopted by Indian cooks. It is not recommended except in emergencies. When necessary, the use of a few Number 10 cans, in which to heat additional water for cooking or bake potatoes, may appeal to some modern Indian cooks. Before one uses such cans, extreme care should be taken to make very certain that no dangerous cutting edges remain. Big tin receptacles, such as lard and syrup pails, which have lids, generally make acceptable kitchen utensils. They can be used without danger of cut fingers, because lids usually assure the absence of sharp edges.

Scouring Brushes

One of the best ways of scouring pots and pans with wildwood material is one that has been in use for many centuries. All that is needed is a bunch of green stalks of the weed known as horse's tail, which is also called mare's tail. It is quite a common plant and may often be found growing in damp places and along the banks of brooks and streams. This rush contains minerals which form a sort of natural metal polish which helps to make pot and pan cleaning fairly easy. Tie a bunch of these green stalks into a scouring brush, as shown in the drawing, and rub the ends of the stems on the surfaces to be cleaned. The work may be finished with a handful of the weed, to complete the job.

BRUSH

Most outdoor cooks know that when the outsides of pots and pans have been rubbed with a cake of soap, before using them, they clean more easily.

Pothooks

The pot hook can be a very important gadget in an outdoor cookhouse. The author has seen many gallons of soups, stews, and hot beverages spilled into cooking fires because the improvised, wildwood pot hooks split or broke, or were not well made enough to hold heavy pots safely over a fire. Pot hooks made from tough, green branches, as illustrated, are fine when made by real woodsmen but those made by tenderfeet are usually not so effective. This difficulty can be removed by doing what Indians did, after the coming of the white men— making pot hooks from galvanized or any other strong, tough wire, about ⅛ inch in diameter. For lightweight pot hooks, hooks made from ¼-inch wire or strong wire coat hangers will serve very well, and will prove most practical and serviceable for suspending light pots.

Chippewa Kitchen Rack

This is a useful rack on which to hang cooking utensils. The drawing shows how the rack is made and set up. It is best made from four straight green poles from 6 to 8 feet long, lashed together at the top to form a tripod. Strong wands of green wood are lashed across it at intervals to hang things on. The peak of the tripod should be about 5 feet from the ground. Sometimes Indians used similar tripods from which to hang a cooking pot, and at such times the green tripod legs straddled the cooking fire.

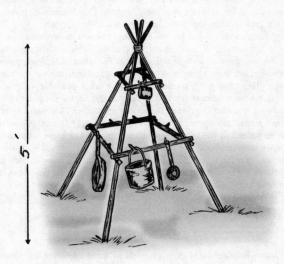

17

Playing Like Indians: Land Games

Indians, young and old alike, were very fond of games of all sorts. They had special games to play at certain seasons of the year and indoor games for the long winter evenings in their lodges. After active games, which were the favorite pastime among all but the older men, came guessing games, and they were played with a patience and persistence that is unbelievable. The Indians ran, wrestled, jumped, putted heavy stones, and contested in swimming, canoe races and water games when tribes were close to a lake, river, or ocean.

Indians of nearly all tribes and of all ages were fond of raiding games, especially those which involved risk. Skill in silent and stealthy movements was acquired by many lessons and much practice under competent instructors of that art. Young braves-to-be delighted in trying to steal out of the village or encampment in order to join a war party, and the Dog Soldiers of many Plains tribes were kept busy trying to outwit these would-be warriors.

Raiding games were played in which young warriors gained coups by entering their village unnoticed, wearing enemy clothing. This clothing, in a number of cases, might consist of a slight difference in the feather headdress, moccasins, or breechclout; but these changes did not deceive the keen eyes of the people in the village. They had been warned in advance of a probable infiltration of "enemy" scouts on a certain day and, consequently, kept a sharp lookout. The advance notice was also to prevent the enemy scouts from becoming targets for war arrows as they attempted to slip into the village. Any braves who were able to arrive unnoticed in the village would count coup, and those who also managed to leave unnoticed could claim grand coup. This high award is explained by the fact that once the scout entered the village unseen, he made himself known and was then closely watched in order to make certain that he did not sneak out again without being intercepted and "taken prisoner" while making the attempt.

Many other Indian Games, 150 of them, have been described in a recent book[1] by the writer, and none of them is repeated here.

GIVE AWAY GAME

The Comanche played this game to celebrate some important happening in a family, often connected with a boy's success on the war trail. All those invited, warriors and women, formed a big circle. A chief, usually a member or relative

---

[1] See *Book of American Indian Games*, by Allan A. Macfarlan (New York: Association Press, 1958).

of the family giving the celebration, stood just outside the ring of guests. He threw small sticks about 4 inches long and ½ inch thick, one by one, into the middle of the circle. Each stick represented a horse or a fine blanket and the first person to run from his place in the circle and pick up the stick, only after it first hit the ground, could collect the prize. This is a good game to teach young braves to be on the alert—and it may be played without giving the winners either horses or blankets.

HIDE SLIDE

This was a game dear to the hearts of youth in the Comanche and other tribes of the Plains. It is a race between two or three teams with three boys in each. Two boys, playing spirited ponies, pulled a driver, sitting on a sled made of a piece of stiff buffalo hide, behind them. They towed the "sled" by means of two strong thongs, about 4 feet long, cut from buffalo hide, with one thong fastened to each side of the front of the sled. Such sleds glided over the smooth prairie grass at high speed, and to make the races more exciting and difficult for the driver the course was around some markers, which caused the sleds to swerve violently as the swift ponies rounded the turns in a race to the finish. At times, to provide additional thrills, the race was down fairly steep, smooth slopes, with the chance of the sled's overtaking one or both ponies and knocking them down in the course of the race.

Modern Indians will find this an exciting race over a smooth, stone-free course 25 yards in length. Here the ponies race around a marker and return to the starting point, making a race of fifty yards in all. Sleds can be made from various things found around a camp, such as pieces of old, heavy carpet runner or heavy canvas, cut into pieces measuring from 36 to 42 inches long and from 24 to 30 inches wide, or bits of thin plywood, of the same measurements, steamed and turned up slightly at the front end. Even very tough pieces of cardboard will serve the purpose, but such sleds will not last for more than a few races. A stout rope about 4 feet long is firmly sewed or fastened in some other way to each side of the sled at the very front. A double knot at the pulling end of each rope will keep it from slipping through the puller's fingers. A very close race, or a tie from the viewpoint of speed, may be decided in favor of one team because of the driver's ability to sit upright, without holding onto the sled, throughout the race, and an extra point may be awarded for his Indian-like nonchalance as his ponies round the marker to lunge into the second stretch of the race.

CHIPPEWA STICK GAME

This easy-to-play guessing game is played with anywhere from 17 to 29 straight, thin sticks or slim, strong reeds, about 3 inches long. There must always be an odd number of sticks.

One player takes the bundle of sticks into his hands and, without counting them, divides the bundle into two handfuls of about equal size. He then holds out both closed hands, each of which contains a bundle of sticks, to his opponent, with the backs of his hands upward. The opponent then quickly chooses either of the bundles and both players count the number of sticks which they hold. The player with the pairs, that is, an even number of sticks, wins one point toward the game's total score, which can range from three to thirty. He continues to present the sticks as long as he keeps getting pairs. When he fails to do so, his opponent takes the entire bundle and does the dividing and presenting of sticks, until he fails to get pairs.

RAVEN TAG

Recently, the author watched small bands of ravens playing various tag games high above the treetops on Graham Island, in the Queen Charlotte Islands, British Columbia, Canada. Watching them at play, it was easy to see why not only the Indians of the Northwest Coast but also other tribes from many habitats, credited these big, black birds with a sense of intelligence, craftiness, and humor. Among the tag games these birds played was the simple form of *Tag* enjoyed by human beings. One raven was *It* and he endeavored to tag any one of the flock of about ten players from above or below, or some unexpected direction. The bird tagged took up the chase instantly without question. It was thrilling to watch the great birds farthest from the tagger soar and circle in apparent unconcern until threatened, and then drop swiftly through the air or take off with powerful wingbeats to avoid the pursuer. Some ravens tagged with their beaks, but many of the taggers seemed to enjoy plummeting on a victim from above and striking it so sharply with their feet that it was thrown off balance for a moment before it could take up the chase.

One of the games played by these raven bands has been enjoyed by modern Indians. This is how they played. One raven, chosen as *It*, would carry a short stick or pine cone in its beak. All of the other players would then wing off in full flight. *It* flew swiftly after the fleeing flock and, when he came *alongside* any one 'of the players, held out the stick, which the other raven took immediately. The new *It* then took up the chase while the pursued dodged and sideslipped so that *It* could not come alongside. The birds *cawed* and croaked with delight as they played, and especially when some unlucky bird was taken off guard or was nearly knocked out of the air by an energetic tagger.

Here is the game suggested for modern Indian bands. *It* carries a stick about 6 inches long and 1½ inches in diameter, rounded at both ends. When he actually comes *alongside* any one of the players pursued, he slips the stick into that player's hand and the new tagger takes over without question. This stick-passing tag is a test of good sportsmanship, since a tagger neither pokes the player whom he is after in the back nor expects him to turn around and take the tagger's stick as he races along just behind him. *It* also has the chance not to show impatience when the hoped-for victim suddenly swerves unexpectedly, making it impossible for the pursuer to come directly alongside.

HOP BALANCE RACE

This is a not-too-easy hopping race which Indian boys enjoyed in various forms as they hopped on one foot, or frog-hopped on both, over different patterns marked on the ground. A modern chief can devise various patterns but the one shown below is a simple, practical one, which illustrates how the game is played. This challenge can be contested by two braves, each hopping only on one foot, or by teams of three or more braves, each member of the relay team following the other in sequence immediately the player ahead of him reaches the exact end of the hop pattern. Each brave or team starts from opposite ends of the oblong, as shown in the drawing. This game helps to develop speed and balance, both being needed to avoid collision between two hoppers at some point as they hop over the pattern squares. Indian boys did not worry about colliding and at times the challenge was carried out so that the young brave who counted coup was the one who shouldered the other off the pattern when meeting, provided both braves did not lose their balance. But modern braves will find that more skill is needed to avoid competitors than to collide with them in crossing some square. This can be brought home to players, when necessary, by disqualifying the one who brings about the collision en route. Chiefs, when directing the challenge with younger or not-too-husky contestants, can allow the contesting braves to hop into *any part* of the square in which the two meet, instead of landing directly in the corner, which must be done in all other squares. This rule not only eliminates possible collision but adds the excitement of being able to judge accurately and speedily where the meeting will take place. The chief must keep a sharp lookout to spot the brave who judges wrongly, as most likely only one of them will, so that coup may be awarded to his opponent. As a rule, the misjudgment is on the part of a player who fears collision and takes advantage of the collision-avoiding rule by jumping into any part of the square just before the actual point of possible collision is reached. The contestants may hop from wherever they landed to avoid colliding, to the exact corner point in the next square, in order to continue the race correctly.

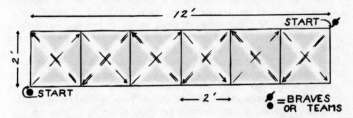

Variations are easily devised by changing the pattern, adding squares to make the race longer, or making the squares larger or smaller than those suggested in the drawing, in order to make the race easier or more difficult. In the case of only two contesting challengers, they may be asked in advance to turn and hop back to the starting point, thus racing twice over the squares to decide who counts coup.

STEP HIGH, STOOP LOW

This is a training game played by the young and old of a number of Indian tribes. It helps to develop limber bodies and quickness of co-ordinated movement and eye. This is how the Indians played this game. They cut six lightweight saplings, each about 8 feet long and 1¼ inches in diameter, from a *thick stand* of saplings (an addition of six more poles, for use as uprights, is suggested to make the game easier for modern braves). These six poles were held in sets of two by a brave at each end. The first set of two poles was held horizontally, with one pole 2 feet above the ground and the other pole 4 or 5 feet above the ground and directly above the lower pole. The height of the upper pole varied according to the average height of the players. The second set of poles was held 10 feet behind and directly in line with the first set, while the third set was held 10 feet behind the second.

The players lined up in Indian file, with 6 feet between contestants, the first player in line being 10 feet away from the first set of raised poles. Each brave walked, one at a time, at a steady pace to the first set of poles, stepped over the lower pole while ducking under the top pole, without touching either. He continued in the same way until he had passed the third set, then turned and went back to the starting point in the same way. Any brave who touched a pole with either foot, his head, or any other part of his body was disqualified and dropped out of the contest. The other braves continued until only one remained to count coup.

Perhaps the most difficult part of this contest fell to the braves who held the horizontal poles in position throughout the contest. Because of the great difficulty in maintaining both poles at a fixed height for so long a period, the author devised the much simpler method of supporting each set of two horizontal poles on two upright poles. This is how modern braves can contest.

Six poles each 8 feet long and about 2 inches in diameter are used as uprights. These poles are driven, in sets of two, 2½ feet into the ground directly in line with each other and 7 feet apart. There is a distance of 10 feet between each set of two poles, in line, one set directly behind the other. Wooden pegs or nails, to support the lighter horizontal poles, are driven into each upright pole at the desired heights—about 2 feet above ground level for the lower pole and about 4 or 5 feet above ground level for the top pole. Both poles should be placed at the height which suits the average contestant, and the position of the crosspieces should be such that the contest is neither too difficult nor too easy. Using the upright poles has the great advantage that the supporting nails for the horizontal poles can be driven into the upright poles at different heights, but fairly close together, to suit contesting groups of braves, each group being of braves of about the same height. Additional pairs of uprights and horizontals can be added so that the braves have to pass from four to six barriers, instead of three.

Four tenders of poles will be found useful, two on each side of the barred lane, in order to replace the poles dislodged by one contestant prior to the arrival of the next.

TRAVOIS RACE

This amusing and exciting race teaches the contesting braves something about travois constructing and knot tying, while providing fun for the spectators. The only equipment required for each team of two contestants is: two light poles about 6 feet long and 2 inches in diameter at the butt end; two straight sticks about 30 inches long and one inch thick; a blanket stuffed with grass or leaves and tied into a roundish ball; and five lengths of thick cord or thin rope, four of them 12 inches long, and the fifth 4 feet long.

Two long lines are marked on the ground directly opposite each other, 30 yards apart. One line is used as the start of the race and the gear of each team is placed just behind it, beside the two braves on the team, who stand side by side with their heels touching the line, facing the finish line. There should be a space of 8 feet between each team. On the "Go!" signal, both contestants on each team start to build the simple travois, as illustrated, and tie the blanket-bundle onto the crosspieces. Once that is completed, only one brave must pull

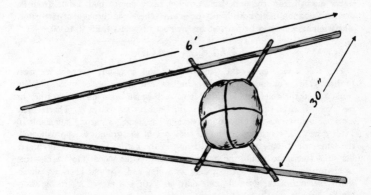

the travois to the finish line, while the other runs directly behind the travois to retie the bundle, should it fall off or drag on the ground. Immediately a bundle touches the ground or falls from the crosspiece, the brave in the rear must seize the travois and hold it back, calling to the travois puller to stop. The travois must not move forward while the bundle is being tied in place, and only when this is secured can the team race forward again. The team to reach the finish line with the bundle lashed to and riding on top of the crosspiece counts coup.

This race can be made more difficult and exciting for older braves by length-ening the distance and having the teams race once or twice around markers set in line with each team. One marker is about one third of the distance from the starting point and the other about one third from the finish line. This form of race offers more chance for complications. When space is limited, the teams can race around one marker placed directly in front of them halfway between the two lines and, after reaching the marker, speed back to the starting point, which becomes the finish line. The markers used in this race *should not* be stakes driven into the ground but ones made from cardboard or cloth, stapled to the ground.

BALL THROW

Indians of the Northwest Coast liked to play this and similar games, using the round, inflated bladder of a sea mammal as a ball.

A circle 3 feet in diameter is plainly marked on the ground with white chalk or a circle of rope. Directly in the middle of this circle a block of wood or a ball, measuring not more than 6 inches in diameter, is placed. Players stand just outside a circle 40 feet in diameter, marked on the ground, with the target directly in the center. Instead of standing outside a circle, each player can stand behind a short line marked on the ground 20 feet distant from the 3-foot circle. Each player, in turn, throws the ball, about the size of a basketball, high into the air in an endeavor to make it fall directly onto the block of wood, or at least within the target circle. Players who hit the block score 10 points, and those landing their ball within the target circle without striking or displacing the block score 5 points. The chief in charge of the game can direct all players to throw the ball from the underhand position, using one or both hands, from an overhead position using both hands, or in any other style throughout one game. The winning score can be fixed at any number of points from 30 to 60.

FEATHER RACE

This was a race enjoyed by Indian boys and each boy brought his own feathers. The ones used by modern Indians can either be crow or chicken feathers, and the chief should either have each brave bring his own feather or have enough clean-tip chicken feathers on hand for several races. The feathers are stuck lightly into the ground in a straight line, facing a starting line about 20 yards distant. The feathers should all stick out of the ground to approximately the same height, only the quill end being in the earth. The contesting braves line up 4 feet apart behind the starting line and on the word "Go!" each races to his feather, which should be in line with him, and, without kneeling, plucks the feather out of the ground, using only his teeth, and races back to the starting line with it.

This race can be made harder and more exciting by placing three feathers, each 2 feet behind the other, which the racing braves bring back to the starting line one at a time. Should feathers be scarce, a chief can use the same feathers a number of times by covering the tip of each feather with a piece of clean paper, about 4 inches long and 1½ inches wide, folded in two over the top of each feather, which can be squared off at the top so that the paper shield will remain in place more easily should there be a breeze blowing.

ARROW THROW

This was a game keenly contested by men and boys of the Comanche and other tribes. The throwing arrows used were from 3 to 4 feet long and were made of any suitable, straight tree shoots available. They were feathered with three feathers, the sections used being rather longer than those used for arrows shot from bows, and the feathers were also rather closely trimmed as compared with those of the shooting arrow. The arrows were tapered so that they were considerably heavier toward the point, and they were beautifully balanced. The Indians tipped their throwing arrows, and the adult contestants were so remarkable that in top-flight arrow-throwing contests no arrow counted in the distance throw which did not travel at least 200 feet.

Arrow-throwing contests were also held in which these arrows were hurled for accuracy at targets or thrown upward to land within a circle marked on the ground at least 60 feet distant.

BLANKET AMBUSH

Younger Indian boys of various tribes liked to play a guessing game in which one or two boys were hidden under a big blanket and two other boys had to guess which two boys the blanket covered. The guessers were allowed to poke, not too hard, and they were given a short time to decide who they thought was under the blanket. Though this was a "fun game," it taught the hidden boys self control, as the best players never squeaked nor made any identifying sounds, while being poked in the ribs, which made things difficult for the guessers.

HAWK EYE

A chief has from eight to twenty braves form a large circle around a grassy area of the encampment, or in a clearing. The distance between the braves is not important, but they should be evenly spaced around the circle which should be about 30 feet in diameter. The chief holds from six to ten sticks each measuring 4 inches in length and ⅜ inch thick. The sticks should be colored in camouflage fashion, with dull shades of green and brown blending, or all green or brown in color, to resemble as closely as possible the color of the terrain on which this eye-testing game is played.

Standing just behind any part of the circle of braves, the chief tosses the sticks, one by one, into various central portions of the circle. On the word "Go!" the braves *lope* into the circle and each one picks up as many sticks as he can see and reach first, holding them until the chief calls "Stop!" The braves then take the sticks which they have found to the chief and count coup or grand coup according to the number of sticks which they have found.

Each time the sticks are thrown, to commence a new game or decide a tie, it is done from a different part of the circle. Should all of the sticks thrown not be found by the time the chief stops the search, he reforms the circle and gives the four braves who found the most sticks another search period, commenced by the word "Go!" The braves finding one or more of the missing sticks count grand coup.

The braves participating in this challenge should not be allowed to search on hands and knees nor stoop with the head held lower than the waist.

The game can be made more difficult, as the braves become more hawk-eyed, by using smaller sticks or increasing the size of the circle, or both. Still another way of increasing the difficulty of the challenge, while giving the braves further eye-training under different conditions, is to stage it at twilight or some other time when light conditions are poor.

STAR JUMP

Indian boys were naturally good jumpers, and the adventurous lives they led made it necessary for them to become even better. They increased their jumping skill by the same method that any modern Indian can increase his—practice. They would see how high a branch they could touch on a tree by making a standing high jump and also by taking a running jump. As their skill increased, they aimed for still higher branches. Here is a way in which modern chiefs can encourage their braves to practice high jumping and at the same time have the satisfaction of knowing how much higher they can jump each week, both from the standing and running positions.

The drawing shows the simple device required to carry out the tests. A top bar 10 feet long is fixed at a height of 9 feet above the ground, on smooth, flat terrain. The markers are 6 inches long and 2 inches wide, spaced one foot apart and fastened by a strong cord to the horizontal bar. The bar can be longer or

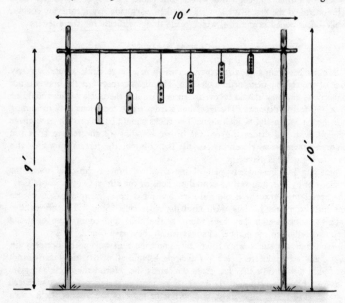

shorter and fixed at the height above ground most suitable to the heights and ages of the braves who do the jumping, though the drawing shows the first Star Jump marker suspended at a height of only 7 feet 3 inches above ground level, and each jump from there on to the final 8-foot-6-inch Star Jump is 3 inches higher than the one before it. When a brave can touch the first Star Jump marker, he leaps for the next star in an endeavor to increase and measure the height of his jumps. He continues along the star-blazed trail of achievement until he has reached the highest point possible.

The bar can then be raised 2 or 3 feet and the brave progress from coup to grand coup.

RACE ON PLACE

This is an amusing contest which not only tests speed and endurance but also balance. Smaller and younger braves can race against bigger and older braves with such surprising results that chiefs will have to establish their own series of handicaps to give bigger braves a chance and assure keen competition between the various categories at the different heights suggested. The only equipment required is four straight, lightweight rods, each 2 feet long and not more than ½ inch in diameter, and eight stout stakes, rounded at the heavy ends, four of them 16 inches long and the other four 10 inches long. All stakes are tapered from a 2-inch-in-diameter heavy end to a point, so that they may be driven into the ground easily. The terrain for the race is prepared by driving the stakes in series of four into the ground, as shown in the drawing. Two stakes 10 inches long are driven exactly 4 inches into the ground one behind the other and exactly 2 feet apart. The remaining two 10-inch stakes are driven into the ground in exactly the same way as the other two but with a distance of 18 inches between these two and the first two, as shown in the drawing. A rod is now lashed inside and at the top of each pair of stakes, as shown.

The set of four 16-inch stakes are driven exactly 4 inches into the ground in exactly the same oblong-like positions as the shorter set of stakes, with a distance of 36 inches between the two, as illustrated.

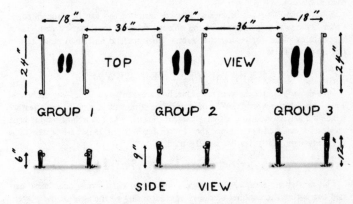

A chief can add an extra oblong or two, so that more braves can contest at the same time, or use rods 5 feet long, instead of the 2-foot ones, so that two braves in the same category, using the same rod height, can race one behind the other. In this fashion, six braves can race at the same time in three of the longer oblongs.

Distinct, easily established categories are necessary in this race to assure the contestants' being fairly evenly matched. These categories are decided by the height of the rods from the ground and the height of the contestants, as follows:

GROUP 1

Braves 4 to 5 feet tall:
Rods 6 inches from ground

GROUP 2

Braves 5 to 5½ feet tall:
Rods 9 inches from ground

GROUP 3

Braves 5½ feet and over:
Rods 12 inches from ground

The number of steps raced can range from 100 to 450. As a guide to the time required in different categories, the approximate time taken for 225 steps in Group 1 is 1¼ minutes. In Group 2, the time required is approximately 2½ minutes. In Group 3, the approximate time required is 3 minutes. These times will vary according to the speed, balance, and stamina of the contesting braves.

The race is run as follows. The chief has the runners take up their positions inside the oblongs, each brave facing in the same direction, as the footprints in the drawing show. One or two keen-eyed braves kneel outside each oblong to count the running steps taken and make sure that each foot is lifted to a position at least just above the rods. The feet need not be raised any higher but they must rise high enough to just clear the top of the rods. The chief can explain that time will be lost, and most likely the race too, by raising the feet needlessly high. On the words "Two hundred and twenty-five steps—*Run!*" each runner, on the word "*Run!*" races, on place, the number of steps given, lifting the feet as speedily as possible but no higher than can be helped above the height indicated by the rods. A chief and an assistant should verify the number of steps "run" by each contestant.

A brave who loses his balance and strikes against a rod can be disqualified, as can a brave who steps outside of the oblong, either at the front or rear. These races are excellent for testing the "racers'" balance and ability to move fast in this *Race on Place*.

BREATH FEATHER CHASE

On a day when breezes were favorable, half a dozen boys would line up behind a mark and on the word "Go!" would start out in pursuit of a fluffy eagle feather which a chief released just before his signal to start. The boy who brought back the feather counted coup. Since the "breath feathers" of eagles are scarce these days, any light, fluffy feather may be used.

FOLLOW-THE-CHIEF CHASE

This was either a rather long-range Follow-the-Leader event or a chase carried out within the confines of the village, according to the ages of the players. An older boy or instructor led a group of from six to eighteen boys following in Indian file. They did whatever the leader did, and he always did a great number of things; another instructor, in the rear of the file, checked on whether each boy was doing exactly what he was supposed to. This game, like many of the games taught Indian boys, was used to develop observation. The leader did a number of little things as he ran and it required observation on the part of the players to imitate them.

With older braves-to-be, such chases usually led across rugged terrain and those taking part had some rough jumping, climbing, swimming, and stream-fording to do before the training period was over.

HOOP AND BALL

Many Indian tribes played games with hoops of various kinds. The game which follows was a favorite with a number of tribal groups.

The players form two straight lines about 30 feet apart and with about 2 feet between the players in each line. Each line of players is given a large ball and an instructor rolls a small wooden hoop, large enough for the ball to pass through fairly easily, between the two lines of players. Modern Indians can use a metal hoop, about 18 inches in diameter, as a substitute when necessary. The leader rolls the hoop with a short stick, keeping it within his reach and under control. He either rolls it up and down halfway between the two lines or weaves in and out toward each line, daring the braves to throw the balls through the hoop as it rolls. The players must remain in line, *especially* when they throw a ball at the hoop. Any player who puts a ball through the hoop when he has stepped out of line is dropped from the game. This stresses the discipline aspect of the game, as it is hard not to step out of line in order to get a better, or closer, throw at the moving hoop. The balls should be thrown or rolled to and from between the two lines so that as many braves as possible get the chance to try their marksmanship. When a ball strikes the hoop rim and knocks the hoop over the game stops until the hoop is rolling again.

This game is more difficult when the instructor orders that the ball be thrown with both hands from the overhead position or in some other special way. No player should throw at the hoop twice in succession. The task of the hoop roller is to keep the hoop in constant motion as trickily as possible, stopping it for a moment unexpectedly or making it swerve suddenly so that a thrown ball misses its mark.

TROPHY HUNT

At the end of the first moon in the encampment, and again at the end of the summer activities, are good times to have the braves go on an observation test of this sort. The trophy, which will be won by the most observant brave, should be something worthwhile, such as a good hand ax, which he will treasure as a proof of his prowess. In the category of minor trophies, a melon or cantaloupe can be cleverly concealed to await the happy finder.

The area in which the trophy is concealed should be well-defined and not too large. Finding a trophy which has been cleverly cached in a wooded, half-mile-square tract of land is test enough for any but mature and seasoned braves. Should a trophy such as a watermelon be hidden, there is almost as much fun in hiding it as in finding it. They can be cached in small clumps of long grass or weeds, *not* in a poison ivy area, or balanced on a low crotch of a tree or bush in such a way that, taking advantage of protective coloring, they can be made very hard to locate.

Whatever the chief in charge of the hunt hides, it should be cleverly hidden but, of course, not impossibly so. Burying the object or lashing it to a high branch in a tree would be unfair ways of putting the braves' observation to the test. Hiding it in a hole in a tree stump or suspending it with a string just inside a hole, within reach, in the trunk of a tree are two ways which make finding not too easy but still possible. To take advantage of protective coloring to hide an object, such as a sheathed ax or a sheathed knife, is advisable, as such objects are hard to spot when blended with a suitable background. Hiding an object in long grass in a grassy area should be avoided, as it makes finding the trophy more a matter of chance than skill and the trophy should never be hidden in a tepee or indoors.

NATURE NO·HOW

This is a little trick-game which teaches braves to observe, in addition to learning how trees, plants, and flowers really look. It can be staged on an elaborate or very simple scale.

In a comparatively small area, prepared in advance, the chief fastens a number of birch leaves carefully onto different willow trees, wild cherry leaves on different alders, dandelion leaves on marigold stems; he exchanges the flowers on different weeds or plants and makes as many similar and scattered changes as the flora of the area permits, without injuring rare or near-rare plants of any kind. The various attachments should be made carefully, green and brown threads being used to camouflage the "grafts." The band is then taken to the faked nature terrain, the boundaries of which should be marked with white cloth or paper streamers fastened to branches or tree trunks. The braves should be given a period of about twenty minutes, longer if the area is fairly large, to discover as many substitutions as possible in the time allowed.

The brave spotting the nature switches should snip off the tied-on leaves or flowers, leaving the thread attached to the stem which he takes back to the chief.

ANIMAL AND BIRD MIMICRY

This type of game was enjoyed by Indians of all ages and of far-spread habitats. The mimicry of birds and animals was in evidence throughout a great number of their dances and ceremonies. Here are some ways in which the game was played by sound and sight. In the first version, a leader imitated the sounds made by an animal or bird and the players, standing in a circle around him, tried to guess which animal or bird was being imitated. The one who guessed correctly first was either given the chance to make the next call or whistle, or was praised by the chief, who continued the mimicry. Some of the sounds were quite easy to make and identify, such as the grunt of a woodchuck, the alarm whistle of a deer, or the unmistakable call of a killdeer or bob white. Other sounds, though well imitated, were much harder to identify. A number of animal calls have been described in Chapter 12.

Another way in which this training game was played that amused both young and old players was to have the leader silently imitate the actions of an animal or bird. This was not an easy form of the contest. Though there may be a certain striking similarity in some of the movements of different animals, there is always enough difference for a keen observer of wildthings to know just what species is being mimicked. Players of all ages watched with fascination as an old hunter showed by clever movements of the hand how certain birds flicked their tails up and down or from side to side, and portrayed the rare bird which could do both.

RUN THE GAUNTLET

This is a game based on the practice of some Indian tribes of making a number of their prisoners "run the gauntlet." The captives, one by one, were forced to run between two lines of their enemies who were armed with sticks, clubs, quirts and, sometimes, tomahawks and lances. Though the braves on each side of the rather narrow lane were just within striking distance of those who ran the gauntlet, chiefs took great care that the lines were kept the same distance apart throughout the test and that none of the armed warriors closed in on the unarmed running captives. Any prisoners who succeeded in reaching the end of the line, whether wounded or unscathed, were given every care. Their wounds were dressed by a medicine man and the best food was given to them. It is surprising how many captives ran the dread gauntlet safely, many of them not even receiving a wound as they raced and dodged the length of the line toward safety. Some of the successful runners were given their freedom, but the majority were adopted by the tribe.

Nowadays Indian boys make their volunteer "captives" run the gauntlet while the boys who form the two lines, one on each side of the lane, strike at the prisoners as they run, with light willow withes and cornstalks. Though this is not likely to cause injuries, there is always the chance of an eye's being poked with the end of a cornstalk or a willow wand. Because of this risk, the author has devised a gauntlet game to be played by using two, three, or four big, semi-hard balls, such as volley balls—if they can be borrowed from a paleface camp. Otherwise balls can be made from a number of loosely rolled-up paper balls sewn into a circular piece of cloth to make one large ball.

A chief marks two straight lines on the ground 20 feet apart and from 30 to 50 feet long. The captors stand behind these two lines, half on each side of the lane and with about 8 feet between braves in the line. Each line is given one or two balls. A box the width of the lane and 8 feet deep is drawn on the ground at each end of the lines marking the throwing area. The captives are safe in either of these two boxes but can be put out of the game by being struck anywhere below the shoulders as they run along the lane seeking the safety of either box. When a runner is hit he is out of the game and the last captive in the game can count coup and regain his freedom. In this harmless form of the gauntlet, the captives run back and forth between the two boxes, one, two, or three at a time, though not running all together. When the runners hesitate for too long a time, the chief in charge of the game counts up to six and those who do not run from the box before the counting ends are out of the game. The players in each line throw the balls at any runner at any time but they must not waste time by taking elaborate aim. No player should throw the ball twice in succession. Since the balls pass back and forth between the lines, a line may have two balls at one time.

18

Playing Like Indians: Water Sports

Many Indians belonging to tribes which lived beside lakes, rivers, or an ocean, were fine swimmers and the boys were taught, from an early age, to feel at home in the water. The author has often watched Indian boys on the Northwest Coast swim in rough, swift water and much too close to jagged rocks for safety but they seemed neither to realize nor to mind the dangers involved. Doubtless their apparent fearlessness was based to a large degree on their self-confidence and the ability to gauge their water prowess in heavy seas. Such swimming practices should be avoided by modern Indians, no matter how well they swim, and alert chiefs will immediately beach any of them who take needless risks or fail to keep close to their partners.

SWIMMING AND LIFESAVING

Today, every modern Indian should be able to swim at least reasonably well and have some knowledge of lifesaving practices, carried out in the water, for use in emergencies.

Safety Measures

No brave, even though an expert swimmer, should be allowed to swim alone on any distance test. He should be accompanied by a canoe paddled by a water-wise brave.

Each swimmer, whether expert or novice, should be paired off with another swimmer of equal ability, and each one should be made responsible for the other's safety in so far as lies in his power. At least one water-wise chief should be constantly on watch, in a canoe or boat or on the bank, with a long, stronge pole, to be able to help immediately if one of them appears to be in difficulty.

WARNING! No member of band should be allowed to enter lake, river, pond, or other unknown water to be used for swimming, or even wading, until it has been thoroughly investigated by a sub-chief or senior brave who is a good swimmer. Another good swimmer should stand by. The inspection is made to assure that there are no dangerous stumps, rocks, currents, broken bottles, glass, tin cans, or other dangerous litter on the bottom. Careful visual scrutiny from the bank or shore will often help to assure this.

Lifesaving Breaks and Towing Methods

Chiefs wise in water safety need not teach their bands all of the breaks and carries detailed in Red Cross and lifesaving handbooks, but one should at least instruct his braves in one or two of the easiest and most effective breaks and methods of towing a drowning or exhausted swimmer.

The easiest breaks to execute are, fortunately, among the most effective ones. Every brave should be taught to break away from a person in danger of drowning who clutches the would-be rescuer's wrists or forearms. This is done by exerting a sharp, jerking, downward movement toward the thumbs of the clutching hands. Strong knee pressure on the grappling person's stomach, coupled with the palm of a hand exerting sharp, upward pressure just under the person's chin, proves effective when the rescuer is clutched around the waist from in front, which is the usual grapple of the person in difficulty, as the would-be rescuer who is a novice at lifesaving generally uses a frontal approach. The rescue approach from the rear is often more effective but much depends on the state of mind, including presence of mind, and actions of the person to be rescued. Quick thinking and instant action on the part of the rescuer are essential in all lifesaving attempts. Violent strugglers may have to be "knocked out," but this is sometimes easier said than done. Ducking the head of a struggling person under water, while keeping a tight grip on his hair, may end resistance to rescue, but again, this depends on the person in trouble.

There are a number of good methods of towing ashore a person in danger of drowning, and two of the easiest ones are carried out as follows. A brave who is too tired to swim further, but does not panic, can float on his back and rest a hand firmly on each shoulder of his helper, who swims a forward basic breast stroke, facing the brave being towed. By the pressure of the hands on the shoulders of the rescuer, the tired brave, who should hold his arms nearly straight, is pushed forward to safety.

The method whereby a good swimmer swims on his back and tows a tired swimmer, who is floating on his back, by grasping him under each armpit, is perhaps an easier rescue system than holding the person being rescued by the biceps of each upper arm. The most important thing in towing and rescue work in general is practice—and then more practice.

Artificial Respiration

A chief should be able to instruct his band in simple artificial respiration techniques. There are several good methods, among the 119 known, including the long-used Schaefer Method and the more modern Holgar Nielsen system. While the author does not recommend any method in which the victim has to be placed on his back and worked on by inexperienced rescuers, it is necessary to make exceptions for the two newer, so-called "Rescue Breathing" methods which are described following the Schaefer and Nielsen systems. In *all* methods, the tongue must *never* be allowed to slip back into the throat.

Schaefer Method. The victim is placed in a prone position, stomach down, on the ground with the head lower than the body. This is done by placing a rolled blanket or jacket under the breast. After the mouth has been cleared of possible foreign matter the tongue is drawn forward and one side of the victim's face is placed on his forearm. The person applying artificial respiration then kneels on both knees, close to the waist and on the left side of the victim, placing the palms of both hands, with fingers spread out, on the lower ribs and swaying backward and forward, exerting steady rhythmic pressure from 10 to 12 times a minute until normal breathing is restored.

The Holgar Nielsen Method. This method is like the above method until the victim's face rests on his forearm. The person applying artificial respiration then kneels on one knee in front of and close to the head of the victim, placing both hands with fingers spread out and thumbs almost touching on his back and just below the shoulder blades. He now presses steadily and evenly downward on the back, then sways backward to relieve the pressure. He now grasps the victim's arms just above the elbows and raises them upward and forward until he feels the pull at the shoulders. Lifting the arms forces air into the lungs, and the rescuer's arms should be kept straight while he performs this movement. The rescuer then releases the victim's arms and again places his hands, as before, on the victim's back and recommences the motions described above. Each motion should occupy about 1½ seconds, with a brief pause between motions. This ends up with a timing similar to that of the method described above, from 10 to 12 times a minute.

In both methods it is important to watch the victim closely after he has apparently recommenced breathing, as respiration may stop and the artificial respiration must then be continued.

Unless the day is very warm it is wise to cover as much of the victim's body as practical with blankets to retain body heat and offset shock.

The so-called "Rescue Breathing" methods of resuscitation must be given a place here on account of their distinguished sponsorship and the successful results obtained by the use of these methods. Some of the major first aid organizations, branches of military services, lifeguards, and other authorities on artificial respiration have adopted the mouth-to-mouth method as practical and effective. It is recommended by them for all cases where breathing has ceased as the result of near-drowning, smoke or gas suffocation, or loss of consciousness from electric shock. To restore breathing, the rescuer simply blows his breath, by the mouth-to-mouth method, into the victim's lungs. The chief point in its favor is the fact that it forces far more air into the patient's lungs than any of the other methods. Another major advantage is that no mechanical equipment of any sort is needed for the simpler form of this type of resuscitation. This is how it is applied.

Rescue Breathing. The unconscious victim is placed on his back, with head tilted back and lower jaw pulled forcibly forward. His chin must never be allowed to sag. His mouth and throat are cleared of any foreign matter by wiping with cloth or fingers. The rescuer then places the thumb of his left hand between the victim's teeth, closes the patient's nose with the fingers of his right hand, takes a deep breath and places his mouth tightly over victim's mouth and his own thumb. He then blows into the mouth forcibly enough to make the chest rise and fall and continues to breathe hard *or blow* his breath into the lungs of the patient every three or four seconds, until normal breathing is restored. The rescuer's mouth should be lifted from time to time so that the victim has a chance to exhale as his breath returns.

Immediately following the recent adoption of rescue breathing by prominent authorities, many practical devices appeared on the market to supplant the direct mouth-to-mouth contact of this means of resuscitation. One is a small resuscitating tube, called an "airway," and this S-shaped tube has a mouthpiece for the rescuer and a breathing tube for the victim, inserted above his tongue, which eliminates the direct oral contact between the rescuer and patient. Several other effective tubes are now available and all of them offer hope for successful and speedy resuscitation. As each airway or tube comes with full instructions for its use, it is only pointed out here that the rescuer's lips should be removed from his end of the tube after each blow in order to get a fresh supply of air and allow the patient to exhale. It may be said that practically all of these tube devices are easy to operate.

Some camps are well equipped with modern, effective mechanical devices, such as pulmotors of various kinds, for applying artificial respiration but such equipment is usually kept on the main waterfront. A number of such devices are excellent when operated by someone who is well versed in their use.

Wherever swimming or water sports are in progress there should always be constant, alert, lifeguard supervision. These guards can be stationed on rafts, in boats or canoes, in the water, or on the bank of a lake or stream, in close touch with the swimmers. The guards should be provided with long, light poles, heavy ropes, knotted at the end which is thrown to the person in difficulties, and, when available, life belts should be kept handy.

AQUATIC GAMES

Only braves who swim well should be allowed to participate in the aquatic games which follow, and lifeguards should patrol the water where the games are being held throughout the entire period of these activities.

Log Push Race

Two, three, or four swimmers push a log, broadside on, in front of them, holding the top of the log with both hands and swimming forward only with the feet. Each team contests against one or more teams. All teams start from the same starting line and each team pushes a log of the same wood, the same length, and, as far as possible, of about the same weight and girth.

The distance for this race can range from 20 to 50 yards, according to the ages of the bands participating. Races with only one brave to a short log can also be contested, using light logs of about the same size.

Log Push-O-War

From two to six braves can compete on each team for this challenge. A big, long, light log is floated into position and one team gets on each side of it, holding the log with one or both hands on top of it, and the feet ready to drive the log forward on the word "Push!" A float-marker is placed 20 yards behind each team and the objective of each team is to drive the log forward toward the marker in front of it, despite the push of the rival team on the opposite side of the log. The log must be pushed broadside on throughout the race.

Log Obstacle Race

From two to four challengers who are good swimmers start from a given line, swim 30 yards to a big, long, smooth log, swim under it and then continue to a finish line, marked by a float, 20 or 30 yards further on. When no suitable logs are available, shorter, individual logs can be used. Additional logs placed at six-yard intervals can be added as additional handicaps when the best swimmers are contesting. Only the breast stroke should be used throughout this race, except in the final spurt when no logs are in the way. A course master, in addition to a lifeguard canoe or canoes patrol, can push the logs with a pole into favorable positions, that is broadside on, to the approaching swimmers.

Dog Paddle Race

The challengers race 50 yards, using the Dog Paddle Stroke only.

Loon Race

The swimmers take a deep breath and try to swim 20 yards, breast stroke, just under water all the way. When a swimmer comes to the surface he is disqualified. The length of this race is decided by the ability of the contestants.

CANOE RACES

For braves with some canoeing experience, the following will prove challenging and exciting.

Marker Canoe Race

Each canoe in this race is paddled either by a brave in the stern or by one brave in the bow and one in the stern. The canoe crews race a distance of 100 yards, paddling *completely* around float-markers about 3 feet in diameter, placed in a straight line 20 feet apart, with one line of markers for each canoe. This race can be made more strenuous and difficult by increasing the distance, or by adding additional markers to the 100-yard course.

It is interesting to note that in all races requiring markers of various sorts, effective markers can be cut from heavy cardboard. When painted on both sides with a bright yellow or white paint and dried in the sun after use, they can be used many times throughout the season.

Canoe Portage Race

This event can best be contested on a lake with a bow and stern paddler in each canoe. From a starting point the braves paddle 50 or 100 yards to shore, land, make a 30-yard portage, hand-carrying their canoe along the shore, embark, and paddle back to the starting point.

This race can be contested with only one paddler in each canoe, who pushes the canoe in shallow water close to the shore, instead of making the 30-yard portage, since no brave should make such a heavy portage alone.

Primitive Paddle Canoe Race

There should be two paddlers but no paddles in each canoe for this race. On the word "Go!" the paddlers hand-paddle their canoe from a starting mark to a point 50 yards distant on the lake shore, beach their canoe correctly, go ashore, improvise two paddles out of any wildwood material or driftwood available, embark, and, each brave using his improvised paddle only, race back to the starting point.

A little thought on the part of a canoe crew can assure winning the race. The question to be decided is, how long should a crew search for suitable material with which to improvise two paddles? A canoe crew which first reaches shore may hastily snatch up two thin sticks which not only have practically no propelling power but may also break en route to the winning float. Another crew may spend a little extra time looking for more effective "paddles" and end up by winning the race.

Canoe Tracking Race

(How to "track" canoes is explained in Chapter 10.)

This race is equally interesting as a one- or 2-man event. It can best be contested in this way. A long pole-marker with a streamer tied on top is driven into the water's edge at a point on a lakefront which has a clear shoreline extending for at least 50 yards in each direction from the pole. A "clear shoreline" is one that is not too strewn with rocks and is comparatively free from bushes along the shore, though low rocks close off shore can prove assets, as obstacles, provided there are about an equal number on each side of the starting marker. A big stake is driven in at the lake's edge 50 yards from the pole, on each side of it.

For the first few races there should be only one canoeman to each canoe so that he handles both tracking lines. A contestant, with the bow of his canoe in line with the big stake, starts from each stake on a flag or whistle "Go!" signal. With his tracking lines shipshape, he sets off, moving his canoe as fast as possible, and at the distance from shore which is determined by the way he handles his lines, towards the finish pole.

After the initial races, the contestants begin the race at the pole, track to the stakes and then back again to the pole. This makes a course of 100 yards and, of course, longer ones may be used when the lake shoreline permits. The canoes should not touch shore at any point in the race and, occasionally, it takes a little maneuvering on the tracker's part when making the turns away from shore. Each contestant will find that both of his tracking lines have to be used well in order for his canoe to make good speed and hold a straight course whenever the shoreline permits.

Novices will soon find that with a little practice they will be able to track either a canoe or rowboat safely, and at good speed. When skill has been developed in the art, races will have to be contested over considerably longer stretches.

When there are no rocks just offshore to provide natural hazards to surmount, a few stout stakes driven into the bottom about 20 feet offshore, with their tops sticking up about 6 feet above the surface of the water, can take the place of rocks. An equal number of stakes should be placed the same distance apart on each side of the starting pole on the way to the stakes at which the turn is made.

It is fascinating to watch an expert tracker track his fragile canoe around sharp rock outcroppings, some of them 60 or 70 feet offshore, with even worse stretches of rock inshore, which make it impossible to track the canoe closer to land. Of course, tracking is done on rivers, both upstream and downstream, usually with currents and eddies making the work more difficult. Great precision and sureness of eye and hand are essential in such circumstances.

Canoe Tow Race

How to tow one canoe behind another correctly is told in Chapter 10. The braves taking part in this challenge must know the method and be able to make the bridle required fairly quickly, in order to add interest to the race. The race can be held on the edge of a lakeshore, where the two canoes required for each team of two braves can be drawn up, side by side, close to the water's edge. The start of the race can also be made from a boat dock, where the two canoes for each team are moored, one behind the other, to the dock.

There should not be more than three teams contesting at the same time and all of the braves participating should swim fairly well and be dressed in breech-clouts. A floating marker, painted yellow or white for good visibility, should be moored 60 yards away from shore at a point as nearly as possible the same distance away from each team. Each team of two is given a 24-foot length of light-weight but strong rope and two paddles. The teams stand alongside their two canoes, ready for action.

On the word "Race!" the braves on each team hitch the canoe to be towed, by the improvised bridle method, to the towing canoe, in which the two braves ride, each with a paddle. The brave in the stern, in addition to paddling when he gets the chance, is responsible for the manipulation of the towing line to which the rear craft is tied. The braves must paddle around the buoy-marker, towing the rear canoe around it, without letting either canoe touch the marker, then paddle as swiftly as possible back to the starting point. Here the towed canoe is unhitched and the towing line neatly rolled; and the two team members line up alongside the canoe in which they contested. The first team to finish wins and counts coup, provided everything is shipshape.

A team forfeits 10 points if the canoe in which they ride touches the marker, and an additional 5 points is lost if the towed craft touches the marker; should both canoes bump the marker, the team is disqualified.

This contest can be made more difficult by increasing the distance, adding a second marker to negotiate, or including both of these suggestions in the challenge.

CANOE GAMES

For braves who are more skilled, there are some strenuous and tricky canoe games to enjoy.

Canoe Club-Ball

Two canoe crews contest in this game with two paddlers and a club-wielding brave in each craft. The club-man kneels in the bow and is armed with a light, flat, wooden racquet shaped like a ping-pong paddle, lashed to the end of a 6-foot, stout, lightweight pole. The ball used for this game can be either any rubber ball about the size of a volley ball or smaller, or a round, inflated bladder of some sort.

A central float-marker is anchored and two markers are placed in line with it, one at each end at a distance of 20 to 30 yards, to mark the game boundary. The object of the game is to drive the ball from the center float-marker, each club-man only propelling the ball to his opponents' goal-marker.

This somewhat strenuous game is not only a test of the club-man's judgment and skill but also that of his canoe crew of two, who have to follow the ball as he manages to drive it forward, turn the canoe speedily when the opponents force the ball in the opposite direction, and at the same time avoid collision with the other canoe. Only the club-man hits the ball, and any other crew member who hits it with his hand or paddle disqualifies his team. Two or three goals can decide which crew count coup.

The author has staged this strenuous game when several old but staunch canoes were available, and at such times two or three canoes, instead of one, contested on each side.

Medicine Ball Canoe Tag

This is a good game for canoe-wise modern Indians who know how to handle canoes very well, when some older canoes are available for this sport. A canoe with bow and stern paddlers and a ball thrower kneeling amidship sets out in pursuit of one to six other canoes, each with a crew of two paddlers and a ball thrower. The brave who throws the ball is armed with a large bladder, taken from a sea mammal—but in these modern times this can be replaced by a large inflated ball of almost any kind, such as a basketball or volleyball. The thrower tries to throw the ball into the nearest, or any, canoe, and when he succeeds in doing so, that canoe becomes the tagger canoe and the game continues. Of course, the two paddlers as well as the thrower try to knock the ball away before it can actually fall into their canoe but once it is in, that canoe becomes the new tagger. The ball can be tossed from any range decided on by the thrower, and quite often balls tossed high score more easily than ones thrown at a low angle, which bounce off the canoe.

There are a number of variations of this game, such as making a rule that the crew of the canoe being chased cannot strike the ball to prevent it from falling into their canoe. Another way to play the game, which makes it much easier for younger players, is to rule that a canoe need only be hit with the ball, instead of the ball's having to drop into the craft. The game can also be played with only one paddler and a thrower in each canoe, but this slows the contest down considerably.

Medicine Ball Canoe Tag, like all games played on the water, should be most carefully supervised by chiefs in canoes or boats, who follow the action of the game as closely as possible.

Coup Stick Canoe Tag

This is another good game for modern Indians who are canoe-wise. As in all aquatic games, careful supervision is necessary.

One canoe, with a paddler fore and aft and a brave kneeling in the bow, chases from one to four other canoes, each with a similar crew. The bowman in each canoe does not paddle but is armed with a light, straight, springy coup stick about 5 or 6 feet long, made from a willow branch or other supple stick, which is held by the butt in one hand only. It is the coup stick bearer's task to touch the canoe being chased by his craft, and of course he may also try to touch any other canoe which is unwary enough to come too close in the excitement of the game. When he succeeds in touching any part of another craft, the crew of that craft become the new chasers and the sport continues.

Coup Stick Canoe Cross Tag

This is an exciting variation of the above game, suggested only for skilled canoemen. The rule is that any canoe crossing between the pursuing canoe and the canoe being chased becomes the canoe which must be chased. While there is some risk of an uncautious crew being bumped in this version of the game it provides much practice in handling a canoe well in case of emergency. With so many craft on the water these days, any practice which helps to develop skill in handling a canoe in case of sudden emergency may prove to be a life saver.

Canoe Tug of War

For this strenuous contest, two canoes are fastened together at the sterns by 12 to 16 feet of stout rope. A strip of cloth is hung from the center of this rope, and it must hang down above the starting mark as the signal to "Tug!" is given. This saves the canoe from the strain of a strong jerk at the start. The two or more paddlers in each canoe try, by strong paddling, to tow the rival canoe backward for a distance decided on and marked before the tug begins. This distance can range from 12 to 20 yards and the canoemen try to keep the craft on as straight a line as possible. A canoe veering off at too much of a tangent can be disqualified and the coup awarded to the other crew.

LOG RIDING AND ROLLING

When choosing logs with which to build a raft, one can set aside a pair for the exciting sport, known to lumberjacks as *birling*. A log suitable for log riding and rolling is best made from a 12- to 14-foot length of a dry, dead pine tree, preferably white pine, which ranges from 2 to 3 feet in diameter. The log should be straight, smooth and as completely round as possible. The bark is left on. Finding suitable dead trees or logs close to the shore of a lake solves the problem of getting them into the water easily. How to roll logs without difficulty and how to carry them easily across ground on which they cannot be rolled is told in Chapter 6.

Once the log is prepared and in the water, the would-be birlers, older boys in bathing trunks, who can swim, can start the none-too-easy job of trying to outwit the rolling log as they balance upright on it and try to remain on top.

Great care must be taken by birlers that when they lose balance they dive or jump clear of the log. Even greater safety in clearing the log is assured by jumping immediately when one senses that he is losing balance. Of course, the trick and thrill of birling is actually in recovering balance and mastery of the log, but that comes later.

Birling should *never* be carried out without strict supervision by at least one mature chief. His position should be in the water on the shore of the lake, close to the birlers, or in a rowboat or canoe only a few feet away from the activity. It is only rarely that a birler will strike himself against the log, because when he discovers that he is losing control of the log he will usually instinctively jump or dive from it. The logs should always be in deep, or fairly deep, water.

Those who engage in this exciting sport should become well acquainted with their mounts before attempting to ride them while standing upright. Begin by leaning on the log, letting the chest and body rest on the log. After starting in this way one can gradually reach the stage of sitting astride, then sideways, which is considerably more difficult, on the log. From there on, one gradually learns to stand upright and balance easily on the log, and eventually not only to keep it rolling quickly underfoot but also to drive it backward or forward—broadside on, of course—in the direction desired.

Log rolling and riding contests can be carried out in a number of ways to test the skill of the birlers. Simple balance contests for beginners may be held, in which each boy sees how long he can remain balanced on the log, without trying to make it roll under him. To make competition keener, two logs can be introduced at this point, with a boy attempting to keep balanced on each log, and with the logs floating at least 20 feet apart. The next stage is racing the logs forward for distances ranging from 20 to 100 yards, the distance being based on the skill of the braves contesting. Later, these logs can be rolled backward.

When the log rollers become really expert, contests can be held in which two braves, one balanced on each end of the same log, can try, on the "Go!" signal, to throw each other off the log by forward and reverse rolling, sudden stops, and other tricks of the lumberman, which they will acquire through practice. Tenderfeet braves may be allowed to wear sneakers, but *only with non-skid soles*, instead of birling in bare feet; but then all contestants should wear them in order to assure fair matches of skill.

Lumberjacks competing in such contests have the decided advantage of wearing sharp, heavy calks on the soles and heels of their heavy boots, which makes staying on a log very much easier. Though beginner contestants in log rolling are sometimes allowed to mount the logs from a boat or landing stage, it is actually far safer for log rollers in the amateur class—which includes nearly everybody except seasoned lumbermen—to get aboard the logs directly from the water.

OTTER SLIDE

A synthetic Otter Slide, built into a lake or river bank, provided there is a suitable spot for it, is a source of fun which every brave will enjoy.

The slide should be cut into a rather high bank at a sufficient angle to assure a speedy ride down the chute from the top of the bank into the lake or stream, which should be fairly deep at the spot where the "otters" hit the water. It is

difficult to find a really suitable bank for the slide, but one can usually be found somewhere in the vicinity of the encampment. A chute with a heavy clay content is the best and easiest to keep in good shape for sliding. The slide should end where the water is at least three feet deep and clear of rocks. The depth can be much greater and is best decided by the ability and age of the otters using the slide. Strict supervision is required at all times when the slide is being used, not only to make certain that no brave gets into difficulties in the water at the end of the slide but also to keep the sliders far enough apart during the descent to assure safe, smooth sliding. While the slide down the chute can be made sitting down and with no other equipment than that provided by nature, the ride down can also be made on boards. These slide-boards should be perfectly smooth, strong and thin, about 2½ feet long and from 14 to 18 inches wide. There should be a 6-inch length of fairly heavy rope, knotted at the holding end, fastened to the edge of the floor of the board on each side, to serve as a hand hold. The sliding boards must be slightly turned up in front, and a little steaming and bending will do this. The width of the chute should not be more than 3 feet. On a really good clay slide which is frequently inspected by a chief, sliders can slide down lying on their bellies as well as in a sitting position, the clay which they pick up on the way down being speedily washed off when they hit the water.

When suitable planks are available and there is a carpenter to supervise the building of the slide, one may build a wooden-surfaced slide onto an earth or any other sort of bank, provided the slant is suitable, but this artificial chute is not nearly so satisfactory as one provided by nature, with a little help from the chiefs. When a plank chute is constructed, it is always much safer to build it on top of a sloping bank, which serves as a sure foundation, because a chute built on trestles can be unsafe unless built by chiefs with a thorough knowledge of carpentry. Some smooth metal can also be used to surface a slide, provided it has neither rough edges nor joins.

19

Indian Crafts, Signalling, and Storytelling

The Indians of practically all habitats were skilled craftsmen, excelling in various fields, often determined by the area in which they lived. Most tribes were also expert in various forms of signalling. Storytelling is included in this chapter because stories, though not tangible artifacts, are actually built and woven from the minds of storytellers and many of the tales devised in the magic mirror in the mind of a storyteller have proved more lasting than many of the ancient articles created by the skilled hands of master craftsmen.

PARFLECHES AND DECORATED
STORAGE BOXES

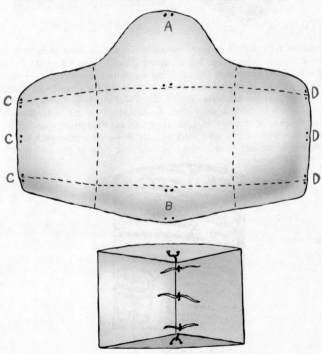

The so-called *parfleche* of the Indians was usually rawhide made into a flat, fold-over case in which blankets and other gear were carried. These cases, sacks, and bags—also made from rawhide—were frequently decorated with beautiful designs. A good imitation of such fold-over cases can easily be made by a modern Indian by simply making the carrier from an oblong piece of strong, white canvas of the size required, and painting Plains designs on one or two sides of it. Leather thongs or strong tapes can be used either to lace the parfleche after it is packed or to tie it in place instead of lacing it.

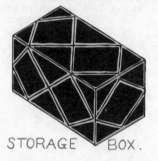

STORAGE BOX.

PARFLECHE.

A durable type of rigid *parfleche* can easily be made by using as the base an ordinary, lightweight, wooden box measuring about 24 inches long, 14 inches wide and 10 to 12 inches high. Of course, the size of the box can vary when there is not much choice of empty boxes. A strip of pliable leather about 2 inches wide and the length of the box makes a good hinge. Nail this hinge firmly onto the lid and top side of the box, using short, flat-headed nails or big tacks. Use fine sand or rough sandpaper to smooth the entire box and then give it a coat of flat white or light buff-colored paint, inside and out. When the paint has dried, draw the decorative outlines desired on the box and then paint on the designs with

FRONT   OF
STORAGE   BOX

bright colors. A better job can be done by covering the entire outside of the box with heavy cloth or lightweight canvas and then painting it and adding the decorations. The Plains Indians were the chief users of *parfleche* containers. The Northwest Coast tribes made magnificent wooden containers which they painted with colorful designs. They used such boxes for storing food and as potlatch gifts. One of these storage boxes is illustrated.

LEATHER AND CANVAS WORK

Many Indian men were expert leather workers, since they often had to make things from leather, such as *parfleche* for medicine bundles, medicine shields, and other things which the women were not permitted to make. The men also liked to work with various sorts of leathers in forming part of their weapons, so modern Indians can take up leather work at their encampment without feeling that they are doing the work of women.

There are many articles to be made from leather and leather strips, such as hatbands, belts, headbands, parts of war bonnets, medicine bags, quivers for arrows, and decorative fringes for leggings and shirts. The Indians used buckskin for many of these things and it is interesting to note that no tanning agents were used in preparing buckskin from rawhide. The rawhide was smoke-treated and then "worked" until it became soft and pliable. Sometimes these skins were dyed. Real buckskin is lightweight, the only leather that can be blown through, and it is very comfortable to wear. The Indians also made so-called buckskin not only from the hide of the male deer but also from the skins of buffalo, elk, antelope, and other animals.

Today buckskin is expensive, and modern braves will have to use whatever substitutes they like best. Fortunately, there are a number of them, including the so-called chamois leather and other, thicker leathers which can be bought fairly cheaply. Another good replacement is cotton flannel of the right color or dyed to buckskin color, which ranged from white through ivory to rather dark beige, according to its preparation. Even cotton cloths can be dyed and used as "buckskin," as can various weights of canvas, which may be made into *parfleche* covers, tepees, and other useful things which modern Indian bands require.

Ax Sheath

Making a protective leather sheath for an ax is not difficult, but it is well to make a paper pattern first. Fold a piece of paper in half and place the axhead on it. Make allowance for the width of the back of the ax blade and trace around the blade with a pencil, allowing ½ inch extra along the lower edge and also for the cutting edge. Before drawing the flap, allow for the top width of axhead, then sketch in the flap. Cut a ⅜-inch-wide strip of heavy leather, shaped like the front of the sheath, to be sewn in position there to protect the lacing from the keen cutting edge of the ax—or instead, a strip of tough leather one inch wide can be doubled and sewn into place where the cutting edge of the ax touches the sheath.

Place the paper pattern on the piece of leather which is going to form the sheath and trace the pattern onto it. Punch four small holes through the leather on the flap part of sheath, as shown in the drawing, and then join each pair of

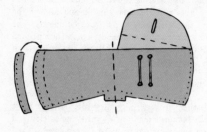

holes, vertically, with a narrow slit, to slip a belt through. A narrow slit is cut through the flap, as illustrated, so that it may be fastened in place with either a small hardwood toggle or a leather knot attached to the front part of the sheath directly under the slit, or coming through from the other side of the leather in the form of a leather thong, knotted to pass through the slit fairly easily. Corresponding holes along the cutting edge and lower part of the sheath, as marked in the drawing, allow the sheath to be laced together with a tough, round thong or leather lace.

A fringe should be cut from a straight or curved strip of soft leather, about 1¼ inches wide and long enough to reach from the top of the sheath to the hole left for the ax handle, as shown in the drawing. The length of the strip will vary according to the size of the axhead. The strip should have holes punched down one side to correspond with the holes in the sheath, so that it may be laced into place between the two halves of the sheath with the same leather thong which holds the sheath together. The fringe is made by snipping from an outer edge of the strip to ⅜ inch from the other edge. This is done before insertion between the two halves of the sheath and the lacing.

Breechclouts and Aprons

Long trousers have already been mentioned as best for expeditions through rough country, and today the men of many Indian tribes wear blue jeans on similar terrain. Despite this, it is well to know how to make a Plains breechclout and Woodland apron for council fire and ceremonial use.

Breechclout. This loin cloth is best made from red or blue flannel, or heavy, colored, cotton material will serve. The breechclout should be as long as the brave is tall and as wide as about one third of his waist measurement. It is worn between the legs and pulled over a belt which holds it in place, with an equal length of cloth hanging down front and back, as shown in the drawing. It may be decorated with painted designs or beads or both.

Apron. The Woodland type of breech cloth is really an apron, made from two squares of cloth, attached around the waist with thongs or tapes. It can also be worn over a belt. An apron should be worn with long leggings or long trousers, though it can be worn with the front and back flaps of the apron sewn to a pair of snug-fitting, colored, short underdrawers. Woodland designs can be painted or beaded on the apron.

WOODLAND
APRON

PLAINS
BREECHCLOUT

Bear-Eared Headband

This easy-to-make headband was worn by some tribes of the Northwest Coast Indians on special occasions and especially by braves belonging to a Bear Society. Members of Bear Societies in other habitats also wore a similar headdress, when they did not wear a bear head mask. This headband can be made of fairly

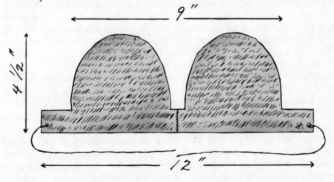

stiff brown or grey felt, or some stiff cloth or leather, which will allow the ears to remain erect when the headband is worn. Short thongs are fastened to each end of the band so that they can be tied behind the ears to hold the headband in place.

The diagram represents this bear headdress in adult size, so when making one for a younger brave a paper pattern should be cut out first to assure the headband's being of the correct size before being cut from the material chosen.

Moccasin Making

Little material and few tools are required to make a pair of good looking, serviceable moccasins. As buckskin becomes scarcer and more expensive, these days, a piece of any tough, but supple leather about 12 inches by 20 inches and at least $\frac{1}{16}$ inch thick may be used. A spool of strong linen thread, a blunt needle, a small cake of beeswax, and an awl or ice pick are needed.

A pattern should first be made. Fold a 12-inch square of strong paper in half. Place one foot on it so that the inside of the foot is $\frac{1}{4}$ inch from the fold and the heel is one inch from the end of the paper, then draw around the foot with a soft pencil. Draw another outline around the first and $\frac{1}{4}$ inch outside it, as shown in Figure 1. When Point A, the widest part of the foot, is reached, draw a line straight back to the heel and extend it one inch beyond the heel, to Point C, at the end of the paper. Starting at Point B, cut out along the outside outline only as far as Point C. When the paper is opened out flat, both halves of the pattern will look alike.

Place the opened pattern flat on the leather and trace around both halves with a soft pencil. Cut out this moccasin. Now trace and cut out another moccasin. So far, there is neither a left nor right moccasin.

Fold the smooth side of the leather *inside*, keeping the edges even with each other. Then, from Point B in Figure 1, punch four to eight holes $\frac{1}{8}$ inch apart and about $\frac{1}{16}$ inch from the edge. Sew them together with the overcast stitch, shown in Figure 2, with well-waxed thread. Keep stitches even, pulling each one tight as the work progresses. Punch four to eight more holes and continue the sewing. The holes are not all punched at the same time, as the work will be neater when they are punched a few at a time. When the sewing is completed, turn the moccasin inside out and press the seam with some smooth, hard object to flatten it out. Up to this point, there has, as stated above, been no left or right foot moccasin, so take either one of them for the left foot from now on. Place this moccasin flat, as shown in Figure 3, and make a vertical, center cut about 4 to 4½ inches long, then a cross, horizontal cut about 2 inches long, as illustrated. Now do the same with the other moccasin, but place it in *reverse* position, so it will fit the right foot. Try on each moccasin, forcing the foot well down into the toe, while wearing the same weight socks as those which will be worn with the moccasins when they are completed. Press the leather together at the heel and, with a pencil, mark the curve of the heel on one half of the leather, then pencil another line $\frac{1}{4}$ inch outside the one just made. It is not necessary to mark the other side of the heel. Trim along the outside line on the half marked, then flatten it against the other side and trim the other side like the first. Now fold moccasin down center of sole so that the edges meet evenly along the center cut and heel and make a ¾-inch slit parallel to the folded sole and

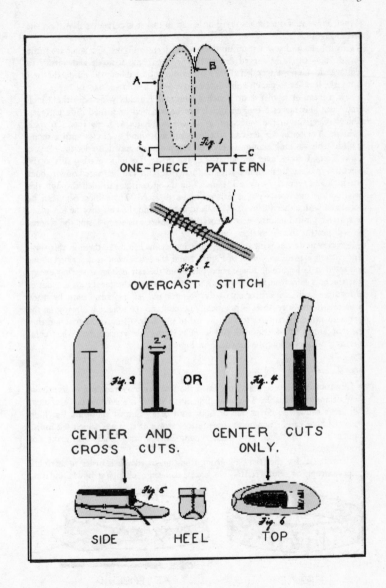

ONE-PIECE   PATTERN

OVERCAST   STITCH

CENTER AND CUTS.
CROSS

OR

CENTER ONLY.   CUTS

SIDE   HEEL   TOP

¾ inch above it. Trim the resulting little flap so that it is curved as shown on the heel in Figure 5.

Punch holes and sew a seam up the heel, as seen in Figure 5, sewing from the outside. Sew the little curved flap to the heel, stitching it inside and outside to reinforce it. Using a wooden darner or an old solid rubber ball inside the heel will make it easier to punch holes in the curved flap and lower part of heel.

Sew a piece of leather 1 or 2 inches long and 2 inches wide onto the 2-inch cross cut. This makes a tongue which can be rounded or shaped differently, as desired. Cut slits in the moccasin, as shown in Figure 5, for a thong to pass through. A scrap of leather can be cut round and round in circles until a thong is made which is long enough to encircle the moccasin and tie under the tongue. Turn the cuff down over and all around the thong. To avoid cutting slits in the moccasin in order to accommodate the thong, the cuff can be turned down about one inch and securely sewn all round. The thong can be threaded through this hem, and as one wears out it can easily be replaced. These moccasins can be decorated with either Plains or Woodland designs, and the cuff may be left plain, or fringed, pinked or otherwise decorated. An inner sole worn inside the moccasin will protect feet from stone bruises.

Braves who do not wish a cuff on their moccasins can make them in this way. The pattern is made as shown in Figure 1 and the leather cut as described above and sewn as in Figure 3. There is no change in the assembling or sewing *except* that the cuts shown in Figure 3 are not made. Instead, the moccasins are cut as in Figure 4 with *two* center cuts only. A right and left moccasin must be made as before. In this way, there is practically no cuff and the tongue is already on the moccasin and only requires to be trimmed to the desired length. Apart from this, the moccasin is fitted, trimmed, and sewn as in the first version; but when completed, it will look like the moccasin in Figure 6.

Tom-Toms

Tom-toms are easy to make, provided the few materials required to improvise these drums are available. The most difficult to secure is a suitable piece of rawhide large enough to cover one or both ends of a drum or tom-tom. Rawhide, untanned hide, can be bought at some leather stores or at stores which sell Indian supplies to camps. When procurable, young calfskin or goatskin also make fine drum heads.

The material for the frame of drum, tom-tom or tombe is easier to assemble. Empty, strong or reinforced cheese boxes, nail kegs, chopping bowls, old tubs

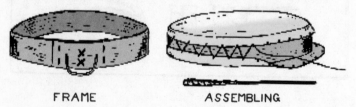

FRAME   ASSEMBLING

and even, as a last resort, big tin cans can serve the purpose. Nail kegs can be made into the tombe form of drum, with two rawhide ends. Big, round cheese boxes can be formed into tom-toms with either one or two rawhide ends. Old tubs, especially cedar ones, can be made into big pow-wow drums, such as the ones used by the Chippewa. When the drums are well painted and decorated, it is difficult or impossible to tell their origin. The long thongs which bind the drum heads to the frames can be cut from a suitable piece of supple leather by cutting round and round in a circle, in the width required for the thong, until a long enough lace is made.

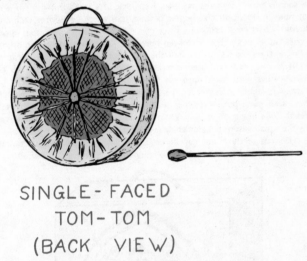

SINGLE - FACED
TOM - TOM
(BACK VIEW)

The rawhide covers of the drums are always soaked in water for at least 24 hours and are stretched tightly and laced onto the drum head while still wet. They will take about thirty hours to dry and should not be beaten at all while drying—in warm shade or in a room which has a moderate temperature. The covers can be painted, as can the drum frame, but only powder paints, which mix with water, should be used on the covers.

Beaters

The beaters can be made from sticks of oak or other hard wood. They range in length from 12 to 30 inches and taper from about $\frac{3}{4}$ inch to $\frac{3}{16}$ inch. The butt end of each drumstick is wrapped around with several thicknesses of gaily colored cloth, about 3 inches wide, which is bound onto the stick with a thin piece of thong or twine. This stick is pictured with the single-faced tom-tom. Another beater is made by wrapping a one-inch strip of buckskin or other light-weight leather around the heavy end of the beater and fastening it there with a thin thong. This beater stick is shown with the double-faced tom-tom.

Offbeat Drums

Two rather unusual types of drums are added because one is easy to make when no suitable round boxes are available to make a hoop drum and the other drum is interesting, as it permits tonal and sound-carrying experimentation.

Square Drum. Square drums were used a great deal by Northwest Coast Indians and sometimes used by tribes of Plains Indians, though most of the tribes preferred the round drums, because a circle was considered a perfect form by them. The advantage of this square, two-headed drum is that it can be made from square boxes of almost any size, from that of a small tom-tom to a large drum. Since most drums take quite a beating, it is wise to reinforce each corner with either short cross struts or a piece of wood cut to fit each corner, once the top and bottom of the box have been removed. The two heads of the drum are laced on in the same way as those of the round tom-tom illustrated. For decorative effect, when two skin heads are laced together in this way, the ends being pulled together with the thongs, the heads can be scalloped, instead of being cut straight; supple skin heads when tightly laced assume a scalloped effect without scalloping, but the former results in a more pronounced scallop effect. When the two heads are made large enough, there is little wooden frame visible when the square drum is completed, ready for decoration. Both the heads and visible sections of the frame can be decorated with suitable designs painted in bright colors and a few feathers can be hung from the corners, if desired.

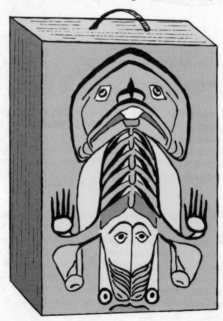

Round and square drums, especially big ones, give a much better sound when hung. They can be hung from branched poles or hung in specially built frames, such as those used by the Chippewa and Ojibway, among others.

Water Drums. Comparatively few tribes made use of this sort of drum. The Seneca used it for signalling, since it could be heard for surprisingly long distances. The Navajo made their water drums by stretching the head over either a big pottery jar or a watertight wooden frame. The easiest way to make a water drum is from a well-made nail keg, which can be made waterproof by soaking in water. The heads of such drums can be covered with buckskin or chamois leather, soaked in water and stretched into place. These drum heads were kept wet while the drum was being played.

Special sound effects were sometimes produced by putting a handful of round, smooth pebbles inside an ordinary drum and using water drums with varying quantities of water inside.

BOW AND ARROW MAKING

Modern chiefs will find that there are a number of books available which are devoted entirely to the craft of making bows and arrows, should they wish to add this art to their bands' handicraft program projects.

Making A Bow

The Indians made not only strong and effective bows and arrows for hunting and war, but also decorative ones of great beauty and craftsmanship for ceremonial purposes; arrows for dual use were rarely made. Modern Indians can make bows suitable for decoration and ceremony from 4-foot lengths of hickory, ash, or other suitable hardwoods, about 1½ inches wide and between ½ and ¾ inches thick. With a sharp jackknife, file, and sandpaper, the wand may be shaped and tapered, cutting the nocks down to ¾ inch from the foot of each end. A thong, sinew, or strong, waxed cord can be used for a bowstring.

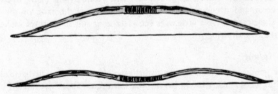

If the bow does not bend evenly and pull smoothly, the stiff sections which interfere with the proper bending of the bow should be filed and sandpapered until the weapon bends well. Indians usually bent bows when the wood was still green but the white man's bow is generally left to dry and season, then oiled and greased before being bent. Modern Indians can steam the wood thoroughly when the bow is cut to size, and then bend it around some heavy nails driven into a piece of two by six in order to shape the bow as desired. The pull of bows range from 20 through 30 pounds for target pull and up to 45 pounds for hunting bows, which can be fired only by a strong-armed bowman. If the finished bow has too weak a pull to be effective, modern braves can do as the Indians did and wrap a good part of the bow with thin strips of rawhide or leather, first soaked in water, which will add considerable strength and resiliency to the weapon.

Red or black strips of cloth, or both, glued onto the bow at top and bottom, or Indian designs painted on the wood, will add considerably to the bow's appearance. The bowstring can be fastened to the bow by a close hitch in the lower nock and a bowline in the upper nock. Of course, the bow should be kept unstrung when not in use.

Bow Cases

The Indians lavished great care on their precious bows, always kept them unstrung when not in use and often sheathed them in artistically decorated cases. These containers were usually made from buckskin which, it should be remembered, was made from a number of leathers, including elk and buffalo, as well as deerskin. The Indians sometimes made two bow cases, one made of rugged leather with little decoration, for carrying the unstrung bow through very rough but not hostile country, and a second case, made from fine leather and beautifully decorated for show and ceremonial purposes. Such a bow case was leather fringed, beaded, or adorned with painted decorations of the habitat of its owner. Some tribes liked cases made from various furs and colored feathers were frequently used in the decoration of bow cases.

Modern Indians will find the making of a bow case a good project, making the case to fit their bow. Such cases can be made from strong cloth, dyed in the desired color and decorated in Indian fashion to suit the taste of the owner. Usually these cases were a little over four feet long and about three inches wide, as shown in the drawing.

Arrow Making

While good arrows which require little trouble to make can be made from $5/16$-inch birch dowels, modern braves will learn more about the Indians by making their arrows from willow shoots and other suitable arrow woods. Dogwood or viburnum and strong, tough reeds can also be used as substitutes for willow wood. All shoots used in arrow making must be quite straight or be straightened before the shafts are fired. The willow shoots should measure from 24 to 28 inches long and measure about $1/4$ inch to $3/8$ inch at the point end. When sandpapered carefully they make good, smooth shafts. They have to be carefully feathered to look well when used as decorations. Indian arrows were feathered in many different ways, but the easiest way to feather modern arrows is to cut suitable feathers, goose, turkey or big chicken feathers into lengths ranging from 3 to 5 inches long. Split them exactly down the center and glue or lash them on, with strong waxed thread, at the top and foot of each section, one being on each side of the arrow directly above and below the notch, with the top end of the feather being about 1¼ inches from the end of the arrow. As seen in Chapter 3, the Indians greatly disliked using crow feathers for fletching arrows. The red men were convinced that these feathers caused the arrows to zigzag or fly off at a tangent. An interesting project for modern Indians is to make an arrow or two and feather them with the wing feathers of a crow, then see if their flight is true. The author has a feeling that modern Indians may be forced to agree with the red men of yesterday.

The Indians used flint, bone, quartz, and other chipped stone arrow tips. These points were lashed securely onto the end of the arrow with thin, strong sinew. When the Indians were able to get metal, such as barrel hoops, from the white man they soon tipped their arrows both for hunting and war with metal points, cut in various shapes. Modern Indians can use metal tips of various kinds or make their arrows heavier, and rounded at the tip end instead of pointed.

Chiefs should strongly impress on all braves who wish to make bows and arrows that the combination of bow and arrow is a deadly weapon which should be used with extreme care and never within the encampment area, unless there is a target zone where they can shoot only under strict supervision.

Quivers

Most Indians carried their arrows in a quiver, which was decorative as well as useful. The quivers were usually made from stout leather, with the bottom of the quiver strongly reinforced inside with tough leather, such as buffalo hide, to keep the war-headed arrows from working their way through the foot of the quiver. Quivers varied in size, to meet the arrow-carrying needs of their

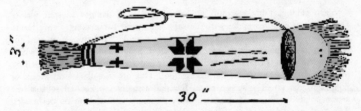

owners. The quivers ranged in length from about 30 inches to 36 inches, and from 3 to about 5 inches wide at the top, tapering toward the bottom of the case, as shown in the sketch. Modern quivers can be made without difficulty by cutting a piece of strong cloth or other material to the size desired and sewing it strongly down the side, where a leather fringe, or a cloth one, can be added. An oval of heavy leather or thin wood can be inserted at the bottom of the quiver before the case is sewn at that point. This quiver can be decorated with painted designs, fur, feathers, beads, or fringes, in true Indian style, as decided by the owner.

Bowman's Wrist Band

Many Indians wore a buckskin band on the wrist of the left arm to prevent bruises from the released bowstring when the arrows were fired. A good bowman in a modern Indian band can be granted permission from his chief to wear a distinctive, decorative band as a sign of his prowess.

Speaking of arrow release, various tribes used three methods of releasing arrows from their bows but invariably the thumb and forefinger held the arrow's nock when the shaft was being fired.

Making Natural Arrow Heads

Modern Indians whose encampments are in sections where real arrow heads can still be found are fortunate. A craft project which can be carried out by modern braves is that of making arrow heads which can be fitted and lashed to war and hunting arrows. These are not too easy to make, from some natural substances, and when one flakes glass in arrow point making for the first time, it is wise to have a bandage handy in case of a chipped or cut finger. Indians chipped arrow heads from flint, jasper, obsidian—a sort of volcanic granite—and other rocks which, despite their hardness, flaked fairly easily. The bones of various animals were also made into effective arrow points.

When flaking, a big roundish stone was used as a hammer to split smaller flakes from the larger nodules of the substances used for making arrow heads. A piece of bone, the tip of a deer antler, or a suitable, hard stone was used for chipping arrow points into shape. As the work progressed, the hammer which was used to drive the chipping tool was discarded and the point was finished by merely exerting pressure on the flaking tool. This pressure flaked off pieces of flint from the under side as well as the side actually worked on so that the arrow points were turned over frequently to assure even flaking on both sides. The final work done on the otherwise completed arrow head consisted in flaking the notches around the point, which is done in the same way in which the arrow head is worked. This notching can be avoided when one is content with the good-looking but un-notched points used by a number of Indian tribes, including several of those of the Six Nations. Three of these points are shown in the drawing.

Arrow heads can also be chipped from glass, especially heavy glass, but this sometimes proves a more difficult task than when using natural materials. Unless the chief in charge of the band wishes to make a regular project out of arrow point construction, most modern Indians may be content to make a few rough arrow heads from flakes of flint or suitable, thin, flaky stones which do not require too much technique and patience to complete.

MAKING A COUP STICK

In case anyone believes that coup stick making by Indians is a thing of the past it is interesting to know that Chief Calf Robe, a Blackfoot, recently showed the author a coup stick which he had just made to carry when he was presented to the Queen. He displayed his stick proudly, as it told of his achievements.

The most necessary possession before starting to make a coup stick is the memory of actual deeds of valor and worth performed by the brave who would make the achievement stick. When such coups exist, even if there are only a few, there is little difficulty in making the actual stick. Coup sticks were short lances of varying lengths, with blunt ends, often used to strike an armed foe.

A straight, smooth stick ranging in length from 4 to 6 feet and about one inch in diameter, is the first thing required. Usually a 4-foot-long stick or dowel is the most suitable. The decorations for the coup stick are a strip of red flannel or other heavy cloth about 3 feet long and 2 inches wide. This cloth strip is attached to the coup stick as shown in the drawing in Chapter 3. The coup feathers and any other decorations desired are fastened to the cloth strip so that they hang downward as illustrated. The feathers shown in the center of the row are for the performance of grand coups. Such feathers are made by attaching long tufts of "horsehair," dyed red or some other bright color, to the tip of the feathers.

A brave who has earned the right to carry a coup stick at ceremonies can draw on his imagination in decorating it. He can paint the stick in some bright color, or in narrow paint-bands of different colors. Varicolored tassels of cord or narrow strips of gaily colored cloth or buckskin may hang from between the feathers suspended on the strip. A well-made coup stick can be artistic and decorative, in addition to telling a story.

PEACE PIPES

These pipes are not only decorative but can be used for peace pipe ceremonies and others. The bowls can be cut without too much difficulty from a maple or birch branch. The fact that neither the bowls nor stems require to be hollowed out adds to the ease with which these calumets can be made by those with even

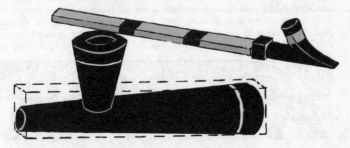

a slight knowledge of wood carving. The stems can be made from a suitable willow branch or any other straight, soft wood and carved in various attractive shapes. The stem should be about 18 inches long, and the bowl about 6 inches long and 3 inches high. A round, shallow hole may be burned on the top of the bowl to add realism to the pipe. The bowl can be painted a dull red and the stem a lighter color, such as yellow, encircled with a few black stripes. The drawing shows a completed calumet.

CANOE PADDLE DECORATION

The drawing shows a decorated canoe paddle of the Northwest Coast. Tribes of various territories ornamented their paddles in a similar manner, the designs used being those of their habitats.

Paddle decoration is an interesting project for braves who own their own paddles or where there are a number of old paddles available at the main camp or encampment which can be improved in appearance with a little artistic decoration. Almost any paint obtainable will serve as the decorative medium and the colors chiefly used can be black, various shades of red, yellow, and blue. Older paddles with the varnish worn from their blades can be sandpapered before painting. The blade only should benefit by the main decorative theme, as the handles of paddles should not be decorated above the grip when they are going to be used for paddling. Decorators will find it easier to sketch or trace the design onto the paddle in soft pencil before starting to paint.

TOTEM POLES

Though totem poles were made only by Indian tribes of the Northwest Coast, there is no reason why a Plains or Woodland tribe or band should not carve and display a totem pole as a link in Indian brotherhood and crafts. Chiefs can make it clear to the younger and novice braves that the pole has nothing to do with their own tribal or band totems, but is set up in the encampment as a tribute to that very special craft of their brothers of the far Northwest.

As the author has dealt at length with various totem poles and how to make them, in some of his other books, such details need not be repeated here. A simple Haida totem pole, added to the author's collection of argillite, miniature

totem poles collected on the Queen Charlotte
Islands, is illustrated here as an easy one to carve.
Such poles are best cut out of soft pine or similar
woods, because they can be worked so easily,
and any parts of carvings which project from
the pole can be cut out separately, from softwood
planks, and dove-tailed into the pole where required. Such additions include the beak of a
raven or thunderbird, the horns of a thunderbird
when it tops a pole, a stick held horizontally by
a beaver, or ears and other parts of human or
animal figures. The pole can range from ten to
thirty feet in height, and the diameter of the pole
will be decided by the girth of tree available.

One good way to let all band members feel
that they have contributed to the making of a
totem pole is for a chief to heavily outline the
figures to be carved on a prepared pole and let
all braves carefully cut, under the supervision of
a chief, some portion of the wood, surrounding
the outlined figures, from the pole. When the
pole is completely carved, it can be painted in
suitable, weatherproof colors and set up somewhere in the encampment with due ceremony.
The colors used on the pole can be red, yellow,
blue, black, white, green, and orange, as can be
seen today on the replicas of original totem poles
being set up in Thunderbird Park, Victoria, B. C.,
by Kwakiutl Indians. If the foot of the pole
which is sunk in the ground is first coated with
cresote or tar, the wood will not deteriorate
easily and the pole will brave the elements for
many snows. The illustration shows a pole outlined and wedged on each side, on two supports,
and ready for carving.

TORCHES

Indian ceremonials were, of course, usually enhanced by torchlight, and
torches were used in connection with other night activities, such as fishing and
hunting, or activities within the encampment.

Birch Bark Torches

These bright-burning torches can be made in a number of ways. It is good to
use *only* the bark taken from dead paper birch trees. One kind of torch is made
by simply rolling a piece of bark about 12 inches wide and 16 inches long into
a rather loose roll and wiring it onto a thin, straight green sapling about 3 feet

long, after its end has been pushed about 3 inches through one end of the bark roll.

Some Indian tribes used another sort of birch bark torch for fishing and hunting. They folded a strip of bark several times and then stuck it into a slit on the end of a green sapling, as illustrated. A good size for such strips is about 6 inches wide and 36 inches long. These torches give most light when the bark is doubled twice and inserted into the slit in such a way that the same amount of bark sticks out on each side of the torch-holding stick. Extra bark strips should be prepared to replace those burnt out.

Cattail Torches

A green cattail with the stalk cut off flush with the cattail makes a good torch. The word 'green' means that the cattail is not dried but cut from the growing stalk whenever the tail is big enough to make a good torch. A green stick, about 3 feet long and pointed at one end is thrust into the cattail exactly where the stalk was cut off. The cattail is then thoroughly soaked in kerosene, the surplus oil shaken off before use, and the torch is ready to burn for approximately half an hour.

Melted paraffin makes a good substitute for the kerosene and the wax burns without dripping.

Paraffin Wax Torches

These are best made by winding a strip of absorbent cloth about 3 feet long and 3 inches wide around one end of a green, straight stick and wiring it in place. When the cloth has been thoroughly soaked in the melted paraffin wax, the torch is ready for use. It will be found that the torch burns a little brighter if the cloth is steeped in the melted wax before winding it onto the stick.

Pitch Pine Torches

These torches give a fair amount of light, but unfortunately they drip and smoke quite a lot. They are made by dipping one end of a green pole about 4 feet long and one inch in diameter into melted pitch, turning it around a few times to collect a fair sized ball of pitch on the end and then letting it dry. It is easier to make a larger pitch ball by several dippings. Indians pounded the end of the sapling which was dipped into the melted pitch, in order to break up its fibres so that the pitch coating was picked up more easily and burned more evenly. A cloth strip wound several times around the end of the pole before it is dipped in the pitch is also a good method of making this torch.

With torches such as these, there is little need to make any of the many sorts of tin can torches, which seem out of place, unless well camouflaged, in an Indian encampment.

BEADWORK

The subject of beadcraft requires several chapters and there are a number of good books available which are devoted to beads and beadwork. Some modern chiefs, too, may well be able to instruct the braves of the encampment in beadwork skills. Here are suggestions explaining how a couple of simple basic stitches can be done without the use of a loom.

The beadwork of skillful Indian craftsmen is often breathtakingly beautiful, the loveliness of colors being equalled by harmony of design; yet a beginner at beadcraft need not be discouraged by such masterpieces. There are many beautiful designs which he will be able to copy onto the leather or cloth which he decides to decorate. It is best, first of all, to draw a full-scale model of the desired design on white paper, filling in the main outlines first, then sketching in the other details afterward. The colors and sizes of the beads chosen can be marked on the drawing either with colored crayons or the color of bead groups can be marked above or below them in pencil. Using colored crayons or chalks is best, as a better idea of the color schemes and the harmony of the colors can be worked out and appraised by this method. The design can now be marked on the material which is to be beaded and the beads sewn over the tracing.

Lazy Stitch

The beads chosen can be sewn onto the design by using this easy stitch, favored by so many of the men beadworkers of the Plains tribes. This stitch is done, as illustrated, by sewing one end of a strong thread onto the material at a starting point, threading from two to nine beads on the thread, passing the needle down through the material at the end of the beads and then bringing it up through the material, close to the last bead. The needle is then threaded

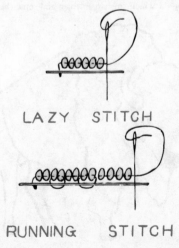

LAZY STITCH

RUNNING STITCH

through about the same number of beads, more or less, and the process is repeated until the end of the row is reached. A very strong thread, or a sewing sinew, is required so that it can be pulled tightly, to prevent the beads from bulging out from the material instead of resting flat and snug against it.

Running Stitch

The so-called running stitch is very similar to the lazy stitch except that after the needle has been pushed down through the material, it is brought up, then passed through the last two beads which have just been sewed on, as illustrated, whereupon the bead threading and sewing continues as before until the end of the row, when the thread is made fast and another row begun.

There are many decorative purposes to which beadwork can be put, such as decorating breechclouts, dance aprons, shirts, belts, headbands, anklets, cuffs, knife sheaths, *parfleches*, peace pipes, and pipe cases, all of which can be artistically and effectively ornamented with beads of varying sizes and colors.

Instead of working directly on larger objects to be beaded, the beading may be done on smaller strips, squares or circles which can then be sewn onto the main piece.

CHARCOAL DRAWING

This simple Indian art is not only decorative but useful, and it can be practiced very easily. All that is needed are a few charred hardwood sticks, a rough, sandstone-like stone on which to sharpen them and some sheets of heavy, rough

paper or lightweight rough cardboard. Even sheets of brown wrapping paper or heavy brown paper bags serve the purpose quite well. One way to prepare the drawing sticks is to cut a number of hardwood sticks about a foot long and from ½ to ¾ inches in diameter and place them on top of a not-too-hot fire of glowing embers. Let the sticks burn for a minute or so then cover them with earth so that they will char all the way through. One can tell when they are ready for use by taking a stick from the fire and examining and trying it when it is cool enough to handle. They are kept pointed when in use by rubbing the ends gently on the sharpening stone.

Indians used these sticks not only for drawing designs of various sorts but also for making maps which were carefully studied by those about to set out on an undertaking which meant traversing little known or unknown country.

MASK MAKING

This is an interesting as well as useful craft for braves, and in the course of a rainy afternoon or evening one or more masks can be made which can be used later on in ceremonial and at council fires. Masks can be easily made from paper, cardboard, cloth, paper bags, corn husks, and bark taken from a dead elm or

birch tree. Spirit and animal masks made from cylinders of cardboard can be most effective. Ears, horns, noses, and other decorations are fastened onto the cylinder which fits over the head. Sturdy masks of all sorts can be made from papier maché, which is merely paper. Newspaper will do, soaked in water, then ground or pounded into pulp and, while wet, moulded into the shape desired and then allowed to dry. All of the masks mentioned can be painted and decorated with various designs to suit the band and tastes of the wearer.

COLORS AND DESIGNS

Since designs, painting, and colors are mentioned from time to time in this chapter, it is well to point out that colors had very definite meanings and values for all Indians, but these varied greatly among the far-flung tribes. Usually, white meant peace, red indicated war, while black was a sign of mourning and death. The principle colors used by most Indian tribes, before European paints were secured by trade, were red, black, yellow, brown, green and blue. White was also used to highlight the colors mentioned, and sometimes as a background.

There were six distinctive American Indian design areas throughout the United States and Canada though, naturally there were certain similarities at the borders of these territories where the various habitats met and sometimes overlapped. These were the six divisions, though often considered as nine for ethnological reasons.

- The Northwest Coast of Canada and Alaska
- The Pacific Coast (California area)
- Pueblo and Desert habitats (Southwest area)
- The Great Plains
- Most of Canada (with the exception of the Northwest Coast) including Eastern woodland and Great Lake areas
- The Southern States, Coast and Gulf Regions

Many of their colors and designs are spoken of and illustrated in other books by the author.

INDIAN SIGNALS AND SIGNALLING

Indian tribes had many silent ways of announcing and expressing things. There were Mirror Talk, Robe Talk, Blanket Talk, Pony Talk, Smoke Talk, Trail Sign Talk, and Water Trails Sign Talk, among others. The scouts of some tribes rode or ran in a Discovery Circle, so that the lookouts in the encampment or village knew as the scouts approached that they had discovered something important, buffalo, other game—or enemies. Scouts of the Omaha signaled "We have seen them!" by riding or running in a criss-cross pattern, that is, moving rapidly from side to side as they approached their village. One runner made the sign in this way but two runners made it even more distinctive by criss-crossing each other as they sped forward.

Secret Signals

These signals of many sorts, from *caution* to *attack*, were given by the imitation of insect, bird, and animal calls and sounds. Many other signals were made by simulating noises of the woods, stream and forest. Modern chiefs can establish their own special code of secret signals for their bands, to be used in addition to the usual Indian signals.

Drum Talk

Indians also used drums and tom-toms at times to signal to the people or to call them together for councils.

Smoke Talk

Smoke Talk was carried out in various ways, by lighting several smoky fires in line or lines, the number and position of fires conveying the message, or by sending up smoke puffs from a single fire. A little fire was built with dry wood and when it burned bright it was covered with a layer of damp grass or moss and instantly covered with an old blanket or big animal hide, which was usually operated by two Indian signalers who sent up signal puffs of smoke which had various meanings. Sometimes the number of puffs, of the same volume, carried a message; at others, the puffs were big and small, comparable to the contrasting dots and dashes of the Morse Code. Expert Indian signalers could easily send and read intricate messages without difficulty or misinterpretation.

Fire Talk

At night, flames often replaced the daylight smoke signals. A small, bright fire on a bluff or cliff, or more than one fire, sent a message which was understood by those who were waiting for it, though it meant nothing to an enemy. At times the fire was screened or covered at varying intervals, which was one way of sending a fire message.

Torch Talk

Bright-burning torches were used in the same manner as fires in sending messages at night. At times, torches were set up on the top of a cliff, hill, or other point from which they could be clearly seen for a long distance, and occasionally they were screened for short intervals behind wet blankets or a square of rawhide as part of a tribal message-sending code. The use of wet blankets indicates the caution used by Indians to prevent any chance of fire. A prairie fire or a fire in Woodland areas meant the death and destruction of Indians and their property as well as the extermination of wildlife. The Indians made and observed conservation laws as a very necessary means of self-preservation, and it is tragic that so many white men now ignore them.

Mirror Talk

This was a form of signalling which many Plains and other tribes used most effectively. The flash of the sun rays, even from their mica mirrors, could be seen at a great distance and, like the heliograph, it had the advantage of not being seen by the enemy even at fairly close range on either side of the sending and receiving points. Not only could Indian mirror signallers send and receive messages speedily and accurately but chiefs often directed the movements of mounted and dismounted warriors in battle by means of mirror signals.

Blanket Talk

Another effective method of signalling, used especially by Western tribes, was carried out by blanket signals. Usually Indian blanket signallers held one corner of the blanket tightly in one hand and another corner in the other hand and often swung the blanket in front of them in a vertical curve during the message sending. Tribes often used different signals from those of their neighbors, though there was a generally familiar series of signals which could be understood by many tribes when gathered for special events such as a buffalo hunt or mass tribal ceremony.

Here are a few of the signals frequently used. *Halt!* the blanket is waved in front of the signaller several times toward the ground. *Peace!* was generally announced by waving the blanket in circles above the head, then tossing it upward and letting it fall, open, on the ground. *Discovery!*—"I have discovered something!"—was signalled by waving an open blanket high above the head while running in a circle. A scout signalled "Many men, or animals, in front of me," by waving the blanket up and down, the upward wave taking it high above the head a number of times.

People of many tribes also used a code of blanket signals to take the place of the spoken word in various situations, such as courting, the making of friends, the wish to participate in a formal debate, and other phases of tribal life. These moods and desires were indicated by the manner in which the blanket was worn or held.

Sign Language and Chinook Jargon

Sign language was more or less the universal means of communication used by the Indians of the Plains. Those who did not master this means of speech made visible were often able to get along by speaking the extraordinary Chinook Jargon, known to all tribes throughout the far-flung Northwest and Northwest Coast.

Handbooks on Indian Sign Language are available for chiefs who wish to develop this skill among their band members. Study and practice of this language will provide a useful way of passing time when the weather keeps the band indoors.

STORYTELLING

Last, but certainly not least, of the thrills and fun which a tribe or band can experience is that of storytelling. This activity need not be confined to the council fire. A circle or semicircle can be formed by the braves under a shady tree or on the bank of a stream at any hour of the day, and the band may swiftly take the trail to storyland.

The author has found that storytelling requires greater skill by daylight. It requires considerably more know-how to transport the listeners to hunting or war trails or into the mystic land of legend without the immense aid of darkness and fire glow—but it can be done.

A chief who is gifted in the art of storytelling blazes the trail and then less gifted tellers of tales can take over for a while, until interest wanes. Unless a really striking story can be introduced at this point to revive interest, it is time to stop. One way to continue interest is to have braves with a gift for storytelling contest in storytelling for coups. Not more than two or three weavers of words should compete at each storytelling session and a grand finale can be planned in order to allow one of the story coup winners to be awarded grand coup.

Only one Indian story is given here as an example of the type of tale which Indians liked. There are many sources of suitable stories to draw on.

A Tsimshian of the Northwest Coast of Canada told the author this amusing story. It is possible that this tale was based on the great Chinook chief, Komkomly. Though, like all great chiefs of that rugged habitat, he went barefoot, he took certain precautions to ward against rock bruises. Chief Komkomly had about 400 slaves who walked ahead of him and spread priceless sea otter skins on the ground to carpet his path.

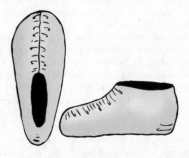

The First Magic Moccasins

A great Plains Indian Chief had very tender feet. Other mighty chiefs laughed openly, lesser chiefs smiled secret smiles, and the rest of the people enjoyed the big chief's discomfort in smileless silence. They were all in the same canoe—all of them had bare feet and no horses, but few of them had tender feet. The unhappy medicine man, who was the Chief-of-the-Tender-Feet's adviser, was greatly troubled because each time he was summoned by the chief he was sternly asked, "What are you going to do about it?" The "it" referred to the tender feet of the chief.

Driven to desperation, the medicine man hit upon a plan which he knew was not the final solution to the problem, but was nevertheless a fine makeshift. He had some women of the tribe weave a long, narrow mat of reeds and when the big chief had to go anywhere, six braves unrolled the mat in front of him so that he walked in comfort. One day the braves, who were worn out from seeing that the big chief's feet were not worn out, carelessly unrolled the mat over a place where flint arrowheads had been chipped. The arrow heads had long since taken flight but needle-like chips remained. When the chief's tender feet were cut by these splinters he let out a series of whoops that made the nearby aspens quiver so hard that they have been doing so ever since.

That night the medicine man was given an impossible task by the enraged chief. "Cover the entire earth with mats so thick that my feet will not suffer or you will die when the moon is round."

This was an order which the frightened medicine man knew he could never carry out, even if he had been commanded to do so before five snows had come and gone. When he returned to his lodge he saw the hide of an elk which he had killed pegged out on the ground with two women busily scraping the hair from the skin. An idea flashed into his groping mind. He sent out many hunters, many women were busy for many days, many braves with hunting knives cut and women sewed with rawhide sinews.

Just before the "moon was round" the medicine man appeared before his chief and told him that he had covered as much of the earth as possible in so short a time. When the chief looked from the door of his lodge he saw many paths of skin stretching as far as the eye could see. Long strips, which could be moved from place to place, connected the main leather paths and even the chief thought that this time the magic of the medicine man had solved tenderfoot transportation for all time—but this was not to be!

One day as the big chief was walking fast along one of his strong, tough, smooth, leather paths, he saw a beauteous maiden of the tribe gliding ahead of him. She glanced back when she heard his feet patter on the elkhide path and lighted his heart with an encouraging smile. She was going in the same direction as he and she was so lithe and agile that she seemed to float rather than walk, though her trim bare feet trod Mother Earth. The chief set off on the run to catch up with her. His eager eyes were fixed on the back of She-Who-Smiled and so his tender feet strayed from the narrow path—and landed in a bunch of cacti! The maiden ran for her life when she heard the hideous howls of the chief, and Indians in the distant village rushed outdoors, fearing the worst.

Two suns later, when the chief was able to speak again, he sent for his medicine man and told him that when the sun was high, next day, he would be sent with all possible ceremony and speed to the Land of Shadows. The chief was still so upset that he could not be spoken to, even in Sign Language.

That night, the medicine man went to a high hilltop on a Power Quest. He waited for a dream-vision which would help him to solve immediately the only problem that would save his life: how to cover the entire earth with leather. In a flash of lightning the answer was shown to him, soon after his vigil had begun. He sped down the hillside, out-howling the big chief at times, as jagged rocks connected with his big feet, but stopping not until he was within his lodge. He worked all night and till those who were to send him on The Shadow Trail came for him just before noon the next day. He accompanied the war-club-armed guards, clutching to his heart something tightly rolled in a piece of deerskin. His cheerful smile surprised the onlookers.

"He is brave!" said the braves who watched his coming. "He is very brave!" said the women of the tribe. The big chief was waiting just outside his lodge and he gave the guards swift, stern orders. Before the maker-of-magic could be led away he asked leave to say a few words to the chief. "Speak!" Said the chief, who was sorry to lose an able medicine man who was very good at all minor magic—for even the chief knew that covering the entire earth with leather was an impossible task.

The medicine man quickly knelt beside the chief, unrolled the objects from his bundle and slipped one of them on each foot of the chief. The chief appeared to be wearing a bear's hairless feet, instead of bare feet, and he was puzzled as he looked at the elkhide handcraft of the medicine man. "Big chief," the medicine man exclaimed joyfully, "I have found the way to cover the earth with leather. For you, O chief, from now on, the earth will always be covered with leather." And so it was!

20

Activities for Indian Villagers

These activities are limited only by the scope of the imagination of the chiefs who direct the pursuits of the tribes and bands of modern Indians. Leaders of American Indian youth had much imagination and originality, and they usually applied it in ways which taught the boys in their charge useful things in as easy a way as possible. A short hike, a walk to the shore of a lake for a supervised swim, can be worth-while activities when a chief points out interesting things *en route* and encourages members of his band to point out interesting things which attract their attention. There is much to be seen, and a practised eye is developed only through observation.

There are many worthwhile Indian activities for modern Indians which come under a number of categories, such as education, utility, and amusement. The best are those which combine at least two, if not all three, of these qualities. An outline of a few such occupations is given here as ideas for chiefs, who will be able to develop and enlarge the pursuits which suit their bands best.

SWIMMING

This should prove one of the most popular activities, especially on a hot day or after a hard hike. Braves should be encouraged not only to improve their swimming style but also to increase the distance which they can swim and the ability to swim well on the back and side as well as on the breast. They should be taught to float with ease and for several minutes at a time, gradually increasing the length of time during which they can stay afloat without effort. Floating can be done on the back and in an upright, treading water, position. The ability of a brave to help another brave who is in difficulty and the knowledge of the easiest way to bring him ashore should be taught and developed. When braves who cannot swim reasonably well are not allowed to use canoes, boats, or rafts, they will experience a sudden urge to learn to swim well.

Modern Indian braves should know that the boys and men of many Indian tribes who lived on the shores of a sea or lake, or on the banks of a river, were expert swimmers. They developed speed, distance swimming, and water skills by contesting one against the other and band against band. The Arkira, who were allied with the Mandan and wore the same striking, ceremonial horned headdress, were fast and tireless swimmers. The braves swam out into the strong currents of the Platte River and, with knife or lance, killed the disabled buffaloes which tried to swim across the river with the mighty buffalo herds.

Pow-wows

Chiefs can arrange for a number of pow-wows on interesting and practical subjects. These talks can be made more interesting by demonstrations and they can be held either outdoors or indoors. Some suggested subjects are: Fire Prevention—Indian Lore—Conservation—First Aid—Swimming and Life Saving—Watercraft—Woodcraft—Woodlore—Knots and Lashings—Nature Lore—Nature Trails—Use of Ax, Saw, and Knife—Ax and Knife Safety—Orientation—Map Reading—At Home in the Dark—Noises in the Night—and similar topics. Many ideas and much information for such pow-wows will be found throughout this book and many of these sessions can include useful and practical displays, with members of different bands taking an active part. These pow-wows are especially fine for indoor programs on rainy days or when held to provide breathing space after a strenuous field program.

Orators

Indian chiefs used this as a play-way of teaching young warriors to become fine orators. A chief had to be a good speaker in order to impress his warriors in council, to effectively address all of the people in his village when the need arose, and match his words against those of the orators of other tribes when a pow-wow was held to settle important intertribal matters. Often exchanges of wily, witty words settled disputes which otherwise would have been settled by war.

Many Indian chiefs—Brant, a Mohawk; Tecumseh, a Shawnee; Chiefs Red Cloud and Red Bear of the Sioux; Red Jacket, a Seneca; Chief Joseph, a Nez Percé—and numerous others were as famous for their magnificent speeches as for their exploits in war.

Here is a good way for modern Indians to develop an eloquence which will stand them in good stead throughout the rest of their lives. When the Indians of a band are seated in a circle, the chief asks any member of the band to give a brief talk on any topic of general interest, such as stalking, hunting, pathfinding, animals, orientation, weather, or Indian games. The talk is given by the brave chosen, who stands in the center of the circle and addresses the entire band. At first, the chief allows each speaker a period of about three minutes, extending the length of the periods as the aspiring orators become more fluent and interesting to hear. More serious orations or debates may be contested between each half of a band, which chooses its best orator as representative.

Humorous speeches can be called for on such subjects as: "What to do if one meets a skunk, or porcupine, on a narrow path," or "What happens after a grizzly bear chases a brave up a tree." The latter topic illustrates one of the Indian ways of teaching Nature Lore; after a young brave had related the adventure in detail, a chief or instructor congratulated the young orator on his eloquence but deplored his lack of knowledge of the ways of the wild—because a grizzly bear, unlike black bear, cannot climb a tree.

SPECIAL PURPOSE HIKES

Any hike, long or short, taken for a specific reason other than exercise, comes under this heading.

Sun-up Hike

The chief leads his band to the top of a high hill, or part way up a mountain, to greet the rising sun with an Indian prayer of thanks for its Medicine Power. Arrangements are made in advance for a breakfast to be eaten directly after sunrise.

Sundown Hike

A hill is climbed by the band in order to watch the sun set, and an Indian prayer is offered that it may come back again next morning. Such a hike should be taken only when there is a reasonably well-defined trail leading down to the foot of the hill and a trail which is well known to the leader of the band leading back to the encampment. An additional safety measure, if the going is rough in places, is to take along several effective torches to light the way back.

Moonrise Hike

A band is taken to the top of the hill to watch the moon rise. This hike is especially spectacular when a great, golden, harvest type of moon makes its appearance, or at least when the moon is full or nearly so. As in the sundown hike, precautions should be taken to assure the band's getting back to the encampment without twisted ankles. Indian cook-outs, providing a light but nourishing meal, can be an enjoyable part of either of the above hikes.

Orientation, Compass Hike

When a lone hiker or a band has a chance to hike in open country, an interesting cross-country trip can be made by hiking directly in a fixed compass direction to a point decided on. When there is more open country to the north, the hike proceeds in that direction. To get the most experience and fun out of a hike of this sort there should be as little deviation from the route decided on as possible. Of course, one has to skirt marshes or private properties but otherwise the outing may lead over hill and dale, through woodland or forest; and streams and rivers encountered en route should be crossed in the most direct and safest way in order to hold to the direction. One gets to know the country really well after a few such hikes in different directions.

MAKING A ROPE LADDER

Various sorts of handy rope ladders can be improvised, with or without wooden rungs. The strongest and longest-wearing ladders of this sort are made by using two strong, rough ropes, with strong, 12-inch-long wooden rungs firmly tied in place 12 inches apart and securely held between the two ropes by being seized immediately *above* and *below* each rung, on either side, with strong cord. To avoid tarring these cords so that they are sure to remain in position without slipping, a clove hitch can be tied on the rope directly above each rung before the ends of the cord are wound around ropes and rung to complete the lashing. The ropes should be stretched from time to time as the work proceeds so that the rungs hang evenly. Naturally, the length of the ladder is decided by the double length of rope available for each side.

With heavier rope, only one strand of heavy rope need be used on each side of the ladder, the rungs being carefully bound to a single rope on each side. Tying a knot in each rope at 12-inch intervals, to which the rungs can be more easily fastened in a non-slip fashion, will assure the rungs' remaining in place despite considerable use, but this method of construction requires much more rope.

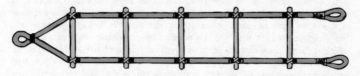

BUILD A WILDWOOD BRIDGE

Enjoyment and utility can be combined in bridging a narrow gorge or stream, using only wildwood material. Sometimes a convenient island in the middle of a not-too-wide stream will serve as the center support for such a bridge, if the stream is not likely to rise as high as the bridge and carry it away. The suspension bridge is most easily made by using two long, strong saplings to support each side of a two-foot roadway across these saplings. The roadway can be built of strong, green poles, or if old planks are available they can be used, provided they are strong enough to support the weight of the users of the bridge. When green crosspieces are used they should be placed about 2 inches apart and lashed in place to each side of the two supporting poles. Once again, the motto should be DARE WITH CARE! and if the bridge is built over a narrow gorge or suspended some distance above a stream, either a light but strong handrail should be built on at least one side of the improvised bridge or a rope with one end tightly tied at each end of the footbridge should be fastened to each side of it so that the younger braves can hold on as they cross.

CRAYFISH HUNT

This is a nighttime expedition for night-wise chiefs and braves which can be both exciting and interesting. The only equipment required are one or two long-handled fish landing nets, one or two long poles, and an effective flashlight for each of the crayfish hunters. There should be not more than eight in a group. An experienced chief should be in charge, as such hunts are often on rocky terrain and through stone-strewn gorges through which the streams flow where crayfish are to be found. The band of hunters should move in Indian file, with the leader ahead, along the bank of a stream, until a pool in which these miniature lobsters are to be found is reached.

Only three hunters should go into action at once when the prey is located. This is done by lying on the edge of the pool and flashing the light down into the water until a crawfish, as they are often called, is caught in its beam. These crustaceans are fast movers but the fact that they shoot backward instead of forward helps the wary hunter to let the crayfish back swiftly into the net, so that it can be scooped up out of the water. They can either be caught by two braves using a net fore and aft of the crayfish chosen for capture or by moving one of the long poles just in front of the little lobster *after* the net is in place behind it. The chief should see that all members of the band have a chance to land a few crayfish, and he directs the moves from pool to pool, in search of better hunting, when necessary.

The chiefs leading these expeditions have to take care that the braves do not suffer twisted ankles on the loose rocks and stones along the stream and that, in their excitement, they do not tumble headfirst into a pool as they try to net their supper. Care must be taken before setting out that the flashlight batteries are fresh, as failure of the flashlights on such a trip can prove dangerous. Batteries which suddenly burn dim can often be given new, if brief, life by heating them.

Upon the group's return to the encampment, the crayfish are easily prepared for the pot by pulling off the very end of the tail, which takes the entrails out. The fish are then boiled in salted water until they turn red. They are then peeled, the heads removed, and the crayfish eaten like lobsters, by dipping them into a seasoned, melted butter sauce or into vinegar seasoned by the addition of a little salt and pepper.

COUNTING THE WILDTHINGS

These expeditions are actually Wildlife Census Field Trips and Bird Counts combined. They can prove of considerable value to a camp, in addition to developing observation on the part of those making the count. When there is only one chief to a band of eight braves and no mature assistant to be responsible for four of the braves, the chief will have to take full charge of the band and work with his braves, each armed with a shrill whistle, spread out and advancing in open formation. This method will cover the maximum terrain and flush the most wildthings. Some of the methods used for flushing birds and beasts, given in Chapter 12, will prove useful. Braves may work singly or in pairs, as decided by the chief, and each brave or pair of braves will keep a record of the different animals and birds and the number of each species seen on the expedition. Probably a number of braves will be unable to identify some of the birds or even beasts seen *en route*, but they will be able to describe them, more or less, and will develop a healthy curiosity regarding these strangers from woodland friends.

LURING THE DANCERS OF THE DUSK

These "dancers" are, of course, moths of all sizes and other night-flying insects. These insects are most readily found around the *edge* of woodland or forest tracts and can most easily be lured, without "sugaring" trees, by using a white screen and flashlights, as described in Chapter 13. On a dry, clear night, and with some luck, a considerable number of moths of various species and other night-flying insects should be attracted to the lure. A big, beautiful Cecropia Moth may be a visitor or the even more lovely, ethereal Luna Moth, luminous, with a pale, greenish light glowing from its huge wings may join the other Dancers of the Dusk. This is especially likely if there are walnut or hickory trees growing in the vicinity of the encampment. These lovely Insects of the Night should neither be collected nor injured and the braves will get far more satisfaction from watching them flit away on gauzy wings, when the lights are dimmed, than from seeing them, perhaps with torn and tattered wings, in a collecting box.

BUTTERFLY LURE

Various species of butterflies can sometimes be lured from their airy flight by spreading pieces of colored paper, of about handkerchief size, on grassy ground, which they fly over to reach flowering fields or trees. The colors which meet with most success are yellow, white, and red, though at times nothing more is needed than a few white paper plates scattered at intervals on grassy ground. Whether these decoys are mistaken for flowers or whether the butterflies visit them out of curiosity is hard to decide. The best time to try this experiment is on a sunny, windless day and the visitors attracted may include the humble, Cabbage butterfly, the regal Monarch or Viceroy, a Sulphur, Fritillary, or Skipper.

MERRYMAKER ACTIVITIES

Practically all Indian tribes had clever merrymakers, or clowns, who kept the braves amused, and quite often took their minds off coming or present troubles by their witty words and droll antics. They told funny stories, did amusing imitations, such as pantomiming a clumsy brave on his first hunt, auctioned off worthless things to the highest bidder, and sometimes gave hilarious performances of fake juggling, conjuring, hypnotism, or ventriloquism, as take-offs on skills at which many medicine men were really expert. A detailed description of their craft appears in an earlier book by the author.[1]

For the make-believe hypnotic and ventriloquial acts, the modern Indian brave who entertains in either of these ways will require an alert accomplice or two. For the hypnotic act, the partner acts as the one hypnotized. The real Indian hypnotists used a small mica mirror, which they shone into the eyes of the person whom they put into a hypnotic "trance." The pseudo-hypnotist can use a real mirror as a prop for his act, which can be given at a Merrymaking Session, when several merrymakers can contest for the most laughs. What the hypnotist makes his "victim" say can be worded out in advance—with the help of a chief, if necessary—and the act can be made really funny.

In the ventriloquist act, the accomplices are hidden, out of sight, in strategic places, and take their cues from the words spoken by the ventriloquist. This act can, like practically all of the others, be carried out in the afternoon, which sometimes make a pleasant change from the evening performance.

KNOTS, HITCHES, AND LASHINGS

Indians tied many clever knots to serve different purposes, and they also used varied lashings and hitches to hold things in place, such as harness, tepee and travois poles, packs on horses' backs, travois bundles and war heads on arrows and lances. The great advantage of their knots and lashings was that they stayed

[1] See *Campfire and Council Ring Programs*, by Allan A. Macfarlan (New York: Association Press, 1951).

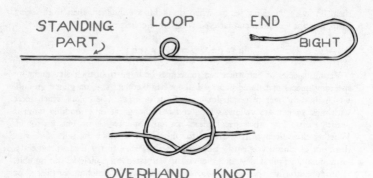

STANDING PART   LOOP   END   BIGHT

OVERHAND KNOT

put. Knots are of such great importance in many outdoor activities that they played a vital part in the lives of the Indians. Knots which were sure and secure often meant the difference between life and death in their adventurous lives. Their knots had to meet three major tests: to be quickly and fairly easily tied; to effectively serve the purpose for which they were used; and to remain knotted and hold despite pull and strain. The factor of knots' being easy to untie was not one of great importance to the Indians, though good knots should untie easily, permitting good cord and rope to be used again and again. The indifference of the Indians to this feature of knot tying is explained by the fact that they had plenty of rawhide thongs for knotting and lashing—and a keen knife was always handy for cutting them loose when they had served their purposes. Another reason why many Indian knots were frequently hard to undo was that they had been made with green rawhide thongs, which set like iron when dry, or wet buckskin strips, which possess the same quality.

Indians were able to tie knots quickly and under unfavorable conditions, such as darkness, or on the run, and while galloping on horseback. They believed that many knots worked magic and cast spells. They had good fortune knots, knots to loose fair winds, and web knots to "tangle the feet of enemies."

A few of the lesser known, useful knots and some hitches and lashings for modern Indians are described and illustrated here, though all knots and lashings are best learned from a knot-wise chief, as this sure method eliminates the chance of learning to tie knots incorrectly, and there are a number of ways of doing this.

Knotting Terms

Two general terms used in knot tying should be mastered before any attempt to tie knots is made.

Standing Part is the inactive part of a rope, which is worked *on* but not *with*.

Bight is the doubled portion of a bent rope, not including the ends.

As these terms are used on land and sea, they are used here in describing how to tie the following knots, hitches, and lashings. Modern Indians will do well to be able to tie all of them quickly—and in the dark.

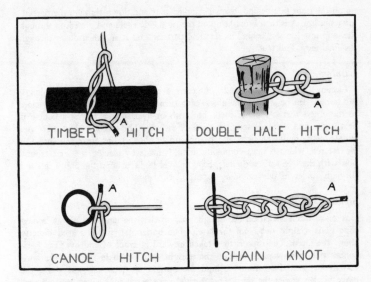

Timber Hitch

The end A of the rope is passed around the pole, brought over and around the standing part—the long piece of rope. End A is then wound three or four times around its own standing part and the rope pulled taut.

Double Half Hitch

End A is passed around the post, looped over and around the standing part and passed down through the bight toward you. This is repeated a second time and the rope pulled taut.

Canoe Hitch

This hitch is also known as the Slippery Half Hitch. The end A is passed down through the ring and brought up over and around its standing part so that a bight is formed, as illustrated.

Chain Knot

This is an ornamental knot sometimes used for shortening a rope, since good rope should never be cut unless it is unavoidable. To start, make a small loop with the rope passing over its own standing part. A short length of stick, a few inches long, is passed between the standing part and the loop thus formed, to hold the links in formation in place. Pass end A up through the loop from the left side, around and up through the new loop just formed. Repeat this process as often as desired, tightening each link as the knotting progresses. To complete the chain, reverse the final loop, as shown in the drawing, by bringing end A up on the right side behind its own standing part and down through the preceding loop. End A is then brought up on the right side again and passed up through the loop just formed, behind its standing part, around it and then down through the final loop. Pull taut.

Lashing

Lashing is not a difficult skill, but there are good and badly made lashings. No lashing can be a good one unless each turn is drawn tight and kept so close to the others that it touches them, but without overlapping. Unless a lashing is neat, tight, and the ends snug, it is a poor lashing. The hitches which start and end lashings should be tight and begun and finished at the correct point. The clove hitch, which is most commonly used, is made by placing the rope around post with the free end on the left; bring it over bight, around the post again and through, under its own standing part; pull cord taut.

Square Lashing

A clove hitch is tied on the upright spar so that the long end of the lashing rope pulls straight out from the hitch. The horizontal spar is placed directly above the hitch. The rope is then taken upward in front of and over the horizontal spar. It now passes behind the upright spar, down in front of the horizontal one, and then around behind the upright spar, passing just above the clove hitch made at the start. This method is repeated four times, keeping outside the earlier turns on the horizontal spar and inside them on the upright spar. This lashing is finished by taking three or four tight frapping turns around the turns binding the two spars together, and ending with a clove hitch on the horizontal spar, close to the lashing. This lashing, like most others, can be snugged by beating it with a short, heavy stick or the back of a light axblade.

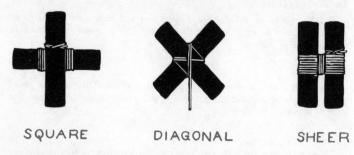

SQUARE   DIAGONAL   SHEER

Diagonal Lashing

Diagonal lashings start with a timber hitch around both poles. This hitch is tightened to pull the two poles as close together as possible. Three or four turns of the rope are then taken entirely around one fork, where the poles touch, and then three or four turns are made entirely around the other fork. Two frapping turns are then tightly made between the two poles at the point where they cross, seizing the turns which hold the poles together. The lashing is finished with a clove hitch around the pole most convenient for the rope end which finishes the frapping.

Sheer Lashing

This lashing begins with a clove hitch on one of the two vertical spars and the turns taken around both spars begin just under the clove hitch. When six or eight turns have been made around the two spars, the lashing ends with a tight frapping between the two spars, around the turns which bind them together, the end of this rope being tied with a double half hitch, pulled very tight, at the bottom of the lashing, on the spar opposite the starting clove hitch.

CONTESTS

Many American Indian Games suitable for encampment activities and contests are given in Chapters 17 and 18. Here are some hunting forms of contests which were popular among Indian boys and which are still in vogue among braves interested in or possessed of hunting skill. Modern Indians, too, like to exhibit their prowess. Contesting is one way of giving them that opportunity. To incite braves to develop skills and then prove their ability is one good reason for holding contests. Alert chiefs will have words of praise and encouragement for modest braves who show marked improvement, rather than those who are likely to form too high an opinion of their prowess and require no coup-feather words of encouragement.

Lariat Making and Roping Contests

Many Indian tribes had crack ropers in their bands and these expert wielders of the lariat proved of good service when horse raiding among rival tribes was under way. The Comanche were especially expert with a *riata*, and a favorite sport of the older boys of 12 and 13 years of age was to slip out of the encampment at night and rope and ride any horse they could get a lariat over. Part of the adventure was eluding the alert camp guards, who made every effort to keep the boys from sneaking out of the village. Once out among the herd, the boys were still in danger of capture and punishment, as mounted guards tried to catch them while they were enjoying their forbidden fun.

Modern Indians who try lariat making and roping will find that it is easier to make a good rope than to make a good throw. From 20 to 35 feet of ⅜-inch manila or other good quality rope are needed for making a lariat. Cotton-braided rope will soon become pliable without much "working" but manila rope has to be worked a great deal before it becomes really supple. Cowboys often run a folded square of very coarse cloth over a new rope, from end to end, many times. This helps to take the kinks out of tightly-laid rope and also remove fiber slivers which are rough on the fingers. A cowboy pulls, twists, stretches and, sometimes, drags behind his horse, a new rope which he is breaking in. Though the authentic cowboy rope has usually an oval piece of metal inside the "honda" loop, so that the rope will pay out without friction, a small honda knot can be made on the end of the rope without using a metal part. The honda knot, shown in the

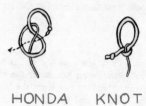

HONDA   KNOT

drawing, is easy to make. There are two ways of forming hondas. The first is by doubling about 2 inches of the end of the rope and lashing it smoothly and securely to the long part of the rope, known as the "stem," thus forming a honda about one inch in diameter. Pass the other end of the rope through the doubled-back honda and the rope is ready for the first cast. The second method of honda making is to double about 1¼ inch of one end of the rope over a medium weight, round, metal ring and then lash the short end of the doubled rope to the stem. The rope will run out well, more easily than when the honda is formed with the rope end. The drawings show these two methods of making a honda.

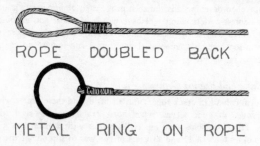

ROPE   DOUBLED   BACK

METAL   RING   ON   ROPE

Good lariat throwing can only be achieved by much practice. When one shakes out a loop, the spare rope is coiled in the left hand and the loop shaken out with the right hand, which should be about in the center of the loop and holding it so that the noose does not tighten before it is on its way. Extending the arm brusquely and stepping forward quickly one step will speed up the throw and help to lengthen the cast. The sighting eye should be kept fixed on the object to be roped and the rope thrown as a ball is tossed, from an overhead position.

When members of the band have practiced roping sufficiently to be able to hold contests, these can be arranged and attended by the band and visitors. Settling the noose over posts driven into the ground, of various heights and at various distances, can be the first entries on the program. These casts are made from a standing position. Volunteers will easily be found to provide moving targets for the more advanced ropers, who have good control of their ropes.

The chiefs should strongly impress on all would-be ropers that the lariat is a dangerous weapon when used carelessly. A "successful" cast made at an unsuspecting, running person can, for example, cause a broken leg or other injury.

Flint and Steel Firelighting Contest

Some Indian tribes used the difficult hand drill method of lighting a fire. This was done by twirling a short length of wood rapidly between the hands, with the point of the stick resting on a block of wood, in order to cause enough friction to make the wood smolder, until it could be used to ignite tinder.

Still other tribes used the so-called plowing method of causing fire by friction. A dry, hardwood stick was pushed back and forth along a groove in a piece of dry board until the friction caused the wood to smolder, or generated sparks, which were used to set a piece of tinder alight.

The bow drill method of fire lighting has been described and illustrated so often that it is well known to all modern chiefs, and for this reason a contest of fire lighting by the use of flint and steel is given instead. Chiefs can also hold contests in which the bow drill is used.

The braves of a band compete to see who can first light a fire built only of wildwood material—or merely a small bunch of dry grass will serve instead of a fire. The only gear allowed in lighting the fire should be flint and steel. Of course, quartz, agate, or jasper, if found in the vicinity of the encampment, can replace flint and the steel used can be the back of a knife, a piece of a file, or any other small piece of steel. As chiefs know, the sparks are first directed downward onto a piece of charred rag which is placed on other tinder of some sort, such as very dry grass, dried white pine needles, shredded birch bark, or dried fluffs, such as dandelion down. When the sparks fall on the rag they should be blown into the flame and the fire or bunch of grass ignited.

Log Rolling Contest

This activity makes an exciting contest between two or three teams of braves, with two contestants on each team. All that is required before the word "Go!" are three fairly heavy logs, each about 6 feet long and one foot in diameter. They can be longer and thicker, or less thick, but they should be approximately the same weight. Three strong, pointed stakes, each about 14 inches long and 2 inches in diameter; a hand ax for each team; and, also for each team, a 30-foot length of rope, which need not be very strong—complete the necessary gear.

On the call "Get ready!" each team stands facing its log, with their backs toward a visible marker placed from 50 to 100 yards behind each team and directly in line with its log at the start of the race. (How to handle the log and roll it is described in Chapter 6.)

On the word "Go!" it is the job of each team to roll its log to the team's marker as quickly as possible. The log must be rolled only by the rope and must not be touched or pushed at any time, except to raise the ends so that the rope slides under it easily at the start and when it is rolled up to the stake and a fresh start is required. One or both contestants on each team can handle the ax used to drive in the stakes in the course of the race. Good team work can double the speed with which the log rolls over the course and add considerably to the length of each roll in the series necessary to take the log up to the marker.

Chiefs can stage this race in a number of ways, having all teams race for only one marker, for instance, and by increasing or decreasing the length of the roll and of the ropes. This race can also be run by providing each team with two stakes which, in a long roll, can be driven in alternately by team members, if they believe that they can gain time on a two-stake roll, which they will not unless they can judge the distance at which the second stake is driven with considerable accuracy.

Rappelling Races

The useful art of rappelling is fully dealt with in Chapter 9, and when the simple technique has been developed by braves in a band, the chief can hold a contest to see which brave deserves to count coup. It is best not to have more than three or four braves contesting at the same time unless the spot selected by the chief is very favorable for rappelling work and offers about the same climbing difficulties along the entire length of the course used for the contest. A very steep hill, slope, embankment, or safe cliff is the prime requirement. In addition to the strong, long rope required for each contestant, a strong metal or pointed hardwood stake at least 2 inches in diameter and 2 feet long is needed. Part of the contest should be having each brave drive his stake at the top of the hill or embankment *before* the contest begins and a chief should inspect each stake to make certain that it is driven very securely into suitable ground or a crevice, so that the weight of the climber cannot dislodge it.

With older braves, the race can be down a long, very steeply inclined slope, where the rope is passed around trees, tree stumps, or the base of strong bushes, on the way down, the rope being pulled off one and changed to a new support lower down and at various heights until the climber reaches the ground. The climbers must use only the rope *throughout* the descent, and those who descend on foot over any part of the climb without the support of the rope even for a few feet, or in order to find a new support for the rope, are disqualified. A survey of the steep slope on which the contest is held should be made by each climber contesting in order that he may know the position of trees, stumps or bushes around which he can pass his rope on the way down. The best places on the slope can be secured by drawing straws, or the chief may allot the points from which the climbers descend, so that the younger braves may have the easiest positions on the way down the slope.

Interesting races of this sort can be held, when more mature braves contest downhill on a long, steep slope without using even one stake, the rope being placed around trees, stumps, or bushes from the top to the bottom of the descent.

This is another comparatively safe sport and completely so when well supervised, but the motto DARE WITH CARE! should never be forgotten by chiefs or braves in this or any other activity where even a minor risk is involved.

Index